Reading Religions in the Ancient World

Supplements to Novum Testamentum

Executive editors

M.M. Mitchell
Chicago

D.P. Moessner
Dubuque

VOLUME 125

Robert McQueen Grant

Reading Religions in the Ancient World

Essays Presented to Robert McQueen Grant
on his 90th Birthday

Edited by

David E. Aune & Robin Darling Young

BRILL

LEIDEN • BOSTON
2007

This book is printed on acid-free paper.

Library of Congress Cataloging-in-Publication Data

A CIP record for this book is available from the Library of Congress

ISSN 0167-9732
ISBN 978 90 04 16196 2

PRINTED IN THE NETHERLANDS

CONTENTS

Part Two

New Testament Studies

Part Three

Patristic Studies

LIST OF CONTRIBUTORS

Larry J. Alderink, Professor of Comparative Religions, *emeritus*, Concordia College, Moorhead, Minnesota

David E. Aune, Professor of New Testament & Christian Origins, Department of Theology, University of Notre Dame

Hans Dieter Betz, Shailer Matthew Professor New Testament, *emeritus*, The University of Chicago

L. William Countryman, Sherman E. Johnson Professor in Biblical Studies, Church Divinity School of the Pacific in Berkeley, Calif.

A.J. Droge, Professor, Department of Humanities, University of Toronto

O.C. Edwards, Jr., Dean and Professor of Preaching, *emeritus*, Seabury-Western Theological Seminary, Evanston, Illinois

Bernard McGinn, Naomi Shenstone Donnelley Professor *emeritus*, Divinity School, University of Chicago

Margaret M. Mitchell, Professor of New Testament and Early Christian Literature, The University of Chicago

Mark Reasoner, Associate Professor of Biblical Studies, Bethel University

Graydon F. Snyder, Dean and Professor of New Testament, *emeritus*, Chicago Theological Seminary, Chicago, Illinois

Tabor, James D., Professor of Religious Studies and Chair, Department of Religious Studies, University of North Carolina, Charlotte

Johan C. Thom, Professor of Classics, Department of Ancient Studies, University of Stellenbosch

Leonard L. Thompson, Professor of Religious Studies, *emeritus*, Lawrence University, Appleton, Wisconsin

Robert Lee Williams, Professor of Biblical Theology, Southwestern Baptist Theological Seminary

Robin Darling Young, Associate Professor of Theology, University of Notre Dame

Peter Zaas, Professor of Religious Studies, Director, Kieval Institute of Jewish-Christian Studies, and Chair, Dept. of Religious Studies, Siena College, Loudonville, NY

FOREWORD

David E. Aune

The inspiration for producing a *Festschrift* honoring Bob Grant on his 90th birthday came initially from Margaret M. Mitchell in consultation with Leonard L. Thompson. The first *Festschrift* honoring Bob was published in 1979 and read like a Who's Who of international patristic scholarship. In this second *Festschrift* it was tacitly agreed that the contributors would be limited to Bob's students and colleagues. After agreeing to take over the editorship of the *Festschrift*, it was a natural step to ask Robin Darling Young, my colleague in the Department of Theology at the University of Notre Dame if she would serve as coeditor, which she graciously agreed to do. When the proposed topics began to come rolling in, it became clear that they covered a broad spectrum of subjects and periods in the ancient world. We regarded this diversity as a positive testimonial to the breadth of Bob's own scholarship and the various ways in which he inspired his students. Special thanks is due to Matthew Bates, my Graduate Assistant, who has worked long and hard reformatting and correcting all of the essays presented in this book.

INTRODUCTION

Robin Darling Young

Teacher and Scholar

Robert Grant was a puzzle to many of his students. Ignorant, we wanted a clear answer to a question: How many martyrs died under Diocletian? How did the school of Alexandria begin? He demurred; or he shrugged or raised his eyebrows; sphinxlike, he turned the question back upon the questioner.

At the University of Chicago, in the late 1970s, we fretted because we knew we could never learn everything about early Christianity. We also knew that Grant knew much of it, because he had the evidence in his jacket pocket and we could see it. He brought stacks of note cards from his study to the Shirley Jackson Case seminar room. They were the results of his expeditions into the texts and monuments of early Christianity, and he collected them in arrangements of his own. He did not share them all.

We had been told that texts had contexts, and that there were methods for discovering the connection between the two. But how to find that connection? In a seminar, Grant sent us off like explorers without maps or guides. He expected us to return in five weeks—we thought—with a polished scholarly essay firm in conclusion and founded upon solid evidence. His most likely response, though, was another question: how could we know?

Robert Grant sails close to the wind: his style was just as terse in his seminar as it is in print. The diffident graduate student was not sheltered, and the puffed-up was fast deflated. He often presided at Sunday liturgy in the Church of St. Paul and the Redeemer in Hyde Park, but gave us no epic tale of early Christianity, and invoked no spiritual reasons for its expansion. He was aware that money and sex moved that world, too. His questions were clipped and abrupt; he spurned method.

And because he did not interpret elaborately, or claim too much, his teaching became deeply valuable and his scholarship has lasted. Unlike many books written about one aspect or another of early Christianity, his are still worth reading; in their oddly chaste approach, they make the more experienced scholar—now more cautious herself—think again.

Justly called "the *doyen* of ancient church historians" not long after he had already received his first Festschrift,[1] Robert M. Grant investigated and wrote with steady industry. His sixty-five-year-long career yielded a long shelf of books interpreting the first three centuries of Christianity in the Roman Empire. Some of these works have been examinations of texts, and others have been broader surveys of specific topics as they develop over time. Yet others have been studies and translations of particular authors. A common feature of them all, though—and one familiar to all Grant's students—is their insistent attention to the particular event or person, and to the primary text or ancient monument. Like his remarks in class, his writing displayed an asperity and dry wit, and an honesty about the state of the ancient sources, those *disiecta membra* well expressed in the title of one reprinted volume called *Second Century Christianity: A Collection of Fragments*.[2]

If in his thirty-six books and many articles, and in his classroom teaching, Grant has refused to present a grand and coherent narrative of antiquity and Christianity—and he has so refused—his sly and clear-eyed questions have the accumulated force that allows, eventually, for the growth of a habit of inspection among his students and readers, and self-discipline that might result in the caution about both self as historian and object as immediately understandable. His account keeps close to the documents and monuments of the ancient world and Christian groups within that world as they have been collected by earlier historians, archaeologists and textual scholars.

Robert Grant's career spans a period of time, however, in which history-writing itself has changed along with social and intellectual fashions. Not only has "early church history" been replaced by the study of the less-ecclesiastical "history of early Christianity;" the latter has, in some quarters, been replaced by the subject of "late antiquity," inspired by Peter Brown and other historians concentrating upon the cultural world shared by Christians and pagans after 313. And inasmuch as his scholarly interests have not been confined to the ancient world, it is worth recalling that Grant's long life has also spanned the period from the beginning of the end of the old empires of Europe to the American occupation of those colonial empires, in between which

[1] E.M. Yamauchi, review of Robert M. Grant, *Eusebius as Church Historian*. Oxford: Clarendon Press, 1980, in *The American Historical Review* 86:5 (1981): 1079–1080.

[2] *Second Century Christianity: A Collection of Fragments* (Philadelphia: Westminster John Knox, 2003).

were the political and cultural changes and conflicts that echoed, and sometimes were begun, in the academic world.

Life and Training

In two ways, the story of empires is also the story of Grant's lifelong interests. Born on November 25, 1917, about six months after the *Unterseeboote* of the first Battle of the Atlantic brought the United States into World War I, Robert Grant seems to have settled before his twentieth birthday upon the two areas of study that have fascinated him all his life. The first, Christianity in the Roman Empire, has in common with the second, the German submarine campaign of the Great War, two notable features: the expansion of empire and the military battles that accompany it, and the importance of translation from encrypted languages.

To introduce his *U-Boat Hunters*, Grant wrote that the book was "a study of some of the ways in which the Royal Navy was able to decipher German U-boat signals in what was known as "Room 40" in the Admiralty's Old Building," after those ciphers had been found in sunken submarines or downed zeppelins. Of his lifelong interest he noted:

> [the] famed U-boats and their opponents were of great interest after the Great War of 1914–1918. In 1936 I was able to study documents in the Office of Naval Records and Library in Washington and later to publish three articles in the United States Naval Institute Proceedings.[3]

Thus Grant has also had a career as a military historian, begun as the European and American world order envisioned under the dispensation of the Paris treaty of 1919 was beginning, in his late adolescence, to come apart. During the years of the war that followed that collapse, Grant became a scholar and a priest; after the war he helped to revive the study of early Christianity and patristic theology when the scholarly communities of Germany, France and England had been disrupted by World War II.

---

[3] Robert M. Grant, *U-Boat Hunters: Code Breakers, Divers and the Defeat of the U-Boats, 1914–1918* (Annapolis, MD: Naval Institute Press, 2003). Two previous works were called *U-Boats Destroyed: The Effect of Anti-Submarine Warfare 1914–1918* (London, 1964), and *U-Boat Intelligence: Admiralty Intelligence Division and the Defeat of the U-Boats* 1914–1918 (London, 1969) (both reprinted 2002, Penzance: Periscope Publishing).

The complexities of Roman society and religion are never set far from his considerations of the Christian assemblies, and his knowledge of the rhetorical and philosophical codes of the Graeco-Roman world came from his profound knowledge of its *paideia.* As with his U-boat research, he could crack the code of the literary elite of the ancient world to see how Christianity re-encoded its habits and its ethos. His abilities here probably came from his thorough, classical training and four great mentors that he himself has acknowledged: his father, Frederick C. Grant at Union Theological Seminary, W.L. Westermann at Columbia, and A.D. Nock and H.J. Cadbury at the Harvard Divinity School, where church history flourished.

When Grant began his research, in the late 1930s, a church historian entered the guild of scholars who could continue to build upon the foundation of great nineteenth century historians, the text scholars and archaeologists of Europe—notably, France, Germany and England—and the United States. Their universities and scholarly publishing houses issued critical editions and lengthy studies because they were still lavishly supporting humanistic training. In the case of church history, most particularly in the Protestant and Roman Catholic churches, clear denominational lines provided the equally clear institutional consciousness both served and created by chronicles of church leaders, teachers, and ideas. In a field that was habitually conservative, scholars of church history often saw church and university, not unlike church and empire (or even republic), as partners. Grant was well aware, however, of the temptations of church history. Church historians could ignore the context of ecclesiastical institutions and of theology, and to write as if their own denomination were the true church, safely insulated from influence by other ecclesiastical groups whether schismatics, heretics or just competitors. He avoided that kind of parochial viewpoint, perhaps thanks to his scholarly upbringing.

Trained in classics at Northwestern University (A.B. 1938) and in church history at Columbia, Union Theological Seminary (B.D., 1941) and Harvard, Grant learned from masters in the field. His father, Frederick Clifton Grant (1891–1974), was a scholar of New Testament and Early Christianity who published studies of those subjects as well as a handbook on Hellenistic religions, and taught biblical theology at Union Theological Seminary and became president of Seabury-Western Theological Seminary in Evanston, Illinois. At Columbia University, Grant Studied under W.L. Westermann, a historian of the Seleucid period and the Roman empire in its political and economic aspects.

Grant left Columbia to study at Union Theological Seminary, going from there to Harvard Divinity School. After earning his S.T.M., he married Margaret Huntington Horton (1940); generations of students, in addition to the Grant family, have appreciated her good humor and kindness.

Professor Grant was ordained in the Protestant Episcopal Church of America (1942) and continued his degree work while serving at St. James Church in nearby South Groveland, Massachusetts (1942–44). For his doctorate, a Th.D. (1944), he studied with Arthur Darby Nock, a Cambridge-trained historian who taught at Harvard from 1929 to 1963 and is best known for *Conversion* (1933), *Saint Paul* (1938), editing the first *Oxford Classical Dictionary* (1949) as well as for contributing to the first *Cambridge Ancient History*. Grant's other Harvard mentor was Henry Joel Cadbury, a Quaker whose scholarly works were devoted to studies on Luke-Acts, the historical Jesus, and Quaker history, including a comparison of Quakerism and early Christianity.

Throughout his long career, Grant held only two teaching posts. For the first, he was appointed professor of New Testament studies in the School of Theology, an Episcopal seminary at the University of the South (Sewanee), Tennessee. He taught there from 1944 to 1953. He then moved to the University of Chicago Divinity School, where he taught church history for nearly thirty-five years, until his retirement in 1987. He was named Carl Darling Buck Professor of Humanities in 1973. Although at Sewanee he had trained candidates for the Episcopal priesthood, at Chicago he worked almost exclusively with graduate students working toward their doctorates. Here he began to emphasize more strongly the study of the social world of early Christianity, while not completely leaving behind the study of the New Testament which earlier had occupied him more centrally. In the fifties, the sixties and the early seventies, the postwar economy prompted a sustained expansion of American universities, and provided numerous graduate students to train, and the Divinity School increasingly emphasized doctoral training.

With scholars from the Classics Department at the University of Chicago, Grant also supported the Department of New Testament and Early Christian Literature, hoping to train masters' and doctoral students to study all the literary works of early Christianity, regardless of whether they were included in the canon. Grant knew that the study of early Christianity had suffered from at least two scholarly habits. The first was the habit of allowing the religious distinction between canonical and noncanoncal texts to persist in the study of first and second century Christian literature.

The second habit was the equally parochial one of studying Christian texts composed in Greek and Latin without reference to the literature of their social or cultural context, the Graeco-Roman world formed by the Roman conquest of the eastern Mediterranean. Grant consistently studied them in their proper context. In these ways his views anticipated and made possible the more popular studies and collections of texts that promote the same unified study of the first one hundred years of Christian writings.

Yet a new intellectual trend challenged this approach. The upheavals of the 1960s that troubled the both the city and the University of Chicago faculty, as lamented in the diatribe of Allan Bloom[4] and fictionalized in a novel by Saul Bellow,[5] echoed the ascendancy in Paris of the poststructuralist thinkers whose works led so many American scholars to reject history as an empirical practice, and intellectual history with it, in favor of theory. The "linguistic turn" was the latest trend in among historians, and further complicated the subdiscipline of early Christian history.

In the space of thirty years, the discipline of history had already absorbed the influences of anthropology and sociology, psychology, and feminist history. Like history in general, the history of Christianity also, changed to accommodate its new context, and has absorbed similar influences.[6] Early Christianity was the subject of numerous such reinterpretations, in which theory held more interest than literary texts in their historical context.

Nonetheless, Grant's works bear repeated readings. Margaret Mitchell's learned essay in the reissued *Augustus to Constantine* discusses the continuing cogency of and interest in the work of Robert Grant; in addition, it is, perhaps, his avoidance of methodology and his modest refusal to create a grand narrative that has contributed to the lasting worth of his work. As Professor Mitchell points out, Grant pioneered a congeries of approaches to the history of early Christianity that were rightly impatient with the settled and even complacent divisions of scholarship that together obscure a full account of early Christianity. She lists five approaches that have been consistent pursuits of Robert Grant and that are still being pursued in current scholarship: his integration of New

[4] Allan Bloom, *The Closing of the American Mind: How Higher Education has Failed Democracy and Impoverished the Souls of Today's Students* (New York: Simon and Schuster, 1987).

[5] Saul Bellow, *The Dean's December* (San Francisco: Harper and Row, 1982).

[6] For a pithy discussion of the changes in European and American historiography over the past forty years, see Keith Thomas, "New Ways Revisited," in the London Times of October 13, 2006; see also fn. 8, below.

Testament and Early Christian Studies, his insistence on social history, his attention to the "historical Jesus" and the history of Christians under Rome, his exploration of connections among Paul, Christian literature and Greek rhetoric and philosophy, and his enduring emphasis upon local histories and varieties of Christianity.

As Mitchell notes, historians have usually treated the appearance, expansion and finally the installment of early Christianity as the religion of the empire in one of two ways. For some historians and philosophers, and among some denominational historians, this apparent conquest is the tragedy of Christianity, either because they regret that it weakened and brought down the empire. Others regard it as Christianity's conquest and triumph.[7]

In either case, the ancient belief, that fate as doom or providence guides history, haunts their stories. This is not the case for Grant. For reasons of training and inclination, Grant's examination of literary potsherds has kept his assertions modest and his narrative spare. Furthermore, his perennial skepticism has resulted in the open-minded regard for contingency and chance that some church historians or historical theologians lack. Grant has always been aware that the ancient church was complicated, its leaders' purposes sometimes inscrutable, and the records they left incomplete or partisan.

Reviewing one scholar's book on Irenaeus, for instance, Grant raised a question. The book, he noted:

> ends on a religious note. "Yet divine Intellect, economy and recapitulation cannot be seen in abstract. The beholder must fall to prayer and by faith share, participate, in the glory which God gives in exchange for the humanity which God shares in Christ." Does this cast any light on the process by which Irenaeus tried to coordinate the materials he selected from scripture and selectively created as tradition?

Grant was sympathetic to the *ressourcement* movement among European Catholics (mostly French, although German scholars also participated, notably Professor Josef Ratzinger). The final section of The Spirit and the Letter reflects on the relationship between the historical critical method and the role of scripture in the thinking of the church; here, his interests were very close to theirs. Just before and after World War II,

[7] Margaret M. Mitchell, "Foreword," pp. xiii–xxxv in Robert M. Grant, *Augustus to Constantine. The Rise and Triumph of Christianity in the Roman World* (Louisville and London: Westminster John Knox Press, 2004) First published (with a more warlike title) as *Augustus to Constantine: The Thrust of the Christian Movement into the Roman World* (San Francisco: Harper and Row, 1970, 1990).

and before the second Vatican Council, those scholars promoted patristic theological works as a way of rejuvenating theology; one of their number, Jean Daniélou, was a personal acquaintance. He approved and supported their work. Yet Grant was not known to be a sympathizer of a similar, earlier effort: the Oxford movement that led John Henry Newman into the Roman Catholic Church. In his own writings, he has generally steered clear of the study of theology, and seemed sometimes to regard it as a the end product of the activities of the church; thus he once amused a class by comparing with approval the Prayer of Humble Access in the 1929 Book of Common Prayer, recited in the Episcopal eucharistic liturgy, to the supplications of a petitioner at the court of Constantine.

The Present Work

Nearly thirty years have passed since the publication, in 1979, of the first Festschrift in honor of the work of Robert McQueen Grant. The editors wrote, in the introduction to that volume, that "the interaction between Christianity and Greco-Roman culture has been the most alluring, and the most persistent," of the "issues [dominating] the study of early Christian literature and thought since the nineteenth century."[8]

Grant, they pointed out, had shown already how Irenaeus did not reject the Greek philosophy that he described and condemned in its dualist distortion by the "falsely-so-called Gnostics," but adapted selected elements of it to his needs as a Christian teacher. Therefore the essays in the 1979 volume would reflect the way in which numerous early Christian authors blended the culture of "a Palestinian Jewish sect" with Hellenistic *paideia* to make "a universal religion." In doing so, they would both pay tribute to, and extend, one aspect of Grant's work as a scholar.

The lasting attraction of their subject, early Christianity and classical culture, and their approach—theological and philological—is illustrated by many of the essays in the present volume as well. These essays investigate problems in classical texts and the societies that they mirror, at least partially; they explore passages in the Gospels and the writings

[8] William R. Schoedel and Robert L. Wilken, eds., *Early Christian Literature and the Classical Intellectual Tradition. In Honorem Robert M. Grant* (Paris: Editions Beauchesne, 1979), p. 9.

of Paul and Hebrews; and they consider early Christian literature and biblical interpretation.

The 1979 volume and this one most resemble Grant's studies in the context of the New Testament and first century Christian writings. Like his *Paul in the Roman World*, they address literature both within and surrounding the writings of the New Testament and later early Christian writings. In the *Paul* volume, Grant wrote about three topics: business and politics, religion and ritual, and sexuality; in it he also juxtaposed ancient writers like Juvenal and Josephus with Christian writers like Clement and Ignatius. By these means he tried to supplement and balance Paul's account with the accounts of others—but not, it should be noted, the approaches of other scholars, although they are not lacking. First and foremost, the writings of Paul were balanced against the testimony of other writings.

Both volumes—this one and its predecessor—participate in a tradition of scholarship that is deeply textual and interpretive, and that, far from originating in the nineteenth century, stretches back to the sixteenth and earlier centuries because it is not only scholarly but scholastic. It depended upon both the skills derived from the field of classics and upon the concepts and traditions of theology, both Protestant and Catholic.

That discipline could fairly be called "intellectual history," and despite recent predictions of its demise, it is still strong and healthy.[9] Both Festschriften are essentially essays in intellectual history with a particular focus on the theology, philosophy, exegesis and polemical rhetoric.

The strength of that field, labeled "patristic" when it is conducted within an ecclesiastical context, and "early Christian thought" when it takes place in a more secular setting, derives from its coherence and its audience. If this approach is less attentive to the social world of early

[9] For discussions defending intellectual history see Richard J. Evans *In Defence of History* (London: Granta, 1997) and Malachi Haim Hacohen, "Leonard Krieger: Historicization and Political Engagement in Intellectual History," *History and Theory* (1966): 80–130; for an account of theorizing challenges to "objective" historiography see, with ample bibliography, Elizabeth A. Clark, *History, Theory Text: Historians and the Linguistic Turn* (Cambridge and London: Harvard, 2004) and now Gabrielle Spiegel, ed., *Practicing History: New Directions in Historical Writing* (in the series Rewriting History) Loindon: Routledge, July 2005 (and their fathers, Michel Foucault, *The Archaeology of Knowledge*, trans. A.M. Sheridan Smith (New York: Random House, 1972) and Pierre Bourdieu, *Outline of a Theory of Practice*, tr. Richard Nice (Cambridge and New York: Cambridge University Press, 1977).

Christianity, or to more novel and recent approaches to the literary, documentary and archaeological remains of that world, it nonetheless represents one major aspect of Grant's work.

It is no criticism of either volume, however, to point out that their topics and approach do not adequately represent the entire scope of Grant's interests, as described above. For the activities of Christian teachers ike Irenaeus, or the apologists about whom Grant has written, took place within a political entity that frames his scholarship and links it with the work of other scholars beyond those who are primarily theological or textual. Finally, his work in sum accounts for the adaptation by Christian groups to the expansionist state that remade the culture and society of the Mediterranean basin from Gibraltar to Dura Europus.

The policing of the Mediterranean and the Middle East accomplished by Roman armies, governors and tax-collectors yielded a stable urban life without which early Christians would not have been able to organize their assemblies, collect libraries and translate texts in different languages, appoint officers, stage liturgies and charities, fight amongst themselves, correspond with each other over long distances, and hold regional councils to exercise discipline and chastise their opponents.

If there were occasionally official prosecutions for sedition, and occasional executions producing heroic martyrs, these were just local until the mid-third century, and did not prevent imperial tolerance of Christianity most of the time. Indeed, the Constantinian court's interest in Christianity was foreshadowed already in that of the court of Alexander Severus and his mother Julia Mamaea residing Antioch in 231 due to the threat of Persian invasion under Artaxerxes I; Julia had consulted Origen about religious matters and he, apparently, was eager to be consulted.

All of this activity, carefully examined by Grant, is related to the ancient historian who may be Grant's muse: Eusebius the church historian.[10] The latter's life, too, spanned a period of turbulence and changes in the empire and in Christianity. Born in 264/265, Eusebius was a student of a student of Origen and a curator of his writings in the library at Caesarea Palaestina; he lived through the persecutions of Diocletian, became a bishop of the same city, tried to influence the court of Constantine with new, Christianized rhetoric, and died, probably in 340, when Christian teachers and bishops had broken into factions because of theological controversy.

---

[10] Robert M. Grant, *Eusebius as Church Historian* (Oxford: Clarendon Press, 1980).

Perhaps the spirit of Eusebius has prompted some of Grant's famous apophthegms on the necessity of sources in the evaluation of early Christianity. Anathema to him are the temptation to abstractions to which theology sometimes yields; though he admits that studying early Christianity can have theological implications, they may be sought only after "digging in the sources, literary, archaeological, and whatever other kind may turn up."[11] Perhaps the apophthegm that best captures his mind on the subject is, "when the last theologian dies, a church historian will record the fact!"

Grant's interest has been, however, in Eusebius' construction of a literary legacy, and particularly his *History of the Church*, the first complete Christian version of the much older Greek historical genre. Eusebius' topics have, to a great extent, been the object of Grant's own research. If other scholars of early Christianity have turned to Syriac and Coptic sources, particularly the Coptic Gnostic literature, to explore the transmission of Christianity to the borders of the empire, Grant's scholarship has remained strongly within the Graeco-Roman tradition. Likewise, Grant has not developed an interest in the connections between early Christian leaders and their Jewish context—both Second Temple and early rabbinic—that has appeared strongly in the last thirty years of the twentieth century.

From his earliest research to the present, rather, Robert Grant has continued, as a careful detective and historian, to interpret the Latin and Greek sources for early Christian history with a depth and skill unparalleled in the United States. He stands in the company of church historians like Henry Chadwick, and of Roman historians like A.H.M. Jones, Mikhail Rostovtseff, and Fergus Millar. In this way he has developed and extended the traditions of scholarship in which he was trained, and like his mentors has stood as an example to his students to continue his work of investigation and interpretation. Thus it is by some of these students, to him, that this work is dedicated.

[11] *Augustus to Constantine*, p. viii.

PART ONE

CLASSICAL STUDIES

PERSONAL RELIGION?

Larry J. Alderink

> The old [poets] made people speak like citizens, but the recent ones make them speak like rhetoricians.
>
> Aristotle *Poetics* 50b5

One of my fond memories of Robert M. Grant I trace to his course in "Gnosticism" in 1966. The research topic I chose was possible connections between ancient Orphism and early Gnosticism, and everyone in the class accepted my negative conclusions about either historical or typological relations between the two ancient religious movements. Prof. Grant pushed a step further. As he furrowed his brow and peered above the lens of his spectacles, he asked a question that implied an answer: "have you read Ivan Linforth's negative arguments about the very existence of Orphism?" "Yes," I replied, "if Linforth has it right, there could be no connections, and if he has it wrong, there would be no connections." A faint smile broke across Robert's face, and he winked! Yes, he winked!

My objective in this paper is to think with the skeptical historical methods I came to appreciate in courses and conversations with Prof. Grant. I want to raise a question and to move toward an answer: how did the tragedians of fifth-century Athens think about and portray selves or persons?

Several excellent studies have been devoted to the terminology the ancient Greeks used to designate various aspects of human beings, but unfortunately they do not include tragedies within their scope.[1] Studies of native terms are useful, but my goal is to ask whether we can find in ancient Greece a form of religion we might consider "personal religion." I shall be concerned above all to detect a change from epic to tragic selfhood and religion as different ways Greek writers constructed their views at various moments in their culture. My goal, then, is to raise a conceptual problem: how can we—indeed, can we—fashion a concept of the person which will serve us fruitfully and well for the interpretation

[1] David B. Claus, *Toward the Soul: An Inquiry into the Meaning of Psyche before Plato* (New Haven: Yale, 1981) and Jan Bremmer, *The Early Greek Concept of the Soul* (Princeton: Princeton, 1983).

of selected materials in ancient Greek religion, and particularly Greek tragedies?

In his Sather Classical Lecture on ancient Greek religion, André-Jean Festugière used the term "personal religion" to designate an aspect of Greek religion that subsequent scholars have not seen fit to use.[2] Whether his concept of personal religion can serve some purpose or be put to some new use is a central question for this paper.

When Festugière began his search for personal religion among the ancient Greeks, he initiated a project at once classical and Christian. The materials he examined as well as the procedures he employed qualify his study of personal religion among the Greeks for the designation "classical studies." The theological assumptions he brought to his project were Christian, however. Consider the traits Festugière identifies as he defines the object and the objective of Greek religion:

The first draws attention to beliefs:

> Religion [is]...belief in a fourth dimension which takes us out of material space, where everything changes, disorder reigns, and we are lonely and unhappy, to attain *something which is*, a Being who exists absolutely, in all perfection and splendor. To feel that we are bound to that Being, to aspire to find Him, to hunger and thirst after Him: that is the religious sense. (1)

The second focuses on sensing rather than believing, sensing

> ...a Presence beyond earthly things, and needing to feel that Presence, without which all is emptiness and the world not more than a desert in which one is lost...such feeling is personal in its nature. There is no true religion except that which is personal. (1)

A third indicates the crucial feature that makes religion personal:

> "True religion is, first of all, closeness to God" (1) and "The highest form of religion is that which unites us with the very being of God." (2)

That closeness or union may be direct through the mystical union sought by Plato as well as Christian mystics, such as St. Thomas, St. Bonaventure, and Meister Eckhart "who sought God directly." (3) Other mystics concentrated their devotion in "visible, perceptible objects, akin to ourselves, Jesus in his humanity, Our Lady, and the Saints..." (3) A

[2] André-Jean Festugière, O.P., *Personal Religion Among the Greeks* (Berkeley: University of California, 1960).

third group "was content to spend long hours in contemplation before a statue of the Virgin, the infant Jesus, or the crucified Christ." (3) In all three cases the point remains the same: procedures and means may differ, but the goal of union between worshipper and deity remains constant.

With the terms of the project defined and its conceptual tools fashioned, Festugière moves to the question he asks us to ask: was such personal religion known to the Greeks? His own answer is an unambiguous yes. Thus, Festugière combines Plato and politics, tragedy and popular piety, and theological desire and political stress, to cast the entire history of Greek religion within the single frame of personal religion.

The focus Festugière preserved throughout his study, his use of evidence, and the conclusions he derived from his inquiry are remarkable in their consistency and economy. We must note that by "personal religion" he does not mean reflective as opposed to popular religion, or individual as opposed to group religion, as though his search for personal religion among the Greeks would require him to search for a small elite rather than the vast majority of Greeks.[3] "Personal religion" *includes* the popular piety in which people contemplate statues, engage in devotional ritual, and participate in public worship as well as the reflective piety which enables individuals to identify the god of popular belief and worship as the God who orders the world and human affairs, guarantees justice and ethics, and displays every perfection. Personal religion, as Festugière construes it, is a pervasive theme that runs throughout ancient Greek religion.

The vexing problem Festugière has bequeathed us concerns less the Greek gods than the Greek human beings and the types of writings in which they are conceived and portrayed and interpreted. A narrative which portrays the trials and travails of an entirely fictional character may be used in the way Festugière uses Apuleius' portrayal in *Metamorphoses*

---

[3] Jon D. Mikalson, *Athenian Popular Religion* (Chapel Hill: University of North Carolina, 1983): 1–8, identifies popular religion as the religion of the townspeople or the majority of Athenians, apart from the poets and philosophers. In *Honor Thy Gods: Popular Religion in Greek Tragedy* (Chapel Hill: University of North Carolina, 1991): xi and 129 he distinguishes popular from tragic religion. He also distinguishes religion in tragedy, which will be popular religion, from the religion of tragedy, which he considers a challenge to popular religion. Martin P. Nilsson, *Greek Folk Religion* (Philadelphia: University of Pennsylvania, 1961): 4 focuses his attention on folk religion as the religion of the masses with their concrete concerns of everyday life, as distinct from the elite and the literary figures, with their aristocratic interests.

of Lucius' love for and liberation by Isis to document the human search for god. A philosophical text that discusses desire may be used in the way Festugière uses Plato's *Symposium* to characterize religion as a thirst for an absolute reality. But do the same standards of utility and fruitfulness apply to Euripides' *Hippolytus* and *Ion*? That is, the assumptions Festugière made—and must make—about the characters in tragedy must be questioned. Apuleius works for Festugière because the leap from narrative episode to religious search the narrative portrays is short and safe, and the *Symposium* works for Festugière because its philosophical narrative appears both to explain and incite the desire for "something more."

The move, however, from *Hippolytus* and *Ion* to possibly real people whose religious yearnings and actions they represent is problematic. Can one read either play, or could an Athenian attend a performance of either, and then make a fairly natural move from the text or the actors to people who walk the streets? That is, can we read *Hippolytus* and *Ion* from the stage to the street? Is Hippolytus a real person...or a play person? One may question Festugière's concept of religion and his assumptions about deity/ies, but one may also probe his notions of human beings. Obviously Festugière has thought a great deal about gods and theology, but he hasn't attended to the role of human beings in creating their theologies and in constructing their self-concepts, let alone situations in which gods and humans are on display. Since conceptions of human beings are as influential in scholarly work as conceptions of deities, attention to this matter will be important as we probe the utility and promise of the notion of personal religion. Thus we move to examine concepts of self or person in ancient Greece.

We have no reason to suppose that we could offer a definition of "self" or "person" let alone the "essential traits" of "human nature" that would serve as a cross-cultural invariant in the search for a "common humanity." We can have little confidence in our ability to construct a universal "human person." Some scholars disagree. Consider the assertions of a recent study of Greek tragedy:

> Greek tragedy is about people, and what they do to each other. It deals with human relationships, such as those between father and son, husband and wife, ruler and suppliant. Human behaviour in these plays is not of some special, uniquely 'Greek tragedy' kind. It concerns those fundamental human passions which are reflected to a greater or lesser degree in the literature of all nations at all periods. In Greek tragedy people love and hate as we do; they protect or destroy as we do; like us, they deceive each other, abuse

> language or beliefs to suit their own ends. They are no less concerned than we—or our descendants, hopefully—with personal integrity, justice, and political health.[4]

Love and hate as we do? Greeks like us? Maybe, maybe not. A more fruitful assumption for historical and literary inquiry is the possibility—or assumption—that concepts of persons and even categorizations of persons will vary from culture to culture and from time to time within a particular culture.[5] Perhaps we moderns and post-moderns would include at least three distinct items in our list of the traits that identify persons: (1) self-awareness or some realization that a person is a bounded identity different from rocks, trees, animals, and other humans; (2) agency or actions chosen and performed for some reason to achieve some goal; and (3) continuity across time. Likely our own notions of persons would hardly serve us well if we want to understand Hippolytus or Agamemnon. Could we find a straight line from them to us or us to them? Even were we able to ask an imaginary ancient Athenian, "What sort of person is Agamemnon?" we'd likely not get a satisfactory answer, and were we to discuss Agamemnon with our imaginary Athenians, we'd possibly talk beside each other. Suppose we ask where Agamemnon lives or when we could meet him in the agora or the temple. Might the Athenian respond, "οχι, οχι, the only place you can meet Agamemnon is in the theater!" Agamemnon is a figure in a poem or a character in a play. Agamemnon is an *ethos*. Why? Because, I suggest, Agamemnon is *not* a real person or even *like* a real person... Agamemnon is a *textual* person. The question we want to ask, then, is not an everyday, common sense question of personhood or human identity, for an Agamemnon cannot be read off the page or the stage, as Festugière thinks possible. We might be able to identify an Agamemnon after a recitation of Homer's *Iliad*, since that poet was singing the deeds and problems of a hero, but would we recognize an Agamemnon after attending a performance of Aeschylus' *Agamemnon*? I doubt it, for Aeschylus' Agamemnon is a character in a text rather than a person in a society.

---

[4] Brian Vickers, *Towards Greek Tragedy: Drama, Myth, Society* (London: Longman, 1973): 3.

[5] See, for example, to the essay of Marcel Mauss, "A Category of the Human Mind: The Notion of Person; the Notion of Self," and the essays devoted to its significance in Michael Carrithers, Steven Collins, and Steven Lukes, *The Category of the Person: Anthropology, Philosophy, History* (Cambridge: Cambridge University Press, 1985).

If our concept of a "real," that is socially real, person differs significantly from a concept of a "play" person who walked the Greek stage, how shall we be able to understand *that* person? What will make a tragic figure intelligible to us? Here a distinction developed by Roland Barthes may be useful for us, the distinction between a *person*, "a moral freedom endowed with motives and an overdetermination of meanings" and a *figure*, "an impersonal network of symbols combined under the proper name."[6] Another distinction made by Mikhail Bakhtin may also be useful, between *character* as a "monologic, finished-off, generalized category that is given and determined—all aspects of "anotherness" and *person* as "a dialogic, still-unfolding, unique event that has the "made-ness" and unpredictability rooted in conditions relating to 'self'."[7] These distinctions are useful if understanding an Agamemnon and an Achilles are our objectives. With Barthes, we can consider a text as a "site" and the *name* Achilles will be a mark on the site and "take its place among the alibis of the narrative operation, in the indeterminable network of meanings."[8] And with Bakhtin, we can need not concern ourselves with literary figures as though they were representations symmetrical with real people... they may well have been something quite different. We can then use the term "textual figure" or "textual self" or even "textual person" if we want to reconstruct or resurrect the idea of "personal religion," or think about various models of human personality.

One problem, as I mentioned, is that the concept of the person will vary not only from culture to culture, but also from time to time within a particular culture. Thus, different Greek figures may be distinguished. Figures such as Agamemnon and Odysseus, Achilles and Hector, and the others who populate *the Iliad* and *the Odyssey* bear several marks of the epic hero:

1. Human beings are fated to be mortal; mortality sets the limits to human being
2. For a hero, honor can compensate for mortality, especially if the honor is lasting in the form of glory and fame
3. Honor, glory, and fame are unstable and at risk; they are gained and lost in battle

---

[6] Roland Barthes, *S/Z*, tr. Richard Miller (New York: Farrar, Straus and Giroux, 1974), p. 94.

[7] Michael Holquist, *Dialogism: Bakhtin and His World* (London: Routledge, 1990): 162.

[8] Barthes, p. 94.

4. The hero who competes for honor and glory on the battlefield will be highly esteemed and thus elevated above other Greeks, as his courage to risk death will mark him as distinct from other Greeks.
5. The hero will avoid unseemly behavior/αἰσχρός and above all the loss of honor, which adds up to his shame.
6. In brief, the Homeric hero is one who achieves excellence by risking life in a deathly contest with another hero. The reward is prized precisely because only one or the other will gain it, the risk distinguishing the hero from other men and death the very reason for striving for glory.[9]

It follows that the reason excellence, courage, honor, glory, fame, and all the other noble values were so desirable precisely because of human mortality. Within the epic frame, mortality finds compensation in glory and fame; indeed, mortality motivates the noble aims. Heroic excellence—ἀρετή—is the name for the cultural values that pervade the epic tradition, a celebration in song and memory of the aristocratic achievement and reward.

Applying the concept of personal religion to the Homeric poems motivates us to venture an identification of the "persons" or "figures" we find in the epics. We search in vain, I fear, for a notion of the self that resembles our own—a discrete and unified self distinguished from all that is non-self and especially other similar selves, an individual marked by unique features—or a body and soul which are distinct from each other and constant in their identity. We do, however, recognize that each hero displays a persistent and, from our point of view, excessive concern for honor/τιμή, a value that is, one may say, a quantity to be increased or decreased in competition and depending on acknowledgment

[9] A clear illustration of these points occurs just before battle when Sarpedon addresses Glaukos by asking:

Why is it you and I are honoured before others
with pride of place, the choice meats and the filled wine cups
in Lykia, and all men look on us as if we were immortals,
and we are appointed a great piece of land by the banks of Xanthos,
good land, orchard and vineyard, and ploughland for the planting of wheat?
Man, supposing you and I, escaping this battle,
would be able to live on forever, ageless, immortal,
so neither would I myself go on fighting in the foremost
nor would I urge you into the fighting were men win glory.
But now, seeing that the spirits of death stand close about us
in their thousands, no man can turn aside nor escape them
(*Iliad*, 322–328; pp. 266–267 in Richmond Lattimore, tr., *The Iliad of Homer*).

by others. The quantity of honor and shame will depend for their existence on acknowledgment by others and may be increased or decreased as figures compete with each other in battle but also in games. Around this core a cluster of supporting values are arrayed. One hero will be stronger than another, and as they engage in contests with each other, anger/νέμεσις will be the justified anger expressing public disapproval, shame/αἰσχρός will be the emotion a hero feels as his honor is taken by another, and fear/φόβος his emotion in the presence of someone stronger than he and threatening to him. Whereas the hero will avoid cowardice or neglect on the battlefield, he will feel mercy/ἔλεος when considering someone weaker or less fortunate than himself, for he need not fear retaliation.

The conclusion I reach is that the epic self or the epic person or the "textual person of the Homeric epic" is not construed as an individual among individuals or an item defined by particular traits, but instead a self defined as a social self, even to the point of being non-personal or at least interpersonal. Achilles and all the others like him do not mull over secret thoughts or conceal their motives or harbor hidden and private emotions; their persons or selves are known in action and displayed as they act upon each other. If honor is to be gotten above all, shame is above all to be avoided: the self is constituted by recognition from others in a public without which evaluation is not possible. Internal qualities and virtues so characteristic of our modern times are hardly in evidence. Excellence/ἀρετή as the standard of value is public and variable rather than internal and generally distributed as a constant throughout the culture.

When we turn from considering an epic self to think about a tragic self, we are immediately struck by the way the tragedies of Aeschylus, Sophocles, and Euripides typically focus on figures from the heroic past and put them on stage. Early in the fifth century the theater of Dionysos on the southeast foot of the Acropolis was the site for performances on the occasion of the City Dionysia in the early spring. Of course, the theatrical performances were among the many other activities in what we may call a performance culture, but one example of performance in ancient Greek culture.[10] We can identify some features peculiar to

[10] Every month the citizens of Athens gathered on the Pnyx as the Assembly met; the Council, a smaller political forum met to set the agenda for the Assembly; juries in Athenian lawcourts, numbering from 100 to 1,500 heard speeches and reached verdicts by taking votes; in the agora debates and lectures were commonplace; Athe-

the tragic presentations, such as the use of masks, suggesting a greater interest in public persons that in individual personalities; the use of the ekkyklema and the skene, suggesting a fluidity between public and private; and the emphasis on dramatic strategy or plot, suggesting a connection between action and character. We can hardly call ancient Greek tragedy a "realistic theater" whose goal is convincingly to represent social life or "psychological theater" whose goal is to present "whole or balanced or perverse personalities." The tragedies present characters whose elements or component parts are selected and organized to explore a conflict or a course of action, as Simon Goldhill persuasively argues.[11] We also note that individuals were situated in both family and city, and thus we should to consider Greek individuals as members of groups rather than as individuals. The presence of barbarians and females on stage has led some scholars, such as Edith Hall, to the conclusion that tragedy, such figures were important means of Greek self-identification.[12] John Gould has shown how dramatic persons are constructs of language and gesture and thus that dramatic personality derives from the theatrical action. He also shows how theatrical language and gesture draw "...a boundary round the dramatic figure that separates him or her from the confusing continuities and complexities of our everyday acquaintance with persons...[it is] framed by a principle of limited existence.[13] Thus, the distance between ordinary and theatrical will be an important principle for the interpretation of "person" or "self" in Greek tragedy.

---

nian calendars demonstrate that a hundred days each year were devoted to public festivals organized around religious cults of the city, the grandest of which was the Panathenaia; pan-Hellenic athletic contests in Olympia, Nemea, Isthmea, and Delphi were attended by Athenian delegates and victories were celebrated by the singing and dancing of victory-odes (epinicians); and rituals of weddings and funerals were city as well as family affairs. Contests for reciting the Homeric epics came to be included in the Panathenaic festival by the last half of the 6th century, with a rhapsode making oral presentations from memory. See Rush Rehm, *Greek Tragic Theater* (London: Routledge, 1992): 3–12.

[11] Simon Goldhill, *Reading Greek Tragedy* (Cambridge: Cambridge UP, 1986) and especially pp. 101–02 of "Character and Action, Representation and Reading Greek Tragedy and its Critics" 100–127 in Christopher Pelling, ed., *Characterization and Individuality in Greek Literature* (Oxford: Oxford, 1990).

[12] Edith Hall, *Inventing the Barbarian: Greek Self-Definition Through Tragedy* (Oxford: Oxford, 1991).

[13] "Dramatic Character and 'Human Intelligibility' in Greek Tragedy," *Proceedings of the Cambridge Philological Society* 24 (1978): 43–67.

We should note one more feature of many if not most of the heroic figures that populate Greek tragedies. Whereas the heroic figures of epic are characterized most clearly by their actions, the heroic figures of tragedy—Agamemnon, Oedipus, Jason—are characterized as facing and making choices. For example, in Aeschylus' *Oresteia*, Agamemnon must decide whether to sacrifice Iphigeneia, and Orestes knows that the cost for obeying Apollo's order to kill his mother will invite revenge by the Erinys; his energetic self-assertion will be punished. Writing characters who decide and whose decisions make plots possible is one way to perform an experiment on the nature of persons, for the results will vary according to the choices made.

More generally I suggest that we view the Athenian tragic theater as a social laboratory for conducting experiments, a place where playwrights, actors, and audience participate in various experiments on conceptualizations of what people are and can be. The range of persons will vary widely, beginning with figures inherited from the epic tradition. The themes that were supplied by the epic tradition—figures, war, fate, risk, revenge, etc.—constitute the set of experimental variables, and persons, played by actors on stage, will comprise the experimental object who will change or resist change as the theme is applied to them in the course of the plot. The plot will be the core of the experiment, for it allows many persons or selves to be subjected to treatments of various kinds in order that observations be made, as, for example, Euripides in the *Medea* portrays ordinary conditions of male and female roles in family structures and struggles but subjects gender relations to distortions in order to observe how revenge might work if a woman sought it and a man suffered it. It is as though an ordinary liquid were to be subjected to laboratory distortions of temperature and pressure in an experiment. Let us say tentatively that theater will be a concentration on one or another aspect of social life that is abstracted or extracted for the purpose of analysis and reflection and thought in the effort to imagine alternatives and options.

So we ask a question: how can we think about person or self in the tragic theater? On my hypothesis, the experiments the tragedians, the actors, and the audiences performed required specific skills of each other. Of course, the actors found it necessary to do their share persuasively and convincingly, or the experiments would fail to provoke the audience into following the experiment by thinking step by step through the plot. The audience, too, made a contribution. Those viewing the action and hearing the words would take the show at face value lest they miss the play. That is, when in the theater, the audience must think believingly or it cannot think at all.

The action and speech and pity and terror wrought by the dramatists exhibit more the signs of rhetoric than description. That is, we can recognize the *made and constructed* character of the performances. What were the playwrights making? I submit that they made "play persons" for the purpose of making and remaking belief—experimental and carefully designed beliefs proposed for the consideration and cogitation of the audience for the purpose of examining alternative selves or persons.

Thus we need two steps: (1) it is necessary to *believe* the make-believe in order to think about it and feel its force, and (2) it is necessary to *see through* the make-believe of the stage in order to see through and beyond the stage to the society, and thus to think and learn about it. Believing isn't enough for the tragedians, and merely seeing isn't believing. Seeing though believing is the first and major step toward knowledge. What does seeing through the selves on stage make possible? Seeing that life in the street and action on the stage bear one crucial trait in common: both are made, with the consequence that the social persons observing the play persons could take credit for or reject what they were and what they made, but also to make changes in themselves that they deemed necessary or desirable.

What can we conclude from all this? André-Jean Festugière made intimacy between god/s and humans the central feature of his concept of personal religion among the Greeks. I conclude from my survey of his concept and my own proposals regarding textual persons that we cannot retain the meaning he attaches to the term any more than we can retain the theological assumptions he brought to his inquiry. Yet who persons were and were understood to be is at the center of both epic and tragedy. Perhaps we will want to retain the terminology, and that remains to be tested and argued. But if we do want to find the term useful for thinking about the religion of Greek tragedy, we will not think about the continuity between Greek religion and the religion of Greek tragedy. We will think about the discontinuity between the two and see how the experiments the Athenians performed on persons (and heroes and gods as well!) enabled them to think about the kinds of persons they were and could be and perhaps could not be. As Socrates, they wanted to know who they were.

DEATH AS LIFE AND LIFE AS DEATH: REVISITING ROHDE

James D. Tabor

> I shall of course be standing, as we all stand, on the shoulders of Rohde
>
> —E.R. Dodds

Robert M. Grant's most fundamental and sustained instruction to his students was that one's original research should stem from one's own curious and independent thinking and inquiry emerging from two primary bodies of evidence—*primary sources* and *older classic secondary works.* He often commented that too many modern researchers were carrying out their scholarly work oblivious to the work of their predecessors, resulting in repetition of results often poorer in quality, despite additional and refined evidence, to what had been done fifty to one-hundred years before their time. When I first met Prof. Grant in 1972 he handed me a thick, manually-typed, mimeographed list of well over two hundred secondary readings for the M.A. qualifying exams in the Department of Early Christian Literature over which he served as Chair. One had the impression he had written it out from memory on his personal office typewriter that he used for all his writing. As I glanced through the pages I came to the sober realization that I hardly recognized one-tenth of the secondary works on the list, despite arriving at the University of Chicago with an M.A. in Christian Origins from another institution.[1] The list contained most of the important classic works related to the study of Christians origins set in its Greco-Roman environment over the past one hundred years or so. Prof. Grant explained that these works were considered essential for even a *basic* beginning in the field. He noted that since I already had earned an M.A. degree I had the option of immediately taking my qualifying exams over the reading list. I politely elected to spend the next two years reading. The oldest work listed was a book by Erwin Rohde titled *Psyche*, published in German

[1] Names such as Bieler, Bousset, Colpe, Cumont, Diels, Dieterich, Dodds, Farnell, Festugière, Gressmann, Jervell, Lietzmann, Nilsson, Reitzenstein, Preisendanz, Rohde, et al. I had somehow missed in my training up to that time.

in 1893.[2] I determined to work through the list in order of publication so that Rohde's work was the first one I tackled—in the English translation of W.B. Hillis.

Now over a hundred years since the publication of the first edition of Erwin Rohde's classic study *Psyche* in 1893, I find that the sage admonition that Prof. Grant passed on to me over thirty years ago still serves me well. Accordingly, in this paper I want to revisit Rohde with the intention of offering a summary of his insights and how they have a fundamental relevance to the pioneering work Prof. Grant has given us on the early Christian text *Ad Autolycum* by the second century Christian bishop Theophilus of Antioch.[3]

Erwin Rohde, pupil of Schopenhauer and early friend of Nietzsche, describes his 600 page work in a single opening sentence of his preface: "This book offers an account of the opinions held by the Greeks about the life of the human soul after death." His subtitle was "The Cult of Souls and Belief in Immortality among the Greeks." Despite this description, in fact, Rohde's book is not primarily about Greek views of the "afterlife," in the way of, say, Cumont's *Afterlife in Roman Paganism*.[4] Rather, Rohde develops a fundamental insight—that the view one takes of *death* is an essential interpretive key to understanding the development of Greek thought regarding the human and the divine. W.K.C. Guthrie, who wrote the preface for the English translation of the 8th edition of Rohde's *Psyche*, shares and builds upon Rohde's basic perception in his own classic presentation, *The Greeks and their Gods*.[5]

In this paper I want to revive and apply aspects of Rohde's analysis to the contemporary scholarly analysis of the categories of the human and the divine in Western antiquity, but more particularly to the ways such notions of humanity and divinity were taken up by Theophilus of Antioch as he set forth his view of Christ as a model of salvation.

Recent scholarly discussion of the "divine man" in antiquity has been largely an attempt to descriptively classify an incredibly diverse mass of data spread over about eight or ten centuries. Scholars have attempted to

[2] Erwin Rohde, *Psyche: The Cult of Souls and Belief in Immortality among the Greek* (1893). Harper Torchbook edition with introduction by W.K.C. Guthrie, 2 vols. Trans. from 8th edition (1920), by W.B. Hillis (New York: Harper & Row, 1966).

[3] Robert M. Grant, *Theophilus of Antioch Ad Autolycum* (Oxford: Clarendon Press, 1970).

[4] Franz Cumont, *Afterlife in Roman Paganism* (New Haven: Yale University Press, 1923).

[5] W.K.C. Guthrie, *The Greeks and their Gods* (Boston: Beacon Press, 1950).

draw together all materials which deal in any way with the conceptual, cultic, or socio-political relationship between humans and gods/goddesses.[6] Thirty-five years ago Morton Smith, in a classic article titled, "Prolegomena to a Discussion of Aretalogies, Divine Men, the Gospels and Jesus," surveyed the history of scholarship and warned us (particularly N.T. scholars interested primarily in Jesus and the Gospels) about the complexity of our collective "collecting" enterprise.[7]

> Behind this mob of divine or deified men and their many varieties lay the Greek notion of gods as beings like men, possessing the human virtues to a higher degree, and possessing also gifts that men wanted, above all immortality and eternal youth... nothing in this complex was stable. As men's notions changed, so did their gods, and as the gods changed, so did the ways in which men might be thought to be like them or related to them."[8]

Smith puts it well. Humans want to be like the gods, but gods are, after all, created in the image of the human. The development of the "divine man" figure was part and parcel of the development of that world's imaginations and desires. Accordingly, we encounter many different patterns, with border-line cases and tie-ins from one "type" to another.

Still, with regard to this classifying enterprise we have made good progress in four areas, the last of which offers the most promise.

First, we have been able to compile fairly complete descriptive lists of our general types, or classes, of deities.[9] There are the Olympian and Chthonic deities, who were never human or "mortal," though they might at times appear in mortal "disguise." There are the demi-gods, often born through union of a human and a god (or goddess), who were once "human" but have subsequently achieved true "godhood," of legendary status (Dionysus, Asclepius, Hercules). Then there are the heroes, which are primarily the local tutelary powers among the "dead," having been once human, but now revered for their powers. There are those of

[6] The classic work is Ludwig Bieler, *THEIOS ANER: Das Bild des "göttlichen Menschen" im Spätantike und Frühchristentum*. 2 Vols. 1935–36, reprinted in 1 volume (Darmstadt: Wissenschaftliche Buchgesellschaft, 1976). See also the helpful summary of Hans Dieter Betz, "Gottmensch" *Reallexikon für Antike und Christentum*, vol. 12, s.v. "Gottmensch II".

[7] Morton Smith, "Prolegomena to a Discussion of Aretalogies, Divine Men, the Gospels and Jesus," *Journal of Biblical Literature* 90 (1971): 174–99.

[8] Ibid., p. 184.

[9] See Smith "Prolegomena," pp. 181–82, as well as David Aune, "The Problem of the Genre of the Gospels: A Critique of C.H. Talbert's What is a Gospel?" *Gospel Perspectives: Studies of History and Tradition in the Four Gospels*, eds. R.T. France and David Wenham, 2 vols (Sheffield: JSOT, 1981) 1:20–34.

historical times, whether magician, ruler, prophet, athlete, philosopher, *et al.* who present themselves, or are presented by others, as having become "divine." Finally, we have less extraordinary individuals and groups, who from a variety conceptual perspectives, and through an assortment of means, hope to obtain divine status.

Second, a fair amount of attention has been given to the ways and means of achieving apotheosis or deification. Here the list is varied and somewhat overlapping: divine parentage; drugs and diet; heavenly ascent; resurrection from the dead; cultic initiation; magical incantation; selection by the gods/goddesses; "natural" selection, and so forth.[10]

Third, we have begun to come to better terms with the variety of ways in which our data survives—literary materials in all their genres, cultic remains, magical rites, inscriptional texts of every type and purpose, and so on. We recognize that although one might find certain correspondences between these types of materials, and the ideas they reflect, great care and caution is in order.

Finally, we are aware of the need to work through this complicated mix/flux on a case by case, text by text, context by context basis. Our goal should be to understand how such categories functioned in the "construction" of religious "worlds." Categories of the "divine" and the "human" *function* less as clearly defined slots into which each candidate must be fit than as the opposite ends of a continuum within which many complex, varying, and even contradictory intermediate classifications are possible. Accordingly, attention must be given to "native" or "indigenous" contexts specific to the text or the evidence itself. There is a particular need to pay attention to polemical contexts and apologetics, as claims and counter-claims are often characteristic of our materials, particularly those of a textual nature. Such claims, or the debunking thereof, are put forth to accomplish certain ends. We must give careful attention to what is at stake in each situation. A truly complete picture of any given claim or case can best be understood in the light of contemporary anthropological insights into native systems of thought and classification, thus linking social experience, systems of classification and world-view.[11]

---

[10] Emily Vermeule, *Aspects of Death in Early Greek Art and Poetry*, Sather Classical Lectures, Vol. 46 (Berkeley: University of California Press, 1979): 130–134.

[11] Here the important work of Eugene V. Gallagher, *Divine Man or Magician?: Celsus and Origin on Jesus, SBL* Dissertation series, no. 64 (Missoula: Scholars Press, 1982) provides a standard for a more nuanced and cautionary method of comparision.

Rohde wrote that his book is about the opinions held by the Greeks about the "life" of the human soul "after death." His language here is carefully chosen. He begins with Homer and ends with Plato and the later Greek philosophers. What he is essentially asking is how the Greeks understood *death* itself. Gods are immortal; humans die. The question is, what is the nature of that death? How was it understood? Or to put it pointedly, when did *death* come to be understood as *life*? As early as his preface Rohde explains the heart of his argument:

> The conception of immortality in particular arises from a spiritual intuition which reveals the souls of men as standing in close relationship, and indeed as being of like substance, with the everlasting gods. And simultaneously the gods are regarded as being in their nature like the soul of man, i.e. as free spirits needing no material or visible body.[12]

Later in the book he offers the following summary of this essential point:

> If the soul is immortal, it must be in its essential nature like God; it must itself be a creature of the realm of Gods. When a Greek says 'immortal' he says 'God': they are interchangeable ideas. But the real first principle of the religion of the Greek people is this—that in the divine ordering of the world, humanity and divinity are absolutely divided in place and nature, and so they must ever remain.[13]

Guthrie, like Rohde, describes his book in a single sentence: "an investigation into Greek views of the relations between man and god." He speaks of two contrasting "threads" in Greek thought:

> ...that there was a great gulf between mortal and immortal, between man and god, and that for man to attempt to bridge it was *hybris* and could only end in disaster, or that there was a kinship between human and divine, and that it was the duty of man to live a life which would emphasize this kinship and make it as close as possible[14]

On the one hand humans are told, "Seek not to become Zeus," "For mortals a mortal lot is right" (Pindar); while on the other hand, "Man's chief end is to put off mortality as far as possible" (Aristotle), "the completest possible assimilation to god" is the goal of philosophy (Plato). Echoing Rohde, Guthrie explains that he uses *god*, *divinity*, and *immortal*

---

[12] Rohde, *Psyche*, preface to the 1st edition, p. xv.
[13] *Ibid.*, II, p. 253.
[14] Gutherie, *The Greeks and their Gods*, p. 114.

as equivalents, because they were so considered by the Greeks. Humans are mortal; gods immortal. Accordingly, "to believe the soul to be immortal is to believe it to be divine. According to Guthrie, "if man is immortal, then he is god," this is a universal of Greek thought.[15]

Rohde's discussion of the development of what he calls the "cult of the souls" unfolds with this fundamental perspective in the foreground. In Homer death is the opposite of life, a dissolution of the body, and a descent of the soul to the shadowy world of Hades. In the well-known section of Book XI of the *Odyssey*, Odysseus calls up the dead from Hades, to a pit he has dug, by means of offerings and blood. It is more of a "seance" than a journey to the underworld. He sees the shades of various ones appear. They take a drink of blood to be able to speak. Antikleia, his mother appears, he tries to grasp her, she flutters out of his hands like a shadow. She says:

> ...it is only what happens, when they die, to all mortals. The sinews no longer hold the flesh and the bones together, and once the spirit has left the white bones, all the rest of the body is made subject to the fire's strong fury, but the soul flitters out like a dream and flies away (11.218–22).[16]

The departed shade of Achilles tells him:

> O shining Odysseus, never try to console me for dying. I would rather follow the plow as thrall to another man, one with no land allotted him and not much to live on, than be a king over all the perished dead (11.488–92).

Rohde then discusses the special case of one being *translated* to the "Isles of the Blest." Menelaos is told:

> But for you, Menelaos, O fostered of Zeus, it is not the gods' will that you shall die and go to your end in horse-pasturing Argos, but the immortals will convoy you to the Elysian Field, and the limits of the earth, where fair-haired Rhadamanthys is, and where there is made the easiest life for mortals, for there is no snow, nor much winter there, nor is there ever rain, but always the stream of the Ocean sends up breezes of the West Wind blowing briskly for the refreshment of mortals. This, because Helen is yours and you are son-in-law therefore to Zeus (*Odyssey* 4.560–570).

---

[15] *Ibid.*, p. 115.

[16] Translations of Homer, *Odyssey* from the Loeb Classical Library edition, trans. A.T. Murray (Cambridge: Harvard University Press, 1924).

Rohde stresses that Menelaos does not die. This is important to his point. He is taken away bodily, and given the status, or "benefits" of a god or immortal, but essentially remains the same. He says the same for the so-called "cave deities," such as Trophonius, who experience a "subterranean translation." They are literally "alive under the earth," still close to humans and their affairs. In Homer, there are legendary notions of mortals joining the realm of the gods. Kalypso pleads with Odysseus to live with her and "be an immortal" (*Odyssey* 5.205–214). Ino called Leukotheia, had once been a mortal, but now is a goddess (*Odyssey* 5.333; cf. 6.280f). Ganymedes, "who was the loveliest born of the race of mortals, and therefore the gods caught him away to themselves, to be Zeus' wine-pourer, for the sake of his beauty, so he might be among the immortals" (*Iliad* 20:230–35). They join the realm of the gods, but without experiencing death, i.e., the dissolution of the body. Their status is miraculous and, accordingly, exceptional.

The dominant view of death that one finds in older Ancient Near Eastern texts, and thus running through much of the Hebrew Bible is remarkably parallel to these ancient Greek perceptions of human mortality and "divinity." Gilgamesh is is admonished by the barmaid Siduri, regarding his quest for immortality,

> The life you pursue you will not find,
> When the gods created humankind,
> Death for humans they set aside,
> Life in their own hand retaining.[17]

Enkidu, Gilgamesh's friend who had died had already described the realm below as "The house which none leave who have entered it... wherein the dwellers are bereft of light, where dust is their fare, and clay their food" (*Gilgamesh Epic* 7.4).

In ancient Hebrew tradition humans are mortal and descend at death to Sheol, the shadowy realm of the dead from which there is no coming back (Job 14:10–12). It is described as a region "dark and deep," "the Pit," and "the land of forgetfulness" (Psalm 6:5; 88:3–12). The heavens belong to Yahweh and his court, while the earth he has given to the "sons of men," but "the dead do not praise Yahweh, nor do any that go

---

[17] *The Gilgamesh Epic* 10.3, translation adaped from James B. Pritchard, ed. *Ancient Near Eastern Texts Relating to the Old Testament*, 2d ed. (Princeton: Princeton University Press, 1955), p. 90.

down into silence" (Psalm 115:16–18).[18] Cases of those who escape the fate of Hades or Sheol, such as the Babylonian Uta-napishtim, or Enoch in the book of Genesis, are seen as exceptions, translated to another realm, but not serving as a pattern of salvation for human beings more generally.

Similarly, the Greek "Heroes," which Rohde traces from the 7th c. B.C., he understands to be once living men, who have died, but whose souls, after death, have experienced a higher life, akin to the gods. This he understands in sharp contrast to the Homeric notions. Yet, he stresses that such an idea of heroes and demi-gods has no essential connection with the idea of the immortality of the soul. In every case, the apotheosis of the hero is an exceptional and fresh "miracle," as he puts it. The "great gulf" between human and divine remains.[19]

Rohde traces the origins of the concept of the immortality of the soul, properly speaking, to the experience of "sacred madness" (*hieromania*) within the Thracian cult of Dionysos. The soul leaves the body, is in union with the god, and lives for a moment the life of divinity. He finds the refinement of the essential idea among the Orphics and Pythagoreans, who begin to speak of the divine spark within, of the body as an impediment, and of purifications of the "Titanic" elements. These elements, this essentially new view of the "human," Rohde then traces through Plato and the later philosophers. Rohde would have been pleased to add to his discussion the *lamellai* ("Golden Plates") had he lived to see their discovery in the past century. These "prayers" of the soul in the Hadean world, discovered in tombs in Crete, Thessaly, and Italy, and dating to the 4th century B.C., offer us our earliest glimpse of what becomes the "Great Confession" of late Western antiquity: "I am a child of earth and starry heaven, but from Heaven alone is my Home."[20]

However one might evaluate Rohde's attempt to explain the *origins* of the notion of immortality of the soul, I think his main argument throughout the book deserves reemphasis. For a "mortal," in whatever period, for whatever reason, and through whatever means, to experience

---

[18] See my broad survey, "What the Bible Really Says About the Future," in *What the Bible Really Says*, Morton Smith and Joseph Hoffmann, eds. (Buffalo: Prometheus Books, 1989), pp. 33–51.

[19] Rohde, *Psyche*, I, pp. 137–138.

[20] See Herman Diels, *Die Fragmente der Vorsokratiker*, ed. Walther Kranz, 10th ed., 3 vols. (Berlin: Wiedmann, 1960–61), 1: 15–18.

translation to the status of deity, represents a recasting of what is old and what is new. On a simple level, as the satirist Lucian remarks, it simply makes heaven more crowded and increases strife among men, but more fundamentally there is a redefining of the human situation—that is humans are "immortals" who are "trapped," "fallen," or otherwise subject to mortal *conditions*. We can continue to investigate the ways and means of such transformations, the social and religious contexts in which such indigenous claims operated, and the particular structures of language from which various traditions draw—but the basic "shift" that J.Z. Smith analyzes, appears to be quite ubiquitous throughout the Mediterranean world in late antiquity.[21]

When death is understood, paradoxically, to be *life*, then what we have is not the mere "crossing of the bounds," or any other complex mix of "categories," but the ultimate collapse of the "great gulf," indeed the abolition of the category "human" itself. *There is no human, only divine.* We are left to then consider the various "conditions" into which "divinity" has fallen. The term "mortal," has nothing to do with death, per se, but becomes a *functional term* for Fate, finitude, and alienation from one's true nature and destiny. This, as Jonathan Z. Smith has so well put it, represents a significant and fundamental shift from the "archaic" to a "utopian" view of the human person that begins to increasingly characterize Hellenistic religious texts of the period.[22] As the departed Africanus the Elder, ascended to heaven as an immortal, tells his grandson Scipio Africanus: "Surely all those [who die] are alive... who have escaped the bondage of the body as from a prison; but that life of yours, which men so call, is really death."[23]

One might object that the dichotomy between mortal and immortal is somewhat arbitrary, one distinction among many. However, with Rohde and Guthrie, I understand it to represent the fundamental existential difference between human life as lived and experienced in the world, and the projected "better" life of the gods in heaven. In other words,

---

[21] See in particular, "Good News is No News," in *Map Is Not Territory*, Studies in Judaism in Late Antiquity, vol. 23 (Leiden: E.J. Brill, 1978): 190–207.

[22] See his summary article with bibliography, "Hellenistic Religions," in *The New Encyclopedia Britannica, Macropaedia*, 15th ed.: 8:749–51.

[23] Cicero, *Republic* ("Dream of Scipio") 6:14. Loeb Classical Library, *De Re Publica, De Legibus*, trans. C.W. Keyes (Cambridge: Harvard University Press, 1928). See the analysis of Georg Luck, "Studia Divinia in Vita Humana: On Cicero's 'Dream of Scipio' and its Place in Graeco-Roman Philosophy: *Harvard Theological Review* 49 (1956): 207–18.

the term "immortal" refers not only so much to longevity, but this higher and better life "above" or "beyond." The cipher, "no death," becomes the focus since death is by all appearances the dissolution of life, following injury, disease, or the misery of old age. It is also the dissolution of activity and power in the world. Thus the "immortal life" of the gods/goddesses comes to stand for all that is good, beautiful, enduring, and powerful. In that sense "salvation" can be defined most succinctly as "escape" or "going home."

Rohde focuses on Greek thought, and the corresponding concept of "immortality of the soul." I maintain that the "Hebrew" view of "resurrection of the dead," as developed in Hellenistic times, is fundamentally parallel, despite the surface differences stressed by N.T. theologians.[24] The former view understands death as the release of the immortal soul from the prison of the body. The body is not the Self, but is perishable. Thus death is not death, but life, i.e., release for the divine Self. Resurrection of the dead is an apocalyptic way of affirming the same at the end of history, collectively, for the worthy group (mass apotheosis): release from the "bonds of decay," and transformation to immortal heavenly life (see Rom. 8:20–23).[25] In either case the body is "dissolved," and the essential Self is free from the conditions of Fate and finitude into which it has fallen, or to which it has been subjected. The differences are semantic and minimal. For most writers of late Hellenistic antiquity the Greek doctrine of the "immortality of the soul" permeates ancient Jewish and early Christian thinking about death and human mortality in such a profound way that the "native" category of "resurrection of the dead" is largely subsumed or reinterpreted to essentially mean the same thing—i.e., escape from *the conditions* of mortality.[26]

---

[24] The dichotomy so widely touted by New Testament scholars between the concept of "resurrection of the dead," and the Greek ("pagan") view of "immortality of the soul," is a fundamental misunderstanding. The much celebrated article by Oscar Cullmann, "Immortality of the Soul and Resurrection of the Dead: The Witness of the New Testament," in *Immortality and Resurrection: Death in the Western World: Two Conflicting Currents of Thought*, ed. K. Stendahl (New York: Macmillian, 1965): 9–53, reflects a misguided theological attempt, fundamentally driven by apologetics, to separate "Biblical" thought from that of the common cultural views of Hellenistic late antiquity. It is a distinction without a difference.

[25] See my comparative treatment, "Resurrection and Immortality: Paul and Poimandres," in *Christian Teaching: Studies in Honor of LeMoine G. Lewis*, ed. Everett Ferguson (Abilene: Abilene Christian University Press, 1981): 72–91.

[26] "Returning to the Divinity: Josephus's Portrayal of the Disappearances of Enoch, Elijah, and Moses," *Journal of Biblical Literature* 108 (1989): 225–38.

The hero, philosopher, magician, or "son of God," who experiences the heavenly exaltation of a god or "immortal," becomes not the exception, but the model, an illustration of the "way." Plato's Socrates tells his students to follow in death as quickly as they can (*Phaedo* 61b). Africanus urges Scipio to "Strive on," realizing that his inner being is not the body, which he will shed, but is indeed "a god" that lives and moves, belonging to the eternal world above the mortal spheres. Paul tells the Christians that because "Christ" has escaped the mortal world and shed his mortal "clothing," that those who are attached to him in one spirit, whether living or dead, will experience the same at his Parousia, rising up immortal "to meet the Lord in the air" and thus "freed from their bondage to decay" (1 Thess 4:13–18; 1 Cor 15:51–54; Rom 8:21).[27] Paul is not so much affirming the "resurrection of the dead," as the *participation* of those already departed to Hades in the escape from death and mortality that comes with the appearance of Christ.

The three surviving books *To Autolycus* by Theophilus, sixth bishop of Antioch (c. A.D. 18) witness to an interpretation of the work of Jesus within these most compelling parameters set forth by Rohde. As Robert Grant succintly observed in his critical edition and translation of this valuable work, "In almost every respect his apology is a defence of Hellenistic Judaism as well as of Jewish Christianity."[28] Theophilus gives no special emphasis to the redemptive work of Christ.[29] In his view Jesus is a model of human development, a second Adam, who like the first Adam was to progress, grow, become mature, ascend into heaven, and become God. Commenting on the creation of man in Genesis, Theophilus writes:

> God transferred him out of the earth from which he was made into paradise, giving him an opportunity for progress so that by growing and becoming mature, and furthermore having been declared a god, he might

[27] One indigenous element of Paul's scheme is that the "creation itself" will also be eventually liberated from its bondage to decay as well. This is presumably based upon prophetic texts, such as Isaiah 65–66, that foresee a "new heavens and new earth" in which the mortal elements are completely dissolved and eliminated. And yet Paul still maintains the fundamental dualism of language (upper/lower, above/below, seen/unseen, mortal/eternal) that is characteristic of so many such texts of the period (2 Corinthians 4:18).

[28] Robert M. Grant, *Theophilus of Antioch Ad Autolycum* (Oxford: Clarendon Press, 1970), p. xvii.

[29] See James D. Tabor, "The Theology of Redemption in Theophilus of Antioch," *Restoration Quarterly* 8 (1975): 159–71.

> also ascend into heaven (for man was created in an intermediate state, neither entirely mortal nor entirely immortal, but capable of either state; similarly the place paradise—as regards beauty—was created intermediate between the world and heaven), possessing immortality.[30]

When Theophilus says that humans are in an "intermediate state" he is speaking of their "condition" or placement in the cosmic scheme of things, not their essential nature—which is divine. It is clear that from a "developmental" point of view, Theophilus clearly thinks of humans as "gods" and he seems pleased to find this language in Genesis. Like other Christian apologists of his time he never directly mentions Jesus, though he quotes his teachings in the Gospels (e.g., III.13–14) and he is even familiar with Paul's letter to the Romans (III.14). His understanding of Christology is apparently so thoroughly grounded in his view of humans as divine that salvation is understood as "obedience," that is, a reversal of the "disobedience" of the first Adam in Paradise. What he implies is that Jesus pioneered that way by being obedient and that the same path of "redemption" is open to all humans by right of their divine nature.

Although other more sophisticated and nuanced forumulations of the Christian view of salvation prevail in the centuries following Theophilus, his view of Christ and his work stand to illustrate how easily an essentially Hellenistic view of the divine and the human, coupled with basic "Sermon on the Mount" ethics, and popular Hellenistic-Jewish homiletics (namely polemics against idolatry and sexual immorality), can so well serve a Christian bishop in Antioch in the late 2nd century A.D.

---

[30] Translation by Robert M. Grant, *Theophilus*, II. 24, p. 67.

CREDIBILITY AND CREDULITY IN PLUTARCH'S LIFE OF NUMA POMPILIUS

Hans Dieter Betz

When I joined the faculty of the Divinity School in 1978, Robert Grant gave me a copy of his book *Miracle and Natural Law in Graeco-Roman and Early Christian Thought.*[1] His inscription reads: "Dieter from Bob. Welcome to Chicago." The laconic words combine brevity with duration. The inscription suggests hope of continuity in interest and method, and so it was and still is today. The book was not new to me because my teachers in Mainz and Cambridge had recommended it as an outstanding piece of scholarship, and I had cited it in my doctoral dissertation of 1957. Grant's work was a rarity at that time, so that owning a copy myself felt more like a miracle than law of nature.

1. Some Reflections on Grant's Miracle and Natural Law

As I read the book again recently, I found even the title to be intriguing. "Miracle *and* Natural Law" suggests a connection where the common view sees a contradiction. Miracle comes first because humanity at first had a worldview that was totally given to the miraculous, until the philosophers came along and destroyed that worldview by demonstrating that what may seem to be miraculous is in fact the result of nature and its laws. Philosophical skepticism prevailed and separated what belongs to nature from what belongs to superstition. Since miracles were παρὰ φύσιν, *contra naturam*, believing in them constituted δεισιδαιμονία, *superstitio*. Moderate skeptics who attempted compromises between these extremes were denounced as eclectics and weak thinkers.

Without delving into Grant's book too deeply, it must be said that it exploded the conventional picture just sketched, in Part I, entitled "Science." The basic issues are shown not to be verified facts but concepts of thought, beginning with "Nature" (including "laws of nature" and

[1] Amsterdam: North Holland, 1952.

"matter and motion"),[2] and followed by "Credibility"[3] and "Credulity,"[4] all of them results of "Education."[5]

In antiquity, the notion of "nature" (φύσις/*natura*) was widely debated among philosophers, and as a result there existed many different concepts as well as traditions of them in the different philosophical schools. What was thought to be"nature" depended on school traditions, within which also experiments and research were conducted.[6] Hence, "nature" was not simply the world out there, but an abstraction derived from what was perceived as reality. Even a common understanding of nature as constituted by four elements (fire/spirit, air, water, and earth) plus Chance (Tyche) was a problematic compromise.[7] Further explanations were needed to clarify the relationships among the elements, their composition and motion. Whatever "laws of nature" were detected depended on a force driving or disturbing them. Is this force intrisically a material or a divine power? If it is divine, it claims the religious name of Chance/Tyche. And if that claim is granted, the question is, Why not grant a divine status to the four elements as well? Why not grant that same status to Nature itself?

Whatever the answer to these questions may be, the door to religion and the world of the miraculous was not closed. Indeed, the answer does not depend on indisputable factual evidence concerning "nature." There is no item called "nature" one can lay one's hands or eyes on; what the senses perceive and can examine are intellectual conceptualities.

If so, this brings up the question of "credibility." As conventional wisdom has it, phenomena are credible, if they conform to nature and its forces and if a majority of reasonable people agree on this assessment. Conversely, if a majority of reasonable people disagree, the phenomena are to be judged as "incredible" or "impossible." There are, however, at least three problems that undermine such a simplistic view of "credibility."

---

[2] Ibid., pp. 3–40.

[3] Ibid., pp. 41–60.

[4] Ibid., pp. 61–77.

[5] Ibid., pp. 78–86.

[6] For the major arguments concerning violation of law, and the order of nature, related to the theodicy problem, see Plato, *Leg.* 10, 884ff.

[7] Presented by Plato as the common view of "universal nature" (*Leg.* 10, 889b): πῦρ καὶ ὕδωρ καὶ γῆν καὶ ἀέρα φύσει πάντα εἶναι καὶ τύχῃ, φασί, τέχνῃ, δὲ οὐδὲν τούτων. ("Fire and water and earth and air, they say, exist by nature and chance, and none of them by craft." (my trans.)

First, the presupposition that a majority opinion must include the "reasonable" people leaves the notions of "reason" and "reasonable" undefined. Are "reasonable" people those endowed with superior rationality, or those who merely follow "commonsense"? Why can a minority opinion not be right, and a majority be wrong? Whichever answer one prefers, it is by necessity based on further deliberations concerning "rationality."

Second, there are no hard and fast criteria which can assist to define what is credible or incredible, possible or impossible. In all instances we are dealing with concepts of language and thought, so that testing them ends where the rules of logic and grammar end. Even where the rules of logic and grammar can be tested, there are no absolute, "metaphysical" criteria. Grant concludes this chapter with a telling quotation from the skeptic Sextus Empiricus, stating that all we have are not facts but literary artifacts such as stories and histories. However, "the Grammarians have not furnished us with a criterion of true history, so that we might determine when it is true and when false. In the next place, as the Grammarians have no history that is true, the criterion of truth is also non-existent;..."[8]

Third, since there are no "objective" criteria, the majority opinion depends on "persuasion" (πειθώ). People evaluate credibility according to what they are persuaded to be true or false. This happens in regard to both "rationality" and "commonsense." How then do people get "persuaded"? They acquire their persuasions through "education," i.e. the comprehension and appropriation of tradition, and this means, as a fruit of rhetoric, "the art of persuasion." Credible are those things which cultural traditions in the wider sense value as such, and the same goes for the opposite, things incredible. In other words, phenomena people regard as "natural" conform to what they have become persuaded to be natural. Phenomena falling outside of the "natural" are incredible, impossible, or miraculous. Miracles are those phenomena which challenge conventional standards or demand disclosure as superstitious fraud.

Given the general decline of scientific research in the philosophical schools and the concurrent expansion of rhetoric in later Hellenism, the increasing role of "credulity" cannot be surprising. Credulity is the

---

[8] Sextus Empiricus, *Adv. math.* i.265–68 (tr. R.G. Bury), cited according to Grant, *Miracle*, p. 60.

naive or calculated willingness to bypass rationality and commonsense, in order to believe in the incredible and even absurd. Grant mentions the tremendous "increase in interest in astrology, magic, and a credulous Pythagoreanism."[9] As Grant's chapter on "Credulity" demonstrates by example after example, the rise of credulity is met by ever increasing story collections of things incredible, seemingly impossible or plainly absurd.[10] Mostly, the stories were based not on hard evidence but hearsay, spread to enhance the fame of "divine men" and magicians who claimed they could, by divine empowerment, do "whatever they wished,"[11] and could report extraordinary experiences during phantastic travels to foreign lands and the netherworld. Consequently, they managed to confuse profoundly what was known as science and philosophy. Politicians and demagogues learned from the rhetoric of these story tellers, how to exploit the lack of reliable criteria for what is credible and what is not, and how to impress the credulous masses. As general standards of credibility faded, credulity proved to be useful for those who were able to benefit from it. However, credulity also became a threat destabilizing public and private religion. Dominating the masses by terrifying fears and utopian hopes enabled sinister demagogues as well as well-meaning political leaders to develop new forms of ruler cult in both Greek and Roman cultures.

When in the chapter on "Credulity" Grant summarizes the views of Plutarch, the philosopher at Chaeronaea, he points out that he began as a radical skeptic in his work "On superstition" (περὶ δεισιδαιμονίας), and that he later represented the middle-Platonic "course between atheism and superstition,"[12] arguing "that immoderate credulity leads to superstition and thence to neglect of the gods and contempt for religion." In reaction, Plutarch simply follows the Delphic maxim, "Nothing too much (μηδὲν ἄγαν)."[13] Attributing to him a diffuse Middle Platonism, Grant concludes: "In Plutarch we find no solution for the problem of miracle. His caution in such matters does not reflect a naive piety but a genuine unwillingness to think through his difficulties. His middle ground, 'nothing too much', is an indication that he cannot face the

[9] Ibid., p. 61.
[10] Ibid., pp. 61–77.
[11] Ibid., p. 61.
[12] Ibid., pp. 65–68.
[13] Ibid., pp. 66, 68.

real contradiction between traditional religion and natural science and philosophy. He solves the contradiction for himself by disregarding it."[14] This verdict, however, needs some further explanations.

First, Plutarch's position is determined by his office as highest priest of the god Apollo at Delphi. This god, *una persona*, represents philosophy as its ultimate source and highest authority. Therefore, representing the god as priest and philosopher, Plutarch interacts with the various philosophical schools, although his own position is informed by Plato. According to Plutarch, the Delphic Apollo is to be regarded as the highest god of all, as intellect (νοῦς), law and world order (λόγος, νόμος). Thus, Apollo is also the ultimate guardian of truth, including both the oracle of the Pythia and all scientific enterprise. Plutarch's Delphic theology is systematic: Apollo rules over a world that is full of riddles (αἰνίγματα) and problems (προβλήματα). The problems of philosophy and science pose challenges for reason, while the irrational conundrums of the daily life are the charge of the oracle.[15] This corresponds to anthropology. The human soul (ψυχή) is endowed both with the capacity of reason and with the desire to seek the truth, in order to find out through research and discussion about possible solutions for problematic phenomena anywhere in the world.[16] This Platonic anthropology also explains Plutarch's position regarding stories about things incredible and miraculous.

Second, stories involving miraculous phenomena need to be evaluated for the purpose of "education" (παιδεία). This need recognizes the social reality that morality and ethics in public and private life are formed and maintained by what the majority of ordinary people (τὰ πλήθη), not informed by philosophical and scientific training, believe to be true or false. Therefore, stories involving miraculous phenomena engage the common people's credulity and what we call "popular religion." In principle, these stories can become either the vehicles of superstition, which undermine the health and stability of the population, or, given the right kind of interpretation, they can become tools for moral education. This concern for moral education decides what use Plutarch himself makes of miracle stories in his own writings. Those that propagate mere monstrosities are to be rejected as caricatures of

---

[14] Ibid., p. 68.

[15] See, especially, Plutarch, *De E ap. Delph.* 384E–385D.

[16] See my article "Plutarch, II. Religion," RGG, 4th ed., 6 (2003) cols. 1410–11.

superstition, others can be given an allegorical or moralizing interpretation, and still others can be modified by renarrating or choosing a different version from the tradition.

2. The Example of Plutarch's Life of Numa

Plutarch's ideas about credibility and credulity can best be demonstrated by a concrete example, for which we have chosen his *Life of Numa Pompilius*.[17] First to consider are the purposes and aims of his biographical work. They are in principle different from the conventional expectations of biography[18] as well as historiography.[19] His main interest is not to compile collections of πράξεις (dates, genealogies, big events, and places), but to describe Numa's βίος for the purpose of παιδαγωγία πρὸς τὸ θεῖον (15.1), which involves worship of the gods (θεραπεία θεῶν) and philosophical instruction (θεωρία διὰ λόγου). This leads to the learning of Numa's way of life (βίος as ἦθος καὶ τρόπος), to ethical reorientation (ἐπανόρθωσις τοῦ ἤθους), and acquisition of virtue (ἀρετή).[20]

a. *Credibility*

Whatever biographical and historical material is used for the composition of such a βίος, it must be obtained from the available sources. This is the point at which the problems of credibility must be faced. Plutarch sets forth his own method in his *prooemia*, especially to *Lycurgus* (1.1–3), *Romulus* (1.1–2.6), *Theseus* (1.1–2.2), and of course *Numa* (1.1–4). Notably, in *Numa*'s concluding biographical sections Plutarch returns to the historical uncertainties.[21] Without taking clear positions, he reports

[17] The text is cited according to the edition by Konrat Ziegler, *Plutarchi Vitae Parallelae*, vols. III/1–2 (BT; Leipzig: Teubner, 1970, 1973); the English translation and section divisions used, unless indicated otherwise, are by Bernadotte Perrin, *Plutarch's Lives*, vol. I (LCL; London: Heinemann; Cambridge, MA: Harvard University Press, 1914).

[18] Although *Numa* ist not mentioned, the article by Ulrich von Wilamowitz-Moellendorff, "Plutarch als Biograph" (*Reden und Vorträge*; 4th ed. [Berlin; Weidmann, 1926], 2.247–79; translated as "Plutarch as Biographer," in Barbara Scardigli, ed., *Essays in Plutarch's Lives* [Oxford: Clarendon Press, 1995], 47–74) is most insightful.

[19] For critiques of the historians, see especially *Alex.* 1.1–3, and *Nic.* 2.4–5.

[20] See *Numa* 3.3–7; 8.1–4; 20.6–8. Important studies are Barbara Bucher-Isler, *Norm und Individualität in den Biographien Plutarchs* (Bern & Stuttgart: Haupt, 1972); Françoise Frazier, *Histoire et morale dans les Vies Parallèles de Plutarque* (Collection des études anciennes, 124; Paris: Les belles lettres, 1996); Tim Duff, *Plutarch's Lives: Exploring Virtue and Vice* (Oxford: Clarendon Press, 1999).

[21] *Numa* 21.1–4: Numa's family; 21: 4–22: his death and burial; 22.6–7: his successors.

what the sources tell, distinguishing between contradictions and agreements.[22] By naming major authors (L. Calpurnius Piso Frugi, 21.4; Valerius Antias, 22.4), he indicates his preferences, perhaps because they have more details than Dionysius of Halicarnassus (2.76.4–6).

As ancient historians were aware, there is no certainty regarding the sources for the earliest period of Roman history, the period of the seven kings. This uncertainty involves all dates, names, genealogies, and major events.[23] If there seems to be agreement that Rome was founded on April 21, 753 BCE, that the period of the kings covered the years until 510/509, and that Romulus' rule was succeeded by Numa's (715–673), there is no basis other than legends. The lack of documents was explained by attributing their disappearance to the sacking of Rome by the Celts in 290/289. When Q. Fabius Pictor (3rd c.) wrote the first history of Rome after the catastrophic battle of Cannae (216), Plutarch says (*Rom.* 3.1; 8.7) that Fabius referred as a source to a Diocles of Peparethus, but nothing more is known about this author.[24] This, however, did not stop Fabius from becoming "the father of Roman historiography." Although Plutarch used a wider range of sources, mentioning L. Calpurnius Piso Frugi (48 BCE–32 CE; *Numa* 21),[25] Valerius Antias (1st c. CE; *Numa* 15; 22), Juba II (50 BCE–20 CE; *Numa* 7.5; 13.5), Dionysius of Halicarnassus (1st c. BCE; *Rom.* 16.8), and M. Terentius Varro (116–27 BCE; *Rom.* 12.3), all of them depended on earlier sources of uncertain quality, and all of them disagreed on just about everything without giving verifiable reasons.[26]

---

[22] See *Numa* 1.1–4; 21.1; *Lyc.* 1.3; *Thes.*10.3; *Solon* 27.1: ἀντιλογία; *Numa* 21.3; *Lyc.* 1.1; *Solon* 27.1: ὁμολογεῖν.

[23] As is well known, the source problems are extremely complicated. The standard edition is by Hermann Peter, *Historiorum romanorum reliquiae* (2 vols.; 2nd ed.; Stuttgart: Teubner, 1914; repr. 1993). Helpful is the collection by Hans Beck and Uwe Walter, eds., *Die Frühen Römischen Historiker* (2 vols.; Texte zur Forschung, 76, 77; Darmstadt: Wissenschaftliche Buchgesellschaft, 2001, 2004). Still valuable is Hermann Peter, *Die Quellen Plutarchs in den Biographien der Römer* (Halle: Waisenhaus, 1865).

[24] See the basic studies by Dieter Timpe, "Fabius Pictor und die Anfänge der römischen Historiographie," *ANRW* I.2 (1972), 928–69, especially 938–42; Idem, "Mündlichkeit und Schriftlichkeit als Basis der frührömischen Überlieferung," in: Jürgen von Ungern-Sternberg & Hansjörg Reinau, eds., *Vergangenheit in mündlicher Überlieferung* (Colloquium Rauricum, 1; Stuttgart: Teubner, 1988), 266–88, especially 274–76.

[25] See Gary Forsythe, *The Historian L. Calpurnius Piso Frugi and the Roman Annalistic Tradition* (Lantham, MD; University Press of America, 1994).

[26] This is true also of Cato, Cicero, and Livy; see Timothy J. Cornell, "Cicero on the Origins of Rome," in: J.G.F. Powell & J.A. North, eds., *Cicero's Republic* (BICS, Suppl. 76; London: University of London, 2001), 41–56.

Thus, when the dates for King Numa seemed to have been established accurately (ἀκριβῶς), a certain C. Clodius Licinus[27] showed in a book on chronology that all the old records were lost when the city was sacked by the Celts,[28] and that the records presently circulating were all forgeries. These forgeries competed with each other in grafting the names of the families of the powerful and famous onto fictional lineages (*Numa* 1.1). As an example Plutarch refers to the fanciful claim made by some that Numa had been a companion or student of Pythagoras, but this Plutarch declares to be false propaganda by those wanting to prove the king got his wisdom from the Greeks.[29] Others disputed the idea that Numa had any share in Greek education and held that he was independently gifted by nature.[30] When it became clear that the philosopher Pythagoras came to Italy five generations after Numa, another Pythagoras was proposed, a Spartan winner of the foot-race in the 16th Olympiad, whom Numa met during his wanderings in Italy and who co-designed with him the city. This claim supposedly explained why there were so many Spartan institutions mixed in with Roman ones: the Spartan runner Pythagoras taught them to Numa. Others argued that Numa stemmed from the Sabines, and the Sabines were believed to have been originally Spartan colonists. However, the list of victors of the Olympian games was compiled only much later by the sophist Hippias of Elis who worked with worthless sources (*Numa* 1.2–4).[31]

Given this confusion and the difficulties in correctly establishing times and dates, none of the sources can claim historical credibility. Therefore, what is the biographer to do? Plutarch ends the prooemium by

---

[27] Nothing further is known about this author and his book entitled ἔλεγχος χρόνων. Plutarch does not claim that he actually saw this book.

[28] Vividly described by Plutarch, *Cam.* 19–29.

[29] Even for Plutarch himself, the question of where Numa acquired the wisdom he was known for is very complicated. Plutarch presupposes the long cultural dispute between those arguing for Greek philosophical influences at the beginning of Rome, focusing on Numa the Pythagorean, and opponents insisting on Numa's indigenous prudence and virtue. The former position seems to have been pushed by Pythagoreans in Southern Italy (Tarentum). See Kurt von Fritz, *Pythagorean Politics in Southern Italy: An Analysis of the Sources* (New York: Columbia University Press, 1940); Walter Burkert, "Hellenistische Pseudopythagorica," *Philologus* 105 (1961) 238–43; Christoph Riedweg, *Pythagoras* (Munich: Beck, 2002), 161–62.

[30] See foremost M. Porcius Cato Censorius (234–149) and M. Tullius Cicero (106–43), *De rep.* 2.15.26–2.16.30; also *Tusc.* 1.1; 5.7–11. At any rate, Plutarch read the rebuttal by Dionysius of Halic. (*Ant.* 2.58.2–59.4). See Erich S. Gruen, "Cato and Hellenism," in his *Culture and National Identity in Republican Rome* (Cornell Studies in Classical Philology, 52; Ithaca, NY: Cornell University Press, 1992), 52–83.

[31] The 5th century sophist was a younger colleague of Protagoras, mentioned in Xenophon and Plato.

stating his method (1.4): "What we have received as tradition worthy of recording about Numa, we are going through, taking it as an agreeable starting point" (ἅ δὲ παρειλήφαμεν ἡμεῖς ἄξια λόγου περὶ Νομᾶ, διέξιμεν ἀρχὴν οἰκείαν λαβόντες. [my trans.]). The statement is carefully formulated: The tradition that has been selected and received as worthy of recording about Numa can serve as no more than a convenient starting point to be scrutinized more closely.[32] Even more skeptical is the statement in the prooemium to *Theseus*, the tradition of which is outrightly mythological: "May I therefore succeed in purifying Fable, making her submit to reason and take on the semblance of History. But where she obstinately disdains to make herself credible, and refuses to admit any element of probability, I shall pray for kindly readers, and such as receive with indulgence the tales of antiquity."[33] Plutarch asks readers to tolerate what is apparently a paradox, namely to subject myth to reason, in order to purify and make it over into history.

Even if, therefore, the notion of "credibility" has to be always kept under critical surveilance, the ancient traditions are not completely without value. In Plutarch's interpretation, the notion needs to be treated differently from the way historians use it. Looked at philosophically, biographical materials exemplify character types and ways of life. These can be used to construct different kinds of biography which serve the purpose of learning about human values and ethical virtues and vices. As Plutarch designs them, the βίοι of eminent Greeks and Romans set forth as examples what is both commendable and reprehensible. The arena of history becomes the life context in which the truth of these values is tested by real experiences by both the persons portrayed and the readers.

---

[32] Cf., especially, the similar formulations in *Lyc.* 1.3: οὐ μὴν ἀλλὰ καίπερ οὕτως πεπλανημένης τῆς ἱστορίας, πειρασόμεθα τοῖς βραχυτάτας ἔχουσιν ἀντιλογίας ἤ γνωριμωτάτους μάρτυρας ἑπόμενοι τῶν γεγραμμένων, περὶ τοῦ ἀνδρὸς ἀποδοῦναι τὴν διήγησιν. ("And yet, although the history is in such a state of confusion, we shall make the attempt to deliver the narrative of the man by following the written sources having the fewest contradictions or the best known witnesses."; [my trans.]) *Rom.* 3.1: Τοῦ δὲ πίστιν ἔχοντος λόγου μάλιστα καὶ πλείστους μάρτυρας τὰ μὲν κυριώτατα πρῶτος εἰς τοὺς Ἕλληνας ἐξέδωκε Διοκλῆς Πεπαρήθιος, ᾧκαὶ Φάβιος ὁ Πίκτωρ ἐν τοῖς πλείστοις ἐπηκολούθηκε. ("But the account having the most credibility and the greatest number of witnesses was, regarding its principal details, the one that first Diocles of Peparethus published among the Greeks, whom also Fabius Pictor followed in most parts."; [my trans.])

[33] *Thes.* 1.3: εἴη μὲν οὖν ἡμῖν ἐκκαθαιρόμενον λόγῳ τὸ μυθῶδες ὑπακοῦσαι καὶ λαβεῖν ἱστορίας ὄψιν· ὅπου δ' ἄν αυθαδῶς τοῦ πιθανοῦ περιφρονῇ καὶ μὴ δέχηται τὴν πρὸς τὸ εἰκὸς μεῖξιν, εὐγνωμόνων ἀκροατῶν δεησόμεθα καὶ πρᾴως τὴν ἀρχαιολογίαν προσδεχομένων.

b. *Credulity*

While the term "credibility" signifies a positive value, "credulity" is ambiguous or altogether negative, assessing an "overreadiness to believe, disposition to believe on weak or insufficient grounds."[34] Thus, the former can be more easily reconciled with critical historical and philosophical thinking, the latter cannot. However, this does not exclude that under certain circumstances positive uses can be made even of "credulity." According to Plutarch, Numa's challenge of re-educating the Roman people even required to resort to their credulity as a political tool, a method justified already by Plato.

"For if a city was ever in what Plato calls a 'feverish' state, Rome certainly was at that time.[35] It was brought into being at the very outset by the excessive daring and reckless courage of the boldest and most warlike spirits, who forced their way thither from all parts, and in its many expeditions and its continuous wars it found nourishment and increase of its power; and just as what is planted in the earth gets a firmer seat the more it is shaken, so Rome seemed to be made strong by its very perils." (8.1–2)

When Numa realized that it would be "no slight or trivial undertaking to mollify and newly fashion for peace so presumptuous and stubborn a people, [he] called in the gods to aid and assist him. It was for the most part by sacrifices, processions, and religious dances, which he himself appointed and conducted, and which mingled with their solemnity a diversion full of charm and a beneficent pleasure, that he won the people's favor and tamed their fierce and warlike tempers. At times, also, by heralding to them vague terrors from the god, strange apparitions of divine beings, and threatening voices, he would subdue and humble their minds by means of superstitious fears." (8.2–3)

Plutarch himself saw it as the biographer's challenge to make plausible what the tradition says about Numa's ability to persuade the people to accept the radical reform program he imposed on them. This reform program was nothing less than a new constitution of religious (9.1–15.1) and social institutions (16.1–20.5), including precepts for law and morality. In order to make these radical and detailed reforms acceptable for

[34] So *The New Shorter Oxford English Dictionary*, vol. 1 (Oxford: Oxford University Press, 1993), p. 545.

[35] For the imagery see Plato, *Rep.* 2, 372e; *Leg.* 3, 691e; it is also used in Plutarch, *Lyc.* 5.6; *De fort. Rom.* 9, 321C.

people who were not trained to follow the arguments of philosophers, they had to be based on strong cultural foundations the people were already familiar with. These foundations included the strengthening of Numa's authority as king, the integration of already existing institutions, and the mobilization of popular religion. As a royal figure Numa was strengthened by assimilating him to Pythagoreanism (8.4–5),[36] and by relating him to Nymphs and Muses: Egeria and Tacita.[37] Another move dealt with the legacy of his predecessor, Romulus. While Numa changed many of Romulus's policies, he confirmed his apotheosis and new divine name by installing a special cult and priest for Romulus Quirinus, naming him Φλάμην Κυρινάλιος.[38]

Highly significant, however, is the role Plutarch attributes to popular religion existing among the Romans (δεισιδαιμονία).[39] After reporting on Numa's cult reforms in chapters 9–14, he states that the Roman people accepted these reforms on the supreme authority of Numa. "On account of such education toward the divine the city thus became malleable and struck with wonder because of Numa's power, so that it accepted the legends which along with his strangeness resembled myths and made people believe that nothing was incredible or unachievable for him, if he wanted it." (my trans.)[40] However, Plutarch has good reasons for thinking that such personal loyalty to Numa would not suffice in view of the profound social reforms to which the Roman people would

[36] Plutarch only seems to contradict himself, when he rejects the tradition of Numa having been a companion of Pythagoras (1.2–4), while he does admit their close association in traditions drawn from the Pythagoreans (Πυθαγορικοί, 8.4–10; 14.1–6; 22.2–4). Thus, Plutarch denies that the historical Numa could have been a companion of Pythagoras, but he affirms that later Pythagoreanism assimilated the two figures.

[37] The legend of Numa's consort Egeria, a spring nymph, is told and argued in 4.1–8; 13.1–2; a different name about a mountain nymph Tacita is mentioned in 8.6 in connection with Pythagorean tradition. Apparently, these legends came from separate strands of tradition. Does the phrase in 13.1–2 "Egeria and the Muses" suggest still other Muses?

[38] See 2.1–3; 7.4–5; Plutarch discusses Romulus's deification at length in *Rom.* 27.3–29.7.

[39] For this important concept see Arnaldo Momigliano, "Popular Religious Beliefs and Late Roman Historians," in his *Essays in Ancient and Modern Historiography* (Middletown, CT: Wesleyan University Press, 1977), 141–59; Thomas S. Schmidt, *Plutarque et les barbares. La rhétorique d'une image* (Collection d'études classiques; Louvain-Namur: Peeters, 1999), 224–34: "Δεισιδαιμονία et croyances barbares."

[40] 15.1: v 'Εκ δὲ τῆς τοιαύτης παιδαγωγίας πρὸς τὸ θεῖον οὕτως ἡ πόλις ἐγεγόνει χειροήθης καὶ κατατεθαμβημένη τὴν τοῦ Νομᾶ δύναμιν, ὥστε μύθοις ἐοικότας τὴν ἀτοπίαν λόγους παραδέχεσθαι, καὶ νομίζειν μηδὲν ἄπιστον εἶναι μηδ' ἀμήχανον ἐκείνου βουληθέντος.

have to commit themselves. The commitments needed for accepting the reforms are detailed in chapters 16–20.

Apparently for this reason, Plutarch adds three miracle stories in chapter 15, which he no doubt took from oral tradition reflecting popular religion. Retrospectively, of course, the Romans Numa was encountering were still barbarians mired in primitive superstition.

The first of the three miracle stories belongs to the category of feeding miracles (15.2). After Numa has been inaugurated as king, he invites a considerable number of citizens to dinner. When these people arrive, they are somewhat surprised by the skimpy table ware and miserly food. After they have begun to eat, Numa announces that the goddess Egeria, his consort, has arrived, and all of a sudden the whole scene is transformed, with precious drinking cups circulating and tables loaded with exquisite dishes. To the people this proved that the new king in one moment can fulfill the first and last hope of Romans, to have food of divine quality on the table.

The second and third miracles (15.3–6) involve a consultation of Numa with Jupiter.[41] These stories reveal Numa's magical powers by which he has control not only over lower daimons but even over Jupiter himself. By a clever trick Numa is able to capture two daimons, Picus and Faunus, who were roaming about on the Aventine hill which at that time was uninhabited and outside of the city. Once the daimons realize that none of their escape tricks work against Numa's firm grip on them, they make a deal with him. They tell him many things to happen in the future and a protecting charm against lightning bolts, Jupiter's most dreaded weapon. The charm, however, is unclear; it involves a sacrifice of onions, hair, and sprats. This problem is solved by another version of the story, in which the daimons bring down Jupiter himself for consultation. Angrily he agrees to a dialogue with Numa, during which he willy-nilly reveals the ingredients of the charm; for this dialogue Numa is coached by Egeria who also sees to it that Jupiter leaves graciously at the end. Weird as these stories are, they involve the full display of the magical arts that Numa was believed to be capable of.

The section concludes with Plutarch's own assessment of the stories (15.6): "These stories are, therefore, mythic fables and ridiculous for

[41] Clearly, Plutarch wants to have three stories, but it appears that the third miracle is a different version of the second. Thus, the second shows Numa's magical power over the lower daimons, the third over the highest god, Jupiter.

that, but they show the disposition of the people back then toward the divine, which the customary habits instilled in them." (my trans.)[42] But what is the point of introducing the matter here?

Paradoxically, this superstitious religion attributed to Numa is a necessity nonetheless. It will fire up the people's credulity by injecting into them the elements of fear of punishment and hope for the seemingly impossible. These elements are indispensible for taking oaths, and oaths are the foundation for the first social institutions to which the people must commit themselves. As such, both *Fides* (Πίστις) and *Terminus* (Τέρμων) are mere concepts, but, in order to be continually adhered to, they must be enforced by sacred oaths.[43] Thus, to assure faithful observance of commitments and respect for borders, Numa installs shrines and priests for them (chapter 16).[44] Oaths will be respected only if fear of punishment is real, and this depends on nothing so much as fear of the gods. Consequently, in the final analysis, persuasion (πειθώ) of the people to remain loyal to the constitution of the state in its entirety requires their belief in the existence of the gods, an argument first made by Plato.[45]

What, then, of hope? The question is answered by a final apophthegma concerning Numa himself: "Toward the divine he had such an attachment to hopes that it happened once when a message was brought to him that enemies were approaching, he smiled and said, 'I am sacrificing'."[46] That is to mean that by performing the sacred act of sacrifice

---

[42] 15.6: Ταῦτα μὲν οὖν τὰ μυθώδη καὶ γελοῖα τὴν τῶν τότ' ἀνθρώπων ἐπιδείκνυται διάθεσιν πρὸς τὸ θεῖον, ἣν ὁ ἐθισμὸς αὐτοῖς ἐνεποίησεν.

[43] See Carl Becker, "Fides," *RAC* 7 (1969) 801–39; Giulia Piccaluga, *Terminus. Il segni di confine nella religione romana* (Rome: Edizioni dell' Ateneo, 1974), 177–85.

[44] For the great oath of Fides and the sacredness of borders, see Dionysius of Halic. 2.74–75; Cicero, *de leg*. 2.19; 2.28; Livy 1.21.4–5; for the sacredness of borders, see also Plutarch, *Quaest. Rom*. 15,267C. Cf. the analogous great oath that Lycurgus makes the Lacedaemonians swear, in order to abide by his system of laws (*Lyc*. 29.2–6).

[45] See Plato, *Rep*. 2,382a–c; *Leg*. 4,718b–723d; 10,884a–907e; moreover Isocrates, *Busiris* 24–27; Polybius 6.51–56; 10.2.8–13 (with the commentary by F.W. Walbank, *A Historical Commentary on Polybius*; 3 vols. [Oxford: Clarendon, 1957–79], 741–43); Cicero, *De div*. 1.117–118 (vol. 1, p. 513 ed. Pease, with parallels); *De rep*. 1.2; 1.7; *De leg*. 2.7.15–22, and the commentary 2.10.23ff. On the whole topic, see Wilhelm Fahr, *ΘΕΟΥΣ ΝΟΜΙΖΕΙΝ. Zum Problem der Anfänge des Atheismus bei den Griechen* (Spudasmata 26; Hildesheim: Olms 1969), 172–79; Klaus Döring, "Antike Theorien über die staatspolitische Notwendigkeit der Götterfurcht," *Antike und Abendland* 24 (1978) 43–56* Jerzy Linderski, "Cicero and Roman Divination," in his: *Roman Questions: Selected Papers* (Stuttgart: Steiner, 1995), 458–84.

[46] 15.6: αὐτὸν δὲ Νομᾶν οὕτω φασὶν εἰς τὸ θεῖον ἀνηρτῆσθαι ταῖς ἐλπίσιν, ὥστε καὶ προσαγγελίας αὐτῷ <θύοντί> ποτε γενομένης ὡς ἐπέρχονται πολέμιοι, μειδιᾶσαι καὶ εἰπεῖν· ἐγὼ δὲ θύω. (my trans.)

he could simply dismiss the danger with a smile, knowing that he "had Good Fortune for his true consort, colleague, and co-regent."[47]

All this makes sense as later explanations for Numa's enormous success in turning the belligerent and almost ungovernable city into the peaceful and well-administered model for all times to come. What impresses about Numa's clearly designed reform program is Plutarch's sense for social pragmatism. In order to make reforms acceptable, their social grounding is necessary, and that includes past practices, customs, habitual thought patterns, and even primitive superstitions from an earlier period. This pragmatism is preferable even to Plato's design of the ideal state which is left entirely in the realm of utopian theory.

As far as Plutarch himself is concerned, he distinguishes between Numa's beliefs, reported by the sources, and his own convictions. Plutarch shows respect for Numa's philosophical and social-political goals, and even for his shrewd exploitation of ancient superstitions. However, there is at least one instance in which he admits having a problem. This problem is related to Numa's alleged sexual relationship with Egeria, a divine being. This issue being central to the appreciation of Numa's work needs special discussion and justification even at the philosophical level, and to this he turns in his chapter 4.

First, he reports on the terms of the legend (λόγος). After the death of his wife Tatia, Numa "left the city life for the country-side, wanting to wander around alone most of the time and making his life in groves of gods, sacred meadows and deserted places. Not the least from this the legend about the goddess took its beginning, according to which it was not from some disturbance or aberration of the soul that Numa gave up life among human beings, but because he had tasted a more distinguished company and had been dignified by divine marriage. Living in love and sharing life with a daimon Egeria. he became a happy man inspired by things divine."[48] If these are the words of the legend, they are

[47] This is Plutarch's longer explanation in *De fort. Rom.* 9, 321C: ἀλλὰ Νομᾶς ἔοικε τὴν ἀγαθὴν Τύχην ἔχειν ὡς ἀληθῶς σύνοικον καὶ σύνεδρον καὶ συνάρχουσαν...(my trans.) See the whole context 9–10, 321B–322C.

[48] 4.1–2: Ὁ δὲ Νομᾶς ἐκλείπων τὰς ἐν ἄστει διατριβὰς ἀγραυλεῖν τὰ πολλὰ καὶ πλανᾶσθαι μόνος ἤθελεν, ἐν ἄλσεσι θεῶν καὶ λειμῶσιν ἱεροῖς καὶ τόποις ἐρήμοις ποιούμενος τὴν δίαιταν, ὅθεν οὐχ ἥκιστα τὴν ἀρχὴν <ἐκεῖνος> ὁ περὶ τῆς θεᾶς ἔλαβε λόγος, ὡς ἄρα Νομᾶς [ἐκεῖνος] οὐκ ἀδημονίᾳ τινὶ ψυχῆς καὶ πλάνῃ τὸν μετ' ἀνθρώπων ἀπολέλοιπε βίον, ἀλλὰ σεμνοτέρας γεγευμένος ὁμιλίας καὶ γάμων θείων ἠξιωμένος, Ἠγερίᾳ δαίμονι συνὼν ἐρώσῃ καὶ συνδιαιτώμενος, εὐδαίμων ἀνὴρ καὶ τὰ θεῖα πεπνυμένος γέγονεν. (my trans.)

ambiguous enough to leave room for various interpretations. Notably, Plutarch's examination uses comparative methods in several steps.

First, he mentions the similarity of ancient myths (μῦθοι) such as those told by the Phrygians about Attis, the Bithynians about Rhodoites, and the Arcadians about Endymion, and others. "Quite obviously, these men were thought to be happy and god-beloved, and accepting it loved them in return."[49] The erotic language in these stories is simply to be taken as metaphors expressing "philanthropy" (φιλάνθρωπος), which, in these relationships, the deities are enjoying with human beings of outstanding wisdom and virtuousness. However, Plutarch ironically rejects the idea that such relationships may be taken in the physical sense. "But that this relationship should involve communion and pleasure of a human body and its beauty attributed to some god and daimon, this would take really hard work of persuasion."[50]

Next, Plutarch finds an Egyptian viewpoint worth discussing, according to which a difference is made between a woman and a man: "for a woman it is not impossible that a divine spirit approaches and causes in her the beginnings of pregnancy, but for a man there does not exist either intercourse or bodily communion with a god. But they [sc. the Egyptians] ignore the fact that what is getting mingled is sharing equal community with the one doing the mingling. However, it may by all means be appropriate for a god to have friendship with a human being, and to call it in this sense love that amounts to care for ethical conduct and virtue."[51] This is the figurative way to properly understand also plenty of other mythical examples brought up by poets, such as the love Apollo had for Phorbas, Hyacinthus and Admetus, as well as the Sicyonian Hippolytus and many others. This is where the poets have wide latitude to invent stories.

"There is, to be sure, nothing wrong with the other account, told about Lycurgus and Numa and other men like them, that, since they

---

[49] 4.2:...εὐδαιμόνων δή τινων καὶ θεοφιλῶν γενέσθαι δοκούντων παραλαβόντες ἠγάπησαν, οὐκ ἄδηλόν ἐστι (my trans.)

[50] 4.3: ὡς δὲ καὶ σώματος ἀνθρωπίνου καὶ ὥρας ἐστί τις θεῷ καὶ δαίμονι κοινωνία καὶ χάρις, ἔργον ἤδη καὶ τοῦτο πεισθῆναι. (my trans.) Cf. the discussion in Grant, *Miracle*, 175–77.

[51] 4.4:...ὡς γυναικὶ μὲν οὐκ ἀδύνατον πνεῦμα πλησιάσαι θεοῦ καί τινας ἐντεκεῖν ἀρχὰς γενέσεως, ἀνδρὶ δ' οὐκ ἔστι σύμμειξις πρὸς θεὸν οὐδ' ὁμιλία σώματος· ἀγνοοῦσι δ' ὅτι τὸ μειγνύμενον ᾧ μείγνυται τὴν ἴσην ἀνταποδίδωσι κοινωνίαν, οὐ μὴν ἀλλὰ φιλίαν γε πρὸς ἄνθρωπον εἶναι θεῷ, καὶ τὸν ἐπὶ ταύτῃ λεγόμενον ἔρωτα καὶ φυόμενον εἰς ἐπιμέλειαν ἤθους καὶ ἀρετῆς, πρέπον ἂν εἴη. (my trans.) Cf. the discussion in Plutarch, *Quaest. conviv.* 8.1.3, 717E–718B.

had to manage ill-disposed and hard to please masses, and to impose great reforms on the states, they pretended to have the sanction from the deity, which was fabricated as a means of salvation for these people."[52] In other words, this kind of religious credulity is approved in the sense that it is beneficial to use it politically for the control of the uneducated and volatile masses.

3. Conclusions

"In Plutarch we find no solution for the problem of miracle. His caution in such matters does not reflect a naive piety but a genuine unwillingness to think through his difficulties."[53] This statement by Grant has the flavor of youthful impatience, but it also depends too quickly on the somewhat contemptuous attitude regarding Plutarch characteristic of 19th century scholarship.

For Plutarch, miracles pose a problem that is by definition insoluble. Miracles are occurrences that challenge commonsense assumptions or existing standards of science and philosophy. If miracles are *experienced*, they are to be taken as αἰνίγματα, σημεῖα, and προβλήματα, which call for investigation and verification or falsification. Such investigations will result in rational explanations of some sort, or in classification as superstition. The problem is that these results are themselves relative because they depend on the ever-changing standards of science and philosophy. Ultimately, there is, indeed, no "final solution" to this problem.

Most miracles, however, are *stories*, coming from oral tradition and the narration of occurrences of miracles, that is, they are claims without scientifically acceptable verification. Such stories are by definition rhetorical and literary products classifiable under the genre categories of θαυμάσια, θαύματα/*mirabilia*, or ἀδύνατα/*impossibilia*. To their listeners or readers these stories can serve quite different purposes: religious propaganda, literary entertainment, quasi-scientific interest in curiosities (παράδοξα), and so forth. These miracle stories can either be believed in a naive way, or, more rationally, interpreted as metaphors, parables, and examples. The former would amount to superstition, the latter

---

[52] 4.8: οὐδὲ γὰρ ἅτερος λόγος ἔχει τι φαῦλον, ὅν περὶ Λυκοῦργου καὶ Νομᾶ καὶ τοιύτων ἄλλων ἄνδρων λέγουσιν, ὡς δυσκάθεκτα καὶ δυσάρεστα πλήθη χειρούμενοι, καὶ μεγάλας ἐπιφέροντες ταῖς πολιτείαις καινοτομίας, προσεποιήσαντο τὴν ἀπὸ τοῦ θεοῦ δόξαν αὐτοῖς ἐκείνοις πρὸς οὕς ἐσχηματίζοντο σωτήριον οὖσαν. (my trans.)

[53] Grant, *Miracle*, 68.

may serve philosophical education and even lead to scientific experiments. Naive or sophisticated, even superstition has its uses, especially in politics. No government can be imagined to succeed without some help from superstition, be it on the part of the credulous masses or the powerful rulers. Therefore, the accounts of history and biography abound with a great variety of miracle stories.

In the days of Plutarch, this situation represents the consensus of the Platonic Academy as well as most other philosophical schools, except for the extreme skeptics.[54] Today, contrary to public opinion, the situation is not radically different. *Miracle and Natural Law* are still associated in more ways than can be explored here. More than ever, common superstition is locked in battle with science and philosophy. Especially if one adds political ideologies, superstition becomes a powerful tool in politics. The institutional separation between religion and politics is more an ideal than reality. The highest offices in almost any country require holders to swear sacred oaths, and no such oath can be performed without invoking divine assistance and placing the hand on Holy Scripture. And admittedly or not, every true scientist hopes for the greatest of all experiences, namely the discovery of a new phenomenon, hitherto unaccounted for and overturning the established laws of nature.

---

[54] For Plutarch's philosophical approach to miraculous phenomena, see *De E ap. Delph.* 2, p. 385C; *Quaest. conviv.* I.9, pp. 626F–627A; IV.2, p. 664C; V.7, p. 680C–D; cf. Plato, *Theaet.* 155d; Aristotle, *Met.* 982b11–14 (ed. W.D. Ross).

"THAT UNPREDICTABLE LITTLE BEAST": TRACES OF AN OTHER SOCRATES

A.J. Droge

There's a divinity that shapes our ends,
Rough-hew them how we will.
Hamlet V.ii.10–11

Socrates' *daimonion* is something of an embarrassment in a figure who is otherwise celebrated for his powerful, probing intellect, and whose characteristic elenctic method is said to owe exclusive allegiance to secular ratiocination—in short, to λόγος not μῦθος. But the stubborn fact remains that both Plato and Xenophon make mention of something Socrates and others called his *daimonion*. Here the problems begin. Is the *daimonion* Socrates' tutelary divinity? A mystical experience perhaps? Some deep intuitive sense of things? The voice of reason? Conscience? Or is it merely a way of referring to Socrates' eccentric personality? No less an authority on Greek philosophy than W.K.C. Guthrie thought the matter best left "to students of psychology or religious experience."[1] E.R. Dodds was both, but his explanation of Socrates' *daimonion* as one of the few cases of "spontaneous auditory automatism" in the ancient world has found few adherents.[2] Even the very term leaves the interpreter in a bit of a semantic quandary, as Kierkegaard already observed in his doctoral thesis. By itself, *daimonion* "is not simply adjectival so that one might render it complete by implying function, deed (ἔργον), or sign (σημεῖον), or something of the kind; nor is it substantive in the sense that it describes a particular or unique being."[3] This semantic ambiguity

---

[1] *A History of Greek Philosophy*, vol. 3: *The Fifth-Century Enlightenment* (Cambridge: Cambridge University Press, 1969), 404. Socrates' *daimonion* is an uncomfortable datum for Guthrie's overarching narrative of the progress of Greek philosophical thought from a mythic to a rational view of the world in the period from 600 to 300 B.C.E. Note the subtitle to his third volume.

[2] *The Ancient Concept of Progress and Other Essays on Greek Literature and Belief* (Oxford: Oxford University Press, 1973), 192.

[3] *The Concept of Irony, with Constant Reference to Socrates* (trans. L.M. Capel; Bloomington/London: Indiana University Press, 1965 [1841]), 186, quoting directly from F. Ast, *Platon's Leben und Schriften* (Leipzig: Weidmann, 1816), 483.

has resulted in a staggering array of English translations for *daimonion*: guiding spirit, prophetic monitor, daimonic thing, and so on.[4]

Plato's use of the word is sometimes adjectival, at other times elliptically substantival. He refers only twice to τὸ δαιμόνιον. In one passage Socrates explains to the seer Euthyphro the charges Meletus has just brought against him—that Socrates corrupts the youth because he is the creator of "new gods" (καινοὶ θεοί) and does not believe in the old ones—to which Euthyphro responds: "I get it, Socrates. This is because you say that τὸ δαιμόνιον keeps coming to you. So [Meletus] has written this indictment against you for making innovations in religious matters" (καινοτομοῦντός σου περὶ τὰ θεῖα).[5] However elliptical δαιμόνιον may be in general, it is hard to see how the use of the substantive in this passage can refer to anything other than a "deity" or "divinity."[6] The same would seem to be the case at *Theaet.* 150d–151a where Socrates describes his art of midwifery. Though denying any claim to wisdom, Socrates acknowledges that those who associate with him do make "amazing progress," not because they have learned anything from him but because they have discovered within themselves "many beautiful things" and "given birth" to them. "But," Socrates says, "the delivery is due to the god and me" (τῆς μέντοι μαιείας ὁ θεός τε καὶ ἐγὼ αἴτιος, 150d). Those associates who drift away from Socrates' care lose whatever progress they have made, and some eventually plead to be taken back. Yet this is not a matter Socrates can decide for himself: "When such men come back," he says, "begging for my company and ready to do wonders, τὸ δαιμόνιον comes to me and forbids me to associate with some but allows others, and these once more make progress" (151a). Here again the substantive seems to have a meaning very close, if not equivalent, to ὁ θεός even if the identity of the god remains mysterious.[7]

---

[4] A glance at *LSJ* reveals the wide range of possible meanings for δαιμόνιος ("marvelous," "miraculous," "heaven-sent") and τὸ δαιμόνιον ("divine power," "divinity," "fatality," "fortune"), and illustrates the difficulty of finding precise English equivalents for their use by Plato and Xenophon. Everything depends on context. For the moment I prefer to leave the word untranslated, though on occasion I gloss it with the term "supernatural." This is intended merely as a place holder and only to indicate that in the texts under consideration here *daimonion* signals "(something) more than human."

[5] *Euthyph.* 3b.

[6] See R.E. MacNaghton, "Socrates and the ΔΑΙΜΟΝΙΟΝ," *The Classical Review* 28 (1914): 187–188: "When Plato uses the word δαιμόνιον as a substantive, he uses it as an alternative to θεός."

[7] *Pace* G. Vlastos, *Socrates, Ironist and Moral Philosopher* (Ithaca: Cornell University Press,

Given the importance of the Delphic oracle to Socrates' mission, some have conjectured that it is the god Apollo who is meant by τὸ δαιμόνιον.[8] But I have my doubts as to whether this identification will withstand scrutiny. Indeed, this is perhaps the major puzzle of Socrates' "defense:" for someone accused of not recognizing the gods of the city, nowhere in Plato's *Apology* does Socrates explicitly profess a belief in any of them, not even Apollo, whom he ostensibly spent his life serving.[9] As a matter of fact, it was not Socrates who had gone to consult the god of Delphi, but his younger friend, Chaerephon. Bear in mind, too, that when Socrates' received the report of Chaerephon's oracle he did not respond with immediate belief; on the contrary, he carried out an investigation of Apollo (ἐπὶ ζήτησιν αὐτοῦ ἐτραπόμην, 21b). Socrates does not so much try to refute the charge of "atheism" as he does evade it, and a majority of the jurors appear to have recognized this for the ploy that it was.

If τὸ δαιμόνιον is an alternative to ὁ θεός, then "the god" being referred to seems to be Socrates' own personal deity and not precisely identifiable with any of the gods of the city. This may allow us to reinterpret several

1991), 280, who repeats the following claim of J. Burnet, *Plato's Euthyphro, Apology of Socrates and Crito* (Oxford: Clarendon Press, 1924), 16: "There is no such noun-substantive as δαιμόνιον in classical Greek. That makes its first appearance in the Septuagint, where it is pretty clearly a diminutive of δαίμων rather than the neuter of δαιμόνιος." Vlastos wants to deny that the *daimonion* is in any sense a "divine progonosticator" for Plato's (i.e., according to Vlastos, the historical) Socrates, and insists that "we should always read the word [δαιμόνιον] as a contraction for the phrase we see filled out in *R.* 496c, 'the divine sign' (τὸ δαιμόνιον σημεῖον)," adding in a footnote that "there is no textual foundation for the assumption . . . that in Plato τὸ δαιμόνιον is a contraction for 'the divine *thing*'" (*Socrates*, 280–281 and n. 141). I return to Vlastos' interpretation below, but just on the basis of the two passages cited above one can see there are problems with it. See further E. De Stryker and S.R. Slings, *Plato's Apology of Socrates: A Literary and Philosophical Study with a Running Commentary* (Leiden: E.J. Brill, 1994), 154 n. 6: "From Herodotus onwards (II 120, 5, etc.), the adjective δαιμόνιος can be used substantively, to denote, like τὸ θεῖον, a divine agent whom one does not want to name. . . . The notion that δαιμόνιον means 'little daemon' is erroneous." Cf. Herodotus 5.87; 6.84; Isocrates 1.33; 5.149; 12.174.

[8] So e.g. M.L. McPherran, *The Religion of Socrates* (University Park: Penn State University Press, 1996), 137, 140; cf. C.D.C. Reeve, "Socrates the Apollonian?," in *Reason and Religion in Socratic Philosophy* (ed. N.D. Smith and P.B. Woodruff; New York: Oxford University Press, 2000), 24–39.

[9] *Apol.* 35d notwithstanding, where there is no direct object for Socrates' profession of belief. What Socrates says is: "For I do recognize (νομίζω) [but what?], men of Athens, as no one of my accusers does, and I entrust to you and to the god [Socrates' *daimonion*?] to judge me in whatever way will be best for me and yourselves." *If* this line is historical, Socrates is being too clever for his own good. On this passage, see the instructive, if somewhat speculative, discussion in McPherran, *Religion of Socrates*, 162–167.

statements in which ὁ θεός is invoked (without it being clear which god is meant) as a reference to the *daimonion*—that is, to Socrates' personal deity—and not to any member of the conventional pantheon. Here are just a few examples from the *Apology*: "For know well, this [i.e. Socrates' mission] is what *the god* commands, and I think that no greater good has ever befallen you in this city than my service to *the god*" (30a); "I am a kind of gift from *the god* to the city" (31a); "Now, as I say, I have been ordered by *the god* to do this [i.e. his mission], both as a result of oracles and dreams [καὶ ἐκ μαντείων καὶ ἐξ ἐνυπνίων], and in every way in which any other divine dispensation ever commanded a human to do anything at all" (33c); "I entrust to you and to *the god* to judge me in whatever way will be best for me and yourselves" (35d); and the famous "Now it's time to leave, I to die and you to live. Which of us goes to the better circumstance is unclear to everyone but *the god*" (42a).[10] *If* these passages are historically reliable, then it could be argued that the reason for Socrates' conviction was the failure of his strategy of double-speak: of saying one thing (albeit sincerely) and hoping the jurors would hear something else. A majority seems to have been sorely troubled by Socrates' references to his personal deity and by his sketchy attempts to render it compatible with conventional belief. But more on this below.

Now if τὸ δαιμόνιον designates a deity, and more precisely Socrates' own god, then Plato employs a variety of expressions to describe *how* this divinity communicates its will to Socrates. Put differently, it is important (*pace* Vlastos and others) to recognize and maintain a distinction between references to Socrates' *daimonion* and descriptions of its means of communication—its "voice" or "sign."[11] At *Apol.* 31d Plato has Socrates say: ὅτι μοι θεῖόν τι καὶ δαιμόνιον γίγνεται ("something divine and supernatural comes to me"), and ἐμοὶ... φωνή τις γιγνομένη ("a sort of voice comes to me").[12] Again in the *Apol.* Socrates refers to

[10] Cf. the ending of the *Crito*: "Then give it up, Crito, and let us act in this way, since it is in this way that *the god* leads" (54e). I am tempted to say that the appearance of the Laws, their conversation with Socrates, and their prohibiting his going into exile is Plato's (if the *Crito* is Platonic) dramatic representation of the way the *daimonion* worked for Socrates. But I cannot not pursue this here.

[11] On this, see L.-A. Dorion, "Socrate, le *daimonion* et la divination," in *Les dieux de Platon* (ed. J. Laurent; Caen: Presses universitaires de Caen, 2003), 183 and n. 41. As Dorion points out, interpreters tend to conflate Plato's references to the *daimonion* and his descriptions of how it communicated itself to Socrates.

[12] Cf. *Phaedr.* 242c: καί τινα φωνὴν ἔδοξα αὐτόθεν ἀκοῦσαι ("and I thought I heard a voice coming from this very spot").

τὸ τοῦ θεοῦ σημεῖον ("the sign of the god," 40b), τὸ εἰωθὸς σημεῖον ("the customary sign," 40c), or simply τὸ σημεῖον ("the sign," 41d).[13] Elsewhere he refers to τὸ δαιμόνιον σημεῖον ("the supernatural sign," *Rep.* 496c), τὸ δαιμόνιον τε καὶ τὸ εἰωθὸς σημεῖον ("both the *daimonion* and its customary sign," *Phaedr.* 242b; cf. *Euthyd.* 272e), and τὶ δαιμόνιον ἐναντίωμα ("a sort of supernatural hindrance," *Alc. I* 103a [if authentic]). But there is one passage in particular which deserves special attention. In his speech to the jurors who voted for acquittal, Socrates addresses them as his "friends" and attempts to explain to them the meaning of what has just taken place.

> An amazing thing has happened to me. In previous times, my customary oracular skill from the *daimonion* [ἡ εἰωθυῖά μοι μαντικὴ ἡ τοῦ δαιμονίου] was always very frequent, opposing me even on trivial matters, if I was about to do something that wasn't right [μὴ ὀρθῶς]. Now, however, as you yourselves can see, something has happened to me that one might think to be... the greatest of evils. Yet the sign of the god [τὸ τοῦ θεοῦ σημεῖον] did not oppose me when I left home this morning, or when I came up here to the law court, or anywhere in my speech when I was about to say anything, even though in other discussions it has often stopped me in the middle of what I was saying. But now, in this affair, it has not opposed me in anything I said or did. What then do I suppose is the reason? I'll tell you. What has happened to me is doubtless a good thing, and those of us who suppose death to be an evil must be mistaken. I have a great proof [μέγα τεκμήριον] of this: for the customary sign [τὸ εἰωθὸς σημεῖον] would surely have opposed me if I were not about to accomplish something good (*Apol.* 40a).

What emerges into partial light in this and other passages is an altogether different picture of Socrates: not the paragon of rational inquiry, as he is so often represented,[14] but a "soothsayer," a man possessed of

---

[13] *Apol.* 40b offers yet more support for construing τὸ δαιμόνιον as an alternative for ὁ θεός.

[14] Vlastos is certainly not the only representative of this position, but he is without question the most eloquent and prolific. His Socrates is a knight of reason, not of faith, and the "prompting" of the *daimonion* is always subordinated to Socratic elenctic reason. Vlastos writes: "Think, for example, of a command like that which Abraham gets in Genesis 22: 'Take thou thy son, thine only son, Isaac, whom thou lovest. Get thee into the land of Moriah and offer him as a burnt offering.' While Abraham could have taken, and did take, the surface content of the sign he got from God as its real meaning, Socrates could not. Both Abraham and Socrates believe that God is good and wills only good for those who serve him. And this would give both Abraham and Socrates a reason for doubting that God could be commanding something so horrendously iniquitous as killing an innocent child. But for Abraham faith trumps reason.... Not so in the case of Socrates, who lives with a commitment to argumentative reason... for

prophetic powers because of his *daimonion*, his personal god. His assertion that death is no evil is *not* established on rational grounds but is delivered as an oracular pronouncement.

Socrates is represented as a figure skilled in "the mantic arts" (ἡ μαντικὴ τεχνή).[15] At *Apol.* 39c he "prophesies" (χρησμῳδῆσαι) judgment against those jurors—his "executioners"—who voted against him. In his conversation with the seer (μάντις) Euthyphro, Socrates is told that Meletus' indictment is attributable to the envy people have in general for "*anyone like ourselves*," that is, people who have the gift of prophecy (*Euthyph.* 3b). To Phaedrus Socrates himself declares, "Now I am a seer" (μάντις), and then playfully adds, "though not very good at it, still—like those who are poor at reading and writing—I am good enough for my own purposes" (*Phaedr.* 242c). In these passages we discern a Socrates who is much more of a *religious* figure than is usually supposed, and we perhaps understand better the reasons for his conviction. During the Peloponnesian wars, soothsayers, as Eythyphro mentions (*Euthyph.* 3bc) and Aristophanic comedy confirms, were mercilessly satirized and treated with outright suspicion by the populace.[16] Furthermore, as Robert Garland has demonstrated, "new gods and their sponsors were by no means assured of a warm welcome when they petitioned for entry into a Greek community, and Athens was no exception."[17]

---

which there is no parallel in Abraham or any other Old Testament figure. The god Socrates serves has only the attributes which Socrates' elenctic reason would approve. If the *daimonion* were ever to give a message which contradicts the character Socratic reason establishes for the gods the message would thereby condemn itself as a vagary of his own fancy instead of a true command from his god" (*Socrates*, 285–286). All of this is an argument from silence. Cf. M. Nussbaum, "Commentary on Edmunds," in *Proceedings of the Boston Area Colloquium in Ancient Philosophy* 1 (1985) 234–235: "The *daimonion* of Plato's Socrates is no tutelary deity at all.... The *daimonion* is called *daimonion*, a divine thing, because human reason *is* [*sic*] a divine thing.... Socrates is telling us that reason, in each one of us, *is* [*sic*] the god truly worthy of respect." I confess that I find the strategy of rationalizing the *daimonion* not only oxymoronic but flawed by far too much special pleading.

[15] Note esp. the reference to μαντεῖα καὶ ἐνύπνια at *Apol.* 33c.

[16] Aristophanes, *Av.* 521, 959–988; *Eq.* 1080–1085; *V.* 380; *Nu.* 332; cf. Thucydides 2.17.2; 5.26.3–4, 103.2. On Aristophanes, see N. Smith, "Diviners and Divination in Aristophantic Comedy," *Classical Antiquity* 8 (1989): 138–158; on Thucydides, see N. Marinatos, "Thucydides and Oracles," *JHS* 101 (1981): 138–140.

[17] R. Garland, *Introducing New Gods: The Politics of Athenian Religion* (Ithaca: Cornell University Press, 1992), 146. He goes on to argue that there were "sound religious reasons, too, for regarding the *daimonion* of Plato's Sokrates with the gravest suspicion, first because it made its communications exclusively to one individual, secondly because it demonstrated not the slightest interest in the welfare of the rest of the citizen body, and thirdly because it could be contacted without recourse to the traditional channels

To summarize, then: Socrates' experience of the *daimonion* began in childhood and manifested itself frequently throughout his life; it acted in matters great and small, though only in a negative fashion, dissuading him from what he proposed to do and never urging him on (*Apol.* 31d, 40a). It kept him from embarking on a political career (*Apol.* 31d; *Rep.* 496c), prevented him from leaving a discussion that eventually turned out well (*Euthyd.* 272e), and from another conversation until he had made some atonement to the gods (*Phaedr.* 242cd). The *daimonion* might warn Socrates not to take back a student who had left him in the past (*Theaet.* 151a). It might even check him in the middle of a sentence (*Apol.* 40b). It kept him from speaking to his beloved Alcibiades for many years until at long last the restraint was lifted (*Alc. I* 103a [again if authentic]). Socrates also acknowledged that his *daimonion* was exceptional: it had happened to few or none before him (*Rep.* 496c). This far Plato.[18]

Our other major source of information about the *daimonion* is Xenophon, who employs a much more consistent terminology than Plato: τὸ δαιμόνιον (*Mem.* 1.2, 4; 4.8.1, 5; *Apol.* 4, 5; *Sym.* 8.5), δαιμόνιον (*Apol.* 13), and φωνή (*Apol.* 12). Like Plato, Xenophon attributes Meletus' charge of introducing καινὰ δαιμόνια to a misrepresentation of Socrates' *daimonion*: "For it had become notorious," Xenophon writes, "that Socrates claimed the *daimonion* gave him a sign (τὸ δαιμόνιον ἑαυτῷ σημαίνειν). It was for this reason above all that he was accused of introducing new divinities" (*Mem.* 1.1.2).[19] Even so, according to Xenophon, Socrates was not introducing anything new, "any more than those who practice divination (μαντική) by relying on augury, oracles, chance occurrences, and sacrifices.... But whereas the majority claim that it is the birds or the people whom they meet that dissuade or prompt them, Socrates said exactly what he meant: for he said that the *daimonion* gave him a sign" (i.e., communicated *directly* with him, *Mem.*

---

of communication between man and god, namely sacrifice, votive offering, prayer and so on.... Sokrates was undermining three of the basic tenets of Greek religion" (149). Garland's distintion between the political and religious threats Socrates presented is anachronistic, but his point is important nevertheless.

[18] At *Tim.* 90a Plato has Timaeus say that "God has given to each of us, as his δαίμων, that kind of soul which is housed in the top of our body and which raises us...up from earth towards our kindred in heaven." Yet Plato makes no attempt to explain Socrates' *daimonion* in terms of this indwelling personal "daemon." That is something the Platonists of late antiquity would do (on which see below). According to Plato, Socrates' *daimonion* was exceptional.

[19] Repeated at *Apol.* 12; cf. Plato, *Apol.* 31d; *Euthyph.* 3b.

1.1.3–4). Given the fact that elsewhere Xenophon uses τὸ δαιμόνιον, οἱ θεοί, and τὸ θεῖον interchangeably,[20] it would appear that the *daimonion* is for Xenophon what we surmised it was in Plato: not an intermediary being (or type of δαίμων), much less the voice of conscience, but in fact a deity—Socrates' personal god.

In contrast to Plato, however, for whom the *daimonion* communicated with Socrates *alone* and only indicated to him what *not* to do, Xenophon reports that the *daimonion* gave positive advice as well as negative and—this is extraordinary—was at the disposal of others. "[Socrates] often warned many of his companions to do this or not to do that, as the *daimonion* indicated, and those who followed his advice benefited from it, and those who rejected it regretted it" (*Mem.* 1.1.4; cf. 4.3.12; *Apol.* 12). In the parallel passage in Xenophon's *Apology*, Socrates states: "I have revealed to many of my friends what the god has advised (τὰ τοῦ θεοῦ συμβουλεύματα), and I have never been found to be wrong" (*Apol.* 13).[21] While Socrates' oracular infallibility is repeatedly emphasized, Xenophon is curiously silent when it comes to providing any examples or anecdotes of the *daimonion* actually communicating to Socrates. Whereas Plato mentioned six or seven occasions of the *daimonion* at work, Xenophon offers only one example: it twice intervened to prevent Socrates' from preparing a defense speech (*Apol.* 5; cf. the parallel passage at *Mem.* 4.8.5). According to Xenophon, then, Socrates' *daimonion* functioned as a semi-private oracle, dispensing prophecies to his "friends," and his mantic skill differed from conventional divination only in technique: his personal god spoke *directly* to him.[22]

Whether Plato or Xenophon gives the more accurate picture of Socrates' *daimonion* is perhaps beyond our grasp, but we can be reasonably confident that the historical Socrates claimed have some sort of personal deity, and that this was in part the basis for his indictment. Most interpreters are inclined to credit Plato's careful delineation of the *daimonion* as more historical than Xenophon's general description, which is alleged to have "a more definitely apologetic purpose."[23] Yet if both Plato and Xenophon are correct, that the charge of Meletus and

---

[20] See e.g. *Mem.* 1.4.2, 10; 4.3.14–15; *Hell.* 4.4.3.

[21] Again, note the interchangeability of τὸ δαιμόνιον and ὁ θεός in these parallel passages.

[22] That is, without any need for interpretation or exegesis.

[23] So Guthrie, *History of Greek Philosophy*, 403. Vlastos considers (early) Plato the more reliable witness in this and every case (see *Socrates*, 282, 297–300).

his fellow prosecutors was related to the *daimonion*, then it seems that Xenophon's account explains a little better why Socrates got into the sort of trouble he did. If Socrates was suspected of dispensing oracular pronouncements among a circle of friends with oligarchic or crypto-oligarchic leanings (Critias, Charmides, and Alcibiades, for example), this would have struck Meletus and no doubt many others as anything but innocuous.[24] According to Hermogenes, Xenophon's source in the *Apology*, the jurors responded to Socrates' boast of his oracular infallibility with shouts of disbelief and jealousy. Furthermore, the kind of terminology Plato puts into Socrates' mouth to describe the *daimonion* ("a *certain* divine or supernatural something," "a *sort* of voice," "a *certain* supernatural opposition," etc.), his insistence that it served Socrates *alone* and then only as a deterrent, and often in quite trivial contexts, all imply a concern to treat the *daimonion* with considerable circumspection. Xenophon's line of defense, on the other hand, admits the wide scope of the *daimonion*, but attempts to assimilate it to traditional modes of divination. It seems more likely to me that Plato reduced the role of the *daimonion* for apologetic reasons than that Xenophon expanded its role for similar reasons.[25]

But this is only the beginning of the story. The fascination with Socrates' *daimonion* manifests itself in at least two distinct, though not entirely separate, traditions, neither of which corresponds exactly with the evidence of Plato or Xenophon. By the second century C.E. we find Platonists discussing at great length the nature of Socrates' *daimonion*, and there are treatises on the subject by Plutarch, Apuleius, Maximus of Tyre, and others.[26] All of them treat the phenomenon by downplaying the uniqueness of its connection to Socrates, and by placing it in the larger framework of a complex hierarchy of cosmic beings. Thus the *daimonion* is no longer taken to be synonymous with ὁ θεός; it has now become an indwelling personal δαίμων, a sort of spirit guide or guardian

---

[24] Xenophon (*Mem.* 1.2.9–47) expends considerable energy trying to deflect the charge that Socrates taught his associates to "despise the established laws" and that he was the covert mastermind behind the public deeds of Critias and Alcibiades (cf. Isocrates 11.5; Aeschines 1.173).

[25] Plato may have made the *daimonion* act only in a negative or prohibiting fashion because otherwise it would have compromised (Plato's) Socrates' disavowal of knowledge.

[26] Plutarch, *De gen. Socr.* 9–12, 20–24; Apuleius, *De deo Socr.* 17–20; Maximus of Tyre, *Or.* 8 and 9 (τί τὸ δαιμόνιον Σωκράτους); cf. Proclus, *In Alc. I* 78, 7–85,14 (pp. 34–38 Westerink); and Olympiodorus, *In Alc. I* 21,1–22,5 (p. 16 Westerink). Olympiodorus equates δαίμων (and by implication Socrates' δαιμόνιον) with the Christian "guardian angel."

angel, intermediate between gods and men. Plutarch's dialogue *On the Daimonion of Socrates* seems to be the first instance of the identification of δαιμόνιον with δαίμων, although this probably occurred much earlier. Plutarch disassociates Socrates' *daimonion* from popular means of divination and explains it as Socrates' perception of the unspoken language of higher powers, the δαίμονες, who mediate between the divine and human worlds.

One of the interlocutors in the dialogue, Simmias, reports the myth of a certain Timarchus, who consulted the oracle of Trophonius to learn the true nature of Socrates' *daimonion*.[27] In his vision Timarchus discovered that the stars he saw overhead were the δαίμονες. As corks float above a net, so a person's individual "demon-star," the purest part of the soul (or νοῦς), floats above him, his soul fastened to it. A soul that obeys its δαίμων from its earliest years is one which belongs to "the race of seers and divine men" (τὸ μαντικὸν καὶ θεοκλυτούμενον γένος), and such was Socrates.[28] Though differing in detail, Maximus of Tyre presents a similar interpretation of Socrates' *daimonion*. He transforms Hesiod's reference to "the thirty thousand immortal watchers of mortal men" into "a great herd of δαίμονες," each dwelling in a different human body: "One (δαίμων) chose this body, and the next another, one Socrates, another Plato, this one Pythagoras, that one Zeno, still another Diogenes.... For as numerous as are the dispositions of men, so also are the natures of the δαίμονες."[29]

In contrast to Plato and Xenophon, these later authors display remarkably little interest in Socrates himself or his oracular abilities. Whereas Plato affirmed the uniqueness of Socrates' *daimonion* (it had happened "to few or none before [him]," *Rep*. 496c), and both Plato

[27] Simmias was, according to Plato and Xenophon, a Pythagorean and a member of Socrates' circle of friends; see D. Nails, *The People of Plato: A Prosopography of Plato and Other Socratics* (Indianapolis: Hackett, 2002), 260–261. Timarchus is otherwise unknown. For a description of the oracle of Trophonius, see Pausanias 9.39.2–14.

[28] Plutarch, *De gen. Socr.* 21–22 (590a–92e); cf. Apuleius, *De deo Socr.* 17–20. This view may go back to Posidonius; see the classic study by K. Reinhardt, *Poseidonios* (Munich: C.H. Beck, 1921), 464–71; and the discussion in J.M. Rist, *Stoic Philosophy* (Cambridge: Cambridge University Press, 1969), 265–72; J. Dillon, *The Middle Platonists* (Ithaca: Cornell University Press, 1977), 219–224, 317–320; and K. Döring, "Plutarch und das Daimonion des Sokrates," *Mnemosyne* 37 (1984): 376–92.

[29] Maximus of Tyre, *Or.* 8.8, quoting Hesiod, *Op.* 252–53. Among still later Platonists this "demonology" appears to grow increasingly complex, such that there is even a hierarchy among the δαίμονες. According to Proclus, *In Alc. I* 79,1–14 (p. 35 Westerink), Socrates' *daimonion* belonged to the highest rank of δαίμονες, the so-called "divine demons."

and Xenophon supplied instances of its prophetic power, the Platonists of a later period were much more concerned with Socrates as an exemplum—a divine man to be sure, but only one among others of this élite corps. Possession of the *daimonion* is no longer what made Socrates unique; this is true of all those who are characterized by surpassing wisdom and purity of soul. Indeed, it is a mark of the extent to which Socrates' *daimonion* has been made to serve the interests of middle Platonic "demonology" that these later authors cite almost no specific instances of Socrates' oracular capabilities. Apuleius mentions the episode from the *Phaedrus* (242cd), as does Maximus, who also alludes to the *First Alcibiades* (103a). Only Plutarch supplies us with a few examples of Socrates' *daimonion* at work, examples furthermore unattested in either the Platonic and Xenophontic writings. One is a quite trivial anecdote, the other two accounts are of much more serious consequence.[30]

Plutarch's treatise *On the Daimonion of Socrates* is cast in the form of a conversation within a conversation. Caphisias, the brother of Epameinondas and Theban envoy at Athens, describes to Archedamus and some other Athenians the events of the liberation of his city from Spartan control in 379 B.C.E., as well as some philosophical discussions that took place among the conspirators on the eve of their plot. Among the latter is a rather lively debate about the *daimonion* of Socrates, from which Plutarch's treatise gets its title. Theocritus, a companion of Socrates and seer (μάντις) himself, relates that although Socrates pursued the truth "with sober reason" (λόγῳ νήφοντι), he also relied on his *daimonion* to "illuminate matters dark and inscrutable to human wisdom." As evidence of the *daimonion*'s power and prophetic accuracy, several anecdotes from the life of Socrates are cited. Theocritus reports firsthand that when Socrates and some of his friends were en route to the house of Andocides, Socrates suddenly stopped in his tracks and

[30] Of course, the later identification of the *daimonion* with an intermediary δαίμων has its origins in Plato himself. In the *Symposium* (202de) Diotima describes Eros as a Δαίμων μέγας, an intermediary between mortal and immortal realms. She then goes on to say: καὶ γὰρ πᾶν τὸ δαιμόνιον μεταξύ ἐστι θεοῦ τε καὶ θνητοῦ. It is clear that Diotima is describing none other than Socrates himself, and, in fact, an exasperated Alcibiades will unintentionally confirm this when he calls Socrates δαιμόνιος at 219b. Cf. Dorion, "Socrate, le *daimonion* et divination," 192: "La démonologie platonicienne, qui s'élabore en marge et indépendamment des passages qui traitent du signe divin de Socrate, offre donc déjà tous les principaux éléments qui permettront, dans la tradition ultérieure, l'assimilation du signe de Socrate à une forme de démon."

fell deep into thought for a long time. "At last," Theocritus reports, "Socrates turned back, taking the way through the street of the cabinetmakers, and called out to his friends who had already gone on to return, saying that the *daimonion* had come to him" (αὐτῷ γεγονέναι τὸ δαιμόνιον). Most of the company turned back with him, but a few did not, imagining that they would thereby discredit the *daimonion*. As they continued on their way they were trampled by a herd of pigs being driven through a narrow passageway. When they finally returned, clothes torn and covered in mud, the Socratic faithful enjoyed a good laugh, but marveled all the same that "the divine (τὸ θεῖον) never neglected or deserted Socrates."[31]

Next, Polymnis, the father of Caphisias, mentions two other incidents, albeit more briefly but of considerably more significance. Both are said to be based on oral tradition (ἀκούω), although partial confirmation can be found in information Plato presents. The first episode occurred during the withdrawal of Athenian forces from Delium in 424 B.C.E. While the defeated Athenians retreated along three different routes, only the one chosen by Socrates at the urging of his *daimonion* proved to be safe. He, along with Alcibiades and Laches, escaped with their lives. Those who disregarded Socrates' *daimonion* and took a different route were killed by the Theban cavalry.[32] The Delium episode had been reported by Alcibiades in Plato's *Symposium* (221ab; cf. *Laches* 181e), though no mention was made of the occurrence of Socrates' *daimonion*. Socrates managed to escape because of his bravery and cool demeanor rather than through any supernatural intervention. Did Plato deliberately omit reference to the *daimonion*, or is Plutarch's version an embellishment of Plato's account? The other incident reported by Polymnis is as astonishing as it is brief. "I also hear," he says, "that [Socrates] foretold (προειπεῖν) to some of his friends the destruction of the Athenian force in Sicily."[33] The Athenian expedition to Sicily in 415–413 B.C.E. resulted in one of the greatest military disasters in Athenian history. Socrates' prediction is mentioned rather matter-of-factly by Polymnis, but his nonchalance should not cause us to lose sight of what a remarkable piece of information it is. Here is the trace of a tradition that Socrates' prophetic powers were not just for himself and his circle of friends, but

---

[31] Plutarch, *De gen. Socr.* 10 (580df).
[32] Plutarch, *De gen. Socr.* 11 (581de).
[33] Plutarch, *De gen. Socr.* 11 (581d); cf. Plutarch, *V. Nic.* 13.9 (532b); *V. Alc.* 17.5 (199f).

could be deployed in the wider arena of Athenian politics and foreign policy. If true, it makes even more apparent the religious *and* political threat Socrates presented to the city.

Stories like these seem to have circulated widely in antiquity. They constitute a second tradition about Socrates' *daimonion*, a tradition which seems much less interested in the theological implications of the *daimonion* than in the supernatural and miraculous character of Socrates himself. Reports of Socrates' prophetic powers, such as his prediction of the failure of the Sicilian expedition or the retreat from Delium, are typically dismissed by modern scholars as "apocryphal tales" because they present a picture of Socrates so at variance with the Platonic version.[34] But if, say, the Delium episode is apocryphal, it was not Plutarch who introduced Socrates' *daimonion* into the story. The same account appears in the first of the pseudepigraphic "Socratic Epistles," which are of uncertain date but have been placed as early as the first century B.C.E.[35] Though the recipient of this letter is not named, he appears to be a head of state who has offered Socrates a considerable fortune if he will leave Athens and become his teacher. Socrates replies in language reminiscent of Plato's *Apology*: he cannot abandon his philosophical mission to Athens because "the god has appointed [him] to this task." As the letter continues, however, ὁ θεός is equated with τὸ δαιμόνιον, not the god of Delphi. "I would not be surprised," Socrates writes, "if you did not believe me when I speak of the *daimonion*, for already not a few others have acted in this way towards me. A great many did not believe me at the battle of Delium." In the description that follows the *daimonion* is referred to as "the customary sign" (τὸ εἰωθὸς σημεῖον) and as "the voice" (ἡ φωνή). This section of the letter then concludes with a general statement about the function of the *daimonion*, which is again referred to as ὁ θεός: "To some men privately I also predicted many of the things that would happen to them, thanks to the god instructing me."[36]

The Delium episode appears yet again, along with two other anecdotes, in the first book of Cicero's treatise *On Divination*, published about

---

[34] So e.g. Dodds, *Ancient Concept of Progress*, 193 n. 1; and R.B. Rutherford, *The Art of Plato* (Cambridge: Harvard University Press, 1995), 59.

[35] The critical questions are discussed by H. Dörrie, "Sokratiker-Briefe," *Der kleine Pauly* 5 (1975), 257–58; for the text, see *The Cynic Epistles* (ed. A.J. Malherbe; SBLSBS 12; Missoula: Scholars Press, 1977).

[36] Ps.-Socrates, *Ep.* 1.7–9 (Malherbe).

45 B.C.E. The first book is an extended philosophical argument in favor of divination, put into the mouth of Cicero's brother, Quintus. The prophetic power of Socrates' *daimonion*, so frequently mentioned *in libris Socraticorum*, is attributed, Quintus says, to his special "purity of soul."[37] But instead of this becoming an occasion to discuss demonology in the manner, say, of a Plutarch or Apuleius, Quintus illustrates his argument with specific examples from the life of Socrates. We learn, for instance, that Xenophon consulted Socrates as to whether he should accompany Cyrus on campaign. Socrates replied affirmatively but with the qualification that the Delphic oracle ought to be consulted for confirmation.[38] "It is also related [*scriptum est item*] of Socrates," Quintus continues, "that one day he saw his friend Crito with a bandage on his eye. 'What's the matter, Crito?' Socrates asked. 'As I was walking in the country the branch of a tree... struck me in the eye.' 'Of course,' said Socrates, 'for after I had had divine warning [*praesagitio divina*], and tried to call you back, you did not listen.'"[39] An account of the episode at Delium follows, and then Quintus supplies a footnote: "Antipater has gathered a mass of remarkable premonitions by Socrates, but I shall pass them by, for you know them and it is useless for me to recount them."[40] The Antipater referred to here was a Stoic philosopher from Tarsus, who composed a treatise (c. 150 B.C.E.) in two books, Περὶ μαντικῆς, which evidently included numerous accounts of Socrates' prophetic powers.[41] That would mean that already by the first half of the second century B.C.E. biographical anecdotes like these were in wide circulation, and the view of the *daimonion* that emerges from them is somewhat closer to Xenophon's description than to Plato's.

The trail of the *daimonion* leads us back even further to the little Platonic dialogue called *Theages*. Before addressing how it might contribute to our investigation, the matter of its authenticity and date must be confronted. In antiquity there was no question about the genuineness

[37] Cicero, *De div.* 1.54 (§122). The term *daimonion* is written in Greek and rendered in Latin by *divinum quiddam*, not *genius*.

[38] Cicero, *De div.* 1.54 (§122). Quintus does not explicitly say that Socrates' advice came at the prompting of the *daimonion*, but that is what the context seems to imply. Cf. Xenophon, *Anab.* 3.1; *Mem.* 1.1.6–8; Diog. Laert. 2.49–50.

[39] Cicero, *De div.* 1.54 (§123)

[40] Cicero, *De div.* 1.54 (§123), *permulta collecta sunt ab Antipatro quae mirabiliter a Socrate divinata sunt.*

[41] For the fragments, see *SVF* III.37–42 (pp. 249–50). Antipater's views on divination are discussed by H. Cohn, *Antipater von Tarsos: Ein Beitrag zur Geschichte der Stoa* (diss. Giessen, 1904), 50–51.

of the work. Thrasyllus (d. 36 C.E.) placed it at the head of the Fifth Tetralogy, along with the *Charmides, Laches*, and *Lysis*.[42] In the mid-second century C.E. Albinus says that "some" began their reading of Plato with the *Theages*—underscoring the dialogue's prestige in the Platonic corpus—and this customary sequence of reading is confirmed by Diogenes Laertius.[43] Despite the ancient testimony, however, most scholars, beginning with Schleiermacher in 1826, have come to regard the dialogue as spurious.[44] Just when the *Theages* was composed, and by whom, have been much discussed. At one extreme, Paul Friedländer presents as good an argument as can be made for its authenticity;[45] at the other, Morton Smith places it in the second century B.C.E.[46] The *Theages* was almost certainly not written by Plato, but I am inclined to believe that it was composed in the period between 370 and 345 B.C.E., and thus probably during Plato's lifetime.[47]

In a prologue (121a–122e) the three main characters in the dialogue are introduced: Demodocus, accompanied by his son Theages, approaches Socrates in the agora to inquire about his son's education.[48] To give such advice, Socrates says, is something sacred, to educate is something divine, and the name "Theages" ("god-led") is significant. The first

---

[42] Diog. Laert. 3.59.

[43] Albinus, *Eisagoge* 4; Diog. Laert. 3.62.

[44] See the discussion in J. Souilhé, *Platon, oeuvres complètes*, 13.2 (Paris: Les Belles Lettres, 1930), 137–42, and the literature there cited. Not surprisingly, Vlastos (*Socrates*, 282) dismisses the historical value of *Theages*, "except as a monument to the level of credulity to which some of Socrates' superstitious admirers could sink after his death."

[45] *Plato, 2: The Dialogues, First Period* (trans. H. Meyerhoff; New York: Bollingen Foundation, 1964), 147–54, 326–29; cf. the remarkable M.A. thesis of a young S. Benardette, "The Daimonion of Socrates: A Study of Plato's *Theages*" (University of Chicago, 1953).

[46] "On the History of the 'Divine Man,'" in *Paganisme, Judaïsme, Christianisme: Influences et affrontements, Mélanges offerts à Marcel Simon* (Paris: É. de Boccard, 1978), 342.

[47] Following the argument of C.W. Müller, "Weltherrschaft und Unsterblichkeit im pseudoplatonischen Theages und in der Eudemischen Ethik," in *Politeia und Respublica* (ed. P. Steinmetz; Palengenisia 4; Wiesbaden: Steiner, 1969), 135–47. Essentially Müller's argument rests on two points: he sees in *Theages* 129e–130a the development of a theme set forth in *Theaetetus* 150c–151b (which he dates to 369 B.C.E.), and he detects a reflection of *Theages* 125ef in the *Eudemian Ethics* 2.10.1225b32–35 (dated to 345 B.C.E.). He attributes the *Theages* to a student of Plato. Müller's dating is endorsed by P. Hadot, *What is Ancient Philosophy?* (trans. M. Chase; Cambridge: Harvard University Press, 2002), 30–31, 287. See further Souilhé, *Platon*, 141–42; and especially H. Thesleff, *Studies in Platonic Chronology* (Commentiones Humanarum Litterarum 70; Helsinki: Societa Scientiarum Fennica, 1982), 217–18. Thesleff places it "in the context of the *Alcibiades I*, i.e. in the 370s."

[48] Probably the Demodocus mentioned by Thucydides (4.75.1) who was a general and tribute collector serving with Aristides; see Nails, *People of Plato*, 123–124.

section (122e–127a) of the dialogue is an elenchus to determine the kind of *sophia* Theages desires. Theages says that he wants to learn the wisdom necessary to govern the citizens of a state—in a word, politics. The second section (127b–130e) is introduced by the re-appearance of Demodocus, who appeals to Socrates to undertake personally the education of his son. The discussion now arrives at the central question of the dialogue, namely, the nature of Socratic *paideia* and the role played in it by the *daimonion*.

Socrates' initial response to Theages is playfully evasive. He points out that Theages already has one kind of *paideia*: he has learned his letters, the lyre, and wrestling (122e). But Theages wants more than this; he wants to rule. "I should indeed pray," he says, "that I might become a tyrant over all people, and failing that, over as many as possible . . .; even more, I would that I might become a god" (θεὸς γενέσθαι, 126a).[49] If Theages wants to learn politics, Socrates advises, he should seek out the politicians. In response Theages quotes Socrates' own words back to him: "Even the sons of such men are no better than the sons of shoemakers" (126cd).[50] Once more Socrates deflects. If not the politicians, then Theages should seek out the sophists. At this point the nature of Socratic *paideia* begins to emerge and is set in sharp contrast to politics and rhetoric. Socrates says, "I do not know anything about these blessed and fair subjects; would that I did! But what I always say, you know, is that I am in the position of knowing nothing except one little subject: matters pertaining to love (τὰ ἐρωτικά). In this subject, however, I claim to be skilled above anyone who has ever lived or is now living in the world" (128b).[51]

Theages takes this to be another evasion. He points out that not only have some of his peers benefited very quickly from Socrates' instruction but many others as well. If Socrates would only agree to take him on as a student, Theages too would make similar progress (128c). At this Socrates ceases his play-acting. The decision to receive a student and that student's subsequent progress are matters beyond Socrates' ken. Everything depends on the will of the *daimonion*: "There is something supernatural (τὶ δαιμόνιον)," he says, "which by divine fate has accompanied me from my childhood on. It is a voice (φωνή) that, when it

[49] Presumably the sort of deification possible for rulers.
[50] Cf. Plato, *Protag.* 320ab; *Alc. I* 118e.
[51] Cf. Plato, *Sym.* 177d; *Lysis* 204bc.

occurs, always indicates to me to avoid something which is about to happen, but it never urges me on." Yet the *daimonion* does not speak to Socrates alone: "If one of my friends consults me and the voice occurs, the same thing happens: it prohibits and does not allow him to act" (128d). The description seems to be half-way between what Plato and Xenophon report about the *daimonion*. Like Plato, the *daimonion* only acts negatively; like Xenophon, it is at the service of Socrates' friends.

Witnesses are called. The notorious Charmides, nephew of Critias and a leader of the oligarchic revolution in 404, consulted Socrates about whether to train for the Nemean races. Almost immediately the voice of the *daimonion* occurred: "No, you must not train." Charmides ignored the oracle and came to a bad end (128e). Next Socrates mentions a certain Timarchus and his accomplice Philemon, who had secretly plotted the assassination of Nicias. Twice, as they rose to leave a symposium at which Socrates was present, the "voice" occurred and Socrates warned Timarchus not to leave. The third time they evaded Socrates and committed the crime, but they were soon arrested and sentenced to death. On his way to execution Timarchus admitted he had done wrong to disregard Socrates' prophetic warnings (129ac).[52] Socrates then mentions his prediction of the disastrous Athenian defeat at Sicily, familiar to us from Plutarch, adding that "*many* will tell you what I said about the destruction of the army" (129d). Here is evidence that this prophecy is no late apocryphal tale but circulated at a very early date. Finally, Socrates offers an opportunity for Theages to put the *daimonion* to the test. A certain Sannio, himself a survivor of the Sicilian expedition, has just now set out with a military force bound for Ionia, and Socrates fears for his safety, expecting him either to be killed or brought very close to death. These examples confirm that Socrates' prophetic powers were believed to operate both in private *and* public realms. At times of crisis for Athens, Socrates was there, a veritable Cassandra, issuing oracular pronouncements.[53]

But there is more. Socrates mentions yet another function of the *daimonion*, this one of direct relevance to Theages. It plays a decisive role in Socrates' relationships with other men and prospective students in particular.

---

[52] We know nothing else about these two men or the event mentioned here. Nicias cannot be the famous general and leader of the failed Sicilian expedition, who was executed by the Syracusans (Thucydides 7.86.2). Like many of the characters in the *Theages*, Timarchus may have been a Theban; see Nails, *People of Plato*, 215.

[53] See Rutherford, *Art of Plato*, 59.

> Now I have told you all this because the power [δύναμις] of this *daimonion* that attends me also exerts itself to the full in my intercourse [συνουσία] with those who spend their time with me. To many, in fact, it is adverse, and it is not possible for these to get any benefit from conversation with me, and I am therefore unable to spend time with them. And there are many with whom it does not prohibit intercourse [συνεῖναι], yet they get no benefit from it. But those whom the power of the *daimonion* assists in their intercourse (with me) are the persons whom you have noticed, for they make rapid progress there and then (129e).

With some the benefit is lasting; others, however, slip back into their former state as soon as they leave Socrates' company. Another example is cited. Aristides the younger, grandson and namesake of the famous general and politician, made enormous progress in a short time as a result of his association with Socrates, but he experienced a relapse when obliged to go away on naval service (130a). In the *Laches*, Plato reported that Aristides' father Lysimachus had brought him to Socrates in the hope that he would undertake the task of educating him. In the *Theaetetus* (151a) we learn that despite being a quick and able student Aristides was a dismal failure. Now in the *Theages* we discover why, and the information is nothing less than astonishing. Aristides says that as a result of his association (συνουσία) with Socrates he was able to debate (διαλέγεσθαι) successfully with even the most educated, and was never found to be inferior in argument (ἐν τοῖς λόγοις) to anyone (130c). This sounds, oddly enough, like proficiency in conventional rhetoric. Yet Aristides' skill is anything but conventional. It is to be understood in terms of "power" (δύναμις, 130c), a word used twice to characterize the *daimonion* (129e), and one suggestive of the miraculous.[54] Whatever it was that Aristides acquired, it had nothing to do with anything that Socrates *taught* him: "I never yet learned anything from you," he says to Socrates (130d). All this may be an allusion to Plato's *Theaetetus* (150c–51b), where Socrates describes himself as a midwife and confesses that he possesses no wisdom nor has he given birth to any discovery. Those who associate with him, he says, "make progress at a rate that seems surprising to others as well as to themselves," but "they have never learned anything from me." The case of Aristides is mentioned, as is the role of the *daimonion* in taking back lapsed students. I say this *may*

[54] See D.L. Tiede, *The Charismatic Figure as Miracle Worker* (SBLDS 1; Missoula: Society of Biblical Literature, 1972), 35.

be an allusion to the *Theaetetus* because at least one scholar has argued that Plato's *Theaetetus* may be a response to the *Theages*.[55]

In the *Theages* Socrates' *paideia* seems likewise to be without content; a student's association with him does not involve a course of instruction, like that of the sophists. But in contrast to the *Theaetetus* there is no mention of Socrates' art of midwifery (μαιευτική), of his bringing to birth "many admirable truths."[56] Instead, something of the master's person ("wisdom," for example, or "power," or both) is conveyed to the student through *physical* proximity—notably *touch*—and assisted by *eros*. Aristides says,

> I will tell you, Socrates, what is incredible, by the gods, but true. For I never yet learned anything from you, as you yourself know, but I made progress [ἐπιδίδουν] whenever I was with you [συνείην]: if I was merely in the same house, without being in the same room, but more progress when I was in the same room. And it seemed to me to be much more when I was in the same room and looked at you as you were speaking, than when I turned my eyes elsewhere. But my progress was by far the greatest and most evident whenever I sat beside you and held and touched you [ἐχόμενός σου καὶ ἁπτόμενος]. Now, however, that condition [ἕξις] has all oozed away (130de).

Aristides' words call to mind Socrates' arrival in Plato's *Symposium* and Agathon's playful request that Socrates sit beside him so that Agathon might share "the great thought" that has just occurred to him. Socrates replies in the same playful manner: "I only wish," he says, "that wisdom *were* the kind of thing one could share by sitting next to someone" (175cd). The theme is touched on again in the speech of the drunken (but truthful) Alcibiades at the end of the *Symposium*. Socrates entrances people with a unique power, like that of the flute-playing satyr, Marsyas, except that Socrates needs no instrument, "only a few simple words" (215c). "For the moment I hear him speak," Alcibiades says, "I am smitten with a kind of sacred frenzy, worse than any Corybant, and

---

[55] See W. Janell, "Über die Echtheit und Abfassungszeit des Theages," *Hermes* 36 (1901): 427–39; a possibility dismissed too quickly, in my judgment, by Souilhé, *Platon*, 141.

[56] *Theaet.* 151d. Socrates' role as midwife is noticeably missing from the entire pseudo-Platonic corpus, as well as from the early Platonic dialogues. This may support the view that it was an invention of Plato and not attributable to Socrates himself, as D. Tarrant suggested in "The Pseudo-Platonic Socrates," *CQ* 32 (1938): 172; and confirmed in my opinion by M. Burnyeat, "Socratic Midwifery, Platonic Inspiration," *Bulletin of the Institute of Classical Studies* 24 (1977): 7–15.

my heart jumps into my mouth and my eyes well up with tears—oh, and not only me but lots of other men" (215de). Socrates may look like a satyr in his bestial physical appearance, but what lies within him is divine (217a). He is like a Silenus statue which contains within it little statues of the gods (215ab). When Alcibiades once saw Socrates' hidden treasures, they were "so godlike, so golden, so beautiful, so utterly amazing" that it was necessary to do whatever Socrates commanded (217a). Alcibiades had intended to acquire Socrates' power through sexual intimacy, but was thwarted by Socrates' amazing self-control, which is, along with the wisdom he possesses, the truly supernatural thing (δαιμόνιον) about him. It is not completely clear how Alcibiades thought he would acquire Socrates' power by sleeping with him. It could be as simple as gaining leverage to manipulate him into revealing his secrets, like Delilah with Samson, but it may as well be something more, like the transfer of *mana* in a shamanistic sense.[57] I do not suppose that Plato entertained this possibility—in fact, he seems to want to deny it—but the dialogue *Theages* suggests that such a notion was in the air and that the *Symposium* was an effort to diffuse it.

Like Plato, the author of the *Theages* invests Socrates with supernatural power, but with this difference: in the *Theages* Socrates' power is conveyed through his physical person. According to Plato (and, indeed, the later Platonists), Socrates' supernatural endowment was attributed to his purity of soul and his complete mastery of the body. In the *Theages*, by contrast, all the attention is on Socrates' *body*.[58] The confession of the younger Aristides appears to be an explicit rejection of what Socrates says to Agathon in Plato's *Symposium*: wisdom *is* the kind of thing that can be shared through physical intercourse. And this is just what Socrates says to Theages: "Such is the intercourse (συνουσία) you would have with me: if it pleases the god (ἐὰν μὲν τῷ θεῷ φίλον ᾖ), you will make very great and rapid progress, but otherwise you will not" (130e). At the beginning of the dialogue the youthful exuberance

[57] I recognize that there are problems with these terms, but I use them in a deliberately provocative way to create some interpretive space for seeing Socrates in a somewhat different light. Cf. H. Joly, *Le renversement platonicien* (Paris: J. Vrin, 1974), 67–69, who refers to Socrates as "the last shaman and the first philosopher."

[58] Note too the contrast with Socrates' remarks at *Theaetetus* 150b: "My art of midwifery is in general like theirs; the only difference is that my patients are men, not women, and my concern is not with the *body* but with the *soul* that is in travail of birth;" see D. Tarrant, "The Touch of Socrates," *CQ* 8 n.s. (1958): 95–98, though much more could be said.

of Theages had expressed itself in a desire to exercise power over as many people as possible: indeed, he wished that he might "become a god" (126a). If the *daimonion* (now identified as ὁ θεός) is willing, Theages will get his wish, but in a fashion he did not anticipate. Socratic *paideia*, if we may even refer to it as such, is predicated on the divine status of the teacher and implies the subsequent divinizing of the student *through physical contact.*

There is much more in this remarkable little dialogue than can be noted here. More attention might be given, for example, to the explicitly "erotic" dimensions of Socrates' συνουσία with Aristides and it connection with the *daimonion*. In the *Alcibiades* of Aeschines of Sphettos, one of Socrates' closest disciples, Socrates says,

> Because of the love I felt for Alcibiades, I had an experience no different from that of the Bacchants. For when they become inspired, the Bacchants draw milk and honey from wells from which others cannot even draw their water. As for me, though I have learned nothing that I could impart to a man to do him good, I nevertheless thought that if I associated with him I would make him a better man through my love [διὰ τὸ ἐρᾶν].[59]

As in the *Theages*, the emphasis here is again on physical proximity, in sharp contrast to Socrates' denial of this in Plato's *Symposium*. Although it is not precisely clear just how Socrates will benefit Alcibiades (as it was not clear with Aristides in the *Theages*), he insists that he is able to do this not through any "skill" (τέχνη) he possesses but by "divine dispensation" (θεία μοῖρα), just as in the *Theages* Socrates' ability to benefit Aristides or any student was due to his *daimonion*.[60] Whether or not these contradictory representations of Socrates can be reconciled (the one in *Theages* and Aeschines' *Alcibiades* with Plato's), one thing seems certain. The claim that Socrates was transformed into a "divine man" by later writers such as Plutarch, Apuleius, and Maximus of Tyre stands in need of qualification. The evidence of the *Theages* indicates that Socrates had already assumed this role in a much earlier period, and indeed may have been regarded as such during his own lifetime. Any conclusions drawn from the dialogue will of course depend on its date, and certainty about this may be beyond our grasp. Let me conclude by suggesting two possible interpretations of the dialogue,

---

[59] Aeschines F11c (Dittmar); cf. Plutarch, *Alc.* 4.3–4; Xenophon, *Mem.* 2.6.28.

[60] Aeschines F11a (Dittmar); on this, see C.H. Kahn, "Aeschines on Socratic Eros," in *The Socratic Movement* (ed. P.A. Vander Waerdt; Ithaca: Cornell University Press, 1994), 87–106, esp. 89–94.

assuming non-Platonic authorship and depending on whether one dates it early or late.

If we assign the *Theages* to the period, say, between 370 and 345 B.C.E., that would place it within the lifetime of Plato and would increase the probability that some of its anecdotes may have come down from persons who had actually seen Socrates. Thus it may contain information about the *daimonion* as reliable as anything Plato and Xenophon report. If the charge of introducing καινὰ δαιμόνια was related to Socrates' *daimonion*, as Plato and Xenophon both concede, then the *Theages*, in which Socrates is first credited with making oracular pronouncements in the arena of Athenian politics and foreign policy, explains better than either Plato or Xenophon why he would have posed such a threat. The dialogue lends credence to the suspicion that Socrates was in effect the mystagogue of a private, but illicit, mystery cult, whose members included men with known oligarchic and pro-Spartan ideological leanings.[61]

If, on the other hand, the *Theages* should be placed 150 years later, in the late third or early second centuries B.C.E., another possible interpretation presents itself.[62] In that case I would be inclined to regard the συνουσία of which Aristides speaks in a way quite different than appears at first sight. His testimony placed enormous importance on physical proximity to Socrates. "My progress," he says, "was by far the greatest and most evident whenever I sat beside you and held and touched you" (130e). It seems odd to place so much emphasis on Socrates' bodily frame after he has been dead for a century and a half or more. Does the *Theages* provide evidence for a cult of Socrates, a cult which also perhaps delivered oracles? Is the language of seeing, touching, and handling a reference to the veneration of a cultic statue? We know that statues of Socrates existed during his lifetime, and after his death Lysippus was commissioned to make a bronze statue of him which was erected between 340 and 330 B.C.E. in the Pompeion (Hall

---

[61] See the discussion in M. Munn, *The School of History: Athens in the Age of Socrates* (Berkeley: University of California Press, 2000), 284–291, though he makes no mention of the *Theages*. Aristophanes describes Socrates as the ring-leader of a group of Athenian devotees of Spartan ways (*Av.* 1280–1283; cf. Plato, *Gorg.* 515e).

[62] Souilhé (*Platon*, 142) dates it to this period on the basis of the references in the text to world-tyranny and Theages' desire to be recognized as a god, which he takes to reflect the period after Alexander the Great and the rise of ruler-cult. But such views were current in the early fourth century as well. Smith ("On the History of the 'Divine Man,'" 342) assigns it a second-century date without saying precisely why.

of Processions) near the Dipylon gate.[63] But there is no indication that this site served as a place for the memorialization of Socrates. And yet Socrates must have been buried somewhere, his provocative remark to Crito at *Phaedo* 115c notwithstanding.[64] A thorough check of Travlos' *Bildlexikon* proved fruitless.[65] So far as I know, the only evidence for a "Socrateion" or for a cultic statue of Socrates is to be found in the *Life of Proclus* by the Neoplatonist Marinus in the late fifth century C.E. Marinus reports that when Proclus arrived in Athens for the first time he paid a visit to the "shrine of Socrates" (Σωκρατεῖον) and drank from its sacred spring.[66] Is the *Theages* evidence for the existence of something like this at a much earlier date? The possibility of a cult of Socrates remains only that. Still, there is something in the dialogue itself which is quite suggestive. At its conclusion Theages agrees to submit to the will of the *daimonion.* "It seems to me, Socrates," Theages says, "that we should test the *daimonion* by associating with one another." If it does not intervene, so much the better; but if it does, Theages announces his intention "to exhort (παραμυθεῖσθαι) the *daimonion* with prayers and sacrifices and anything else that the seers may prescribe" (131a). This would be evidence that by the late third or early second century B.C.E. the presence of Socrates was believed to be mediated through a cult of his *daimonion.*[67]

These two alternative readings are not necessarily mutually exclusive. The cultic veneration of Socrates, if it existed, may have begun at an early date, perhaps even during his lifetime. And there is no reason why

---

63 Diog. Laert. 2.43. Lysippus' statue became the model on which the so-called "Type-B" portraits of Socrates were based; see M. Bieber, *The Sculpture of the Hellenistic Age* (rev. ed.; New York: Columbia University Press, 1961), 44–47, and the literature there cited.

64 "Crito: In what way shall we bury you? Socrates: In any way you like, if you can catch me and I don't elude you."

65 J. Travlos, *Pictorial Dictionary of Ancient Athens* (New York: Praeger, 1971).

66 Marinus, *Vita Procli* 10. The Σωκρατεῖον seems to have been located outside the walls of the city, because Marinus reports that Proclus stopped there on his way up from the Piraeus. In ch. 23 we are told that Proclus celebrated the birthdays of both Socrates and Plato.

67 In a fascinating esssay S.A. White, "Socrates at Colonus," in Smith and Woodruff, *Reason and Religion in Socratic Philosophy*, 151–175, argues persuasively that within a decade or two of Socrates' death Plato instituted a commemoration of Socrates—a kind of "hero-cult"—near the Academy on the outskirts of Athens, thus elevating Socrates from the status of fond philosophical memory to an active religious force within the school that Plato founded. He makes no mention of the *Theages* but his intepretation is amenable to my own. If White is correct, then this might have been the place of origin of the *Theages.*

a later date would preclude the possibility that the dialogue preserves some historically reliable information about the operation of Socrates' *daimonion*. Admittedly, neither this non-canonical dialogue nor my reading of it is likely to impress many of the modern-day Socratic faithful. Their Socrates is the standard bearer of enlightenment and the hero of a narrative of progress from religion to philosophy (*vom Mythos zum Logos*). His trust in the *daimonion*, that "unpredictable little beast" as Gregory Vlastos has called it, is wholly subordinated to his reliance on the power of reasoned discourse—or a cipher for reason itself.[68] The *Theages* does not invalidate this narrative so much as cause us to linger over some stubborn facts in the evidence where, I submit, we are able to discern traces of an other Socrates—enchanter, seer, magician—whom not even the extraordinarily deceptive power of Plato's art could entirely efface.[69]

[68] This reference to the *daimonion* occurs in his review of T.C. Brickhouse and N.D. Smith, *Socrates on Trial* (Princeton: Princeton University Press, 1989); see Vlastos, "Divining the Reason," *Times Literary Supplement*, 15–21 December (1989): 1393, and the lively exchange of letters among Vlastos, Brickhouse, Smith, and McPherran collected in Smith and Woodruff, *Reason and Religion in Socratic Philosophy*, 176–204. For an analysis of the metanarrative in which the "rational Socrates" plays the role of hero, see the collection of essays in *From Myth to Reason? Studies in the Development of Greek Thought* (ed. R. Buxton; Oxford: Oxford University Press, 1999).

[69] I am indebted to R. Gostenhofer, R. Kotansky, V. Nimmo, and A. Thomas-Elder for their careful reading of earlier drafts of this paper, and for providing invaluable criticisms and suggestions.

TO SHOW THE DIFFERENCE BY COMPARISON: THE *NEW WETTSTEIN* AND CLEANTHES' *HYMN*[1]

Johan C. Thom

> προύργου δὲ ᾠήθην καὶ τοῖς παρ' Ἕλλησιν ὀνομαστοτάτοις γεγενημένοις νομοθέταις τοὺς ἡμετέρους παρεξετάσαι, τοὺς ἁλιέας λέγω καὶ τὸν σκυτοτόμον καὶ τοὺς τελώνας, καὶ δεῖξαι πάλιν ἐκ ξυγκρίσεως τὸ διάφορον.
>
> I thought it useful also to examine our lawgivers (I mean the fishermen, the leather-worker, and the tax collectors) in comparison to those who have become most famous among the Greeks, and to show again the difference by comparison....
>
> (Theodoret, *Graec. affect. cur. praef.* 12, ed. Canivet)

Despite its many potential and actual abuses, the comparison of New Testament (NT) texts with Greek and Latin material remains indispensable for the historical study of the NT: it illuminates the historical context in which the NT authors and its first recipients lived by assisting in the reconstruction of the encyclopedia of knowledge, the linguistic and conceptual frameworks, the worldviews, and the social settings of these authors and readers; it helps us determine the *differentia* distinguishing early Christian traditions from other moral and religious movements of the time; and it is invaluable for identifying the dynamic and developmental relationships between early Christianity and other religions.[2]

---

[1] I am grateful for this opportunity to honor Robert Grant for all that I have learned from him, but especially to read ancient texts, including early Christian material, critically and without preconceived ideas, and to make *sense* of these texts within their intellectual and social contexts.

[2] For recent discussions of, and further bibliography on, the role of comparison of NT and Greco-Roman material, see Jonathan Z. Smith, *Drudgery Divine: On the Comparison of Early Christianities and the Religions of Late Antiquity* (Jordan Lectures in Comparative Religion 14, Chicago Studies in the History of Judaism; Chicago: University of Chicago Press, 1990); Gerald Seelig, *Religionsgeschichtliche Methode in Vergangenheit und Gegenwart: Studien zur Geschichte und Methode des religionsgeschichtlichen Vergleichs in der neutestamentlichen Wissenschaft* (Arbeiten zur Bibel und ihrer Geschichte 7; Leipzig: Evangelische Verlagsanstalt, 2001); L. Michael White and John T. Fitzgerald, "*Quod est Comparandum*: The Problem of Parallels," in *Early Christianity and Classical Culture: Comparative Studies in Honor of Abraham J. Malherbe* (ed. J.T. Fitzgerald, et al.; NovTSup 110; Leiden: Brill, 2003), 13–39. Walter Burkert's Lietzmann lecture also provides a salutary perspective: *Klassisches Altertum und antikes Christentum: Probleme einer übergreifenden Religionswissenschaft* (ed. C. Markschies; Hans-Lietzmann-Vorlesungen 1; Berlin: de Gruyter, 1996).

Most NT students and scholars will find it difficult to navigate their way through the extensive extant corpora of Greek and Latin texts. A collection of comparative material, judiciously selected to illustrate the aspects mentioned above, can therefore be an important tool to guide them through these sources. One of the most ambitious recent collections of this nature is the *New Wettstein*.[3]

1. The *New Wettstein*: A Brief Description

The *New Wettstein* project, to be published in two (or three) volumes with seven or eight parts, started out under the leadership of Georg Strecker at Göttingen in 1986 and has since 1993 been directed by Udo Schnelle at Halle.[4] The aim of the *New Wettstein* is to provide a "reader" ("Lesebuch")[5] containing passages with substantive parallels ("inhaltliche Parallelen") to NT texts, especially regarding rituals and institutions; texts explaining realia found in the NT; texts illuminating important concepts or scarce words; texts illustrating the reception horizon ("Rezeptionshorizont") of ancient readers; and texts explaining fixed word combinations (epithets, word pairs, phrases).[6] As the title

[3] A similar collection, but much less extensive is Klaus Berger and Carsten Colpe, eds., *Religionsgeschichtliches Textbuch zum Neuen Testament* (NTD, Textreihe 1; Göttingen: Vandenhoeck & Ruprecht, 1987); an English translation with additional material is provided by M. Eugene Boring, et al., *Hellenistic Commentary to the New Testament* (Nashville, Tenn.: Abingdon, 1995).

[4] The first volume of *Neuer Wettstein: Texte zum Neuen Testament aus Griechentum und Hellenismus* to be published was vol. 2, which appeared in two parts as *Texte zur Briefliteratur und zur Johannesapokalypse* (ed. Georg Strecker and Udo Schnelle; assisted by Gerald Seelig; Berlin: de Gruyter, 1996). Pt. 2 of vol. 1 appeared as *Texte zum Johannesevangelium* (ed. Udo Schnelle; assisted by Michael Labahn and Manfred Lang; Berlin: de Gruyter, 2001). It has become clear that the remaining NT books will require more space than originally planned: the three Synoptic gospels will each be published as separate parts, and Acts perhaps in two parts; see Udo Schnelle, "Wettstein, Johann Jakob," *TRE* 35 (2003), 726; Manfred Lang, "Die Neubearbeitung des *Neuen Wettsteins*" (2005), § 4, online: http://www.theologie.uni-halle.de/NT/CorpusHellenisticum/Wettstein/neubearbeitung (accessed 3 July 2006). For a brief description of the original project see Georg Strecker, "Das Göttinger Projekt 'Neuer Wettstein'," *ZNW* 83 (1992): 245–52. See now also Manfred Lang, "Geschichte und Programm des *Corpus Hellenisticum*" (2004), § 1.7, online: http://www.theologie.uni-halle.de/NT/CorpusHellenisticum/Geschichte (accessed 3 July 2006).

[5] Cf. Lang, "Geschichte und Programm," § 2.3: "Wie (Strack/)Billerbeck so will auch der Neue Wettstein ein Lesebuch sein, um zur weiteren Lektüre des entsprechenden Materials anzuregen und so selbst das eigene Verstehen zu fördern."

[6] See Gerald Seelig, "Einführung," in *Texte zur Briefliteratur und zur Johannesapokalypse* (ed. G. Strecker and U. Schnelle; vol. 2.1 of *Neuer Wettstein: Texte zum Neuen Testament*

indicates, the *New Wettstein* is first and foremost a revision of Johann Jakob Wettstein's collection of Greek, Latin, and Hebrew parallels to the New Testament.[7] According to the introduction to the first part of the *New Wettstein* to be published, "Es handelt sich hier um nicht mehr als eine Neubearbeitung, eine Revision des 'alten' *Wettstein*, die begrenzt erweitert, d.h. an theologisch zentralen Stellen durch neuere, im 'alten' *Wettstein* noch nicht aufgewiesene Vergleichstexte ergänzt wurde."[8] For practical reasons the *New Wettstein* therefore remains bound by some of the "old" *Wettstein*'s limitations in its selection of comparative texts,[9] but the fact that the *New Wettstein* does omit some of the texts found in the old *Wettstein* and adds some new texts of its own, means that its selection of material remains subject to critical evaluation.[10]

The manner in which comparative material is presented in the *New Wettstein* is straightforward: NT verses or passages to be illustrated are quoted or cited in order of appearance, each followed by one or more parallel passages taken from Greek and Latin texts. The latter are presented in the following order: first Hellenistic-Jewish texts, then pagan Greek texts, and finally Latin texts. The texts in each of these categories are listed in chronological order. These extracts are quoted in

---

aus Griechentum und Hellenismus; Berlin: de Gruyter, 1996), XV ("Gruppen von Belege"). Cf. however Lang, "Neubearbeitung," § 2.2 for changes in vol. 1 ("Diskontinuität zu NW II/1.2"). Hans-Josef Klauck considers the question of what constitutes a parallel as the major theoretical problem in projects like the *New Wettstein* ("Wettstein, alt und neu: Zur Neuausgabe eines Standardwerks," *BZ* 41 [1997]: 94).

[7] *'H KAINH ΔIAΘHKH: Novum Testamentum Graecum editionis receptae cum lectionibus variantibus codicum mss., editionum aliarum, versionum et patrum nec non commentario pleniore ex scriptoribus veteribus Hebraeis, Graecis et Latinis historiam et vim verborum illustrante, opera et studio Joannis Jacobi Wetstenii* (Amstelaedami: Ex Officina Dommeriana, 1751–52; reprint, Graz: Akademische Druck- und Verlagsanstalt, 1962). For a discussion of Wettstein's life and work see Pieter Willem van der Horst, "Johann Jakob Wettstein nach 300 Jahren: Erbe und Anfang," *TZ* 49 (1993): 267–81; and esp. Seelig, *Religionsgeschichtliche Methode*, 23–121.

[8] Seelig, "Einführung," XI. The revision entails among other things that ancient texts are translated into German, and that a larger part of the textual context is included (ibid., XI–XII).

[9] This means, amongst other things, that there is an unequal distribution of parallels between NT verses; see Seelig, "Einführung," XVI. This is also pointed out by Peter Wick (Review of *Neuer Wettstein* I.2, II.1–2, *TZ* 59 [2003]: 90).

[10] For the selection criteria employed in the *New Wettstein* see Seelig, "Einführung," XII–XIV. For subsequent changes see Lang, "Neubearbeitung," §§ 2, 3. In his review of the first volume to be published (vol. 2), Klauck points out that important parallels found in the old *Wettstein* have been excluded, while much more material could have been included, e.g., from Seneca's *Epistulae morales* and from non-literary papyri ("Wettstein, alt und neu," 90–93).

German translation, although some significant Greek or Latin phrases are included. Each extract is preceded by a brief introduction indicating the larger textual context. Despite laudable attempts to include a larger part of the textual context of each extract,[11] the very fact that extracts are used unfortunately tends to destroy the textual coherence and complexity of the original text.[12]

In what follows I will focus on one of the parallels included in the *New Wettstein*, namely, Cleanthes' *Hymn to Zeus*. Some of the questions I want to consider are (a) the rationale for including the *Hymn to Zeus*; (b) the aptness of the description and presentation of the *Hymn to Zeus*; (c) the appropriateness of its present comparative location; and (d) what light the above sheds on the value of the *New Wettstein* in general. The value of a comparative project such as the *New Wettstein* depends to a large extent on the theory on which it is based, on the one hand, and on whether the praxis succeeds in realizing the goals entailed in the theory, on the other. In considering these issues it is important to keep in mind that comparison is an intellectual act, not just the natural result of a "passive" perception: we choose *what* to compare and *how* to compare, that is, from what perspective. Both "what" and "how" are in turn determined by *why* we compare, that is, what we hope to achieve by the comparison.[13]

2. Cleanthes' *Hymn to Zeus* in the *New Wettstein*

In contrast to most of the excerpts included in the *New Wettstein*, the *Hymn to Zeus* (*SVF* 1.537) has the advantage of being quoted in full (i.e., not just as a partial extract). It is item 4 of nine texts adduced to John

[11] See n. 8 above.

[12] Cf. Klauck's criticism that texts are "atomized" ("Wettstein, alt und neu," 94–95).

[13] Cf. Smith, *Drudgery Divine*, 51, 115: "In the case of the study of religion, as in any disciplined inquiry, comparison, in its strongest form, brings differences together within the space of the scholar's mind for the scholar's own intellectual reasons. It is the scholar who makes their cohabitation—their 'sameness'—possible, not 'natural' affinities or processes of history" (quotation from p. 51). The constructive nature of comparison can have a significant impact on the interpretation of the text under consideration because of the context created by the selection of comparative material; cf. Klauck's observation that "der Johannesprolog im Spiegel des hellenistichen Vergleichmaterials als ein zutiefst philosophischer Text erscheint, was auf Grenzen dieses Verfahrens aufmerksam macht" (Hans-Josef Klauck, Review of *Neuer Wettstein I/2*, *BZ* 47 [2003]: 127).

1:1–18.[14] The other texts are (1) Prov 8:22–31; (2) Sir 1:1–4, 6, 8–10, 15; (3) Sir 24:3–9, 12, 19–22, 30–31; (5) Aratus, *Phaen.* 1–14; (6) Plutarch, *Mor.* (= *Is. Os.*) 372e–f; (7) *Orphic Hymns* 10.1–10; (8) *Isis Aretalogy of Kyme* 3–56; and (9) Cicero, *Tusc.* 5.5. For the *Hymn to Zeus* itself the translation by Bernd Effe is used, which is a reliable, scholarly translation.[15] Somewhat surprisingly, the Greek of some crucial terms that also find a resonance in John 1:1–18 are omitted in the presentation, particularly κόσμος (*Hymn to Zeus* v. 7) and λόγος (vv. 12, 21).

It is not quite obvious from the presentation in the *New Wettstein* why the *Hymn to Zeus* was selected for comparison to the Prologue to John.[16] According to the introductory description of the *Hymn*, "Kleanthes erörtert den Gedanken der dem Weltganzen immanenten Gesetzmäßigkeit. Diese bestimmende Kraft kann als Logos, Nous, Seele, Notwendigkeit oder auch als Gott (Zeus) beschrieben werden. Der folgende Hymnus [sc. the *Hymn to Zeus*] entfaltet diese pantheistische Vorstellung."[17] Leaving the accuracy of this description aside for the moment, it suggests that the *Hymn to Zeus* was chosen as illustration of a pantheistic conception of the Logos as the divine power at work in nature. Two related questions immediately present themselves: Why is the *Hymn to Zeus* compared to the whole of the Prologue, instead of just the first few verses?[18] Are there other, as important, points of comparison between the two texts than that implied by the introductory description? Although I will attempt to provide possible answers to these questions after discussing the *Hymn to Zeus*, it can be inferred from the other comparative texts listed above that the *Hymn to Zeus* has also been included for its generic value as a *hymnic* praise text.

---

[14] *Neuer Wettstein I.2*, 3–4.

[15] Bernd Effe, ed., *Hellenismus* (vol. 4 of *Die griechische Literatur in Text und Darstellung*, ed. H. Görgemanns; Stuttgart: Reclam, 1985), 157, 159. This is a vast improvement on the partial and very free translation by Edwyn R. Bevan, which is used by Boring, et al., *Hellenistic Commentary*, 326–27. Other good German translations include that by Peter Steinmetz, "Die Stoa," in *Die hellenistische Philosophie* (ed. Hellmut Flashar; vol. 4.2 of *Die Philosophie der Antike*; Grundriss der Geschichte der Philosophie; Basel: Schwabe, 1994), 577–78; Hans Schwabl, "Aus der Geschichte der hymnischen Prooimien: Homer, Hesiod, Arat, Lukrez—und ein Blick auf den Zeushymnus des Kleanthes," *Wiener humanistische Blätter* 43 (2001): 57–58; and Günther Zuntz, *Griechische philosophische Hymnen* (ed. H. Cancik and L. Käppel; STAC 35; Tübingen: Mohr Siebeck, 2005), 32–33.

[16] The *Hymn to Zeus* is not cited or quoted at this location in the "old" *Wettstein.*

[17] *Neuer Wettstein I.2*, 3.

[18] Cf. Boring, et al., *Hellenistic Commentary*, 240, who cite the *Hymn to Zeus* only *ad* John 1:1 for the Stoic identification of God, Logos, and cosmos.

3. The *Hymn to Zeus*: Introduction and Overview

The *Hymn to Zeus* by Cleanthes (331/330–230/229 BCE), second head of the Stoa in Athens, is the most important witness to early Stoic religiosity.[19] Nothing is known about the circumstances of the *Hymn*'s composition; the text itself is only extant as one of the excerpts in Stobaeus' *Anthology* (1.1.12, ed. Wachsmuth), and it is not directly quoted or cited anywhere else. Scholars have suggested that the *Hymn to Zeus* formed part of one of Cleanthes' other known works (e.g., περὶ θεῶν), that it was an introduction to a lecture series, or that it was written for use in the Stoa's communal worship, but there is no definite evidence to prove or disprove any of these positions.[20]

One of the most remarkable aspects of this text is the interplay of religious, philosophical, and literary motifs.[21] From the text itself it is clear that we have to do with a hexameter poem with a typical threefold hymnic structure, that is, with an Invocation (vv. 1–6), Argument (or Praise) (vv. 7–31), and Prayer (vv. 32–39).[22] The Invocation identifies the addressee by means of a series of epithets as the all-powerful Zeus who is chief of the gods, polyvalent and predominant in nature,[23] the

[19] For a critical text and translation, as well as an introduction and detailed commentary to the *Hymn to Zeus*, see Johan C. Thom, *Cleanthes'* Hymn to Zeus*: Text, Translation, and Commentary* (STAC 33; Tübingen: Mohr Siebeck, 2005). The interpretation of the *Hymn to Zeus* that follows is also based on this work. See further idem, "Doing Justice to Zeus: On Texts and Commentaries," *Acta Classica* 48 (2005): 1–21. The posthumously published study of the *Hymn* by Zuntz (*Griechische philosophische Hymnen*, 27–42) appeared only after my own work was published, but would not have affected my interpretation materially.

[20] See Thom, *Cleanthes'* Hymn to Zeus, 6–7, 11–12.

[21] This is discussed in detail in Thom, "Doing Justice to Zeus," passim.

[22] For the form of a hymn, see Thom, *Cleanthes'* Hymn to Zeus, 8, with the literature cited there (n. 38). To these may be added A. Knittel and I.K. Kolding, "Hymne," *Historiches Wörterbuch der Rhetorik* 4 (1998), 98–106; Lutz Käppel, "Hymnus I: Begriff und Gattung," *RGG* 4 (2000), 1974–75; idem, "Der philosophische Hymnos im Kontext seiner Gattung," in Günther Zuntz, *Griechische philosophische Hymnen* (ed. H. Cancik and L. Käppel; STAC 35; Tübingen: Mohr Siebeck, 2005), XVIII–XIX. The composition of the *Hymn to Zeus* is discussed in detail in Thom, *Cleanthes'* Hymn to Zeus, 13–20.

[23] The epithets πολυώνυμε and ἀρχηγέ are both (perhaps deliberately) ambivalent: πολυωνυμία is frequently used to indicate a god's multitudinous attributes, which enhance his praise. At the same time, the epithet may refer to the fact that the Stoic deity could be viewed from different perspectives, e.g., the universe as a unity, reason, fire, fate, or providence; see Thom, *Cleanthes'* Hymn to Zeus, 46–47. ἀρχηγός was also used with a traditional meaning ("chief, leader"), as well as with a technical philosophical meaning ("first cause, originator"). Cleanthes probably has both in mind; see Thom, *Cleanthes'* Hymn to Zeus, 49–50.

one who rules everything with his law (vv. 1–3a). Human beings have a special relationship with Zeus distinguishing them from all other creatures on earth: they alone can trace their origin to Zeus, because they bear his likeness (i.e., share in his rationality) (vv. 4–5);[24] they therefore have a special obligation to praise him (vv. 3b, 6).

The Argument section, as one would expect, starts out with a laudatory description of Zeus' orderly rule throughout nature (vv. 7–14). The whole cosmos responds with willing obedience to the guidance Zeus provides by means of his thunderbolt, the iconographic symbol representing the ever-active, inexhaustible, fiery force always at Zeus' command (vv. 7–11). The thunderbolt thus alludes to the Stoics' "designing fire" (πῦρ τεχνικόν) or fiery *pneuma*, the material mode of God's creative activity in matter.[25] As such it also acts as the medium or vehicle carrying the divine intelligence (*logos*) throughout matter (vv. 12–13).[26] All of this contributes to establish Zeus' eternal supremacy (v. 14). Throughout this subsection the heavens serve as the ultimate example of the divine order at work in the cosmos, and of nature's obedience to God's rule (vv. 7, 13).

God's dominance is again emphasized in the next two verses: nothing happens anywhere in the world without his involvement (vv. 15–16). Up to this point the poem could be interpreted as a straightforward Stoic hymn extolling the divine order immanent in nature.[27] The next verse, however, introduces a new perspective, which has dramatic consequences for our understanding of the *Hymn*. After the rhetorically emphatic statement of vv. 15–16 that not a single thing happens without God, not on earth, nor in heaven, nor in the sea, the πλήν ("except") at the beginning of v. 17 comes as a shock: there is something that evades God's order, namely, the foolish actions of "bad people" (κακοί). From now on it becomes clear that the point of the *Hymn* is not simply to praise Zeus' orderly rule; instead, it focuses on the problem of the bad people that disturb the world-order.[28] This means that the reader has to

---

[24] Although there still is no widely accepted solution to the crux in v. 4 (ἐκ σοῦ γὰρ γένος ἐσμὲν † ἤχου μίμημα λαχόντες), Meineke and Pearson's combined conjectures γενόμεσθα θεοῦ μίμημα give the best sense in this context; see the discussion in Thom, *Cleanthes'* Hymn to Zeus, 54–66.

[25] See Thom, *Cleanthes'* Hymn to Zeus, 76–83, esp. 77.

[26] See Thom, *Cleanthes'* Hymn to Zeus, 84.

[27] Cf. the *New Wettstein*'s description of the *Hymn to Zeus*, quoted above.

[28] This problem is discussed in more detail in Johan C. Thom, "The Problem of Evil in Cleanthes' *Hymn to Zeus*," *Acta Classica* 41 (1998): 45–57.

revise his initial interpretation of the function of the first subsection of the *Hymn to Zeus*: instead of simply praising Zeus' rule, this subsection provides a positive example of nature's obedience against which the negative behavior of the bad people can be measured.[29]

The next few verses indicate that Zeus himself is able to provide a solution to the problem created by the κακοί: he is able to change disorder into order (vv. 18–19); he has in fact combined things in the world in such a way that the end-result will be a rational order (λόγος) (vv. 20–21).[30] Once again, we may expect a Stoic hymn to draw to an end after this reassurance that God is in control, despite the resistance offered by the κακοί. This is not the case, however; the *Hymn to Zeus* devotes another ten lines (vv. 22–31) to the destructive behavior of the κακοί before it comes to the concluding Prayer section. The solution Zeus can provide is therefore offered as a possibility, not as an accomplished fact: the rational order he has in mind is still "coming to be" (γίγνεσθαι) according to v. 21. Instead of being a closing statement of praise, vv. 18–21 function as a hinge between the positive section on the orderly obedience of nature (vv. 7–17) and the negative section on the wayward behavior of the bad people (vv. 22–31).

The final subsection of the Argument describes in fairly traditional terms the refusal of the bad people to accept God's rational order (the universal *logos* and *nomos*) and its consequences. The unfortunate bad people are blind and deaf to what really constitutes the good life, namely, obedience to God's law (*nomos*) (vv. 22–25);[31] instead, they rush around trying to obtain the conventional goals of life often criticized by ancient philosophers, namely, honor, wealth, and pleasure (vv. 26–29).[32] They end up with the complete opposite of the good life they are searching for, that is, a life of instability and incoherence (vv. 30–31).

---

[29] The topos of nature's obedience as foil for humanity's disobedience is found in other traditions as well; cf. the passages in Second Temple Jewish writings cited by George W.E. Nickelsburg, *1 Enoch 1: A Commentary on the Book of Enoch, Chapters 1–36; 81–108* (Hermeneia; Minneapolis: Fortress, 2001), 152–55.

[30] For a discussion of the several philological issues in vv. 18–21 see Thom, *Cleanthes'* Hymn to Zeus, 98–112. For Cleanthes' probable sources for the formulation, cf. Hesiod, *Op.* 5–9; Solon, frg. 4.32–39 West; Heraclitus, frgs. 1, 23, 25, 26, 27, 91 Marcovich (22 B 1, 2, 10, 50, 51, 102 Diels-Kranz).

[31] Cleanthes' formulation appears to be based on the Pythagorean *Carmen aureum* 54–56; *Hom. Hymn Dem.* 256–57; Orphic frgs. 49.95–97, 233 Kern = 396.14–15, 337 Bernabé.

[32] Cf., e.g., Aristotle, *Eth. Nic.* 1095a20–24; Dio Chrysostom, *Or.* 4.83–84. For more references to ancient sources, see Thom, *Cleanthes'* Hymn to Zeus, 130–33.

It is significant that the subsection on the behavior of the κακοί (ten verses; vv. 22–31) is more or less of equal length to the subsection on the obedience of nature (eleven verses; vv. 7–17),[33] which supports my interpretation that nature functions as foil to the bad people, and that the purpose of the *Hymn to Zeus* is to suggest and request a solution to the problem created by the bad people.

Against the background developed in the Argument (i.e., that Zeus' rule finds a positive response in nature, but is rejected by bad human beings, and that Zeus is able to restore his order) Cleanthes now comes to the final Prayer (vv. 32–39).[34] This Prayer, as usually is the case, is the climax of the *Hymn*;[35] it is therefore important for understanding the purpose and meaning of the poem. The author requests Zeus to deliver human beings from the ignorance destroying their lives and to grant them the insight (γνώμη) on which Zeus' own rule is based (vv. 33–35). They will then be able to reciprocate by praising Zeus' works continuously, as is the duty and privilege of mortals and immortals alike (vv. 36–39). We see here that the problem of the κακοί who disturb God's order by their foolish actions (v. 17) can only be resolved if God himself comes to their assistance. Left to their own devices, the bad people tend to reject the divine, rational order (v. 20) and follow their own inclinations (vv. 26–31). By helping them to understand his world-order (vv. 34–35), Zeus enables them to participate in the just praise of this order (vv. 36–39) and he thus restores the disorder created by the κακοί (cf. vv. 18–19).

There is, however, also a noteworthy shift in perspective in the Prayer section. Previously, in the Argument, the author referred to the bad people as if they constituted a particular section of humanity (κακοί, v. 17; ὅσοι θνητῶν κακοί εἰσι, v. 22) characterized by foolishness and ignorance. In the Prayer Cleanthes asks that humanity *in general* (ἀνθρώπους, v. 33) be saved from their ignorance and granted insight; the goal is that "we," that is, everyone, the author and his fellow Stoics

[33] The compositional patterning of the *Hymn*, including the function of the length of the various sections, is discussed at more length in Thom, *Cleanthes'* Hymn to Zeus, 16–18.

[34] The main function of the Argument section of a hymn was indeed to prepare the ground for the petitions following in the Prayer section; see R. Wünsch, "Hymnos," PW 9.1 (1914): 145.

[35] For the function of the prayer section in ancient hymns, see William D. Furley and Jan Maarten Bremer, *Greek Hymns: Selected Cult Songs from the Archaic to the Hellenistic Period* (STAC 9, 10; Tübingen: Mohr Siebeck, 2001), 1:60.

included, be enabled to respond appropriately (ἀμειβώμεσθα, v. 36) to the privileged status human beings enjoy vis-à-vis God (cf. vv. 36 and 3–5). The implication is that most people, if not all, are in need of God's help to live as rational beings.[36]

Finally, it is clear that the Prayer and the *Hymn* in general function on two different communication levels: internally, there is a communication between Cleanthes and Zeus combining praise and prayer,[37] but externally Cleanthes also communicates with his audience.[38] On this level, Cleanthes wishes to remind people of, and implicitly exhorts them to achieve, their true goal in life, namely, to live in accordance with the divine order (*logos*) manifest in nature.[39]

4. Comparing the *Hymn to Zeus* with NT Texts

In a previous study I discussed the *Hymn to Zeus* in relationship to some NT texts for which the *Hymn to Zeus* is often cited as comparative material, namely, the Lord's Prayer (Matt. 6:9–13), the Prologue to the Gospel of John (1:1–18), and Paul's speech in Athens (Acts 17:22–31).[40] In this paper I want to follow a different approach: instead of trying to identify NT texts with which the *Hymn to Zeus* may profitably be compared, I will explore some of the reasons why the *Hymn* is an

[36] For a discussion of the function of the Prayer in the *Hymn to Zeus*, see Thom, *Cleanthes'* Hymn to Zeus, 10–11, 24–27.

[37] In an attempt to distinguish a hymn from a prayer, Käppel contends that while the latter ("Beten") consists in a dialogical communication with the deity aiming at reciprocity, the hymn is predominantly characterized by praise and adoration ("Anbetung") of the deity, even though these two communicative functions are often combined ("Philosophische Hymnos," XVII–XIX). If this distinction is valid, the primary function of the *Hymn to Zeus* appears to be a prayer aimed at restoring the true praise of Zeus, rather than hymnic adoration.

[38] These two communication levels are typical of prayers in general; see Jerzy Danielewicz, *Morfologia hymnu antycznego: Na materiale greckich zbiorów hymnicznych* (Uniwersytet Im. Adama Mickiewicza w Poznaniu Seria Filologia Klasyczna 8; Poznan: Uniwersytet im. Adama Mickiewicza w Poznaniu, 1976), 118–19 (English summary); Wolfgang Fenske, *"Und wenn ihr betet..." (Mt. 6,5): Gebete in der zwischenmenschlichen Kommunikation der Antike als Ausdruck der Frömmigkeit* (SUNT 21; Göttingen: Vandenhoeck & Ruprecht, 1997), esp. 79–127; cf. also Furley and Bremer, *Greek Hymns*, 1:59.

[39] See Thom, *Cleanthes'* Hymn to Zeus, 13.

[40] Johan C. Thom, "Cleanthes' *Hymn to Zeus* and Early Christian Literature," in *Antiquity and Humanity: Essays on Ancient Religion and Philosophy Presented to Hans Dieter Betz on His 70th Birthday* (ed. A.Y. Collins and M.M. Mitchell; Tübingen: Mohr Siebeck, 2001), 477–99.

important comparative text, as well as some significant potential points of comparison with NT material.

Even without taking the details of its content into account, the *Hymn to Zeus* presents itself as an important comparative text because it is the only more or less intact text extant from early Stoicism. Its prominent position in Stobaeus' *Anthology* (1.1.12) probably indicates that it was still considered an important philosophical school text in later antiquity.[41] This, together with its religious, philosophical, and moral contents, makes it not unreasonable to assume that the *Hymn to Zeus* was known in some early Christian circles,[42] especially in view of the fact that Stoicism was the most widely popularized philosophy in the early Imperial period.

On the level of form, the *Hymn to Zeus* is one of the most important examples of philosophical hymns in antiquity and thus offers a good point of comparison for the hymnic material found in the NT, especially in John 1:1–18[43] and in various letters (e.g., Phil. 2:6–11; Col. 1:15–20; Heb. 1:3–4). A notable formal difference between the *Hymn to Zeus* and the NT material mentioned above is that the former follows the so-called "Du-Stil" in which the deity is addressed in the second person, while the NT texts use the "Er-Stil" in which Christ is described in the third person.[44] In both the *Hymn to Zeus* and in the NT material, however, we find a description of the deity's actions and qualities (cf. esp. vv. 1–21 for

[41] Cf. Matthias Perkams, "Kleanthes," *RAC* 20 (2004), 1258. We unfortunately have no other explicit evidence of its reception in antiquity, although a good case has been made that Lucretius composed the introductory hymn to Venus as an Epicurean counterpart to the *Hymn to Zeus*; see Ulrich von Wilamowitz-Moellendorff, "Kleanthes: Hymnus auf Zeus," in *Reden und Vorträge* (4th ed.; Berlin: Weidmannsche Buchhandlung, 1925–26), 1:328; Ernst Neustadt, "Der Zeushymnos des Kleanthes," *Hermes* 66 (1931): 393–95; and esp. Elizabeth Asmis, "Lucretius' Venus and Stoic Zeus," *Hermes* 110 (1982): 458–70.

[42] The strongest case can be made for Luke in Acts 17:28: although the quotation itself in 28c comes from Aratus, *Phaen.* 5, it is not unlikely that Luke's reference to "your poets" in the plural means that he has other similar poems such as the *Hymn to Zeus* in mind as well; see Rudolf Pesch, *Die Apostelgeschichte II: Apg 13–28* (EKKNT 5.2; Zurich: Benziger Verlag, 1986), 139; Thom, "Cleanthes' *Hymn to Zeus* and Early Christian Literature," 479–80.

[43] One suspects formal considerations also played a role in the selection of the *Hymn to Zeus* as comparative text to the "hymnic" Prologue to John in the *New Wettstein*. For a comparison of some of the hymnic features in the *Hymn to Zeus* and in John 1:1–18, see Thom, "Cleanthes' *Hymn to Zeus* and Early Christian Literature," 495.

[44] This distinction was first made by Eduard Norden in his still irreplaceable book, *Agnostos Theos: Untersuchungen zur Formengeschichte religiöser Rede* (Leipzig: Teubner, 1923).

the *Hymn to Zeus*), which is characteristic of ancient hymns in general, and of philosophical hymns in particular.[45] As we have seen, prayer plays an important role in the *Hymn to Zeus*; the text therefore also offers a valuable comparison to prayers in the NT, including the Lord's Prayer (Matt. 6:9–13). One of the most important points of contact between the *Hymn to Zeus* and the Lord's Prayer is that they are both structured around the combined topic of God's rule in the world and the human predicament, which may be a standard subject of ancient prayers.[46]

This brings us to points of comparison regarding the content of the *Hymn to Zeus*. The worldview reflected in the latter shares to a surprisingly large extent a common core with that of NT texts. There is a world-order established and maintained by God, which may be perceived in the regularity of nature (*Hymn to Zeus* vv. 7–16). Human beings, however, even though they enjoy a privileged relationship with God (vv. 3–5; cf. v. 36), tend to disregard or even reject God's order in their selfish pursuit of short-term goals (vv. 17, 22–31). They can only be saved from the destructive consequences of their actions by divine assistance (vv. 32–35); only God can finally restore the order disrupted by humans (vv. 18–21). The ultimate goal is that all humans will join other heavenly beings in continuously singing God's praise, that is, in living a life in conformity to God's order (vv. 36–39; cf. vv. 3, 6).[47]

Contrary to what one may expect from a Stoic author, Cleanthes' Zeus is depicted in remarkably personalist and theistic terms. He is addressed in the second person throughout the poem[48] as the king and ruler of the world, a divine father from whom all human beings have their origin and to whom they can turn for help, a god who can correct our mistakes, someone with whom we can communicate, and to whom we have an obligation.[49] Stoicism is normally viewed as a

---

[45] Cf. Käppel, "Philosophische Hymnos," XIX: "Die Gattung 'Hymnos' scheint also geradezu prädestiniert zu sein, neben dem genuin religiösen Anliegen der Wendung *an* die Gottheit auch als Medium des Sprechens *über* die Gottheit zu fungieren.... Dies ist sicher eines der wichtigsten Merkmale der Gattung Hymnos, das sie dann auch dazu geeignet erscheinen ließ, neben religiösen auch philosophische Inhalte zu transportieren, so daß es zu einem Phänomen wie dem philosophischen Hymnos kommen konnte" (emphasis original).

[46] For a more detailed comparison, see Thom, "Cleanthes' *Hymn to Zeus* and Early Christian Literature," 493–95.

[47] For praise as metaphor for the appropriate way of life, cf. Epictetus, *Diss.* 1.16.15–16, 18, 20–21; see also Thom, *Cleanthes'* Hymn to Zeus, 158–59.

[48] See vv. 3, 4, 6, 7, 8, 12, 15, 18, 19, 33, 34, 35, 36, 37. The direct address is strengthened by the use of the vocatives Ζεῦ (vv. 2, 32), πάτερ (v. 34), and δαῖμον (v. 15).

[49] This depiction of Zeus in the *Hymn* is treated in more detail in Thom, *Cleanthes'*

monistic and materialistic pantheism, in which God permeates all of nature, from the cosmos as a whole down to the most lowly physical object.[50] He is in fact often identified with aspects of the physical world, such as nature, reason, providence, fate, or the law of nature, or even with the world as a whole itself.[51] Such a view does not appear to allow for a personalist deity. There is, however, a growing acceptance in recent scholarship that Stoicism was, from the very beginning, not purely pantheistic, but an amalgam of pantheism and theism, despite the problem of inconsistency this created.[52] Stoic theism derives from the view that God, as the ultimate form of rationality, in a sense transcends the world structured and ordered by him; he is thus immanent and transcendent at the same time.[53] On the same view God also transcends human rationality, but he may to some extent still be considered a "person" because his rationality is similar in kind to that of humans. It is to such a deity that Cleanthes turns for help in his *Hymn to Zeus*. The poem reflects an awareness of a rationality transcending the limits

Hymn to Zeus, 20–24; "Doing Justice to Zeus," 8–12. For Cleanthes' personalist treatment of Zeus, see Margherita Isnardi Parente, *Introduzione a lo stoicismo ellenistico* (I Filosofi 59; Rome and Bari: Laterza, 1993), 47; Brad Inwood, "L'*oikeiosis* sociale chez Epictète," in *Polyhistor: Studies in the History and Historiography of Ancient Philosophy* (ed. K. Algra, et al.; Leiden: Brill, 1996), 258–59; cf. already Martin P. Nilsson, *Geschichte der griechischen Religion* (3rd ed.; Handbuch der Altertumswissenschaft 5.2.1–2; Munich: Beck, 1967–74), 2:296, 297. The most prominent Stoic representative of such a theistic and personalist approach to God is Epictetus, but he may well have followed Cleanthes; see A.A. Long, *Epictetus: A Stoic and Socratic Guide to Life* (Oxford: Clarendon, 2002), 147–52, esp. 147 n. 4.

50 See Max Pohlenz, *Die Stoa: Geschichte einer geistigen Bewegung* (2 vols.; 6th–7th edition 1990–92; Göttingen: Vandenhoeck & Ruprecht, 1948–49), 1:108.

51 See Thom, *Cleanthes'* Hymn to Zeus, 10, 46, 48–49.

52 See Long, *Epictetus*, 147–48; Keimpe Algra, "Stoic Theology," in *The Cambridge Companion to the Stoics* (ed. B. Inwood; Cambridge: Cambridge University Press, 2003), 167–68; Thom, *Cleanthes'* Hymn to Zeus, 25–26; contra Giovanni Reale, *The Systems of the Hellenistic Age* (ed. and trans. J.R. Catan; vol. 3 of *A History of Ancient Philosophy*; Albany: State University of New York Press, 1985), 247, who views the relationship between pantheism and theism in Stoicism in terms of a historical development from the former to the latter.

53 Cf. also G. Verbeke' view that the deity is for Cleanthes both immanent and transcendent (*Kleanthes van Assos* [Verhandelingen van de Koninklijke Vlaamse Academie voor Wetenschappen, Letteren en Schone Kunsten van België, Klasse der Letteren 11/9; Brussels, 1949], 193–94). For the concept in Stoicism in general, cf. Abraham P. Bos, "Immanenz u. Transzendenz," *RAC* 17 (1996), 1059–60: "Ihre [sc. Stoic philosophy's] Theologie kann mit recht als kosmische Theologie bezeichnet werden. Für irgendeine Form von Transzendenz im Sinne einer höheren Ebene der Wirklichkeit ist darin kein Platz. Sofern Gott aber dem Kosmos gegenüber steht als dessen Urheber u. Lenker, wird er trotzdem manchmal auch als dem Kosmos u. der Materie transzendent dargestellt."

of our own, something, or rather someone, who may assist us in living the rational life and who deserves our worship.[54]

Because of its rationalistic and monistic approach, Stoic theology has a monotheistic tendency, which is also at work in the *Hymn to Zeus*. This does not mean that the existence of other gods are denied (cf. vv. 1, 39), but there is only one single active deity named God or Zeus.[55] The combination of the monotheistic and personalist perspectives has an interesting effect in the *Hymn to Zeus*: although the *logos* and the designing fire (here represented by the thunderbolt, but elsewhere also called the fiery *pneuma*) are normally considered alternative forms or "modalities" of the deity in other Stoic sources,[56] they are here portrayed as the servants or instruments implementing Zeus' plan in nature (vv. 9–13).[57] This provides an important point of comparison to the mediating role of the Logos and of Christ in creation in John 1:1–18 and elsewhere (e.g., Col. 1:15–17; Heb. 1:2); it also points to the complexity of ancient concepts of "monotheism."[58] In John 1, the

---

[54] See Thom, *Cleanthes'* Hymn to Zeus, 27.

[55] See Reale, *History of Ancient Philosophy III*, 246; Jaap Mansfeld, "Theology," in *The Cambridge History of Hellenistic Philosophy* (ed. K. Algra, et al.; Cambridge: Cambridge University Press, 1999), 461–62; Michael Frede, "Monotheism and Pagan Philosophy in Later Antiquity," in *Pagan Monotheism in Late Antiquity* (ed. P. Athanassiadi and M. Frede; Oxford: Oxford University Press, 1999), 51–53; Long, *Epictetus*, 144; Algra, "Stoic Theology," 153–78, esp. 165–70; Thom, *Cleanthes'* Hymn to Zeus, 45.

[56] Cf., e.g., Diogenes Laertius 7.135 (*SVF* 1.102), with the secondary sources cited in Thom, *Cleanthes'* Hymn to Zeus, 46 n. 20, 49 n. 34.

[57] See Thom, *Cleanthes'* Hymn to Zeus, 22, 73–74, 77–90.

[58] Pagan monotheism has recently come under renewed scholarly scrutiny. Collections such as Polymnia Athanassiadi and Michael Frede, eds., *Pagan Monotheism in Late Antiquity* (Oxford: Oxford University Press, 1999), and Barbara Nevling Porter, ed., *One God or Many? Concepts of Divinity in the Ancient World* (Transactions of the Casco Bay Assyriological Institute 1; [Chebeague, Maine]: Casco Bay Assyriological Institute, 2000), signal only the beginning of a new research focus. Monotheism in early Judaism and Christianity is also being reconsidered; cf., e.g., Hershel Shanks and Jack Meinhardt, eds., *Aspects of Monotheism: How God is One* (Symposium at the Smithsonian Institution, October 19, 1996; Washington, D.C.: Biblical Archaeology Society, 1997); Carey C. Newman, et al., *The Jewish Roots of Christological Monotheism: Papers from the St. Andrews Conference on the Historical Origins of the Worship of Jesus* (Supplements to the Journal for the Study of Judaism 63; Leiden: Brill, 1999); Loren T. Stuckenbruck and Wendy E.S. North, eds., *Early Jewish and Christian Monotheism* (JSNTSup 263; London: T&T Clark International, 2004); Wiard Popkes and Ralph Brucker, eds., *Ein Gott und ein Herr: Zum Kontext des Monotheismus im Neuen Testament* (Biblisch-Theologische Studien 68; Neukirchen-Vluyn: Neukirchener Verlag, 2004); Reinhard Gregor Kratz and Hermann Spieckermann, eds., *Götterbilder, Gottesbilder, Weltbilder: Polytheismus und Monotheismus in der Welt der Antike* (2 vols.; FAT II.17–18; Tübingen: Mohr Siebeck, 2006), to cite just some of many recent publications on the subject. See also the survey articles in *Religion im Geschichte und Gegenwart*, vol. 5 (2002), esp. Gregor Ahn, "Monotheismus und Poly-

Logos as mediating agent in creation (1:3, 10) is the only one able to reveal the true nature of God (1:14, 18) and of humanity (1:9), and thus also able to reconcile God and humans, if the latter accept him (1:12–13). In the *Hymn to Zeus*, too, the *logos* plays a mediating role in the formation of the world (vv. 12–13), and constitutes the fundamental expression of God's plan (vv. 20–21). Acceptance of the *logos*, and thus understanding of God's purpose, is the precondition for human beings to be restored to God's world-order and to live a meaningful life (vv. 22–25, 34–35). In both texts, the Logos/*logos* assumes physical form as the concretization of God's involvement in the world (John 1:14; *Hymn to Zeus*, vv. 12–13).[59]

There is no essential difference in the *Hymn to Zeus* between the *logos* and the universal law (κοινὸς νόμος). The *logos* denotes the divine rationality underlying the world-order (vv. 12–13, 21), while the *nomos* refers to the normative regularity inherent in this rationality. From a cosmic perspective, it refers to the inevitable sequence of natural events that constitutes Zeus' rule (cf. vv. 2, 35); from a moral perspective, it refers to the normative order that has to be obeyed by humans and gods alike (vv. 24–25, 38–39).[60] These two perspectives are inseparably linked: the order in the cosmos provides a norm humans ought to be able to perceive and to emulate (cf. vv. 24–25).[61] The revelatory and normative function of God's works in nature (cf. τὰ σὰ ἔργα, v. 37) is applied in arguments by NT authors as well (e.g., Acts 14:15–17; 17:24–28; Rom. 1:19–21),[62] although Christ as the Logos, God's final revelation and the ultimate norm of human behavior, is carefully contrasted to the

theismus I: Religionswissenschaftlich," 1457–59; Hans-Peter Müller, "Monotheismus und Polytheismus II: Altes Testament," 1459–62; Hans Hübner, "Monotheismus und Polytheismus III: Neues Testament," 1462–63.

[59] The reference to the heavenly bodies in *Hymn to Zeus* v. 13 is to be interpreted as representative of all of nature. In Stoicism the divine principle permeates all things giving them their physical coherence, but in different states of tension, depending on the object; see Thom, *Cleanthes'* Hymn to Zeus, 87–90. The comparison between the incarnation of the Logos and the permeation of the Stoic *logos* in nature may not be as farfetched as it appears: one of the reasons the evangelist chose the term Logos might have been to contrast God's revelation centered in one, specific, human being, to the vague diffusement of the Stoic divine principle throughout nature.

[60] See Long, *Epictetus*, 154, who refers to the inner and outer aspects of natural law in the *Hymn to Zeus*; also Thom, *Cleanthes'* Hymn to Zeus, 52, 122–23.

[61] Cf. the discussion above of nature as foil to human beings.

[62] See Thom, "Cleanthes' *Hymn to Zeus* and Early Christian Literature," 497–99. The Stoic background to the Romans passage is emphasized by James D.G. Dunn, *Romans 1–8* (WBC 38A; Dallas, Tex.: Word Books, 1988), 56, 58. Cf. further Wis 13:1–9.

nomos in NT texts.[63] Christ's example of self-sacrificing love cannot be encapsulated in moral prescriptions,[64] nor can it be deduced from the regularity of natural events.

The anthropology encountered in the *Hymn to Zeus* is critical of humanity, but not overly pessimistic. As we have seen, the foolish behavior of the bad people is the main problem addressed in the *Hymn*. Because of their lack of insight and understanding, human beings reject the divine rational order and prefer to follow their own wayward impulses (vv. 17, 22–31). This not only has dire consequences (cf. λυγρῆς, v. 33) for their own well-being (cf. vv. 23, 25, 26, 31), but also disrupts God's order (vv. 15–17; cf. 18–19) and the praise he deserves (cf. vv. 36–39). Human beings are privileged among other creatures, however, because they share in God's rationality (vv. 3–5);[65] they are therefore able to obtain the insight (γνώμη) that will allow them to be saved from their folly and be restored to the divine order (vv. 33–39).[66] Such an ethical intellectualism is of course common in Greek philosophy from the time of Socrates onwards,[67] but what is striking here is the emphasis on the need of Zeus' assistance to obtain the necessary insight. Despite the fact that humans as rational beings ought to be able to find the insight within themselves,[68] they appear unable to do so without

63 Cf., e.g., John 1:17; Gal. 2:16; Phil. 3:9.

64 But cf. the interesting formulation τὸν νόμον τοῦ Χριστοῦ in Gal. 6:2.

65 This is the most probable interpretation of the vexing v. 4; see Thom, *Cleanthes'* Hymn to Zeus, 54–66, esp. 60–61. Robert Renehan provides an excellent survey of the topos of humankind's preeminent position in nature found in Greek philosophical texts ("The Greek Anthropocentric View of Man," *HSCP* 85 [1981]: 247–50); see also Thom, *Cleanthes'* Hymn to Zeus, 66–67.

66 The meaning of γνώμη in this context is somewhat ambiguous, but it is clear that it must denote either an intellectual ability, or an intellectual content; the translation "insight" attempts to captured both. See my discussion in *Cleanthes'* Hymn to Zeus, 153–55.

67 Cf. Albrecht Dihle, "Ethik," *RAC* 6 (1966), 649–52.

68 Several recent scholars have indeed rejected a literal interpretation of the prayer for divine assistance. Reinhold Glei, e.g., contends that the *Hymn to Zeus* is a sophisticated literary allegory by means of which the readers are persuaded to attain insight, i.e., the Good, by using their own *logos* ("Der Zeushymnus des Kleanthes: Ansätze zu einer philosophischen Theo-Logie," in *"Ihr alle aber seid Brüder": Festschrift für A. Th. Khoury zum 60. Geburtstag* [2nd ed.; ed. L. Hagemann and E. Pulsfort; Würzburger Forschungen zur Missions- und Religionswissenschaft II.14; Würzburg: Echter Verlag, 1990], 577–97); while Algra suggests that the prayer is a direct self-address to the god within us, the rational self, to remind us that the rational self ought to be in tune with the cosmic reason ("Stoic Theology," 174–76). See Thom, *Cleanthes'* Hymn to Zeus, 10–11. For support of my own position, see now also Zuntz, *Griechische philosophische Hymnen*, 40.

God's help.[69] Salvation entails divine assistance in order to understand the world-order and to live accordingly. In Paul's Areopagus speech, too, human error is ascribed to ignorance (ἄγνοια) rather than to sin (Acts 17:23, 30), but this is an accommodation to the Athenian Greek audience. Paul does not in this speech refer to the moral consequences of such ignorance, as Cleanthes does (cf. *Hymn to Zeus*, vv. 26–31), but it is an important aspect of the argument in Rom 1:18–32, as is the need for salvation.[70]

5. Conclusion

We may now return to the questions formulated earlier about the *New Wettstein*'s treatment of the *Hymn to Zeus*.

The first question concerned *the rationale for including the Hymn to Zeus as comparative text*. Although the *New Wettstein* does not explain the reasons for its selection of particular texts, it should be evident from the discussion above that the *Hymn to Zeus* provides numerous and significant points of comparison to NT material, and that it is therefore an obvious choice for inclusion in a collection such as the *New Wettstein*.[71] Whether its potential as comparative text has been realized in full, is a different matter.

A more important question for our present purposes concerned *the aptness of the description and presentation of the Hymn* in the *New Wettstein*. As

[69] Cf. also Marcus Aurelius, *Med.* 9.40; Posidonius, frg. 40 Edelstein-Kidd, with the commentary by I.G. Kidd, *(I) Testimonia and Fragments 1–149*, pt. 1 of *Posidonius II: The Commentary* (Greek Classical Texts and Commentaries 14A; Cambridge: Cambridge University Press, 1988), 184.

[70] See my earlier discussion in "Cleanthes' *Hymn to Zeus* and Early Christian Literature," 497–99. As an example of the fact that despite terminological agreements between pagan and NT texts there may still be significant conceptual differences, Seelig contends that Paul only uses the tradition of a natural theology ("natürliche Gotteserkenntnis") found in the many pagan-hellenistic parallels to Rom. 1:20–21 to emphasize the moral blameworthiness ("Schuldhaftigkeit") of the pagans ("Einführung," XIX n. 5; *Religionsgeschichtliche Methode*, 316). It is clear that Cleanthes, at least, is also aware of the moral blame of those not making using of their opportunity to recognize God's works in nature.

[71] It is quoted as comparative text to Acts 17:22–31, and cited as parallel to Matt. 6:7 and John 1:1 in Boring, et al., *Hellenistic Commentary*, 62, 240, 326–27. The *Hymn to Zeus* is also included in C.K. Barrett, *The New Testament Background: Writings from Ancient Greece and the Roman Empire That Illuminate Christian Origins* (rev. ed.; San Francisco: HarperSanFrancisco, 1987), 67–68, although the translation given there is more of a paraphrase than a true translation.

we have seen, the *Hymn to Zeus* has the advantage over many other texts of being quoted in full, which makes it easier for the user to determine its value as comparative text. The translation used is reliable and many of the significant terms and phrases are given in Greek as well. The omission of λόγος is surprising, since the occurrence of this term in the *Hymn* is probably one of the main reasons for its comparison with the Prologue to John (see below). The description of the *Hymn to Zeus* as presenting a pantheistic Stoic wordview in which the regularity underlying the cosmos can be described as the Logos, Nous, Soul, Necessity, or God,[72] is, however, deficient and misleading. My analysis has shown that Zeus is depicted as a personalist, theistic deity rather than as a pantheistic force in the *Hymn to Zeus*. We also find in the *Hymn*, not an identification of God and the Logos, but a clear distinction between them as different agents. The subject of the *Hymn to Zeus* is clearly not a description of the pantheistic force at work in the cosmos, but the problem of human beings who resist the divine rule. A more accurate summary of the theme and content of the *Hymn* would have provided better guidance to the potential users of the *New Wettstein*.

This brings us to my third question, regarding *the appropriateness of the Hymn to Zeus' comparative location* in the *New Wettstein*. It is not clear from the *New Wettstein*'s description of the *Hymn to Zeus* why the latter is quoted as comparative text to the Prologue of John (1:1–18). The only explicit connection (i.e., taking the description as point of departure) is the use of the term *logos* in both texts, but for this connection a link between the *Hymn to Zeus* and John 1:1–3 would have sufficed.[73] It may be that the *New Wettstein* tacitly assumes a hymnic base for the Prologue of John, and that the combination of the *logos* motif and a hymnic form serves as the connecting link between the two texts.[74] Be that as it may, I fully concur with the *New Wettstein* that the *Hymn to Zeus* is an important comparative text to John 1:1–18, but not only for the rather superficial reasons already mentioned. A more significant connection is that in both texts the Logos/*logos* as the visible expression of God's involvement in the world (John 1:1–4, 14, 18; *Hymn to Zeus*, vv. 12–13, 21) is not recognized and is rejected by human beings (John

[72] *Neuer Wettstein I.2*, 3, quoted above.

[73] Cf., e.g., Boring, et al., *Hellenistic Commentary*, 240. See already Norden, *Agnostos Theos*, 157 n. 3, 159 n. 1, 349–50.

[74] This inference is strengthened by the fact that most of the other comparative texts cited in connection with the Prologue as a whole also have a hymnic form.

1:10; *Hymn to Zeus*, vv. 22, 24), who should have known better because of their close relationship to God (John 1:4, 11; *Hymn to Zeus*, vv. 4–5); both texts also offer a solution to the dilemma created by this rejection (John 1:12–13; *Hymn to Zeus*, vv. 18–21, 33–36). The relationships and interaction between the *dramatis personae* of the metaphysical-mythical narrative schema of the two texts thus provide a more important point of comparison than the terminological similarities. This analogy will perhaps not be obvious to most readers and should therefore be pointed out to them in the introductory description of a text like the *Hymn to Zeus*.

It will have been apparent from my discussion of the *Hymn to Zeus* that it may profitably be compared to other NT texts as well, notably the Areopagus speech in Acts 17 and the Lord's Prayer in Matthew 6. Since the *New Wettstein* volumes on Matthew and on Acts have yet to appear, one can only express the hope that the relevant passages will contain references to the *Hymn to Zeus*. It is a pity, however, that there are no references to the *Hymn* in volume 2 of the *New Wettstein* (on the NT letters and the Book of Revelation). As we have seen, at least Rom. 1:18–32 and some of the hymnic passages in the epistles could have contained references to the *Hymn to Zeus*.

What conclusions may be drawn from the way a text like the *Hymn to Zeus* is used in the *New Wettstein*? Despite its good intentions,[75] a problematic feature of the *New Wettstein* is that it tends to promote a one-dimensional comparison between two texts: a specific expression or concept (e.g., the *logos*) is highlighted as point of comparison, whether by the textual extract that is selected, or (as in the case of the *Hymn to Zeus*) by the description of the text. This means that other important analogies between the two texts concerned are pushed to the background, or that the more significant analogies between complexes of relationships are ignored. One-dimensionality is also fostered in another respect: for obvious reasons of economy an Hellenistic text is only quoted at what is considered the most important NT text for comparative purposes, but this means that many significant analogies between the Hellenistic text and other NT texts are lost.

What can be done to counter this? Although it may be important not to expand the *New Wettstein* beyond what is practical and affordable,

[75] Cf. the apologetic formulations by Seelig, *Religionsgeschichtliche Methode*, 18–19; and by Lang, "Geschichte und Programm," § 2.3 (quoted n. 5 above).

the complexity and multidimensionality of a Hellenistic text can be signaled in various ways without increasing the bulk of the published text dramatically.[76] The first is to include important keywords in the description of the pagan text, identifying significant formal and substantive analogies not only to the present NT text, but to other NT texts as well. The second is to make much more use of cross-references to pagan texts quoted at other NT locations than is presently the case. A third possibility is to provide a topical index of the NT and pagan texts concerned. This last approach may indeed be a different project altogether, going far beyond the limited goals the editors and publisher of the *New Wettstein* set themselves.

As my analysis has shown, however, the *New Wettstein* is not a sufficient tool by itself; it needs to be complemented by detailed analyses of the various Hellenistic texts in which the textual integrity and complexity of the latter is preserved. Only then will the comparative task that the *New Wettstein* wishes to promote become truly meaningful.

[76] Cf. Seelig's recommendation that texts be compared on multiple levels because texts are complex objects ("komplexe Gebilde") (*Religionsgeschichtliche Methode*, 315–16).

ISMYRNA 753: GODS AND THE ONE GOD

Leonard L. Thompson

1. Introduction

Inscriptions are invaluable sources of information for social institutions and cultural expressions, but they are maddeningly succinct and laconic.[1] For its original intended audience, the location of the inscription and the situation in which it was set up provided information that is not available to those of us who find inscriptions in museums or collected in books, or even for those who find them broken, often moved and reused in walls or foundations of buildings. Overcoming that "information gap," as B.H. McLean aptly calls it, presents "one of the great challenges of epigraphy."[2]

ISmyrna 753 is a case in point. Today it can be seen in the Epigraphical Museum in Athens: an inscribed, gabled stele of bluish marble, five broken pieces cemented together. It was found about 1875 on the northeastern slope (Sibile Tepe) of Pagos Hill in Smyrna. On the one hand, ISmyrna 753 describes, in detail not found elsewhere, a sanctuary or precinct of a cultic association.[3] On the other hand, as an isolated document, it gives few clues about the theology of that cultic association or its social location in Smyrna. The purpose of this paper is to move the inscription from museum confinement into the lively company of gods and humans in Smyrnaean life and thought from which it came. First, however, the inscription itself.

---

[1] Salut! Professor and Mrs. Grant, for timely kindnesses throughout the decades. This essay is intended as a recognition of, and contribution to, Grant's interest in the second Christian century.

[2] B.H. McLean, *An Introduction to Greek Epigraphy of the Hellenistic and Roman Periods from Alexander the Great Down to the Reign of Constantine (323 B.C.–A.D. 337)* (Ann Arbor: University of Michigan Press, 2002), 2.

[3] For examples of similar dedications, though not so detailed, see Louis Robert, "Inscriptions d'Antalya et de Byzance," *Hellenica* IX (1950): 39–51 and Pierre Debord, *Aspects Sociaux et Économiques de la Vie Religieuse dans L'Anatolie Gréco-Romaine* (Leiden: E.J. Brill, 1982), 223–24. Inscriptions tend to give more attention to the donors and their connections or the amount of money given.

2. The Inscription

The inscription reads as follows:[4]

(1) 'Απολλώνιος Μητροδώρου Σπάρος, (2) ὁ πατὴρ τοῦ γενομένου ἱερέως 'Απολ- (3) λωνίου τοῦ 'Απολλωνίου Σπάρου τοῦ (4) Ἡλίου 'Απόλλωνος Κισαυλοδδηνοῦ ἀ- (5) νέθηκεν τῶι θεῶι καὶ τῆι πόλει τὰ κατασκευ- (6) ασθέντα ὑπ' αὐτοῦ, λαβὼν κατὰ ψήφισμα τὴν (7) ἀναγραφὴν ποιήσασθαι αὐτῶν ἐν στήλῃ καὶ (8) ἔστιν: αὐτὸς ὁ θεὸς ἐπὶ βήματος μαρμαρίνου (9) καὶ ἡ παρακειμένη τῶι θεῶι τράπεζα λίθου Λεσβί- (10) ου ἔχουσα πόδας ἀναγλύπτους γρῦπας καὶ πρὸ αὐ- (11) τῆς ἀβάκηον μαρμάρινον πρὸς τὴν χρῆσιν τῶν (12) θυσιαζόντων, καὶ θυμιατήριον τετράγωνον κα- (13) τεσκευασμένον πέτρας Τηΐας ἔχον περίπυρον (14) σιδηροῦν, καὶ ἄγαλμα μαρμάρινον 'Αρτέμιδος ἐ- (15) πὶ παραστάδι μυλίνῃ, καὶ Μηνὸς ἄγαλμα ἐπὶ βάσει (16) μαρμαρίνῃ, καὶ τράπεζα ποικίλη τετράγωνος, (17) καὶ βωμὸς μαρμάρινος ἔχων ἀετὸν ἐν ἑαυτῷ (18) Διός, καὶ ναὸς ἐξυλωμένος καὶ κεκεραμωμέ- (19) νος καὶ τεθυρωμένος καὶ κεκλειδωμένος, (20) ἐν ᾧ καθείδρυνται ἀγάλματα Πλούτωνος 'Η- (21) λίου καὶ Κούρης[vv] Σελήνης ἐπὶ βήματος (22) ἐμπεφιεσμένα, ἔχοντα καὶ παστῆον ξύλι- (23) νον ναοειδὲς καὶ παστὸν λινοῦν, καὶ παρ' ἑκατέ- (24) ρᾳ τῶν εισόδων βωμὸς Φωκαϊκός, καὶ κλεῖν (25) κεχρυσωμένην καὶ ἐμπεφιασμένην πρὸς (26) τὴν λογήαν καὶ πομπὴν τῶν θεῶν καὶ στεγνὰ (27) ἐπίπεδα καὶ ἐπ' αὐτῶν στοὰν κατῳκοδομημέ- (28) νην καὶ κεκεραμωμένην πρὸς τὴν οἴκησιν τῶν (29) ἱεροδούλων καὶ τὸν θεὸν θεραπευόντων, καὶ (30) τὴν ἐνδώμησιν τοῦ τεμένους καὶ θεμελί- (31) ωσιν ἐν τετραγώνῳ διὰ σπαράγματος, ἵνα (32) ἦν ἐπίπεδον ἐν ὁμαλῷ τὸ τέμενος, καὶ ὅπλα (33) τῶι θεῶι παρακείμενα τοῦ κόσμου χάριν (34) σιδηρᾶ ὀκτώ.

Apollonios Sparos, son of Metrodoros, [2]father of the former priest, Apollonios, [3]son of Apollonios Sparos, priest of [4]Helios Apollo Kisauloddenos, [5]set up as a dedication to God and to the city [6]the things provided by him, having received permission by decree [7]to inscribe them on a stele. They are the following: [8]God himself on a marble pedestal. [9]Adjacent to God a table of lesbian [10]stone with sculptured feet of a griffon and before [11]it a marble dish to use for [12]sacrificing and a square incense-altar, [13]made of stone from Teos, with an [14]iron vessel for containing fire. Alongside, a marble statue of Artemis on [15]a millstone stand. A statue of Mēn on a marble [16]base along with a square, many-colored table. [17]A marble altar with an eagle on it, [18]of Zeus. A temple of wood with tiled [19]roof and locked doors, [20]in which are dedicated clothed statues of Pluto [21]Helios and Koure Selene upon a pedestal, [22]holding a wooden [23]case in the form

[4] For the inscription, see *SIG* 996 or *ISmyrna* 753. E.N. Lane, *Corpus Monumentorum Religionis Dei Menis*, Études Préliminaires Aux Religions Orientales dans L'Empire Romain (Leiden: E.J. Brill, 1971–78) (*CMRDM*). Lane also includes a photograph of the inscription on Plate 16.

of a shrine and a linen embroidered bridal curtain. On [24]each of the entrances a Phokaian altar. A key, [25]gilded and covered, for [26]the collection and procession of the gods. Closely-fitted, flat [27]pavement stones and on them a stoa built up [28]and roofed with tiles for housing the [29]sacred slaves and servants of God. [30]A wall enclosing the temenos and a [31]foundation squared by means of chips of stone, so that [32]the temenos would be on level ground. Shields [33]adjacent to God for ornamentation, made of iron, in number, eight.

This inscription, probably set up somewhere around the entrance to the sanctuary, follows the form of a dedication: benefactor in the nominative case; deity (here also the *polis*, line 5) in the dative; the verb, *anethēken*, which is most commonly found in dedicatory inscriptions. In this inscription the objects dedicated are at first named in the nominative case, then at the end of line 24 (*klein*) they shift to the accusative, the expected case for a dedication.[5]

A dedication served as the last of a series of formalities required for establishing a holy place.[6] Authorization to construct came from God, through dream or omen.[7] Apollonios Sparos does not indicate how God directed him, perhaps it came through his son/priest. A sanctuary was constructed on a site recognized as sacred. Apollonios Sparos's sanctuary was probably located on the northeastern slope of Pagos Hill, where the inscription was found. (Lines 30–32 suggest that the slope had to be leveled out for the temenos wall.) There the goddesses Nemeseis revealed themselves to Alexander the Great when he lay asleep in front of their temple on Pagos Hill.[8] Within the sacred area, statues and altars were essential furnishings (temples were optional), and the sanctuary had to be marked off from the area around it by a temenos boundary. Apollonios Sparos met all those formalities.

---

[5] See McLean, *Introduction*, 246–54.

[6] There was probably not a dedicatory sacrifice. Price comments that such actions, at least for a temple, were apparently not common (Simon R.F. Price, *Rituals and Power: The Roman Imperial Cult in Asia Minor* [Cambridge: Cambridge University Press, 1984], 134). See, however, Walter Burkert, *Greek Religion*, trans. John Raffan (Cambridge: Harvard University Press, 1985), 85, 89, 383 note 59 with references to Aristophanes, *Peace* 922, et al.

[7] Cf. *SIG* 985, lines 4 & 12; G.H.R. Horsley, *NewDocs 1976* (North Ryde: Macquarie University, 1981), 31; G.H.R. Horsley, *NewDocs 1978* (North Ryde: Macquarie University, 1983), 20–26.

[8] Pausanias (7.5.1) tells the story, probably an etiology. That scene appeared iconically on coins issued at Smyrna as early as 147 A.D. under Emperor Antoninus Pius, see Dietrich O.A. Klose, *Die Münzprägung von Smyrna in der Römischen Kaiserzeit*, Antike Münzen und Geschnittene Steine (Berlin: Walter de Gruyter, 1987), Tafeln 39–40, R1–13.

More was required, however, for the sanctuary to be a sacred site. Sacralization requires ongoing performance—devotees who regularly offer sacrifices and eat meals before God.[9] If there were ever to come a time when sacral performances no longer enlivened Apollonios Sparos's sanctuary, then it would become simply a curiosity of archaeologists, classicists, and historians of religion.[10] In this case, Apollonios (and his son) belonged to a cultic association that would regularly offer cult in the precinct.[11]

The inscription gives a glimpse onto the practices, organization, and theology of the cultic association to which Apollonios Sparos presented his gift.[12] For the most part, there is little that sets this association apart from any other. It had priests (line 2) and other temple personnel (line 29). Statues, whose iconic features were fixed by social habit and cultural convention, represented and made present the deities.[13] Sacred meals

---

[9] Cf. Burkert, *Greek*, 92: "The sacred spot arises spontaneously as the sacred acts leave behind lasting traces." More generally, Roy A. Rappaport, *Ritual and Religion in the Making of Humanity* (Cambridge: Cambridge University Press, 1999), esp. 37–46.

[10] Re-ligion assumes re-iteration, as Peter Jackson notes in his perceptive article, "Retracing the Path: Gesture, Memory, and the Exegesis of Tradition," *HR* 45, no. 1 (August 2005): 1–28.

[11] Apollonios Sparos dedicated his gifts "To God and to the city" (line 5). Martin Nilsson even proposed that this inscription marks a transfer of the sanctuary from a private to a city cult (*Griechische Feste von Religiöser Bedeutung* [Darmstadt: Wissenschaftliche Buchgesellschaft, 1906, repr 1957], 428, note 3). Cecil John Cadoux assumes that κατὰ ψήφισμα in line 6 refers to the cultic association, though he allows that it might "possibly" have been the city who gave permission (*Ancient Smyrna: A History from the Earliest Times to 324 A.D.* [Oxford: Basil Blackwell, 1938], 187, note 5). Debord at least implies that the association gave the permission, see Debord, *Aspects Sociaux et Économiques*, 401, note 49. I wonder if "private" and "public" aren't anachronistic. As one can see from other inscriptions, "private" associations were accepted as a part of the city's, or even the empire's, piety. See, for example, a dedication from the Peloponnesos to Heracles and the city (*Supplementum Epigraphicum Graecum* 41:363.1) or a dedication from Ephesus with a threefold dedication: Ἀρτέμιδι Ἐφεσίαι καὶ Αὐτοκράτορι—καὶ τῆι πρ]ώτ[ηι καὶ μ]ẹγίṣ [τηι—Ἐφεσίων πόλει (IEph 460.2).

[12] For a succinct discussion of associations, with bibliography, see Hans-Josef Klauck, *The Religious Context of Early Christianity: A Guide to Graeco-Roman Religions*, trans. Brian McNeil (Minneapolis: Fortress, 2003), 42–47. Also, Arthur Darby Nock, *Essays on Religion and the Ancient World*, ed. and comp. Zeph Stewart (Cambridge: Harvard University Press, 1972), 430–42.

[13] In short, the statues are signs. On that subject much has been written. I note the following: Porphyry, *Agalm.* frag. 1 = Eusebius, *Praep. ev.* 98A: The profane ones "consider statues as nothing but wood and stone, just as those who do not understanding letters view writing tablets as pieces of wood and books as woven papyri." Rappaport, *Ritual and Religion*, 63: "Constructed Indices nevertheless qualify as True Indices in that the relationship of sign to object among them is, no less than among Natural Indices, that of effect to cause or as part or aspect to whole." James Hoopes, ed., *Peirce on Signs:*

were eaten in the sanctuary on a *trapeza* (lines 9 and 16), and sacrifices were offered on a *bōmos* (17 and 24).[14] If the "linen embroidered bridal curtain" held by Plouton Helios and Koure Selene (line 23) was used in some form of a rite of sacred marriage (*hieros gamos*), that, too, was well known. Lines 24–26 refer to a key (to the temple?) "for the collection and procession of the gods." A temple-key had importance, for a *kleidouchos* (keeper of the key) had charge of the temple. Burkert notes that a figure of a priestess "with the big key" is "a constant attribute of temple iconography."[15] Probably the *kleidouchos* carried the key in the procession of the gods and goddesses.[16] In such processions, a *logēan* was taken for temple upkeep.[17]

A few distinctive features may give a clue to the identity of the cultic association. Apollonios Sparos dedicated as part of the furnishings adjacent to God eight *hopla*. The number eight is given emphasis by being in the final, emphatic position (lines 32–33). Incense on a square *thumiatērion* and bloodless sacrifices on a marble *abakēon* were offered to "God himself" (lines 11–12).[18] Most distinctive, however, is the list of six deities which Martin Nilsson called "eine wilde Kultmengerei der nachchristlichen Zeit... auffällig."[19] Yet for the benefactor and devotees in this cultic association, the six must have had some meaningful coherence.

Writings on Semiotic by Charles Sanders Peirce (Chapel Hill: University of North Carolina Press, 1991), 141–42: "A sign is an object which stands for another to some mind.... it [the sign] must have qualities which belong to it whether it be regarded as a sign or not... Such characters of a sign I call its material quality. [Secondly] a sign must have some real connection with the thing it signifies so that when the object is present or is so as the sign signifies it to be, the sign shall so signify it and otherwise not.... I shall term this character of signs their pure demonstrative application.... [Third] it is only a sign to that mind which so considers and if it is not a sign to any mind it is not a sign at all. It must be known to the mind first in its material qualities but also in its pure demonstrative application. That mind must conceive it to be connected with its object so that it is possible to reason from the sign to the thing."

[14] Dining and sacrificing were the primary collective rites in "private" associations, see Debord, *Aspects Sociaux et Économiques*, 223–24.

[15] Walter Burkert, "The Meaning and Function of the Temple in Classical Greece," in *Temple in Society*, ed. M.V. Fox (Winona Lake, IN: Eisenbrauns, 1988), 35.

[16] Cf. *SIG* 900, line 14 where a key is mentioned in a procession during the ten-day festival at Panamara, Caria.

[17] Cf. I Cor. 16:2 for another reference to a collection, here for the saints in Jerusalem. For other examples, see Adolf Deissmann, *Light from the Ancient East*, trans. Lionel R.M. Strachan (Grand Rapids, MI: Baker Book, 1978), 104–07.

[18] David Gill, "*TRAPEZOMATA*: A Neglected Aspect of Greek Sacrifice," *HTR* 67 (1974): 120

[19] Martin P. Nilsson, *Griechische Feste*, 428.

Further, since this cultic association was neither clandestine nor suspect, the six deities marked the association as having some recognizable theological identification in Smyrna.

By reading and re-reading the inscription, we gain some information about relationships among the six deities. In the inventory proper (lines 8–32), the cult deity is given greater status than the other five. Rather than being mentioned by name, he is referred to as "God" (lines 29 and 33) or "God himself" (line 8).[20] Further, "God himself" was present on a pedestal without any sculpted representation, in contrast to *agalmata* for Artemis, Mēn, Pluto Helios and Koure Selene or *aetos* for Zeus. Artemis stood on a *parastas* of millstone (line 15) alongside "God himself." Naming her stand a *parastas*, anything that stands beside, paired her with Helios Apollo. A statue of Mēn was positioned next to Artemis. Along with his statue was a square, many-colored *trapeza*, for dining before Mēn. Only he and "God himself" had a *trapeza*. Zeus was represented in the sanctuary by a marble altar with an eagle, but he is given minimal recognition. Even the phrase "of Zeus" (line 18) appears in the genitive case on the next line after the reference to the marble altar. Here, Zeus is clearly subordinate to "God himself." Plouton Helios and Koure Selene—kept from view in an enclosed, locked temple (the only deities in a temple)—form a pair. Only the two in the temple and "God himself" were on a *bēma*. Helios Apollo and Plouton Helios are contrasted, the former having Helios in first position, the latter, in second position. From evidence in the inscription itself, three of the six deities are associated with planets (Sun and Moon).

In an ideal world of research, further clues would be found in and around Smyrna. Unfortunately, none exists. Of the six deities, only Zeus, a minor deity in this precinct, and Artemis are mentioned in other artifacts from Smyrna. There is no mention of Helios Apollo, Mēn, Plouton Helios, or Koure Selene. Nor does any other inscription or text bring together those six. The name of the benefactor appears nowhere else. As with many inscriptions, this one is difficult to date. Dittenberger at *SIG* 996 suggested tentatively the first Christian century ("c. saec. I p. Chr.?").

If clues are to be found, they will have to be discovered indirectly and further afield. Fortunately, the conservative nature of Greek theology

[20] *Auton ton theon* is found in other inscriptions in reference to, e.g., Apollo (*OGIS* 227) and the emperor, *auton ton theon Sebastion* (IEph 17).

makes such discoveries possible. For example, what Euripides said about Apollo's connection to Helios in Athens sometime in the fifth pre-Christian century can be found eight centuries later in Themistius of Paphlagonia. Although no facsimile brings together the six deities found in ISmyrna 753, there do exist inscriptions and literary texts with some shared resemblances, that is, they contain one or two of the names given to deities in this inscription or make the same kind of relationships—pairings or contrasts—among deities found in ISmyrna 753. By compiling a number of those texts and charting how they are distributed by centuries, we may be able to discover some further evidence for the date of this inscription and the theology of the cultic association.[21]

3. Shared Resemblances

The triple name for the deity, Helios Apollo Kisauloddenos, appears only in this inscription. A slight variant on the last two names occurs in two other inscriptions from Smyrna: Apollo Kisaludenos (ISmyrna 754) and Apollo Kisalaudenos (ISmyrna 755). The suffixes on Kisauloddenos or variants mark it heavily as a gentilic.[22] There may have been an area in or around Smyrna called something like Kisaulos or Kisauloddos. Cadoux thinks that a local Asiatic god from that area had been identified with Apollo.[23] Helios Apollo (with or without Kisauloddenos) is not found in any other inscription, coin, or literary text from Smyrna, though the double name is found on inscriptions from elsewhere in western Asia.[24]

From about 400 B.C. to the beginning of the Roman Empire, the head of Apollo appears regularly on the obverse (head) of coins minted

[21] It is now possible to make global searches of Greek literature with the aid of Luci Berkowitz and Karl A Squitier, *Thesaurus Linguae Graecae: Canon of Greek Authors and Works* (New York: Oxford University Press, 1990) (latest version e). For search software, I have used *Workplace Pack* 9.02 (Silver Mountain Software, 2001). Searches were made from the fifth century B.C. to the fifth century A.D. A list of texts has been given in Table 2.

[22] -ηνός suffix is a Greek gentilic and -oud(d)a suffix in Lydian-phrygian place names. For Greek gentilic, see Herbert Weir Smyth, *Greek Grammar*, rev. Gordon M. Messing (Cambridge: Harvard University Press, 1956), Par. 844.3. For Lydian-phrygian, compare Einouda, Attouda, Aloudda (Petzl's note on ISmyrna 451.2).

[23] Cadoux, *Smyrna*, 207.

[24] E.g., Thyatira (*IGRR* IV.1238), Dionysopolis, on the upper Maeander in Phrygia (*MAMA* IV.279), Patara in Lycia (*Tituli Asiae M*inoris II.1–3).

at Smyrna, but in imperial times, Apollo disappeared from Smyrna's coinage.[25] Apart from *ISmyrna* 755 and 753 mentioned above, inscriptions referring to Apollo are also pre-imperial.[26] For unclear reasons, Apollo did not represent the city in imperial times, so it is unlikely that Apollonios's sanctuary was an official city cult. At the same time, from this inscription as well as the numerous references to Apollo in Aelius Aristides (second Christian century), it is clear that Apollo (not Helios Apollo) continued to have a significant presence in Smyrna. Helios (alone) had but little presence in Smyrna. Theon and Albinus mention Helios in connection with movement in the zodiac.[27] There is one broken, dedicatory inscription with a bust of the Sun and another deity lost (ISmyrna 745).

In literary texts outside of Smyrna, Helios's connection with Apollo occurs frequently. The mythic Phaethon laments, in a fragment of a play of Euripides by that name, "O beautiful shining sun, how you destroyed me, you rightly called Apollo by mortals, the one who knows the secret names of daimons" (lines 224–25). Thirty-one authors from the fifth pre-Christian through the fifth Christian centuries make a connection between Apollo and the Sun.

Artemis is mentioned in a few other inscriptions from Smyrna, all pre-imperial Rome: One of the towers on the city wall was named Artemis (ISmyrna 613b), a cultic association set up a precinct for Artemis Ephesia (ISmyrna 724), and in an agreement between Smyrna and the Magnesians (on the Maeander), both swear by Artemis Tauropolis, among others (ISmyrna 573). In the same inscription, the people of Smyrna placed a copy of the agreement in the sanctuary of Artemis Leukophryene at Magnesia, an epithet peculiar to Artemis of that city. In an inscription from that city, Artemis Leukophryene is apparently related to the moon—the inscription is fragmented (IMagnesia 83).[28] A few coins minted at Smyrna also show Artemis holding a laurel branch and a bow or represented by a bee.[29]

---

[25] For coins with the head of Apollo, see Barclay V. Head, *Catalogue of the Greek Coins of Ionia*, A Catalogue of the Greek Coins in the British Museum (Bologna: Arnaldo Forni, 1964), 238–46, Plate xxv. For disappearance in imperial times, see Klose, *Münzprägung*, 24.

[26] *ISmyrna* 573–574, 750–752, 754.

[27] See Theon of Smyrna, *Mathematics Useful for Understanding Plato*, trans. Robert and Deborah Lawlor (San Diego: Wizards Bookshelf, 1979), 87 and Albinus, *The Platonic Doctrines of Albinus*, trans. Jeremiah Reedy (Grand Rapids, MI: Phanes, 1991), 48.

[28] Ἄρ[τε]μ̣ι̣ν̣ Λ[ευκο]φ[ρυηνὴν—] εἰς σελήνην [—] μετ̣έχειν ἡμ[ᾶς—].

[29] See Klose, *Münzprägung*, 31.

As twins of Leto and Zeus, Artemis and Apollo are often mentioned together. When paired with Helios Apollo, as in ISmyrna 753, Artemis is associated with the moon. References to those two doubles, sometimes along with others such as Hera/aēr, appear in 12 authors. In seven instances, Artemis is mentioned in connection with the moon without reference to Helios Apollo (see Table 2).

There are no other references to Mēn, an Anatolian moon deity sometimes identified with Attis, in inscriptions, coins, or literature from Smyrna. Inscriptions from the imperial period have been found in several cities east of Smyrna in Lydia and Phrygia.[30] At Pisidian Antioch, Strabo describes a large temple of Mēn and a temple estate controlled by his priest.[31] In western Asia Minor, as in this sanctuary at Smyrna, Mēn seems to have been a minor deity in cultic associations.[32] Mēn is referred to in eight authors (see Table 2).

On one other inscription, a broken one, from Smyrna, a picture of an eagle was etched alongside a dedication to Zeus.[33] A series of coins minted at Smyrna from the age of the Antonines has on the obverse a head of Zeus Akraios, on the reverse, an eagle.[34] Zeus Akraios dominated the Smyrnaean scene with his huge temple on modern Dierman-Tepé. Mary Boatwright has made a strong case for that being the second neocoros temple designated under Hadrian.[35] Given the fact that Zeus had such a minor place in the association's sanctuary and is so ubiquitous in Greek literature, I have not attempted to map his distribution among Greek authors.

---

[30] E.g., Coloae (*SIG* 1142) and Eumenia (*Corpus Cultus Cybelae A*ttidisque I.84) in Phrygia; Collyda (*CCCA* I.475) and Maeonia (I.479; *Lois Sacrées de L'Asie Mineure* 19), Lydia. Eugene N. Lane has collected the evidence in *CMRDM*.

[31] Strabo 12.3.31 (cf. 12.8.14). There Strabo also comments that the royal oath was sworn "by the Fortune (*tuchē*) of the king and Mēn of Pharnaces." Later at 12.8.20, Strabo refers to the temple of Mēn Carus, between Laodiceia and Carura, at which there was also a school of medicine.

[32] See Horsley, *NewDocs 1978*, 30, 22. Also Martin P. Nilsson, *Geschichte der Griechischen Religion, Vol. 2*, Handbuch der Altertumswissenschaft (München: C.H. Beck'sche Verlagsbuchhandlung, 1961), 657: "Da Men fast keine bedeutung für die antike Religion gewann, mag es bei dieser kurzen Erwähnung sein Bewenden haben."

[33] Georg Petzl, *Die Inschriften von Smyrna: Teil II,2: Addenda, Corrigenda und Indices*, Inschriften Griechischer Städte Aus Kleinasien (Bonn: Dr. Rudolf Habelt GMBH, 1990), XL, p. 368.

[34] Head, *BMC Ionia*, p. 255, number 165. Zeus Akraios appears on the head of many coin-series, with different images on the coin's tail (e.g., a lion, griffin, prow).

[35] See Mary T. Boatwright, *Hadrian and the Cities of the Roman Empire* (Princeton: Princeton University Press, 2000), 157–62. ISmyrna 680 refers to an aquaduct leading into Zeus Akraion.

Erik Peterson documents the widespread view that the sun sojourns in the underworld.[36] Plouton Helios, however, is not mentioned or represented in any other artifact from Smyrna or in any other inscription that I can find. In three literary texts he is mentioned in connection with Helios Apollo and with Koure Selene (see Table 2).

In ISmyrna 753, Koure Selene, who was abducted and made queen of the underworld, sits with Plouton Helios hidden from view in a closed temple. Her connection with the moon was made because of the importance of the moon in the growth of vegetation, with which she was closely allied. She is mentioned in only seven literary texts (see Table 2).

Table 1: Frequency Distribution by Century

Distribution of authors roughly by Christian centuries is as follows (if one author refers to two or more deities, he is counted under each deity) (Plutarch is counted as early second century):

HA = Helios Apollo; AS = Artemis Selene; PH = Plouton Helios; KS = Koure Selene.

	HA	AS	Mēn	PH	KS	Total	Total Pagan
BC v	3	0	0	1	0	4	4
BC iv	2	0	0	0	0	2	2
BC iii	2	1	0	0	0	3	3
BC ii	1	1	0	0	0	2	2
BC i	0	0	1	1	0	2	2
AD i	2	2	0	0	0	4	2
AD ii	8	4	2	2	2	18	14
AD iii	3	2	4	1	3	13	12
AD iv	9	5	0	1	2	17	5
AD v	1	2	1	0	0	4	4

I have discounted the 19 occurrences in Philo and Christian writers, for they simply reflected what they heard or read about in pagan writers. Thus, we are seeking the frequency distribution only in pagan writers. Of the 50 occurrences in pagan writers, 23 (46%) appear in authors from the reign of Trajan to the tetrarchies of Diocletian, roughly the

[36] Erik Peterson, 'ΕΙΣ ΘΕΟΣ: *Epigraphische, Formgeschichtliche und Religionsgeschichtliche Untersuchungen* (Göttingen: Vandenhoeck & Ruprecht, 1926), 307, fnt. 2. See Apuleius, Pindar, and Virgil in Table 2.

second and third Christian centuries. Moreover, that is the only time period in which all five deities are referred to. If that frequency distribution tells us anything about ISmyrna 753, it points to a date sometime in the latter half of the second or possibly early third Christian century.

4. In Context: Shared Resemblences from Trajan to Diocletian

Now if we limit authors to pagan writers of roughly the second and third Christian centuries, we obtain the following 14: Alexander, Apuleius, Artemidoros, Athenaeus, Diogenes Laertius, Heliodoros, Heraclitus, Iamblichus, Lucian, Maximus, Orphic Hymns, Pausanias, Plutarch, and Porphyry. Perhaps they may give further information about the distinctive features of the cultic association indicated in ISmyrna 753: that is, the curious group of deities; the fact that all of them have solar or lunar connections;[37] the placement of Plouton Helios and Koure Selene in a closed temple; Helios Apollo as "God himself"; the contrast between Helios Apollo and Plouton Helios; the eight *hopla*; and bloodless sacrifices.

Some of these authors refer only in passing to one or more of the deities. Moreover, they do little more than confirm what we knew from ISmyrna 753. Alexander refers to Helios Apollo and Artemis Selene in a statement comparing Greek and Egyptian religions. In the *Metamorphoses*, Apuleius says that Lucius, during an initiation, saw the sun shining brightly about midnight when he approached the gates of Proserpine. Though not so named, the sun could be understood as Plouton Helios. Athenaeus refers to a village in Phrygia named Mēn, which indicates the popularity of this deity in that region. In the novel, Aethiopica, Heliodoros refers to the desecration of the holy precinct of Apollo at Delphi, who, he added, is the same as the sun. Lucian parodies the material of statues by having Hermes (at Zeus' command) place the pure gold statues of Mithras and Mēn ahead of the Greek gods, which irritates Poseidon. Lucian also notes that the Phrygians sacrifice to Mēn. Pausanias comments on Apollo's healing

[37] Even Zeus, whom I have bracketed out of consideration, has solar connections, e.g., Julian's "Hymn to King Sun," Porphyry's "Hymn to Zeus" (Orphic), Frag. 3 = Eus. *Praep. Ev.* 100–101, and Macrobius, *Sat.* 17 (drawn from Porphyry, see Martin P. Nilsson, *Geschichte* 2, 514, note 8.).

power, because the sun, by adapting its course to the seasons, imparts to the air its healthfulness. In the *Orphic Hymn to Artemis* (36), Artemis is identifed with the moon as "torch-bearing goddess, bringing light to all" (i.e., Selene). In *Orphic Hymn to Persephone*, she (Koure) is described as "brilliant and horned," i.e., Selene. Artemidoros, the dream analyst, says that dreaming of Apollo "signifies that secrets will be brought to light. For he is identified with the sun."

Paired Names

The earliest known identification of a deity with some aspect of the physical world, such as the sun or moon, occurred in interpretations of Homer.[38] The first known scholium was done by Theagenes of Rhegium (Italy, sixth pre-Christian century), who glossed the text of the battle of the gods in Chapter 20 of the *Iliad* as referring to contrarieties in the elements of nature (*stoicheia phuseōs*).[39] Maximus of Tyre explains this manner of interpretation as follows: Poets and philosophers say the same thing (*homoiotēta*), but in poets you find names (*onomata*), in philosophers, *logoi*, a difficult term to translate here, perhaps, "forces."[40] Heraclitus gives the name allegory to this form of interpretation: "the trope which says [*agoreuōn*] one thing but signifies something other [*alla*] than what it says receives the name 'allegory' precisely from this."[41] So in *Iliad* 20, Poseidon and Apollo battle to a draw, for the sun (Apollo) is nourished by a salty liquid element (Poseidon), and so as giver and receiver of nourishment, each gave way to the other.[42] Heraclitus asserts that Homer himself identified Apollo with Helios—the allegory is present in the text, not layered upon it—yet Heraclitus realized that to get the allegory, one must delve deep "into Homer's rites and be initiated in his mystical wisdom." Then what appears to be impiety about the gods will

---

[38] Menander Rhetor says that Parmenides and Empedocles wrote *phusikoi humnoi* in which a deity is identified with some element in nature, e.g., "a hymn to Apollo, [in which] we identify him with the sun, and discuss the nature of the sun" (*Menander Rhetor*, trans. and ed. D.A. Russell and N.G. Wilson [Oxford: At the Clarendon Press, 1981], 13–15).

[39] See Porphyry, *Quaest. hom. Iliad.* 20.67. David Konstan considers it plausible that Theagenes is responding to Xenophanes, see Donald A. Russell and David Konstan, eds. and trans., *Heraclitus: Homeric Problems* (Atlanta: Society of Biblical Literature, 2005), xiv. *Iliad* 20 became a commonplace for discussing allegory, cf. Heraclitus, *Hom. Prob.* ¶56.

[40] See LSJ under λόγος III.7.c for use in Neo-Platonic writings. Cf. also Himerius: Sun is to Apollo as light is to *logos*.

[41] Russell and David Konstan, *Heraclitus*, 9.

[42] Russell and David Konstan, *Heraclitus*, Paragraph 56.

be "charged with deep philosophy."[43] John Dillon notes that Heraclitus here shares with Theon and Albinus, both of Smyrna, the metaphor of philosophical understanding as initiation into a mystery.[44]

Koure/Plouton

Porphyry interpreted the Demeter/Koure/Plouton myth along the same lines as Heraclitus interpreted the *Iliad*: Plouton signifies the sun, Koure/Kore, shoots (*koroi*) or seeds. Plouton abducted Koure, that is, when the sun goes down under the earth, it snatches up the shoot at seed-time (*ton sporon*) (Eus. 110d). Or, Plouton, which is the sun as it travels around to the lower hemisphere, draws down (*helkei*) beneath the earth the power in seeds (Koure) at the time of the winter solstice (Eus. 109c). The myth, thus, represents the cycle of vegetation, and that cycle is related to the cycle of Helios, as it moves diurnally and through the seasons.[45]

Plutarch also gives an interpretation of the Demeter/Koure myth. In "The Face of the Moon," brother Lamprias reports what he learned from "a mysterious stranger" (945D). The Greeks are wrong in believing that Demeter and Kore lived together in the same region. Rather, Demeter exists as sovereign over the region of the earth, whereas Kore, over the region of the moon.[46] Koure/Kore cannot leave Plouton who abducted her, for Koure (the moon) marks the boundary of Hades (Plouton). But every six months or so, she is wrapped in earth's (Demeter's) shadow; there they embrace, as they long for each other when apart. Hades is that region between the moon (Koure) and earth (Demeter).[47] The myth also conceals (*epikrupsamenos*) an eschatological dimension: In that region the evil and unclean go and stay, but the

---

[43] Russell and David Konstan, *Heraclitus*, 93 (¶ 53), cf. ¶6.6, "That Apollo is identical with the Sun, and that one god is honored under two names, is confirmed both by mystical doctrines taught by secret initiations and by the popular and widely quoted line, 'the sun's Apollo, and Apollo the sun'" (Russell and Konstan translation).

[44] John Dillon, *The Middle Platonists: 80 B.C. to A.D. 220* (Ithaca: Cornell University Press, 1977), 398. Philo also uses that metaphor.

[45] Porphyry does not directly identify Koure with Selene, but he does say that the moon maintains Koure or keeps her in relationship (Eus. 113d): ἔστι συνεκτικὴ τῆς Κόρης ἡ σελήνη. Συνεκτικὴ is an adjective from συνέχω. The suffix τ-ικος marks "fitness or ability or a relation" (Smyth, *Greek Grammar*, 237).

[46] In *Orphic Hymn* 29, queen Kore (Koure) is described as brilliant (*eupheggēs*) and horned (*keroessa*), that is, she is the moon.

[47] Iamblichus, in Lydus, located the territory of Hades, which he says is Plouton, from the moon (Persephone) to the sun (ὑπὲρ σελήνης ἄχρις ἡλίου). There the souls are purified.

good rise to dwell on the moon until their second death, when they rise to the sun. The tripart human is, thus, a microcosm of the celestial spheres: Earth furnishes the body (*sōma*), moon the soul (*psuchē*), and the sun the mind (*nous*). The first death reduces humans to soul and mind; the second, taking place on the moon, reduces humans to mind, which rises to the sun (942D–943B).

Plutarch's complex interpretation moves beyond a straightforward association of a deity with an element in nature to uncovering enigmatic, hidden meanings in the myth: Physics and human eschatology join together to form a larger whole. According to Menander Rhetor, such enigmatic writings were associated with the Pythagoreans.[48] If something like the thought of Porphyry and/or Plutarch was present in the cultic association at Smyrna, then the meaning of Plouton Helios and Koure Selene, bride and groom in their temple, could have resonated out into the cycle of vegetation, celestial positions, and/or the cycle of life and death of humans.

Helios Apollo

As we have seen, the cultic association recognized Helios Apollon Kisauloddenos as their special deity. He is referred to in the inscription as "God" or "God himself," and, for whatever reason, there is no mention of an *agalma* or any other representation of him on his stand. Here, as in, for example, a fragment of *On Sacrifices* by the Pythagorean Apollonius of Tyana, "the unique dignity of the Supreme Being coexisted with the reality of the various subordinate manifestations of divinity," as Nock puts it.[49]

Among writers from roughly the second and third Christian centuries, Plutarch discusses Apollo and Helios Apollo in considerable detail. He gives a Platonic spin to the double name, Helios Apollo, most succinctly in "The Obsolescence of Oracles." Many of an earlier generation, he writes, regarded Apollo and Helios as the same god, but those who respected analogy recognized that as the body is to soul, vision (*opsis*) to intellect (*nous*), and light to truth, so the sun is to Apollo (*Mor.* 433E).

---

[48] At *Menander Rhetor*, 15 (¶ 337): "The hymns which circulate as Pythagorean are enigmatic, while those we have just mentioned [e.g., Apollo identified with the sun] are overt."

[49] Arthur Darby Nock, "A Cult Ordinance in Verse," in *Arthur Darby Nock: Essays on Religion and the Ancient World*, comp. and ed. Zeph Stewart (Cambridge: Harvard University Press, 1972), 850.

And Ammonius says—back in "The E of Delphi"—that we must awaken as from dreaming those who think that Apollo and the sun are the same so that they may see clearly that the sun is seen through the senses, while Apollo is the creative power of the sun conceived through the mind (393D).[50] In short, the sun belongs to *aisthēsis*, Apollo to *noētos* (393E) or *dianoia* (400D).[51]

In "The E at Delphi," Ammonius, Plutarch's teacher, lectures at length on Apollo as God.[52] He poses the question, "What, then, really is Being (*on*)?". Answer: True Being is found only in God who is eternal (*aidion*), uncreated (*agenēton*), and incorruptible (*aphtharton*) (392E–393A). God should, therefore, be addressed in the singular as εἰ, "you are" (393B).[53] Or, better, εἶ ἕι, "You are One." That is why his name is Apollon, "denying the Many" (A-pollon: alpha privative + an Ionian form of *polus*) (393C). As The One, Apollon contrasts with Plouton, "many"[54] (394A): Apollo is clear, Plouton is unseen; Apollo bright, Plouton dark; Apollo supports memory, Plouton oblivion (394A). Apollo as Helios is lord of the realm of Becoming and plain to see, while at dissolution we pass into the opposite realm, that of Hades, the unseen. (1130A).

By calling Apollo (Being) One, Ammonius also alludes to Pythagorean number theory, for which numbers are the "permanent, prime principles of the world...Their configurations reveal the structure of the universe."[55] Or as Theon of Smyrna states: "According to the Pythagoreans, it is necessary to give precedence to arithmetic since the origin, source, and root of all things is found in numbers."[56] Among numbers, *hen* or *monas* is the most basic: It is the underlying source

---

[50] According to Proclus (*in Ti.* 1.159–60, a gloss on Plato, *Ti.* 24C), Porphyry also places Apollo in the sphere of thought] δὲ εἰκότως φησὶ [Porphyry]...καὶ ὁ Ἀσκληπιὸς νοῦς ἐστι Σεληνιακοί ὥσπερ ὁ Ἀπόλλων Ἡλιακὸς νοῦς.

[51] Apparently Plutarch did not separate *noētos* and *dianoia* into different spheres. If in fact there was no representation of Helios Apollo Kissauloddenos in the Smyrnaean sanctuary, it would further support the connection between that cultic association and Platonism. At Delos, the statue of Apollo "holds a bow in the right hand, and Graces in the left, each of them holding a musical instrument,..." (Plut. *Mor.* 1136A).

[52] His long speech begins at 391E.

[53] Ἐι is also the name of the Greek letter, Epsilon, or E, at Delphi, which the interlocutors are seeking to explain. This is one of several explanation for the meaning of E at Delphi.

[54] Presumably from πλε(F)ω, "to abound, flood, to have an abundant harvest."

[55] Lucas Siorvanes, *Proclus: Neo-Platonic Philosophy and Science* (New Haven: Yale University Press, 1996), 211. Plutarch points out that Ammonius "plainly held that in mathematics was contained not the least important part of philosophy" (391E).

[56] 18.1–2, my translation.

of all things, supreme over all things. "From it come all things, but it comes from nothing."[57] In "Isis and Osiris," Plutarch points out that the Pythagoreans named *monas* Apollon—τὸ τὴν μονάδα τοὺς ἄνδρας ὀνομάζειν 'Απόλλωνα—and that they got that notion from the Egyptians (354F). Later in the same dialogue, he says that the Pythagoreans also called *hen*, Apollo (381F).

In Pythagorean number theory, numbers join together in harmonious relations—present in music, in the celestial spheres, and in the harmonious universe as a whole. According to the Pythagorean Platonist, Eratosthenes, when Hermes rose up into the sky, after having invented the lyre, he was astonished that the harmonies produced by the velocities of the planets were exactly the same as the harmonies on the lyre that he had constructed.[58] More commonly, however, the lyre belongs to Apollo. So in Plutarch's "The Oracles at Delphi," after the participants had passed the house of the Acanthians and Brasidas in their tour of Delphi (400F), one of the gold votive offerings they mentioned was "a golden plectrum" that represented the bright rays of the sun: "Fair Apollo, who gathering together origin and end, tunes them, and holds the light of the sun as his plectrum" (402B). In the *Orphic Hymn to the Sun* (8), the lyre also belongs to Helios Apollo: "Yours the golden lyre and the harmony of cosmic motion... *kosmokratōr* and player of the syrinx."[59] The *Orphic Hymn to Apollo* (34) gives greater detail. Apollo is praised, inter alia, "for tuning the celestial pole with resounding lyre, now the highest pitch, when he goes to the highest point, then the lowest pitch. Then in Dorian mode, tempering the pole for the orderly arrangement of the universe. That enigmatic statement is then explained: giving an equal measure of summer and winter, distinguishing winter with the lowest tones, summer with the highest, and Dorian for the spring season of lovely blooms." That is pure Pythagorean number theory applied to the celestial spheres. Porphyry, gives a slightly different version in his hymn to Helios: They call Apollo the pulsation (*palsis*) of his [the sun's] beams. There are also nine muses singing to his lyre..." (Frag. 8 = Eus. 112b).[60]

---

[57] 99.24–100.6, cf. Theon of Smyrna, *Mathematics (Lawlor)*, 66. *Monas* (unity) may have priority over *hen* (one), but so far as I can tell, Theon does not make a strict separation of the two terms.

[58] Quoted in Theon of Smyrna, 142.7–143.1, cf. *Lawlor*, 93–94.

[59] My translation. Cf. Apostolos N. Athanassakis, ed. and trans., *The Orphic Hymns*, Graeco-Roman Religion Series 4 (Missoula, Montana: Scholars Press, 1977), 13–15.

[60] Cf. the fourth century Sallustius, *Concerning the Gods and the Universe*, ed. and trans.

The Other Distinctive Features

We may treat summarily the other distinctive features of ISmyrna 753. According to Iamblichos, Pythagoreans were admonished not "to sacrifice a white cock, for he is a suppliant and sacred to Mēn."[61] Diogenes Laertius gives a variant: Pythagoreans were prohibited even from touching a white cock, for the same reason. In the introduction to the *Orphic Hymns*, the Phrygian Mother of the Immortals, Attis, and Mēn are invoked, along with several other deities, to come to this mystic rite (*thuēpoliē*) and holy libation.[62] In Orphic and Pythagorean cult, no blood sacrifices were offered. That fits with the furnishings in the Smyrnaean sanctuary: Before "God himself" stood a *thumiatērion* for offering incense and a marble *abakēon* for offering bloodless sacrifices (lines 11–12).[63] Finally there are the enigmatic *hopla*, in number eight, that lay beside God in the Smyrnaean sanctuary. If read in the Homeric tradition, those *hopla* are shields and arms taken in battle and hung in Apollo's temple for ornamentation (*tou kosmou charin*).[64] In Pythagorean number theory, the number eight was significant. The author of the *Theology of Arithmetic* states that "eight is all" (*panta oktō*).[65] And Theon of Smyrna states that the spheres circling round the earth are eight in number and they join together harmoniously, citing the Pythagoreans, Timotheus and Eratosthenes, as authorities.[66] In that Pythagorean

Arthur Darby Nock (Chicago: Ares, 1996, repr of 1926), VI: Of the mundane gods, some "harmonise it out of its varied components...Apollo strings a lyre."

[61] Iamblichus, *On the Pythagorean Way of Life*, John Dillon & Jackson Hershbell (Atlanta: Scholars Press, 1991), 109. Paragraph 84. Dillon & Hershbell translate as "Moon," to which of course the common noun, *mēn*, refers (month or moon). Here, however, the context suggests, if not requires, the name of the deity, cf. Hippolytus who says that the Greeks call Attis ἐπουράνιον Μηνὸς κέρας. Cf. also the directives that Orpheus gives to Mousaios, line 40 of the Introduction to the *Orphic Hymns*.

[62] On the relationship of Mēn to the Mother of the Gods and to Attis, see Lane, *CMRDM*, III.81–82. The epigraphic evidence indicates some kind of relationship among the three, but it is not clear that Mēn is a consort of Mother.

[63] Animal sacrifices were sometimes offered to Apollo, see Lewis Richard Farnell, *The Cults of the Greek States*, vol. I–V (Oxford: At the Clarendon Press, 1896–1909), IV.436, note 276.

[64] See *Iliad* 7.83, cf. Dio Chrysostom, *Discourse* 2.34.

[65] 75.5–6, ἡ περιέχουσα τὰ πάντα σφαῖρα ὀγδόη, ὅθεν ἡ παροιμία "πάντα ὀκτώ" φησι. For a translation, Iamblichus, *The Theology of Arithmetic*, trans. Robin Waterfield (Grand Rapids, MI: Phanes, 1988). Waterfield points out that the author of the treatise is actually unknown (p. 23).

[66] Theon, *Mathematics Useful for Understanding Plato* 105.11–106.2 Τιμόθεός φησι καὶ παροιμίαν εἶναι τὴν "πάντα ὀκτώ" διὰ τὸ τοῦ κόσμου τας πάσας ὀκτὼ σφαίρας περὶ γῆν κυκλεῖσθαι, καθά φησι καὶ 'Ερατοσθένης: ὀκτὼ δὴ τάδε πάντα σὺν ἁρμονίῃσιν

context, the phrase, *tou kosmou charin* in ISmyrna 753, could be translated something like "for the benefit of the world order."

5. In Context: Smyrna

The cultic association behind ISmyrna 753 could not have assimilated all the shared resemblances found in the writers of the previous section. My concern there was to locate a range of possible meanings for the distinctive features in that sanctuary. From those possible meanings, however, one conclusion can be made: a thread of Pythagoreanism runs through them. The "unique dignity" given to Helios Apollon Kisauloddenos also fits with a Pythagorean context, for from the start, Pythagoras was seen as having a special relationship with Apollo.[67]

Pythagoreanism or a Platonism heavily influenced by Pythagoreanism fits with the intellectual setting of Smyrna in especially the latter half of the second century, the heyday of Pythagorean Platonism in Smyrna's museion.[68] Albinus was probably the most distinguished professor there. Galen, a young man in his 20s (c. 150), left Pergamon to study with him.[69] Grave markers have been discovered for three students who died while studying at Smyrna: Agathokles from Nicaia was 20 years old, Domitius Sabinus was 17 (probably from Smyrna), and Diodotos was from Colossae (no age given).[70] Philostratus mentions several *sophists*, that is, orators, who taught there, for example, Rufinus of Smyrna (*VS* 608), Nicetes of Smyrna (*VS* 511, 516), and the great Polemo (*VS* 531). On a tombstone at Pergamon (IGRR 1690, n.d.), a mother proudly wrote on her tombstone that her son, Herodotos, taught philosophy at Smyrna—or perhaps the son directed the stone mason to incise that on her memorial!

ἀρήρει, 106 ὀκτὼ δ' ἐν σφαίρῃσι κυλίνδετο κύκλῳ ἰοντα…ἐνάτην περὶ γαῖαν. Cf. Theon of Smyrna, *Mathematics (Lawlor)*, 69–70.

[67] Some said he was Apollo's son, others, that he was an incarnation of the God. When Abaris, a priest of Hyperborean Apollo, met Pythagoras, "he believed him to be truly none other than Apollo himself, and not just a mortal resembling him." See Iamblichus, *Pythagorean*, 35, 55, 115 (= II.5, VI.30, and XIX.91).

[68] For the revival of Pythagoreanism in the early imperial period and its relation to Platonism, see Dillon, *Middle Platonists*, 341–83. Also Fritz Graf offers a succinct summary in the third edition of *OCD*, under "Pythagoras (1), Pythagoreanism."

[69] Galen, *De libris propriis* liber 19.16.10–15.

[70] ISmyrna 439–441.

Another professor there, Theon, a lesser light, wrote an introductory text for those students who did not have an adequate mathematical background for reading Plato. He elucidated Plato by including large chunks of Pythagorean authors, for they "are necessary to understand the ideas of Plato" (47.17).[71] He justifies his dependency on Pythagoreans by noting that Plato himself often followed the Pythagoreans (12.10). Thus, Theon's Plato, like other Middle Platonists such as Philo of Alexandria, Plutarch of Chaeronea, and Apollonius of Tyana, was dosed heavily with Pythagorean notions.

Pythagorean convictions at Smyrna found expression not only in the academy, but also in associations with their own private religious rites.[72] For example, there is an inscription of a cult ordinance of a Dionysiac temple from Smyrna, probably second century (perhaps early third), that shows clear influence of Pythagorean dietary regulations.[73] So, Arthur Darby Nock concluded that Pythagoreanism offered "a life with a scheme and a brotherhood and religion."[74]

ISmyrna 753 may offer evidence for a late second century Pythagorean sodality at Smyrna, like the one near Porta Maggiore in Rome.[75] The centrality of Helios Apollo, offerings of bloodless sacrifices to him, the solar and lunar designations of the deities, the presence of Mēn in the list of deities, and the enigmatic eight instruments before god all suggest a Pythagorean association.

---

[71] He cites Adrastus's *On Harmony and Consonance*, various works by Eratosthenes, and in the Chapter on music, large blocks from Claudius Thrasyllus's *On the Seven Tones*. He also refers to the work of other Pythagoreans: Philolaus (470–390 B.C.) whose *On Nature* may have been the first book by a Pythagorean and which was the primary source for Aristotle's account of Pythagoreanism. Fourth century Pythagoreans, Eudoxus (390–340) in astronomy, Aristoxenus (b. c. 370 B.C.), and Archytas (400–350 B.C.).

[72] In a reference to Sextus Claudius Aurelianus, a Pythagorean from Smyrna given honorary citizenship at Delphi, Arthur Darby Nock said about Smyrna: "[I]n a community so cultivated and substantial there may well have been others who shared his convictions"(Nock, "Cult Ordinance," 850).

[73] ISmyrna 728 and Nock, "Cult Ordinance." The most telling taboo is that of not eating the heart (Nock 848). A ban on eating eggs or beans is more general.

[74] Arthur Darby Nock, *Conversion* (Baltimore: The Johns Hopkins University Press, 1933), 168.

[75] Nock, *Conversion*, 168.

Table 2: Ancient Authors

Legend: Author. Date by century. Classification. Reference. Deity mentioned.
AS = Artemis Selene. HA = Helios Apollo. KS = Koure Selene. M = Mēn. PH = Plouton Helios. Z = Zeus.

Alexander, son of Numenius. ii A.D. Middle platonist. *Rhetoric* 5.3–9. AS & HA.
Apuleius. ii A.D. Middle platonist? *Metamorphoses* 11.23. (PH)
Artemidoros of Ephesus (also Daldis). ii A.D. Interpreter of Dreams. *Onirocriticon* 2.35. HA.
Athanasius. iv A.D. Christian. *Vita Antonii* 26.949. HA, AS, K(S).
Athenaeus. ii A.D. Sophist. *Deipnosophistae* 2.17. M.
Callimachos of Cyrene. iii B.C. Poet & Scholar. *Hecala* frag. 302. HA.
Chrysippus. iii B.C. Stoic. Frag. 632 in Plutarch, *Obsolescence of Oracles* 425F. HA, AS.
—— *Frag.* 748. AS.
Clement of Rome. ii A.D. Christian. *Homily* 6.2.12. HA, K(S).
Cornutus of Rome. i A.D. Stoic. *De natura deorum* 65. HA, AS.
Cyril of Alexandria. iv A.D. Christian. *Contra Julian* 2.26. HA, AS.
—— 1.36. HA.
Diogenes Laertius. iii A.D. Biographer. *Pythagorus* 8.34. M.
Diogenes of Babylon. ii B.C. Stoic. *Testimonia et fragmenta* 33 (Philodemus, *de pietate* 15). HA, AS.
Empedocles. v B.C. Pythagorean. in Menander Rhetor 333. HA.
Euripides. v B.C. Dramatist. Frag. of *Phaethon* 224–26. HA.
Eusebius of Caesarea. iv A.D. Christian. *Praep. Ev.* 119D. HA, AS.
—— 96B–C. HA, AS. —— 102–03. Z. —— 121C. HA, AS, K(S).
Heliodoros. iii A.D. Novelist, Neo-Platonist. *Aethiopica* 10.36. HA.
Heraclitus. ii A.D. Allegorist. *Homeric Problems* 6.6. HA.
—— 7.2. HA.
—— 7.7. HA.
—— 8.1. HA.
—— 53. HA, AS.
—— 56. HA.
—— 57. AS.
Hesychius of Alexandria. v A.D. Lexicographer. sub divlogcon (1847). AS.
Himerius. iv A.D. Sophist. *Declamationes* 41.1–9. HA.
Hippolytus. iii A.D. Christian, Naassene. *Haer.* 5.9.8. M.
Iamblichus. iii A.D. Neo-Platonist, Pythagorean. *Vita Pythagorae* 18. M.
—— in Lydus, *de Mensibus* 149. KS.
John Chrysostom. iv A.D. Christian. *Exposition Psalm 55.57.* HA.
Julian. iv A.D. Neo-Platonist. *Orat.* 4.136. PH.
Lucian. ii A.D. Epicurean? *Jupp. trag* 8. M.
—— 42. M.
Macrobius. v A.D. Neo-Platonist. *Saturnalia* 1.17. HA.
—— 1.18. PH.

Maximus of Tyre. ii A.D. Middle Platonist. *Dialexeis* 4. HA.
Origen. ii A.D. Christian. *Mart.* 46. HA, AS.
—— *Cels.* 4.48. HA, AS.
—— *Philoc.* 17. HA, AS.
Orion of Thebes, Egypt. v A.D. Grammarian. *Etymologicum* 189. AS.
Orphic Hymns. iii A.D. Orphism. *Heis Hēlion* (8). HA.
—— *Heis Selēnēn* (9). AS.
—— *Apollōnos* (34)
—— *Artemidos* (36). AS.
—— *Humnos Persephonēs* (29). KS.
—— *Orpheus pros Mousaion* (Introduction). M.
Parmenides. v B.C. Pythagorean. in Menander Rhetor 333. HA.
Pausanias. ii A.D. Travel Guide. *Descr.* 7.23.8. HA.
Philo. i A.D. Jewish Middle Platonist. *Decal.* 54. HA, AS.
Philochoros. iv B.C. Historian. in Harpocration, *Lexicon of the ten Orators* 294. HA.
Pindar. v B.C. Poet. Frag. 129. (PH).
Plato. iv B.C. Philosopher. *Leges* 945. HA.
Plutarch. i–ii A.D. Middle Platonist. *Moralia* 386B. HA.
—— 393C. HA.
—— 394A. PH.
—— *400C. HA.*
—— 425E. HA.
—— 433D. HA.
—— 938E. AS.
—— 942D. KS.
—— 1129F–30A. HA.
—— Frag 157 = Eus. *Praep. Ev.* 85a. HA.
Porphyry. iii A.D. Neo-Platonist. *Quaest. hom. Iliad* 1.399. HA.
—— 18.239. HA.
—— 20.67.39–47. AS, HA.
—— *Agalm.* frag 3 = Eus. *Praep. Ev.* 100–01. Z.
———— frag 5 = Eus. *Praep. Ev.* 108d. AS, HA.
———— frag 6 = Eus. *Praep. Ev.* 109b. K(S).
———— frag 7 = Eus. *Praep. Ev.* 109c. KS, PH.
———— frag 7 = Eus. *Praep. Ev.* 109d. KS.
———— frag 7 = Eus. *Praep. Ev.* 110d. KS, PH.
———— frag 8 = Eus. *Praep. Ev.* 112b. HA.
———— frag 8 = Eus. *Praep. Ev.* 113b. AS, PH.
———— frag 8 = Eus. *Praep. Ev.* 113d. KS.
———— frag 10 = Eus. *Praep. Ev.* 115D. K(S).
—— in Proclus, *in Ti.* 1.159.25. HA.
Proclus. v A.D. Neo-Platonist. *in Ti.* 4.251. M.
Sallust. iv A.D. Neo-Platonist. *de deis et mundo* 4. KS.
—— 6 HA, AS.
Strabo. i B.C. Geographer. *Geogr.* 5.431. M.

Themistius. iv A.D. Aristotelian. *Huper tou legein* 2.330D. HA.
Theodoret. iv A.D. Christian. *Quest. et respons.* 130.6–11. HA.
—— *Graec. affect. curatio* 3.45. AS.
Virgil. i B.C. Poet. *Aenead* 6.641. (PH).

PART TWO

NEW TESTAMENT STUDIES

"THE SPIRIT IS WILLING, BUT THE FLESH IS WEAK" (MARK 14:38B AND MATTHEW 26:41B)

David E. Aune

The phrase τὸ μὲν πνεῦμα πρόθυμον, ἡ δὲ σὰρξ ἀσθενής ("the spirit is willing, but the flesh is weak"), found in verbally identical forms in Mark 14:38b and Matt. 26:41b, is a simple but carefully crafted proverb formulated antithetically (hereinafter referred to as the "dominical proverb"). This dominical proverb is preceded, in both Mark 14:38a and Matt. 26:41a, by a hortatory saying: γρηγορεῖτε καὶ προσεύχεσθε, ἵνα μὴ ἔλθητε [Matt: εἰσέλθητε] εἰς πειρασμόν, "Keep awake and pray, that you do not enter into temptation" (hereinafter referred to as the "hortatory saying"). Again, the Matthaean and Markan versions are nearly identical. The sole verbal variation consists in Matthew's preference for the compound verb εἰσέρχομαι in contrast to Mark's use of the simple form ἔρχομαι. The preceding and particularly the following verses in both Matthew and Mark, however, exhibit considerable verbal variation.[1] Luke reproduces only the hortatory saying, which he does twice, once in Luke 22:40 and again in Luke 22:46. In the first instance, uttered before Jesus goes off to pray alone, it serves as a warning: προσεύχεσθε μὴ εἰσελθεῖν εἰς πειρασμόν ("Pray that you do not enter into temptation"). Luke inserts this hortatory saying in place of the Markan phrase "Sit here while I pray" (Mark 14:32), slightly expanded by Matthew to "Sit here while I go over there and pray" (Matt 26:36). The second, as in Mark and Matthew, is uttered when Jesus returns and finds the disciples sleeping: τί καθεύδετε; ἀναστάντες προσεύχεσθε, ἵνα μὴ εἰσέλθητε εἰς πειρασμόν ("Why are you sleeping? After rising, pray that you do not enter into temptation"). Luke has thus used the hortatory saying as an *inclusio* for the short episode narrating the prayer of Jesus in vv. 41–42.

In this essay in honor of my esteemed teacher and dissertation adviser, Robert M. Grant on his 90th birthday, I propose to explore

[1] Matt. 26:40 has fourteen words compared with the slightly shorter parallel in Mark 14:37 with twelve words. But Matt. 26:42, with twenty-one words, is considerably shorter than the parallel in Mark 14:39, which has just eight words.

several issues involving this dominical proverb in relation to the hortatory saying, though they will not be taken up *seriatim*: (1) What is the form of this dominical proverb and how does it function in its Markan (and Matthaean) context and does it have any close literary parallels? (2) Is there any evidence to suggest that either the dominical proverb or the hortatory saying were in circulation before their incorporation into Mark and their subsequent recycling by Matthew and Luke? (3) To what extent were the hortatory saying and dominical proverb recycled in early postcanonical Christian literature? (4) Since this particular anthropological idiom is largely absent from the Synoptic Gospels, was it perhaps at home in other phases of early Christianity independent of their canonical attestation? (5) What is the appropriate religio-cultural context for an anthropological duality which conceives of the human person as consisting of two constituent elements labeled πνεῦμα and σάρξ? Is this anthropological duality consistent with those found in the Hebrew Bible or is it more characteristic of the world of Greek thought, or it is perhaps a syncretistic combination of both? (6) Finally, can the dominical problem be regarded as reflecting the *ipsissima vox Jesu*?

1. The Form and Function of the Dominical Proverb

The grammatical formulation of this dominical proverb is unusual in the New Testament and early Christian literature. The occurrence of the paired contrasting correlative particles μέν and δέ, in which the inclusion of μέν throws the emphasis on the segment headed with δέ, is comparatively rare in the Gospels, but is characteristic of classical style.[2] The μέν...δέ contrast occurs elsewhere in Mark just once and in the same context (Mark 14:21):[3] "For the Son of Man [ὅτι ὁ μὲν υἱὸς τοῦ ἀνθρώπου] goes as it is written of him, but woe [οὐαὶ δὲ] to that man by whom the Son of man is betrayed!" Since μέν, in contrasts with δέ, is a specifically Greek idiom, the possibility of an Aramaic substratum in both passages seems somewhat diminished. Oddly, this grammatical idiom is more at home in Matthew, where it occurs eleven times,

[2] Friedrich Blass and Albert Debrunner, *Grammatik des neutestamentlichen Griechisch*, ed. Friedrich Rehkopf, 16. Auflage (Göttingen: Vandenhoeck & Ruprecht, 1984), §447. See also J.D. Denniston, *The Greek Particles*, 2nd ed. (Oxford: The Clarendon Press, 1954), 369–74.

[3] Excluding the relative form of the idiom in Mark 12:5.

(excluding the relative forms, e.g., ὃ μέν…ὅ δέ, "the one…the other"),[4] though in all passages it is associated with Matthew's Q source (3:11; 9:37; 10:13; 16:3; 17:11–12; 20:23; 21:35; 22:8; 25:33; 26:24, 41). An example: Q 10:2 (Matt. 9:37 = Luke 10:2): ὁ μὲν θερισμὸς πολύς, οἱ δὲ ἐργάται ὀλίγοι ("the harvest is great, but the workers are few"), an antithetical proverb using the contrastive μέν…δε construction with the omission of the linking verb. The same form is found in Matt. 22:8: ὁ μὲν γάμος ἕτοιμός ἐστιν, οἱ δὲ κεκλημένοι οὐκ ἦσαν ἄξιοι, "The wedding is ready, but those invited are unworthy." The idiom occurs seven times in Luke, again excluding relative forms:[5] Luke 3:16, 18–19; 10:2; 11:48; 13:9; 23:41; 23:56–241. The same form occurs in the agraphon inserted into Codex Beza at Luke 6:5: τῇ αὐτῃ ἡμέρᾳ θεασάμενός τινα ἐργαζόμενεον τῷ σαββάτῳ εἶπεν αὐτῳ· ἄνθρωπε εἰ μὲν οἶδας τί ποιεῖς, μακάριος εἶ, εἰ δὲ μὴ οἶδας ἐπικατάρατος καὶ παραβάτης εἶ τοῦ νόμου ("On the same day, when he [Jesus] saw someone working on the Sabbath, he said to him: 'Man, if you know what you are doing, you are blessed; but if you do not know, you are cursed and a transgressor of the law'").

The dominical proverb preserved in Mark 14:38b and Matt. 26:41b reflects a meristic anthropological perspective in which the two basic constituents of the human person are conceptualized in terms of πνεῦμα ("spirit") and σάρξ ("flesh"). It is apparent that these two conceptions are oppositional, reflecting a perception of a tension if not a conflict within human experience expressed by the "willingness" of the spirit which is frustrated by the "weakness" of the flesh. The formulation of this dominical proverb suggests that the flesh is a hindrance to the desires of the spirit, but there is no suggestion that the flesh is in any sense sinful or evil or is itself the seat of negative desires or impulses. Further, it also seems evident that in this dominical proverb πνεῦμα represents a "higher" or "superior" aspect of the person (the seat of thinking and willing), while σάρξ represents a "lower" or "inferior" aspect of the person. Finally, particularly in view of the fact that the terms "spirit" and "flesh," either singly or as a contrasted pair, are conspicuous by their absence in the rest of the Synoptic tradition,[6] it cannot be

[4] Matt. 13:4, 8, 23, 32; 16:14; 22:5; 23:27, 28; 25:15.

[5] Luke 23:33.

[6] In the Synoptics, πνεῦμα usually refers to the Holy Spirit or unclean spirits, and is rarely used in an anthropological sense. To the latter category belong the references in Matthew to the "poor in spirit" (5:3), and the reference that Jesus "gave up his spirit"

assumed that the dimeristic anthropology expressed in the contrast between πνεῦμα and σάρξ is typical or even representative of the ideological context from which it derives.

The context of the dominical proverb in both Mark 14:38b and Matt. 26:41b is that of the passion narrative that Matthew (Matt. 26:1–27:66) has largely reproduced from his Markan exemplar (Mark 14:1–15:47). Whether or not Mark inherited an existing passion narrative that he edited conservatively or created the passion narrative out of disparate traditions remains a disputed issue in New Testament scholarship,[7] though in my view the first option is the more likely. The hortatory saying and the dominical proverb are part of the Gethsemane scene in the passion narrative (Mark 14:32–42; Matt. 26:36–46). Both the hortatory saying and the dominical proverb play a paraenetic role within the Gethsemane scene, and are just two of several passages that serve a paraenetic function within the remainder of the passion narrative and its expansions by Matthew and Luke.[8] It is likely, given the distinctive content of the dominical proverb that both it and the hortatory saying were added to the Gethsemane scene of the passion narrative at a late stage of its development before it was taken up by Mark.[9]

when he died (27:50; cf. Luke 23:46). In Mark, Jesus reportedly knew "in his spirit" what people were saying about him (2:8), and is said to have "groaned in his spirit" (8:12). In the context of the Magnificat in Luke 1:47, Mary says "my spirit rejoices in God my savior." With the exception of Matt. 26:41b and Mark 14:38b, πνεῦμα and σάρξ occur in the same immediate context in the Synoptic Gospels only in Luke 24:39: "a spirit does not have flesh and bones as you see that I have." In John, πνεῦμα and σάρξ occur antithetically in two passages: (1) In John 3:3, "That which is born of the flesh is flesh and that which is borne of the spirit is spirit." (2) In John 6:63, "The spirit is that which enlivens, the flesh profits nothing."

[7] Werner Kelber is one who has argued against the existence of a pre-Markan passion narrative: "Thematically it is difficult to identify a major non-Mkan thrust or theme in Mk. 14–16, let alone extrapolate a coherent pre-Mkan source" ("Conclusion: From Passion Narrative to Gospel," *The Passion in Mark: Studies on Mark 14–16*, ed. Werner H. Kelber [Philadelphia: Fortress, 1976], 157).

[8] Rudolph Bultmann, *Die Geschichte der syoptischen Tradition*, 8th ed. (Göttingen: Vandenhoeck & Ruprecht, 1970), 307, refers to the paraenetic purpose of several sayings in the passion narrative, including Mark 14:38. Detlef Dormeyer, *Die Passion Jesu als Verhaltensmodell* (Münster, 1974) has examined the paraenetic function of the entire passion narrative.

[9] Urs Sommer, *Die Passionsgeschichte des Markusevangeliums* (WUNT, 2.58; Tübingen: Mohr Siebeck, 1993), 104.

2. Spirit and Flesh in the Hebrew Bible and Judaism

In searching for parallels to the contrast between πνεῦμα and σάρξ, it is logical to begin with a consideration of Old Testament and Judaism. The anthropology of the Hebrew Bible generally regards the human person as a composite entity,[10] reflected in a variety of meristic phrases dominated by *lēb* (Gen. 6:17; 7:15; Deut. 28:65; Job 34:15; Ps. 16:9; 73:26; Prov. 14:30; Eccl. 2:3; Isa. 66:14).[11] The human person as a composite of πνεῦμα and σάρξ is found in the LXX (Gen. 6:17; 7:15; MT: Isa. 31:3), but never in contexts implying conflict within the human person.[12] "Spirit" designates God and his world, "flesh" designates human beings with their intellectual or spiritual possibilities and their world. The Greeks distinguish between the "soul" and the "body" but almost never use the terms "spirit" and "flesh" for that dichotomy. Sand argues (against Schweizer) that one cannot speak of an "anthropological dualism" in Mark 14:28B and proposes instead that "the weakness of the σάρξ and the willing spirit correspond rather to the OT understanding of the conflict between good and evil in human beings (cf. Ps. 50:14 LXX)."[13] This is a very strange suggestion, for nowhere in the OT is there any discussion of a conflict between good and evil within the person. According to Schweizer, "Jewish and Greek ways of thinking have in this case been blended into one."[14] In essential agreement with Schweizer, Till Arend Mohr, proposed that while the dichotomistic anthropology in Mark 14:38b appears to reflect Greek thought, the distinction between a willing spirit and the weak flesh is not characteristically Greek.[15] Further, Mohr suggests that the discontinuities between this saying and

---

[10] There is no implicit claim here that OT anthropology is "unified" in any meaningful way. To appreciate the complexity of the issues, see Robert A. Di Vito, "Old Testament Anthropology and the Construction of Personal Identity," *CBQ* 61 (1999) 217–38.

[11] H.-J. Fabry, *TDOT*, 7.412–3.

[12] Eduard Schweizer, *Das Evangelium nach Markus* (NTD 1; Göttingen: Vandenhoeck & Ruprecht, 1967), 181.

[13] A. Sand, "σάρξ," *EDNT* 3.232. However, Sand's reference to LXX Ps. 50:14 is pointless since the phrase πνεύματι ἡγεμονικῷ in the phrase "strengthen me with a guiding spirit" does not reflect the underlying Hebrew of Ps. 51:14.

[14] Schweizer, *Markus*, 181.

[15] Till Arend Mohr, *Markus- und Johannespassion: Redaktions- und traditionsgeschichtliche Untersuchung der Markinischen und Johanneischen Passionstradition* (Zürich: Theologischer Verlag Zürich, 1982) 231.

both Hellenism and Judaism suggests its authenticity,[16] and he goes on to suggest that Mark 14:37–38 as well as 14:33–34 belong to the oldest stratum of the Passion Narrative which Mark took over from tradition.[17] Linnemann, however, argues that 14:38 presupposes vv. 33–34a, and therefore belongs to a later revision of the Markan Passion Narrative, Mark's third version of the pericope.[18] This basic disagreement concerning the relative age of Mark 14:38, while understandable given the subjective bases for critical judgment, makes it difficult to argue for either the authenticity or secondary character of Mark 14:38 based on traditional critical criteria.

There are several passages in the LXX where σῶμα is used to refer to the physical body, while καρδία indicates the thinking and willing capacity of the individual (2 Macc. 3:17; 4 Macc. 13:13; Prov. 5:11–12; Wis. 8:17–20; Sir. 30:16; 47:8–19). In the OT and early Judaism, the heart is the seat of all vices as well as all virtues.[19] The former view is reflected in Rom. 1:24: "Therefore God gave them up to the desires of their hearts [ἐν ταῖς ἐπιθυμίαις τῶν καρδιῶν] to impurity, to the dishonoring of their bodies [σώματα] among themselves." In the anthropology of the Dead Sea Scrolls, human frailty and weakness is concentrated in the heart.[20]

The Hebrew term *baśar* has eight distinct meanings,[21] three of which are relevant for our investigation: (1) "flesh [as substance of the body]" (Gen. 2:21, 23, 24; 17:11; Lev. 12:3; Ezek. 37:6, 8), (2) "body [of (a) person]" (Ex. 30:32; Lev. 6:10; 13:2, 3, 4; 14:9; 15:19), and (3) "human being [in contrast to God]" (Gen. 6:3; Num. 16:22; 27:16; Jer. 17:5; Ps. 56:4).[22] When used with the second meaning, "body [of a person]," it is sometimes contrasted to the spirit or soul (Isa. 10:18; 31:3; Ps. 16:9 [LXX 15:10]; 63:1 [LXX 62:2]).[23] It should be noted that none of the three distinct semantic meanings of *baśar* mentioned above (based on

---

[16] Mohr, *Markus- und Johannespassion*, 231.

[17] Mohr, *Markus- und Johannespassion*, 232, 404

[18] Eta Linnemann, *Studien zur Passionsgeschichte* (FRLANT, 102; Göttingen: Vandenhoeck & Rupprecht, 1970), 29, 32, 179.

[19] Karl-Adolf Bauer, *Leiblichkeit, das Ende aller Werke Gottes: Die Bedeutung der Leiblichkeit des Menschen bei Paulus* (SNT 4; Güterloh: Verlagshaus G. Mohn, 1971) p. 142, n. 14; H.-J. Fabry, *TDOT*, 7.426–34.

[20] H.-J. Fabry, *TDOT*, 7.436.

[21] *DCH*, 2.276–7.

[22] *DCH* 2.276.

[23] *DCH* 2.277 (Lev. 17:11 and Deut. 12:23 are also suggested under the rubric "body of a person," but both refer to animals).

major Hebrew lexicons), include the connotation of weakness, which is therefore a pragmatic rather than semantic meaning of the term, that is it may be suggested by the context but not by the basic meanings of the word itself. The view that *baśar* "embraces the typically Hebraic thought of weakness,"[24] is unfounded. In the LXX, *baśar* (which occurs 266 times in the Hebrew Bible) is frequently translated σάρξ (129 times) and less frequently rendered σῶμα (21 times), the latter largely in Leviticus and Numbers. When *baśar* in the OT means "body [of a person]," it is usually translated in the LXX with σῶμα (Lev. 6:10; 13:2, 3, 4; 14:9; 15:19), though in one passage it is rendered σάρξ (Ex. 30:32).

3. Analogous Hellenistic Anthropological Dualities

It must be frankly admitted at the outset that the terms πνεῦμα and σάρξ are rarely if ever used together in Hellenistic sources to contrast the thinking and willing capacity of the human person on the one hand, with the weak physical body on the other. In *Nicomachean Ethics* 7, Aristotle has an extended discussion of ἐγκράτεια ("self-control, strength of will") and ἀκράτεια ("lack of self-control, weakness of will"), the primary qualities of the ἐγκρατής (the "strong-willed person") and ἀκρατής (the "weak-willed person"). Aristotle is particularly concerned to explain how a person can act against his or her own understanding of what is best to do. The ἐγκρατής sees what must be done and does it, though he is divided and also has contrary impulses to which he may occasionally give in. The ἀκρατής sees what must be done but does not do it, for he is also divided but gives in to his impulses.

One of the closest parallels to Mark 14:38b and Matt. 26:41b in pagan literature is found in Lucian *Tragopodagra* 66–68, where two Greek terms for designating the "soul" and "body," ψυχὴ and δέμας, are used in an antithetical sense. Here, in a contrastive μέν... δέ construction which is part of a brief soliloquy, the "soul" of a man with gout is eager (ψυχὴ μὲν οὖν μοι καὶ προθυμία) to go to the door of his house, but his feeble body cannot serve his will (δέμας δὲ νωθρὸν οὐχ ὑπηρετεῖ πόθοις). Here (probably because of the iambic meter) δέμας is the term used for "physical body," while ψυχή, usually translated "soul," designates the thinking and willing faculty of the inner person.

[24] Dunn, *Theology of Paul*, 64.

4. Πνεῦμα and Σάρξ in Pauline Anthropology

Since Paul frequently contrasts πνεῦμα and σάρξ, it is important to determine whether the πνεῦμα/σάρξ dichotomy in Mark 14:38b and Matt. 26:41b has any relation to this anthropological aspect of Pauline thought, particularly in light of the fact that all of Paul's letters were written before the Gospel of Mark and might therefore indicate the extent to which πνεῦμα and σάρξ, were current in early Christian thought as the two basic components of the human person. Indeed, some scholars have characterized the spirit/flesh contrast in our dominical proverb as "Pauline," while others have taken the opposite position and argued that the spirit/flesh contrast is not at all similar to that found in the Pauline letters.[25] In fact (as we shall see), there is room in Paul's conception of πνεῦμα and σάρξ for the meanings found in the dominical proverb, though they are by no means distinctively Pauline.

Paul contrasts πνεῦμα and σάρξ in eleven different contexts with several variations in meaning. πνεῦμα is used in three different ways by Paul in contrast to σάρξ: (1) the immaterial part of the human person, the seat of the emotions and the will, (2) the Spirit of God which takes over the functions of the human spirit, (3) as a metaphor for the inner, true allegorical meaning of the Torah. On the other hand, σάρξ is also used in at least three different ways in contrast to πνεῦμα:[26] (1) the physical body, (2) human nature as the primary locus of the passions, (3) as a metaphor for the outer, now invalid meaning of the Torah.

There are three groups of passages in the genuine Pauline letters in which σάρξ and πνεῦμα are juxtaposed.[27] (1) In the first group, con-

[25] M.-J. Lagrange, *Évangile selon Saint Marc* (4th ed.; Paris: J. Gabalda, 1929), 390; Ernst Lohmeyer, *Das Evangelium des Markus* (14th ed.; KEK; Göttingen: Vandenhoeck & Ruprecht, 1957), 317–18; Herbert Braun, *Späjüdisch-häretischer und frühchristlicher Radikalismus* (2 vols.; Tübingen: Mohr-Siebeck, 1957) 2.116, n. 4; Ernst Haenchen, *Der Weg Jesu: Eine Erklärung des Markus-Evangeliums und der kanonischen Parallelen* (2. Aufl.; Berlin: Walter de Gruyter, 1968), 492. The most comprehensive discussion of the non-Pauline character of Mark 14:38b and Matthew 26:41b is in Karl Georg Kuhn, "Jesus in Gethsemane," *Redaktion und Theologie des Passionsberichtes nach den Synoptikern*, ed. Meinrad Limbeck (Darmstadt: Wissenschaftliche Buchgesellschaft, 1981), 96–8.

[26] I have omitted the view that the term σάρξ, in addition to the material flesh, could also represent a cosmic or demonic power, the opinion of Hermann Lüdemann, *Die Anthropologie des Apostels Paulus und ihre Stellung innerhalb seiner Heilslehre: Nach den vier Haupbriefen* (Kiel: Universitäts-Buchhandlung [Paul Toeche], 1872), 54, which is now widely held; see Robert Jewett, *Paul's Anthropological Terms: A Study of Their Use in Conflict Settings* (AGJU 10; Leiden: Brill, 1971), 453–4.

[27] A passage which lies outside the three categories is Rom 1:3–4, which refers to

sisting of two passages (and one anomalous passage), πνεῦμα is used of the human spirit and σάρξ is used neutrally of the physical body.[28] A clear example of this type of contrast is found in 2 Cor. 7:1: "let us cleanse ourselves from every defilement of body and spirit [σαρκὸς καὶ πνεύματος]." (2) In a second group of four passages, σάρξ is referred to negatively, but more specifically as a metaphor for those aspects of the Torah which are rendered invalid by the coming of Christ, while πνεῦμα is used as a metaphor for the true meaning of the Torah.[29] Rom. 2:28–29 exemplifies this category:

> For he is not a real Jew who is one outwardly, nor is true circumcision something external and physical [ἐν τῷ φανερῷ ἐν σαρκί]. He is a Jew who is one inwardly, and real circumcision is a matter of the heart, spiritual [ἐν πνεύματι] and not literal.

(3) Finally, in a third group of four passages,[30] Paul uses πνεῦμα of the Spirit of God indwelling the human spirit, and σάρξ as human nature serving as the instrument of sinful desires; conflict between these two antithetical forces is emphasized. A clear example of this group is Gal. 5:16–17 (part of a longer contrast between σάρξ and πνεῦμα in Gal. 5:16–26):

> But I say, walk by the Spirit, and do not gratify the desires of the flesh. For the desires of the flesh are against the Spirit, and the desires of the Spirit are against the flesh; for these are opposed to each other, to prevent you from doing what you would.

According to Paul, the desires of the Spirit are frustrated by the apparently contrary desires of the flesh, impeding Christians from doing what they should be doing. While there are some similarities between this

Jesus Christ who was descended from David "according to the flesh [κατὰ σάρκα] and designated Son of God in power "according to the Spirit [κατὰ πνεῦμα] of holiness by his resurrection from the dead." Here κατὰ σάρκα and κατὰ πνεῦμα are clearly parallel, but unlike other Pauline passages in which σάρξ and πνεῦμα are contrasted, this text has a christological focus.

[28] The other passage in the authentic Pauline letters in which σάρξ and πνεῦμα are contrasted neutrally, with σάρξ referring to the physical body and πνεῦμα to the human spirit is 1 Cor. 6:16–17. The neutral meaning of σάρξ is also found in two pseudo-Pauline letters, including Col. 2:5 ("though I am absent in body I am present in spirit") and 1 Tim. 3:16 ("He was manifest in the flesh, vindicated in the Spirit").

[29] In addition to Rom. 2:28–29, other passages in this category include Gal. 3:2–3; 4:29; Phil. 3:3.

[30] In addition to Gal. 5:16–26, the other passages which belong to this group include Rom. 7:5–6; 8:1–17; Gal. 6:8.

Pauline anthropological conception and our dominical proverb, nevertheless the clear conflict between spirit and flesh in Gal. 5:16–17 is more heightened than the weak flesh impeding the willing spirit in Mark 14:38b and Matt. 26:41b. The most important difference, however, is indicated by the capitalized word "Spirit," reflecting Paul's conviction that the Spirit of God indwells believers.[31] Though some commentators have argued that πνεῦμα in Mark 14:38b and Matt. 26:41b refers to the Spirit of God,[32] it seems quite clear that the human spirit, i.e., the *conditio humana* is referred to here.[33] The conflict between Spirit and flesh is also clearly articulated in Rom. 8:5–6 (a selection from the longer discussion in Rom. 8:1–17):

> For those who live according to the flesh set their minds on the things of the flesh, but those who live according to the Spirit set their minds on the things of the Spirit. To set the mind on the flesh is death, but to set the mind on the Spirit is life and peace.

While this texts seems to divide people into two categories, "those who live according to the flesh" and "those who life according to the Spirit," it appears rather that the possibility of living according to the flesh is a possibility always present for Christians. This conflict between the spirit and the flesh described by Paul paralyzes the person in whom these forces struggle for supremacy.

Paul's view of the σάρξ as a negative influence has a parallel in 4 Macc. 7:18:

> Only those who with all their heart make piety their first concern are able to conquer the passions of the flesh [κρατεῖν τῶν τῆς σαρκὸς παθῶν], believing that to God they do not die, as our patriarchs Abraham, Isaac, and Jacob died not, but live to God. Accordingly, the validity of our argument is not impaired by the fact that some men seem to be ruled by their passions because of the weakness of their reason [διὰ τὸν ἀσθενῆ λογισμόν].

---

[31] Paul clearly expresses this view in Rom. 8:9a: "But you are not in the flesh, you are in the Spirit, if in fact the Spirit of God dwells in you." However, it is sometimes difficult to determine whether Paul understands πνεῦμα as the Spirit of God or the spirit of the human person. In Rom. 8:10, the verse immediately following that quoted above, πνεῦμα refers to the human spirit: "But if Christ is in you, although your bodies are dead because of sin, your spirits are alive because of righteousness."

[32] Josef Ernst, *Das Evangelium nach Markus* (RNT; Regensburg: Friedrich Pustet, 1981), 431. This understanding of πνεῦμα occurs frequently in Paul.

[33] Haenchen, *Der Weg Jesu*, 492.

Paul nowhere uses πνεῦμα and σάρξ as contrasting aspects of the human person in a way precisely parallel to Mark 14:38b and Matt. 26:41b, where σάρξ is a hindrance to the willing πνεῦμα only because of its weakness. Paul does use σάρξ with several distinct meanings or denotations along with a number of connotations, one of which emphasizes the weakness of the flesh.[34] In Rom. 6:19, for example, Paul says, "I speak in human terms because of the weakness of your flesh [διὰ τὴν ἀσθένειαν τῆς σαρκὸς ὑμῶν]." While it is possible to understand σάρξ as a synecdoche for the entire person, construing the Greek phrase to mean "because of your weakness" (cf. Rom. 5:6), it is more natural to understand σάρξ as referring to the physical body which has the quality of weakness. Here Paul makes explicit one aspect of his complex understanding of σάρξ, namely, its physical and moral frailty. A close verbal parallel is found in Gal. 4:13 where Paul refers to his own physical condition when he first preached the Gospel to the Galatians with the phrase δι' ἀσθένειαν τῆς σαρκὸς, "because of a weakness of the flesh," i.e. (more idiomatically), "because of a physical ailment." According to Dunn, "weakness of the flesh" characterizes Paul's understanding of the human condition."[35] A similar emphasis is found in Rom. 8:3, where Paul observes that because of the weakness of the flesh, the Law is unable to counteract the power of sin. In Rom. 5:6, Paul observes that "It was while we were weak [ὄντων ἡμῶν ἀσθενῶν] that Christ, at the appointed time, died for the ungodly." Both Paul and Ignatius used πνεῦμα and σάρξ in tandem to refer to the inner and outer aspects of the human person as a totality (2 Cor. 7:1; Col. 2:5; Ign *Magn.* 13:1; *Trall. inscr.*; 12:1; *Rom. inscr.; Smyrn.* 1:1; *Polyc.* 1:1; 5:1; cf. *Eph.* 8:2).[36]

In sum up, Paul uses the contrastive anthropological terms πνεῦμα and σάρξ in ways that are closely (if not exactly) similar to the dominical proverb in Mark 14:38 and Matt. 26:41, making it clear that such language was potentially extant in Christian circles before the composition of the Gospel of Mark.

[34] James D.G. Dunn, *The Theology of Paul the Apostle* (Grand Rapids: Eerdmans, 1998), 64–66, reviews eight different meaning of σάρξ in the authentic Pauline letters. While Dunn's discussion is not without problems, it does serve to illustrate the complexity of Paul's use of σάρξ.

[35] James D.G. Dunn, *Romans 1–8* (WBC 38A; Dallas: Word, 1988) 345.

[36] On flesh and spirit in Ignatius, see William Schoedel, *Ignatius of Antioch* (Hermeneia; Philadelphia: Fortress, 1985), 23–24.

5. Early Christian Appropriations of Mark 14:38 and Matt. 26:41

Since there are no explicit grammatical features connecting the hortatory saying to the dominical proverb which follows, coupled with the fact that both make sense independently of the other, it is not surprising that they were in fact often separated in subsequent Christian tradition. In addition to Matt. 26:41, one of the earliest appropriations of Mark 14:38 is found in the Lukan version of Jesus' prayer in Gethsemane in Luke 22:40 and 46, in which the hortatory saying is reproduced twice, in a form in which εἰσέλθητε is shared with Matthew and circumstantial participle ἀναστάντες is substituted for the Markan imperative γρηγορεῖτε: ἀναστάντες προσεύχεσθε, ἵνα μὴ εἰσέλθητε εἰς πειρασμόν ("Rise and pray that you might not enter into temptation"), but omits the dominical proverb entirely. A phrase closely parallel to the hortatory saying is μὴ εἰσενέγκῃς ἡμᾶς εἰς πειρασμόν ("do not lead us into temptation"), which occurs in identical form in the three earliest versions of the Lord's Prayer (Matt. 6:13; Luke 11:4; Did. 8:2). This parallel is even more striking once it is recognized that the present imperative προσεύχεσθε introduces the Lord's Prayer in Matt. 6:9 and Did. 8:2 (Luke 11:2 substitutes the present subjunctive προσεύχησθε in a ὅταν clause).[37]

The two sayings in Matt. 26:41 and Mark 14:38 are occasionally quoted or alluded to by later Christian writers, but always in forms suggesting dependence on the canonical Gospel tradition. Polycarp, in *Phil.* 7:2, substitutes an allusion to the temptation phrase from the Lord's Prayer for the hortatory saying,[38] and then quotes the dominical proverb in the same form found in Matthew and Mark, attributing it to the Lord (*Phil.* 7:2): δεήσεσιν αἰτούμενοι τὸν παντεπόπτην θεὸν μὴ εἰσενεγκεῖν ἡμᾶς εἰς πειρασμόν, καθὼς εἶπεν ὁ κύριος· τὸ μὲν πνεῦμα πρόθυμον, ἡ δὲ σάρξ ἀσθενής ("Asking the all-seeing God in our prayers not to lead us into temptation, just as the Lord said: 'The spirit is willing, but the flesh is weak'"). Polycarp's allusion to the dominical proverb, the

[37] There is a tendency to regard the Lukan formulation of the introduction to the Lord's Prayer as representing the form found in Q; see Shawn Carruth and Albrecht Garsky, *Q 11:2b–4*, ed. Stanley D. Anderson (Documenta Q; Leuven: Peeters, 1996) 70–74.

[38] Édouard Massaux, *The Influence of the Gospel of Saint Matthew on Christian Literature before Saint Irenaeus*, Book 2: *The Later Christian Writings*, trans. L.J. Belval and S. Hechi (Macon: Mercer University, 1986) 31–32.

earliest application of this saying outside the New Testament, is striking because he regards the hortatory saying and the temptation phrase from the Lord's Prayer as closely related and he freely exchanges them. While the Oxford Society argued that the dominical proverb was derived from oral tradition or a document similar to the canonical Gospels,[39] rather than from the Gospels themselves, this appears to be one of the few passages in the Apostolic Fathers in which there is a clear allusion to either Matthew or Mark.[40] Since Matt. 26:41b and Mark 4:38b are identically worded, it is not possible to specify which Gospel Polycarp is dependent on, though his use of the temptation phrase from the Lord's Prayer suggests Matthew, for only Matthew contains both parts of Polycarp's allusion.

In early Christian literature subsequent to Polycarp, the dominical proverb is frequently used in martyrological contexts where no particular interest in its anthropological features is in evidence. Irenaeus (*Contra haer.* 5.9.2) cites the dominical proverb reversing the two clauses: "Sicut enim caro infirma, sic spiritus promptus a Domino testimonium accepit" ("For as the Lord has testified that 'the flesh is weak,' so also that 'the spirit is willing'"). Irenaeus applies the saying to martyrs who sacrifice their lives, not hesitatingly because of the infirmity of the flesh, but unhesitatingly because of the readiness of the spirit. Clement of Alexandria quotes the dominical proverb in the same form as Polycarp (*Stromata* 4.7): "And the Savior has said to us, 'The spirit is willing, but the flesh is weak'." Similarly, Tertullian also quotes the two clauses of the dominical proverb in reverse order in *Ad uxorem* 5.4. He begins with the reverse order in *Ad martyras* 4, but quickly observes that the Lord first declared the spirit willing, showing which of the two ought to be subject to the other. Elsewhere he alludes to it in canonical order (*De fuga* 8). He cites the second clause, "the flesh is weak," to explain the fact that Jesus trembled at the prospect of death (*On the Flesh of Christ* 9). Tertullian also quotes the hortatory saying alone in *De baptismo*

---

39 Oxford Society of Historical Theology, *The New Testament in the Apostolic Fathers* (Oxford: Clarendon Press, 1905), 103.

40 Helmut Koester, *Synoptische Überlieferung bei den apostolischen Vätern* (Berlin: Akademie-Verlag, 1957) 114–15; *idem, Ancient Christian Gospels: Their History and Development* (Philadelphia: Trinity Press International, 1990), 20; Doudewijn Dehandschutter, "Polycarp's Epistle to the Philippians: An Early Example of 'Reception'," *The New Testament in Early Christianity*, ed. Jean-Marie Sevrin (BETL 86; Louvain: Leuven University Press, 1989), 288; Wolf-Dietrich Köhler, *Die Rezeption des Matthäusevangeliums in der Zeit vor Irenäus* (WUNT 2.24; Tübingen: Mohr Siebeck, 1987), 103.

20: "'Watch and pray,' he says, 'lest you fall into temptation'." In his essay *On Patience* (13), he argues that "the spirit is willing, but the flesh [without patience] is weak." Hippolytus, in his discussion of the two natures of Christ, uses the dominical proverb in Matt. 26:41b and Mark 14:38b to argue that the flesh of Christ did not become divine in his incarnation (*Against Beron and Helix* frag. 2). Origen, interpreting the Parable of the Tares, observes that "while men are asleep they do not act according to the command of Jesus, 'Watch and pray that you enter not into temptation,' the devil on the watch sows what are called tares, that is, evil opinions" (*Comm. in Matt.* 10.2). Cyprian argues that the Lord was teaching humility in the sayings preserved in Matt. 26:41 and Mark 14:38 (*Treatises* 4.26). In *Const. apost.* 5.1.6, believers are exhorted not to court dangers rashly, "for the Lord says, 'Pray that you fall not into temptation; the spirit indeed is willing, but the flesh is weak'." In a later section, believers are exhorted to receive those fleeing persecution since they know that "the spirit is willing, the flesh is weak," and prefer to lose their property while preserving their allegiance to Christ (*Const. apost.* 8.4.45).

The saying is also alluded to in three Coptic-Gnostic documents, all of which appear dependent on the Synoptic tradition. The Strasbourg Coptic Papyrus rearranges three allusions to the Passion narrative:[41] "The hour is nigh, when I shall be taken from you [Mark 14:41 = Matt. 26:45]. The Spirit <is> willing, but the flesh <is> weak [Mark 14:38 = Matt. 26:41]. <Wait> now and watch <with me> [Mark 14:34 = Matt. 26:38]," quoting the dominical proverb of Mark 14:38 and Matt. 26:41, but omitting the hortatory saying. A Gnostic interpretation of both sayings is found in *Thom. Cont.* 145.8–9:[42] "Watch and pray that you not come to be in the flesh, but rather that you come forth from the bondage of the bitterness of this life." Here the term "temptation" in Mark 14:38a and Matt. 26:41a is construed to mean "being in the flesh," i.e., remaining physically alive or living an ascetic lifestyle. Finally, *1 Apoc. Jas.* 32.19–20 alludes to the second part of the proverbial component: "The Lord said to him: 'James, thus you will undergo these sufferings. But do not be sad. For [γάρ] the flesh is weak'." Here, sadness or fear

[41] Wilhelm Schneemelcher, *New Testament Apocrypha*, trans. R. McL. Wilson (2 vols.; Cambridge: James Clarke; Louisville: Westminster John Knox, 1991) 1. 104.

[42] Bentley Layton (ed.), *Nag Hammadi Codex II,2–7* (NHS XXI; 2 vols.; Leiden: Brill, 1989) 2.205.

in the expectation of suffering is equated with the weakness of the flesh, which refers to the possibility of physical pain and suffering.

The aphoristic character of both the hortatory saying and the dominical proverb, together with the fact that they have no logical or grammatical connection in Mark 14:38 and Matt. 26:41, led to their frequent use in a variety of contexts in early Christian literature. For Polycarp, the hortatory saying cohered well with the temptation phrase from the Lord's Prayer, and that is the context in which he quoted the dominical proverb. For Irenaeus and Tertullian, the dominical proverb is interpreted in a martyrological context, which is a natural development of its use in the passion narrative of Mark and Matthew. For Origen and Cyprian, the dominical proverb functions as paraenesis directed toward the avoidance of temptations to fall into sin. Some Gnostic texts construe the dominical proverb as an encouragement for maintaining an ascetic lifestyle.

6. Concluding Summary

It is likely that the paraenetic character of the dominical proverb in Mark 14:38 and Matt. 26:41 did not belong to the earliest stratum of the pre-Markan passion narrative, but was added when the passion narrative was formulated for use in a liturgical context in the early church. The Greek style of the dominical proverb argues against an Aramaic origin. Further the fact that the terms "spirit" and "flesh," understood as the two basic and contrastive elements that constitute the human person, has relatively close analogies in Judaism and the early church suggests that the dominical saying cannot be regarded as an authentic saying of Jesus. The aphoristic character and lack of close connection between the hortatory saying and the dominical proverb frequently led to their separation as both sayings were recycled a number of ways in various contexts in early Christian literature. There is no compelling evidence that either saying could have been derived from Hellenistic anthropology or aphoristic discourse.

"EVERY SIGNAL WORTH READING": JESUS AND JEWISH SECTARIANS IN MARK

Peter Zaas

At the very least, however, ... every signal could prove to be worth reading.[1]
—Robert M. Grant

As every naval intelligence officer knows, most of the information about what is going on around the ship is to be found under the surface. Sonar operators, at least since the Second World War, typically locate their quarry by triangulating simultaneous signals from multiple sources, sometimes calculating their objective via fuzzy logic, thus "fuzzy triangulation."[2] A superficial survey reveals that exegetes of the New Testament base their research upon nearly-identical principles as the gatherers of underwater intelligence: They similarly prefer multiple views of the same target.[3] It should surprise us not at all that both a prolific American historian of the New Testament and the literature of early Christianity and an eminent British naval historian insist on the same methodological principles in both New Testament scholarship and underwater intelligence, or even that these two historians are the same person.

Mark's Gospel often provides a text whose details can often be revealed by comparing the pings returned from two different hydrophones, the derivative Gospels Matthew and Luke: Examining Matthew's and Luke's redaction of the text of Mark is the bread-and-butter of Synoptic criticism, the "happy hunting ground," in R.M. Grant's phrase.[4] But Mark's account of Jewish sectarians, Pharisees and Sadducees,

---

[1] Robert M. Grant, *U-Boat Intelligence 1914–1918* (Penzance, Periscope Publishing, 2002) 41.

[2] W. Hackmann, *Seek & Strike. Sonar, Anti-submarine Warfare and the Royal Navy 1914–54* (London: Her Majesty's Stationery Office, 1984) 289. *Cf.* K. Demirliand, B. Türken, "Sonar based mobile robot localization by using fuzzy triangulation," *Robotics and Autonomous Systems* 33 (2000) 109–123.

[3] "Only when two or more sources of information are available can the analyst definitely show that a subjective judgement has provided a mistaken interpretation..." Robert M. Grant, *A Historical Introduction to the New Testament*[2] (New York, Simon and Schuster, 1972), 79.

[4] Grant, *Historical Introduction*, 110ff.

likewise provides another aspect of the Gospel that can be examined from multiple sources, sources that normally find a more central place in the history of these sects than does the second Gospel.

What do his accounts of the nature of Sadducees and Pharisees reveal about Mark as an historian of first-century Judaism? After all, this anonymous author is the earliest writer explicitly to define for his readers the nature of both of these sects. Writing almost a generation before Josephus, probably in the decade preceding the First Jewish Revolt,[5] the evangelist portrays Jesus in conflict with a variety of individuals and groups, but in the several stories in which the evangelist portrays Jesus with Pharisees and Sadducees (and only in these stories) does Mark take pains to define for his audience the particulars about Jesus' opponents.

Students of first-century Judaism learn about Pharisees and Sadducees from Josephus, but Josephus's descriptions bear close comparison to those in Mark. In Josephus' familiar morphology, Sadducees believe in free will and deny the persistence of the soul after death;[6] they are concerned to follow only the laws as they are written, uncorrupted by τὰ δ' ἐκ παραδόσεως τῶν πατέρων.[7] They are disputatious,[8] and rude in their disputation.[9] Pharisees are the opposite of all of these things; they play down the importance of the human will;[10] they believe in the soul's immortality and in judgment in the afterlife.[11] They have handed down additional laws which they hold alongside those written in the Torah.[12] Unlike the Sadducees, they are perpetually good-humored.[13] They are largely defined with reference to the other.

Although Josephus certainly describes incidents in which Pharisees and Sadducees (especially Pharisees) act independently of each other,

---

[5] Grant, *Historical Introduction*, 126. Paul Achtemeier, "Mark, Gospel of," in D.N. Freedman, ed. *Anchor Bible Dictionary* (New York: Doubleday, 1992) Vol. 4:543.

[6] *War* 2.164f.

[7] *Ant.* 13.297.5. Παράδοσις occurs seven times in Mark's Gospel, all in chapter 7, all in regard to the Pharisees. The term is more frequent in this gospel than in any other gospel, occurring .38 times per 1000 words, as compared to .14/1000 in Matthew. In the New Testament, only 2 Thess., Gal., and Col. have a greater frequency. The term occurs with a frequency of .02/1000 in Jos. *Ant.*, .1/1000 in *War*, .12 in the Life, and .27/1000 in Apion.

[8] *Ant.* 18.17.

[9] *Ant.* 2.166.

[10] *War* 2.162f; *Ant.* 18.12f.

[11] Ibid.

[12] *Ant.* 13.297.

[13] *War* 2.166.

his definitions of each group largely depend on its denying the precepts of the other. Likewise, in the Gospel of Mark, Pharisees and Sadducees appear almost exclusively (for Sadducees, absolutely exclusively) in dispute narratives, disputing, of course, with Jesus.

Mark portrays Pharisees in dispute with Jesus over a wide range of issues of Jewish ritual observance,[14] and Sadducees in dispute with Jesus over the issue of resurrection. These disputes between Pharisees and Jesus, on the one hand, and Sadducees and Jesus, on the other, resemble to a significant degree the disputes between Sadducees and Pharisees that Josephus, writing a generation later, will imply, and the Tanaitic literature, later still, will describe explicitly.

In Mark 12, Sadducees make their only independent appearance in the Synoptic tradition, entering into what we have come to recognize as a typical dispute story between this group and their opponents, although of course our recognition arises from exclusively later examples. Their dispute concerns resurrection, a subject, the author of Mark's Gospel informs his readers, that is central to who the Sadducees are:

> Sadducees came to him, who say that there is no resurrection. They argued with him: "Teacher, Moses wrote for us 'If anyone's brother dies,' and he leaves behind a wife, 'and he has no children,' then 'the brother takes his wife and raises up offspring for his brother.' Now, there were seven brothers. The first took a wife and died, without producing any offspring. The second brother took her and died, without leaving behind any offspring. Likewise the third. None of the seven produced any offspring. And last of all, the woman died. In the resurrection, whose wife will she be, for all seven had her as a wife?"
>
> Jesus said to them, "Isn't this why you are in error, because you know neither the Scriptures nor God's power? For when they are resurrected from the dead, neither men nor women marry, but instead they are like angels in the heavens. Concerning the fact that they are raised from the dead, have you not read in the book of Moses about the bush, how God says to him 'I am the God of Abraham, the God of Isaac, and the God of Jacob?' He is not God of the dead but of the living. You are greatly in error."[15]

Several things are striking about this brief dispute story in Mark. Jesus meets the Sadducees' challenge, that the levirate marriage law would

[14] Mark 2:15–22 (table fellowship and fasting); 2:23–28, 3;1–4 (Sabbath observance); 7:1–23 (purifying hands before eating); 8:11–12 (heavenly signs); 10:2–12 (divorce); 12:13–17 (paying imperial taxes.)

[15] Mark 12:18–27. All translations are the author's.

lead to any number of illegal marriages,[16] should these marriages continue after the resurrection, with the counterargument that the resurrected life is free of marriage, indeed, apparently, free of gender, if that is the meaning of "all are like angels."[17] In Mark's dispute stories, Jesus usually cites some non-scriptural proverb to cement his point,[18] but here, in the dispute about divorce, 10:2–11, and in the dispute about handwashing in 7:1–20, he invokes the Torah to do so, here citing Exodus 3:6. Equally striking is the very fact of the dispute story, which puts Jesus into the role of the Pharisaic interlocutor familiar from the Pharisee-Sadducee dispute stories of later literature.

Is Mark portraying Jesus as a Pharisee by putting him in a dispute-story with Sadducees? Even on its own terms, Jesus' response to the Sadducees sounds Pharisaic, at least if Josephus is describing the Pharisees accurately. Jesus bases his argument on two points, on the angelological[19] point that in the resurrection there is no marriage and on the scriptural point that God is the God of the Patriarchs. In form-critical terms as well, Jesus takes on the normal role of Pharisees in a dispute story with Sadducees.

Sadducees appear in Mark's gospel only in the Sadduzäerfrage about resurrection, while Pharisees appear often, and are the normal interlocutors in Mark's dispute stories. But it is only in the Markan dispute story *par excellence*, the dispute about handwashing in Mark 7:1–22,[20] that

---

[16] Commentators typically miss the point that the Sadducees in this dispute are talking about law, not propriety. The woman in the story is involved in an unfortunate case of polyandry, a highly illegal marriage. Taylor's comment that the Sadducees intend "to show that belief in the Resurrection leads to an absurdity" (V. Taylor, *The Gospel According to St Mark*[2] [London: MacMillan, 1966] p. 482) is off the mark.

[17] See I. Abrahams's essay, "The Life of the Resurrection," *Studies in Pharisaism and the Gospels, First Series* (Cambridge, Cambridge University Press, 1917, repr. Ktav, 1967) pp. 168–170. Abrahams cites Maimonides's contention that existence in the next world is incorporeal.

[18] Proverbs: The dispute about eating with tax collectors and sinners (2:15–17): Those who are well have no need of a doctor; About fasting (2:18–22): No one sews an unshrunken patch on a new garment or puts new wine into old wineskins; About healing on the Sabbath, 3:1–6: Is it lawful to do good on the Sabbath or to do harm?, if this question presupposes a proverb. The dispute about gathering grain on the Sabbath (2:23–28) includes both a proverb, "The Sabbath is made for human beings, not human beings for the Sabbath," and a biblical narrative, the story of David's eating the showbread, I Sam. 21:1–7. The dispute about hand-washing is rather more complicated, and is discussed below.

[19] Acts 23:8 distinguishes Pharisees from Sadducees based on the Pharisaic belief in angels, but Josephus does not.

[20] I dealt with this pericope extensively in "What Comes out of a Person is What

the evangelist identifies the distinguishing characteristics of the Pharisees for his readers: In a parenthesis that follows the Pharisees' initial query to Jesus, about why his disciples eat without first washing their hands, Mark explains

> For the Pharisees and all the Jews do not eat unless they wash their hands with a fist, holding the traditions of the elders (τὴν παράδοσιν τῶν πρεσβυτέρων), and they do not eat anything from the market unless they wash, and there are many other rules which they have received that they keep, the baptizing of cups and pitchers and bronze pots.

In the pericope, it is clear from Jesus' challenge to the Pharisees, that Mark knows more about Pharisees than their propensity for washing both hands and vessels, specifically, he knows that they dispute with Sadducees. Jesus' complaint strongly resembles the complaints of the Sadducees who encounter Pharisees in the dispute-stories of later literature: The Pharisees teach their disciples to hold "human teachings" above God's commandments. By allowing a Jew to allocate his wealth to the Temple by declaring it to be "Qorban," it allows him to violate the fifth commandment of the Decalogue, thus

> *nullifying the word of God by your tradition which you have received* (7:13).

I have elsewhere[21] tried to sort out the redaction-critical stages of this complex pericope, concluding that we have here a re-interpretation of a dispute story between Jesus and Pharisees whose lines should be familiar from the Tanaitic Pharisee-Sadducee dispute stories. Jesus argues that the Pharisees, by insisting on *netilat yadaiim* for all Jews before they eat, fundamentally misunderstand the purity laws of the written Torah, namely that it

> is not the things that come into a person that make that person impure, but the things that come out of a person that make that person impure. For the evil thoughts come out of the hearts of people: fornications, thefts, murders, adulteries, acts of greed, evils, guile, licentiousness, an evil eye, blasphemy, arrogance, stupidity. All these evils come from inside and make the person impure. (7:21–23)

Makes a Person Impure: Jesus as Sadducee" *Jewish Law Association Studies VIII. The Jerusalem 1994 Conference Volume* (Atlanta: Scholars Press, 1996) 217–226. The magisterial treatment is that of Herbert Basser, *Studies in Exegesis. Christian Critiques of Jewish law and Rabbinic Responses 70–300 C.E.* (Leiden: Brill, 2000) 35–49.

[21] Ibid.

Here, as I have argued, Jesus' argument is no longer that of a Sadducee *manqué*, but rather represents the developed understanding of the early Christian community that what both Pharisees and Sadducees view as purity laws should now be viewed as moral laws; it is sin that makes us impure, and not the proximity to the holy.

But notwithstanding Mark's manipulation of the pericope to reflect the increasing distance of his audience from the biblical purity laws, the passage does incorporate a definition of Sadducees remarkably consistent with Josephus' famous statement in *Ant.* 13 that the Sadducees reject the "traditions of the elders" and the Pharisees affirm them. It is also well worth noting that the pericope that he is manipulating resembles a Sadducee-Pharisee dispute story as strongly as does the dispute about resurrection. Again, Jesus stands in for the Sadduceean interlocutor that we have come to expect from the (later) literature: Jesus criticizes Pharisees for creating rules that allow their disciples to violate the written Torah. Not only is there no religious obligation for ordinary Israelites to wash before eating, the Pharisees make it possible for Jews to make a vow that requires them to violate the fifth commandment of the Decalogue.

It would probably be too much to claim from the evidence in Mark that this gospel is not only the source for Josephus' definitions of Pharisees and Sadducees, but for the *topos* of Sadducee-Pharisee dispute story as well. Nonetheless, if we can make the leap to understanding Jesus as a stand-in for Pharisees when he is disputing with Sadducees, and of Sadducees when he is disputing with Pharisees in this Gospel, then Mark is the earliest location for such stories.

Mark portrays Jesus in conflict with Pharisees and Sadducees, but not with Essenes or Zealots. Perhaps Jesus' lack of apparent conflict with Josephus' other two *haireseis* in Mark betokens nothing more than that while Pharisee-Sadducee dispute stories are (or will become) conventional, disputes with Essenes and Zealots are not. Or we could argue, with S.G.F. Brandon,[22] that Mark was so concerned that Jesus was in fact a zealot, or closely tied to zealot concerns, that the evangelist does everything in his power to obscure that tie. Perhaps we could make the same argument, *mutatis mutandis*, that Mark simply thinks of Jesus as an Essene, and so portrays him, without thinking of Essenes as a group defined by their antagonists. Or we could follow Larry Schiff-

---

[22] *Jesus and the Zealots; a study of the political factor in primitive Christianity* (New York: Scribner, 1967).

man to the conclusion that the Essenes *were* Sadducees, and so when Jesus argues with Sadducees he argues with them. We should at least note that in his argument against divorce, Mark 10:2ff, Jesus takes the position vis-à-vis Pharisaic law that characterizes the sectarian position evidenced from Dead Sea Scroll sources, that marriage is life-long, and that remarriage after divorce constitutes adultery.[23]

In Mark's Gospel, Jesus' teaching about Judaism is a third point on a fuzzy triangle that includes Pharisees and Sadducees at its other two points. The author of the Second Gospel is as knowledgeable about the nature of Pharisaic teaching as is Josephus, and his understanding of the Sadducees resembles that of the historian, despite writing a generation or so before him. We do not have the tools to determine whether Mark's Gospel is one Josephus' sources in describing the teachings of these sectarian groups, but neither can we dismiss the notion.

Whatever its origin, whether or not it was written by a Roman disciple of Peter,[24] Mark reveals a depth of knowledge about Jewish sectarians nearly as detailed as that of Josephus, the canonical source for such information. However we characterize the Gospel, and whether or not it shares sources with Josephus or provided a source for him, we must take into account that its author knows a great deal about the Judaism contemporary to Jesus, and takes pains to locate Jesus in a triangle of sectarian Judaism. He pings Sadducees, and he pings Pharisees, reads the signals, and triangulates. Mark's signals, like all signals, "could prove worth reading". Much of Mark's character as an historian of Judaism lies below the surface, as does a good part of all good information, from the standpoint of underwater intelligence, at least.

---

[23] I.e., CD 4:19–5:3; 4Q159 f2 4:10; 4Q524 f15 22:2.

[24] Grant, *Historical Introduction*, 119.

DIVINE SONS: AENEAS AND JESUS IN HEBREWS

Mark Reasoner

The building materials used in the bricolage constructed by the author of Hebrews has been the object of intense study.[1] While most scholars look to Jewish sources for the theological background of Hebrews, the portrait of Aeneas in Augustan theology also shows clear parallels with Hebrews. In this essay I wish to advance the thesis that three perspectives in Hebrews' christological portrait that are not emphasized in its author's scriptures or in gospel tradition—the pious son, the priestly son and the founding son—are found in the divine son of Augustan theology, Aeneas.

Virgil's *Aeneid* is the primary exemplar of "Augustan theology" for this study, but I do consider Aeneas materials preserved in Ovid and Dionysus of Halicarnassus, as well as the Forum of Augustus and the Ara Pacis. The latter is not an Augustan poet as the former two are; Dionysus considered himself an historian. But still as an historian writing in Rome, his work must be consulted. This is not to say that the author of Hebrews was consciously modeling his homiletical letter on the *Aeneid* as its foundational text, or that he was consciously reacting against or adapting Augustan theology, but I am arguing that along with the previously recognized sources for the heroic presentation of Jesus in Hebrews, the Septuagint and the Heracles story cycle, Hebrews' portrait of the hero Jesus makes sense when read alongside portraits of the "goddess-born Aeneas" in Virgil, Ovid, and Dionysus of Halicarnassus.[2] And far from being an incidental source, the *Aeneid* models

[1] This study begins from the now established viewpoint that a plurality of conceptual backgrounds accounts for Hebrews's distinctive literary and theological traits (L.D. Hurst, *The Epistle to the Hebrews: Its Background of Thought*, SNTSMS 65 [Cambridge: Cambridge University Press, 1990], 131–33; Craig R. Koester, *Hebrews: A New Translation with Introduction and Commentary*, AB36 [New York: Doubleday, 2001], 76–79. I am therefore not claiming that the *Aeneid* is the only literary foundation for Hebrews, as Marianne Palmer Bonz does for Luke-Acts in her *The Past As Legacy: Luke-Acts and Ancient Epic* (Minneapolis: Fortress, 2000).

[2] "Goddess-born" or "nate dea" in Virgil's text, is a standard designation for Aeneas, the son of the goddess Venus and human Anchises, e.g. *Aen.* 3.435; 8.59. See also "sate sanguine divum" (6.125).

for Hebrews what Hebrews's other sources cannot—a hero story that shows how the hero's people are religiously superior to their cultural ancestors. The author of Hebrews taps into the motifs of purification, the divinely favored people in search of a divinely founded city and paideia of the son as Virgil uses them in the *Aeneid*, to show that the hero and his cult surpass their cultural ancestors.

1. Why Cross the Language Divide and Look to the *Aeneid*?

Before exploring the parallels between the *Aeneid* and Hebrews, an objection must first be voiced: why look to the *Aeneid*? There are no direct quotations of the *Aeneid*, and even such a New Testament scholar as oriented to the Greco-Roman bank of parallels as J.J. Wettstein mentions the *Aeneid* only at Hebrews 13:14 in his *Novum Testamentum*. As recently as 1973, William George Johnsson [sic] concludes his dissertation with the judgment, "It must be admitted that the writer's sustained references to the Jewish cult, with corresponding omission of any reference to pagan sacrifices, are in favor of his having a Jewish background. But the point cannot be affirmed with certainty." He goes on to reject suggestions that the letters' first addressees must necessarily be viewed as Jewish, since in his estimation the danger that is poised over the readers is apostasy out of the believing community rather than a return to Judaism.[3] L.D. Hurst guardedly concedes "It should not be denied that 'Greek' influence has contributed at some point to the ideas found in Hebrews," but goes on to dismiss the suggestion of Platonic or Philonic influence on Hebrews' author.[4] Craig Koester cites nine parallels between discrete phrases or ideas in Hebrews and the *Aeneid*, more than Attridge's single parallel.[5] Herbert Braun only cites the Aeneid at the "enduring city" phrase in Hebrews 13:14.[6] Most commentators follow the lead of Otto Michel, who concentrates on Jewish parallels and occasionally offers

[3] William G. Johnsson, "Defilement and Purgation in the Book of Hebrews," (Ph.D. dissertation, Vanderbilt University, 1973), 444.

[4] L.D. Hurst, *The Epistle to the Hebrews: Its Background of Thought*, SNTSMS 65 (Cambridge: Cambridge University Press, 1990), 7–42; quotation from 41.

[5] Craig R. Koester, *Hebrews*, AB 36 (New York: Doubleday, 2001); Harold W. Attridge, *Hebrews*, Hermeneia (Philadelphia: Fortress, 1989).

[6] Herbert Braun, *An die Hebräer*, HNT 14 (Tübingen: J.C.B. Mohr (Paul Siebeck), 1984), 469.

some Greek parallels.[7] Since dependence on Virgil's *Aeneid* is not widely recognized by students of this letter, might I be mistakenly alone with this hypothesis, simply one more New Testament student finding the parallels I want to find?

First of all, questions of chronology and literary provenance must be addressed. The literary divide between Latin and Greek was not as great in the early Principate as it is to us. Grammarians Servius and Macrobius list the places where they think Virgil actually calqued Greek phrases in his works.[8] J.N. Adams's *Bilingualism and the Latin Language* also cites one example of Virgil's Latin diction that alludes to a Greek word.[9] Virgil died in 19 B.C.E. Though he had charged Varius his executor to burn his unfinished *Aeneid*, Augustus decreed that this charge be disregarded and the work published as it was.[10] Dionysius of Halicarnassus was teaching in Rome at this time and writing his *Roman Antiquities* in Greek. He is clearly a bilingual, as evidenced by his discussion of how the term "Penates" is translated into Greek.[11] Some think that the *Aeneid* was translated into Greek at least by 42 or 43 C.E., when Seneca mentions the translation.[12] The "translator" was the freedman C. Iulius Polybius, who had a significant influence in literary circles during the reign of Claudius.[13] It must be admitted that Seneca's references to this Polybius are not conclusive regarding the nature of his translation, so we cannot be sure that a full length Greek translation of the *Aeneid* was published in the first century. Since the composition of Hebrews is dated to a time between 60 and 100 C.E., it is certainly possible that its author had read the *Aeneid* in either Latin or Greek.[14]

---

[7] Otto Michel, *Der Brief an die Hebräer*, KKNT 8th ed. (Göttingen: Vandenhoeck & Ruprecht, 1949).

[8] John Conington, *The Works of Virgil, with a Commentary*, Vol. 1, 4th ed. rev. by Henry Nettleship (London: Whittaker & Co. 1881), xlviii–xlix mentions how in the 18th and following chapters of book 5 of Macrobius's Saturnalia these instances are listed.

[9] J.N. Adams, *Bilingualism and the Latin Language* (Cambridge: Cambridge University Press, 2003), 77–78 n. 173, citing *Aen.* 6.438–39.

[10] C.G. Hardie, "Virgil," *OCD* 2nd ed., 1124.

[11] Dionysius of Halicarnassus, *Ant. Rom.* 1.67.3.

[12] Seneca praises Polybius for translating the *Aeneid* into Greek; this is our evidence for the Greek translation; Seneca, *Consolatio ad Polybium* 8.2; 11.5–6.

[13] Johannes Irmscher, "Vergil in der griechischen Antike," *Klio* 67 (1985): 281.

[14] Harold Attridge, *The Epistle to the Hebrews*, Hermeneia (Philadelphia: Fortress, 1989), 9. Koester, 54, dates the letter between 60 and 90 C.E.

Two pieces of evidence from the surface level of the text's opening justify an initial juxtaposition of Hebrews with Greco-Roman epic. In the elegant beginning of Hebrews, we have two literary features that remind one of Homer's *Odyssey*. First, Hebrews begins with alliteration on the same letter as the *Odyssey*, the letter π. Second, the third word of Hebrews (πολυτρόπως), hapax in the New Testament, is the adverbial form of the *Odyssey*'s distinctive adjectival substantive πολύτροπον, the fifth word of the *Odyssey*. For anyone who had studied the basic elements of literature in a Hellenistic school, the beginning of Hebrews, describing how God formerly spoke to humanity, would remind one of Homer's *Odyssey*. These two connections, common alliteration and the possible derivation of the πολυτρόπως can be seen in the following table. Of course, cognates of Homer's πολύτροπον are used elsewhere by Hellenistic authors, but the placement of this word as the third word, at the very beginning of Hebrews, must be a purposeful nod to the epic.

While I shall go on to argue that the letter of Hebrews shows more affinities with the *Aeneid* than the *Odyssey* in its portraiture of the hero, the similarities between the openings of the *Odyssey* and the letter of Hebrews are a clue that this author is able to display the schooling he has received in the basic text of Greek literature, the *Odyssey*. This clue alerts us to the possibility of literary influence from epic poetry known to the author, a possibility for which I shall argue in the major sections on the pious son, the priestly son and the founding son. It is also beyond argument that Virgil's *Aeneid* is a thoroughly Homeric text,

Odyssey 1.1–5	Hebrews 1:1–2
Ἄνδρα μοι ἔννεπῖε μοῦσα πολύτροοπον, ὅς μάλα πολλὰ	Πολυμερῶς καὶ πολυτρόπως πάλαι ὁ θεὸς λαλήσας
πλάγχθη ἐπεὶ Τροίης ἱερὸν πτολίεθρον ἔπερσεν	τοῖς πατράσιν ἐν τοῖς προφήταις
πολλῶν δ' ἀνθρώπων ἴδεν ἄστεα καὶ νόον ἔγνω,	ἐπ' ἐσχάτου τῶν ἡμερῶν τούτων ἐλάλησεν ἡμῖν ἐν υἱῷ
πολλὰ δ' ὅ γ' ἐν πόντῳ πάθεν ἄλγεα ὅν κατὰ θυμόν	ὅν ἔθηκεν κληρονόμον πάντων
ἀρνύμενος ἥν τε ψυχὴν καὶ νόστον ἑταίρων.	δι' οὗ καὶ ἐποίησεν τοὺς αἰῶνας.

as has been documented in the thousands of allusions that Knauer has identified.[15]

Recent work on Hebrews also suggests that more is invested in its bricolage of an alternate story to Judaism than simply scriptures from which its author quotes. The letter is a diaspora letter, as Barnabas Lindars noted: "The Hellenistic character of Hebrews, combined with the lack of any allusion to participation in the cultus, makes it far more probable that the church of Hebrews is located in the Diaspora in some place as Alexandria, Antioch, Ephesus or Rome."[16] Since Lindars's article, David Aune has observed a number of parallels between the christology of Hebrews and the Heracles myth current in the Hellenistic world.[17] If Heracles might lie behind some of the ways in which the heroic activity of Jesus is presented in Hebrews, might not Aeneas as well? Craig Koester's commentary also notes the similarities in imagery between Hebrews 12:1–2 and the games in *Aeneid* 5: "In an ordinary stadium an honored guest would sit on a platform at the edge of the track, about midway along its course. According to Virgil one of the pioneers of Rome, Aeneas, sat on such a platform (*Aeneid* 5.290), but in Hebrews Jesus the pioneer of faith has the place of honor."[18]

The section titles of Hurst's book on the background of Hebrews are illustrative of the New Testament guild's omission to look as far west as Rome for literary and theological influence on this letter: "Philo, Alexandria and Platonism"; "Qumran"; "Pre-Christian gnosticism"; "The Samaritans"; "The Stephen Tradition"; "Pauline Theology"; and "First Peter."[19] While Croy is open to Latin parallels in his examination of Hebrews 12:1–13, there is no mention of Virgil.[20] The need for Roman backgrounds to illuminate this letter's literary and theological distinctives and the actual attention to such backgrounds that its interpreters have invested is in inverse proportion to such need and attention for

---

[15] Georg Nikolaus Knauer, *Die Aeneis und Homer: Studien zur poetischen Technik Vergils mit Listen der Homerzitate in der Aeneis*, Hypomnemata 7 (Göttingen: Vandenhoeck & Ruprecht, 1964).

[16] Barnabas Lindars, "The Rhetorical Structure of Hebrews," *NTS* 35 (1989): 403.

[17] David E. Aune, "Heracles and Christ: Heracles Imagery in the Christology of Early Christianity," in *Greeks, Romans, and Christians: Essays in Honor of Abraham J. Malherbe* (Minneapolis: Fortress, 1991), 3–19 (especially 13–19).

[18] Craig R. Koester, *Hebrews: A New Translation with Introduction and Commentary*, AB36 (New York: Doubleday, 2001), 536.

[19] Hurst, *Hebrews*.

[20] N. Clayton Croy, *Endurance in Suffering: Hebrews 12.1–13 in Its Rhetorical Religious, and Philosophical Context*, SNTMS 98 (Cambridge: Cambridge University Press, 1998).

most other books of the New Testament. Hurst at least is right that the letter is "a joke played upon a church obsessed with finding complete certainty about its origins."[21]

In this paper I trace three continuities of portraiture between Aeneas in Augustan theology and Hebrews' Jesus. The divinely born Aeneas is presented as pious son, priestly son and founding son in Augustan theology and these categories are emphasized in Hebrews' depiction of its divine son, without consistent emphasis in the scriptures employed by that letter. While it cannot be argued that Hebrews is intentionally referring to Virgil's *Aeneid* or other media of Augustan theology, it is clear that Hebrews employs categories ascribed to the divine son and that son's people that were current in Augustan theology of the first century.

2. The Pious Son

Most evident in a simultaneous reading of the *Aeneid* and Hebrews is their heroes' piety. Unlike Homer's portraits of crafty Odysseus or war-like Aeneas, the Augustan Aeneas is pious. Virgil signals this dominant quality in the portrait of his hero with the phrase "insignem pietate virum" in the tenth line of his epic.[22] Galinsky is basically correct to view piety as distinctly Virgil's addition to the portrait of Aeneas, though he fails to mention Sophocles' description of how Aeneas piously obeys his father, Aphrodite and divine omens when he moves his family to Mt. Ida.[23] Still the transmission of this fragment of Sophocles through Dionysus of Halicarnassus, writing his history during Augustus' reign, fits with Galinsky's overall picture that Aeneas' piety is used to reinforce the emperors' piety in the Principate.[24]

Jesus' prayer is heard because of his piety according to Hebrews 5:7. No traditions of Jesus praying "with loud cries and tears" and being saved from death can be found elsewhere in the New Testament; Jesus'

[21] Hurst, *Hebrews* 1.

[22] Repeated descriptions of "pious Aeneas" may be found at *Aen.* 1.220, 305, 378; 3.75; 4.393; 5.26, 286, 685; 6.9, 176, 232; 7.5; 8.84; 9.255; 10.591, 783, 826; 11.170; 12.175, 311. For the difference between Aeneas, Homer's martial hero and the pious Aeneas of Augustan theology, see G. Karl Galinsky, *Aeneas, Sicily, and Rome* (Princeton: Princeton University Press, 1969), 3–21.

[23] Dionysus of Halicarnassus, *Ant. Rom.* 1.48.2. It is Sophocles' play, *Laocoön*, found in C. Müller, *Fragmenta Historicorum Graecorum* Vol. 1, 61–62, frag. 127.

[24] Galinsky, *Aeneas, Sicily, and Rome* 6–7, 61.

cries from the cross do not seem quite fitting for this description, since they precede a real death. Is the author relying "on biblical and Jewish traditions concerning prayer," as a sort of midrash on what the prayer of a righteous sufferer must look like?[25] Koester convincingly lines up Hebrews 5:7 with Psalm 116 to show how this verse in Hebrews seems built off of that psalm. Most certainly the author of Hebrews is influenced by "biblical and Jewish traditions," but why exclude the most exemplary son in Latin literature, the ultimate model of a divine son in Augustan theology who is described by Virgil as pouring out his soul in prayer more times than the gospels describe Jesus in such prayer? Aeneas cries out in prayer or pours out his prayers and is always heard.[26] The influence of Augustan theology on Hebrews is confirmed by the letter's theology of prayer. Noah is heard because of his piety and the letter's readers are enjoined to pray with piety (Heb. 11:7; 12:28). This requirement for prayer is not found in the author's Jewish scriptures, in earlier letters of the New Testament or in gospel traditions. The best explanation for piety as a necessary ingredient in effective prayer is what was current in the Augustan theology of prayer, exemplified in Virgil's Aeneas.

Aeneas learns his piety from his father.[27] Jesus, though a son, learns obedience from the sufferings ordained by his father.[28] The hero as someone who has learned to obey is not a theme in the author's scriptures, but certainly is a theme in the *Aeneid*. Aeneas makes haste to fulfill all that the Sybil instructs him in preparation for his visit to the underworld.[29] When the pious son finally meets his father in the underworld, Virgil places on Anchises' lips the reason for his son's successful journey: "Have you at last come, has that *pietas* your father counted on conquered the journey?"[30] The *Aeneid* and *Odyssey* both take

---

[25] Quotation from Koester, *Hebrews* 108.
[26] Koester, *Hebrews* 108; *Aen.* 1.92–101; 6.55; 8.67–70.
[27] *Aen.* 2.687–704; 3.102–120, 143–46; 6.719–51.
[28] Heb. 2:10–11; 5:8.
[29] *Aen.* 6.236.
[30] *Aen.* 6.687–88 (venisti tandem, tuaque exspectata parenti vicit iter durum pietas?); Fitzgerald 6.921–22, uses "loyalty" for "pietas" here. (*The Aeneid*, trans. Robert Fitzgerald (New York: Vintage, 1990] has different line numbers than the standard edition, *P. Vergili Maronis Opera*, ed. R.A.B. Mynors, Scriptorum Classicorum Bibliotheca Oxoniensis [Oxford: Clarendon, 1969]. If I use or refer to Fitzgerald's translation, I designate it by "Fitzgerald" with his line numbers following. Otherwise, all references to the *Aeneid* are to the standard line numbers of Mynors' edition, which are also the same as those used by H. Rushton Fairclough in his LCL edition.)

pains to present their heroes as loyal sons and faithful fathers to their own sons. The final book of the *Odyssey* celebrates the connection of filial piety with valor, when Odysseus, encouraged by the theophany of the "daughter of Zeus," spurs Telemakhos into battle in the presence of Laertes, who then exults in seeing his son and grandson striving to outdo one another in bravery.[31] But Virgil celebrates filial love in the *Aeneid* in ways Homer does not. For example, in book 1 of the *Aeneid*, we see Aeneas hurrying to send word to Ascanius of developments in Carthage, motivated by love and parental care, a description unmatched in the *Odyssey*'s descriptions of its hero.[32]

A related quality to piety, and one which antedated piety both in terms of temple construction and numismatic commemoration, is *fides*.[33] I admit that Virgil's depiction of Aeneas's *fides* (*Aeneid* 7.235–236; 8.150) as reciprocated loyalty with another people is not the same as Hebrews's picture of Jesus' πίστις (Heb 3:2, 6; 12:2). The consensus among New Testament scholars would be that Virgil's view of *fides* has nothing to do with πίστις in Hebrews, as Grässer's habilitationschrift makes clear.[34] Still we see what we might expect to see in an author composing a homily of epic horizons whose rhetoric of persuasion must present a son of God who should be followed: the son exemplifies πίστις.

Where would the author of Hebrews get the idea that *fides* is a quality that the heroic son should have? Faith, or faithfulness, is God's own quality in the Jewish scriptures (Exod. 34:6; Lam. 3:23). It does not get the attention in the Jewish scriptures that one would expect simply from reading Hebrews 11. And it is common knowledge that the "heroes of faith" in Hebrews 11 do not match the list of people from the Old Testament that one would choose as exemplifying faith.[35] The rhetorical function of the encomium on faith in Hebrews has more to do with the place *fides* occupies in Augustan theology than with the concept of faithfulness in the Jewish scriptures.

And how well do the portrait of a son faithful over his father's house and the phrase ὁ τῆς πίστεως ἀρχηγὸς καὶ τελειωτής function for those

---

[31] *Od.* 24.502–15.

[32] *Aen.* 1.643–46.

[33] Galinsky, *Aeneas, Sicily, and Rome* 58.

[34] Erich Grässer, *Der Glaube im Hebräerbrief*, Marburger Theologische Studien 2 (Marburg: N.G. Elwert, 1965).

[35] Attridge, *Hebrews* 306: "It is clear that 'faith' has not been chosen as an organizing rubric for these exempla on any inductive principle. It is imposed on or read into a list of biblical heroes."

whose expectations for a divine son come only from the Jewish scriptures and gospel traditions?[36] These descriptions work much better for people who know of temples built to faith and an empire purportedly built on the *fides* its rulers initiate with others, first exemplified in Aeneas. It is Aeneas whose final request in his opening speech to Evander is "Accept and give back *fides*."[37] Yes, Aeneas' *fides* is different from Jesus' πίστις. But the strategy of describing Jesus as faithful over his father's house and an architect and accomplisher of faith seems most likely to arise in a context that considers *fides* a preeminent quality of the prototypical, divine son.

Virgil's Aeneas performs similar actions to Homer's Odysseus, but it is only Virgil who grounds such actions in piety. The conclusion of the scene in which the Trojans bury Misenus before Aeneas enters the underworld illustrates the piety of Aeneas, a trait not mentioned for Odysseus in the comparable scene of necessary burial in Homer's *Odyssey*. Virgil attempts to portray Aeneas as a paradigm of piety:

> Faithfully then
> Aeneas heaped a great tomb over the dead,
> Placing his arms, his oar, his trumpet there
> Beneath a promontory, named for him,
> Misenum now and always, age to age.
> All this accomplished, with no more ado
> He carried out the orders of the Sibyl.[38]

Whether the author of Hebrews is consciously modeling his picture of Jesus in response to Virgil's *Aeneid* or not, the fact remains that "Aeneas was the *exemplum pietatis*" in Augustan theology. Thus, it is Aeneas who occupies the center of the northwestern exedra in the Forum of Augustus, between the Julii and the kings of Alba Longa.[39] The picture of Jesus as pious son in Hebrews would surely strike a resonant chord for first century hearers of the letter who were daily exposed to the symbolic world of Augustus, communicated so effectively by Virgil and Ovid, and reinforced by Augustan sculptors.[40] The specific scenes of

---

[36] Heb. 3:5–6; 12:2.

[37] *Aen.* 8.150: accipe daque fidem.

[38] Fitzgerald 6.324–330; *Aen.* 6.232–236 (at pius Aeneas ingenti mole sepulchrum imponit...).

[39] Paul Zanker, *The Power of Images in the Age of Augustus*, trans. Alan Shapiro (Ann Arbor: University of Michigan Press, 1988), 194, 201–3. "Aeneas was the *exemplum pietatis*" is on 203.

[40] In addition to references already seen in the *Aeneid*, see Ovid. *Met.* 13.626–27.

Virgil's *Aeneid* that were repeatedly used by the artisans for Augustan concerns, Aeneas's rescue of the Penates and his father from burning Troy and the sacrifice at the site of Lavinium,[41] emphasize the piety of Rome's favorite son—obedient to his father and without equal in his role as priest for his people. The divine son is pious, so pious that he effects purification as a priest, according to Hebrews.

3. The Priestly Son

The centrality of purification in the world view of Hebrews can be seen by how the letter is framed. The first specific predication of something Jesus has accomplished begins with a description of the purification of sins—"after effecting purification of sins, he sat at the right of the majesty in the high places, becoming so much better than the angels, since he inherited a better name than them" (Heb 1:3b–4). In the main argument of the letter, the point that is explicitly identified as the most significant (κεφάλαιον) is that "we have this kind of high priest, one who took his seat at the right side of the majestic throne in the heavens, a ministry in the sanctuary, even the true tabernacle that the Lord and not humans set up" (Heb. 8:1–2). The juxtaposition of Jesus as a purifying priest and his session in heaven occurs nine times in the book (1:3; 4:14; 6:19–20; 7:26; 8:1b–2; 9:12, 23–24; 10:12; 12:2). It is related to the quality of his life—Jesus becomes priest, according to this book, because his life cannot be destroyed (7:16). After establishing the centrality of blood and sprinkled water in the purification process in the body of the letter, the benediction includes "the blood of the eternal covenant" as the instrumental means behind Jesus' death and resurrection (Heb 13:20). The letter thus portrays, to a degree unmatched by any other New Testament text, Jesus as the priest and son of God who effects purification for those who follow him.

Augustan theology also expects the son of God to be a priest, and emphasizes the priest-king figure more than the scriptures available to the author of Hebrews. Aeneas and his father meet the priest-king Anius and receive a favorable oracle at his temple, for which Aeneas then offers sacrifices.[42] The priesthoods occupied by Augustus are famously catalogued in *Res Gestae* 67. Zanker writes that well before 17 B.C.E.,

---

[41] Ibid., 201–9.

[42] *Aen.* 3.79–120; Ovid, *Met.* 13.632–33.

"the princeps must have made it known that henceforth he preferred that statues put up in his honor show him togate at sacrifice or prayer.... making it clear that he considered the performance of his religious duties his greatest responsibility and highest honor."[43] Here the progressive orientation of the *flamines* priesthood to Caesar and then the emperors is relevant. Images of the emperor dressed as a priest were common in early imperial propaganda.[44] On the south side of the Ara Pacis, Augustus is shown with priests. On the Altar of the Lares, Augustus is portrayed as an augur holding a lituus.[45] It is true that Aeneas is not called a priest in Virgil's *Aeneid*. But in the Augustan theology that orbits around the same imperial sun as the *Aeneid*, a veiled Aeneas is depicted on the front of the Ara Pacis, where he is standing as a priest, offering a sacrifice to the rescued Penates at the future site of their temple at the location where he would found Lavinium.[46] The author and first audiences of Hebrews no doubt expected that a son of God would be a priest. This expectation came more from Augustan theology than from their Christian scriptures.

In the scriptures available for the author of Hebrews, the chosen priest is usually separate from the king (1 Sam. 2:35; 2 Sam. 8:15–17; 1 Kgs 1:32; 4:1–2; Zech. 6:13). The only places in these scriptures that mention the priest-king Melchizedek are used here in Hebrews. It is the only place in the New Testament where the story of Melchizedek is exegeted (Heb. 7:1–28) and the only place in the New Testament that quotes "You are a priest forever" phrase of Psalm 110:4 (Heb. 5:6, 10; 7:17, 21). The material on the priest-king is significant in the persuasive encounter between the author and early hearers of Hebrews because it addresses a need already created by Augustan theology: the divinely sanctioned people must be led by a leader who functions as priest and king. In the paragraphs that follow in this section, I argue that specifics of Jesus' priestly portrait in Hebrews are influenced by Augustan theology. The emphasis on the purifying nature of Jesus' blood, conflation of ritual purification and atonement of sin rituals, and the session of the priest in heaven all have more definite contact

[43] Zanker, *Power of Images* 127.

[44] J.A. North, "flamines," in *OCD* 3rd ed., 599–600; idem, "priests (Greek and Roman)" in *OCD* 3rd ed., 1245–46.

[45] Zanker, *Power of Images* 124–25.

[46] Zanker, *Power of Images* 194, 203–4.

points with the Augustan theology of the first century than they do with the scriptures explicitly cited by the author of Hebrews.

Hebrews specifies how its hero's purifying mission occurs: it is by his blood. This emphasis on one person's blood being efficacious beyond all others has been noted as a distinctive feature of Hebrews, which sets it off from how blood is depicted in the Old Testament.[47] Other puzzling features of blood in Hebrews include its emphasis only on how blood cleanses, with no acknowledgement of how it can defile; the dominance of blood at the expense of God's role in the action of forgiveness in Hebrews 9–10; and the emphasis on the material nature of Christ's blood.[48]

Beyond its power to purify sins, Jesus' blood also allows access into an otherworldly, divine realm (Heb 10:19), just as divinely sanctioned blood allows Aeneas to enter the underworld unscathed (*Aen.* 6.248–9). Offerings of blood also punctuate other occasions with proper piety in the *Aeneid*. Aeneas pours "holy blood" on his father's funeral mound to honor the gods and prepare for the games on Sicily (5.78).[49] Aeneas's allies in Arcadia are also shown as offering blood to Hercules in a setting of proper piety (8.106). The people to whom this letter is addressed are expected to believe what anyone constructing a theology of purification simply from the law, prophets and writings would not accept: "without the shedding of blood there is no forgiveness of sins"[50]

It is also worth emphasizing how imprecise the author is in describing aspects of purification from the Torah. Attridge suggests that the "inexact reminiscences of the atonement ritual" in Hebrews 9–10 is rhetorically significant as "a way to express disdain for what may be considered antiquated and superficial offerings."[51] This is certainly a correct generalization for understanding how the inaccuracies of Hebrews' description of purification rituals fit with its polemical thrust. But we might also note that the inaccuracies in Hebrews' caricatures

---

[47] Johnsson 234, identifies this feature as the "most striking point" of the representation of blood in Hebrews.

[48] Ibid., 239–250.

[49] Fitzgerald's "two of victims' blood" (5.103), following Fairclough's "two of the blood of victims" (5.78), misses the connotation of Virgil's "duo sanguine sacro."

[50] Heb. 9:22; cf. Lev. 5:11–13; Isa. 6:7; Mic. 6:6–8; Ps. 50:1–15; 51:17–19 (English, 51:15–17).

[51] Attridge, Hebrews 248. Cf. Koester (*Hebrews*, 410), who looks for similarities between the purification rites that the author of Hebrews collapses together in Hebrews 9:13.

of the purification rituals of Mosaic Law include a blurring of ritual cleansing rites with sin offerings and mention of the bull (an animal sacrificed in honor of Augustus' birth)[52] as an animal characteristic of the sacrificial cult (9:13; 10:4). The treatment of impurity as a form of sin is shown by the way in which this author includes rites for ritual purification in the description of the Torah's means for purification of sin. Attridge suggests that the conflation of rituals for cultic purity with rituals for forgiveness of sin is designed to show that Torah provides only outward purification.[53] This is certainly possible, though an equally elegant solution for the inconsistencies between Hebrews and the law of Moses is that Hebrews is influenced by a grammar of purification alien to the Mosaic law.

When we imagine a time when Hebrews was not, we have to acknowledge that the early Christians' scriptures do not clearly anticipate a messiah who will be a purifier of sins. By contrast, this letter presents the central work of Jesus as that of purifying sins, a pure hero who ultimately enters the divine sanctuary after his purifying mission is accomplished (Heb. 9:24–26). Yes, this expectation for a priest might have come from a strand of Judaism that pictured angels as priestly mediators, as Attridge suggests, but note his concluding qualification: "The understanding of Christ as High Priest is probably based on Jewish notions of priestly angels and was already a part of the Christian liturgical or exegetical tradition on which our author draws, but that tradition hardly explains the way in which the motif is developed in the text."[54] Johnnson comments with regard to Jesus' blood in Hebrews that "the author does not intend some spiritual or mystical connotation: the language is religious rather than theological. That is, it is essentially mythopoetic."[55] For this author, Jesus' blood is effective; it has a spiritual power to purify—the author makes no attempt to explain why.

I grant that purification is not as central in the *Aeneid* as in Hebrews. But Augustan theology has clearly influenced Virgil toward portraying his hero as an agent of purification in ways not found in the *Odyssey*.

---

[52] Zanker, *Power of Images* 304.

[53] Attridge, Hebrews 257.

[54] Attridge, *Hebrews*, 103. Attridge's evidence for the Jewish hope in the priestly mediation of angels is: Isa 6:3; *1 Enoch* 39.10–13; *Jub.* 2.2, 18; 15.27; 31.14; *T. Levi* 3.5; *Asc. Isa.* 7.37; 8:17; 9.28–33; *3 Enoch* 1.12; 1QSb 4:25–26; 4QSir 400.2–4, 16 (ibid., 51 n. 24; 100 n. 238).

[55] Ibid., 250.

Sins are a stated issue in the *Aeneid*, unlike the *Odyssey*.[56] In the *Odyssey*, sacrifices are done to please gods and goddesses (1.22–26), not to effect purification. A comparison of similar scenes in the two epics clearly shows this. In both epics' descriptions of the hero's visit to the underworld, the hero is asked to bury a member of his party. Elpenor meets Odysseus in Hades and asks him to bury his body. The unburied corpse may tempt the gods to be angry, but no mention is made of it as a problem of impurity.[57] By contrast, Aeneas is informed of Misenus's unburied corpse by the Sibyl who is speaking for Phoebus Apollo, a god known for his special concern for purity, and enjoined to take care of the pollution this corpse is causing as a condition for entrance into the underworld.[58] The comparison is sharper when one compares how the corpses are buried. Odysseus and his men mourn for Elpenor, burn his corpse and form a burial mound as requested, but no mention is made of the purifying effects of this rite or any involvement by a priest. By contrast, Aeneas's party washes and anoints the corpse of Misenus. The rite is described in much more detail than Homer employs for the matching scene, and Virgil even tells us how the Trojan priest Corynaeus placed Misenus's bones in an urn and then

> with pure water went three times
> Around the company, asperging them
> With cleansing drops from a ripe olive sprig,
> And spoke the final words.[59]

This scene echoes an earlier one in the *Aeneid*, in which Aeneas, when almost defiling the dead Polydorus, is warned to avoid defiling his hand and his men hold a funeral for Polydorus, a Trojan victim of contaminated hospitality ("pollutum hospitium") and use libation cups of holy

---

[56] Si sine pace tua atque inuito numine Troes/Italiam petiere, luant peccata neque illos/iuueris auxilio (*Aen.* 10.31–33); "If without your consent, your heavenly will/ The Trojans crossed to Italy, then let them/Pay for their sins, afford them no relief" (Fitzgerald 10.41–43).

"sed periisse semel satis est": peccare fuisset ante satis, penitus modo non genus omne perosos femineum. (*Aeneid* 9.140–42); "Enough that Trojans perished once? Their sin/That once had been enough, were they not still/Given to hatred of all womankind" (Fitzgerald 9.195–97).

[57] *Od.* 11.71–76.

[58] On Apollo as a god of purity, see Robert Parker, *MIASMA: Pollution and Purification in Early Greek Religion* (Oxford: Clarendon, 1983), 393 in his appendix "Gods Particularly Concerned with Purity." The quotation from the *Aeneid* is from Fitzgerald 6.218–20; *Aeneid* 6.149–50.

[59] Fitzgerald 6.321–24; *Aeneid* 6.229–31.

blood ("sanguinis et sacri pateras") to give rest to his spirit.[60] As we would expect, the *Aeneid* has its own vocabulary for purification.[61]

Another example of the way in which Hebrews blurs "sinful" and "unclean" categories relates to the sprinkling of water. Hebrews 9:19 describes Moses as sprinkling water in a covenant inaugurating ceremony concerned about purification of sins, though in Mosaic law it is only used for the purification of uncleanness (Num. 19:18–21). The references to sprinkled water in Hebrews (9:19; 10:22) thus might be influenced by the religious world of the author and readers, who knew from encounters with Roman religion or the *Aeneid* that sprinkled water purifies from sins.[62] The sprinkling of water is also the last component of the rite that allows Aeneas into Hades, accompanying his placement of the golden bough at its entrance (6.635–6). The Tiber is considered sacred (8.72) and Dionysus of Halicarnassus gives a lengthy description of the two springs of very sweet water that sprang up when Aeneas' company was near the shore at Laurentum, water which in his day is still regarded as the sun's sacred water.[63]

The *Aeneid* does not explicitly present Aeneas as taking a seat in heaven as Hebrews does in its portrait of Jesus.[64] Still, Aeneas is clearly bound for the glories of heaven. His mother appears to him in her heavenly splendor in the opening book.[65] Later we learn that Aeneas is

---

60 *Aeneid* 3.41 ("parce pias scelerare manus"), 60–68.

61 The favorite word for purification in the *Aeneid* is the verb "lustro" (3.279, 6.231, 8.183). Negatively, the *Aeneid* displays significant concern for sins that defile by its use of the verb "scelero" (3.41–42, 604; 8.206) and its adjective "sceleratus, -a, -um" that is often used to form substantives in Virgil's epic (2.231, 576; 3.60; 6.563; 7.461; 9.137; 12.949).

"Incesto," the word for "pollute" or "make impure" is used in 6.150; 10.389.

62 When Virgil describes Dido's attempt to present her suicide as a normal sacrifice, he places these directions on Dido's lips: "have her/Quickly bedew herself with running water/Before she brings our victims for atonement." The pollution that the unburied body of Misenus brings to Aeneas's company (6.150: totamque incestat funere classem; Fitzgerald 6.219: "polluting all your fleet with death") is cleansed when the priest Corynaeus cleanses Aeneas and his men by sprinkling pure water on them at the end of the funeral of Misenus (6.229–231).

63 Dionysus of Halicarnassus, *Ant. Rom.* 1.54.1–2.

64 Hebrews's nine references to Jesus as priest who has entered or taken his seat in heaven are listed at the beginning of "The Priestly Son" section.

65 *Aeneid* 2.589–592—cum mihi se, non ante oculis tam clara, uidendam/obtulit et pura per noctem in luce refulsit/alma parens, confessa deam qualisque uideri/caelicolis et quanta solet; Fitzgerald 2.773–777—"But at that moment, clear, before my eyes—/Never before so clear—in a pure light/Stepping before me, radiant through the night,/ My loving mother came: immortal, tall,/And lovely as the lords of heaven know her."

bound for Elysium, the land of the blessed, as the Sibyl and Deiphobus make clear when they come to a fork in the road with Aeneas (*Aen.* 6.542, 546). When the Sibyl and Aeneas do reach the "place of joy" (locos laetos),[66] we observe the same connection between priestly function and entrance into heaven that Hebrews emphasizes. The *Aeneid* assumes that souls pass from Hades into the sky, as seen in Aeneas's question to his father about this when visiting him in Hades.[67] The narrator tells us that Orpheus is there in Virgil's heaven as "the Thracian priest with long garment" and then identifies "the group of those who suffered injuries while fighting for fatherland, and those who were pure priests while life remained, and those pious poets who spoke worthy of Phoebus."[68] In a similar way, the author of Hebrews participates in the belief that pure priests are destined for heaven and he is impressed with the finite tenure of all human priesthoods captured in Virgil's phrase "those who were pure priests while life remained." This author builds on the phrase, "You are a priest forever" in Psalm 110:4, to emphasize that Christ's priesthood is gained "by the power of an indestructible life," a contrast to all human priests whose priesthoods end at death (Heb. 7:16).

Of course, there are differences between Hebrews's portrait of its priest's work of purification and the priestly activity of purification in Augustan theology. While Hebrews follows the *Aeneid* in its glorification of the divine action of vengeance, it does not blur vengeance and purification as the latter does, especially in the last scene in which sacrifice and vengeance are linked to the victim's blood.[69] The tabernacle imagery used by Hebrews is clearly from its author's scriptures and Augustan theology does not have a clear parallel. But why is this author so free to reconfigure elements of the ceremonial cult of his Old Testament when he describes them? I submit that the author is seeking to portray Jesus as a hero in a way that impresses the letter's first hearers. In order to show that those who follow Jesus have a way to deal with sins that

---

[66] *Aeneid* 6.638; cf. Hebrews 12:2—ὃς ἀντὶ τῆς προκειμένης αὐτῷ χαρᾶς...

[67] 6.719–21.

[68] *Aeneid* 6.645 (Orpheus); 6.660–662—hic manus ob patriam pugnando volnera passi/quique sacerdotes casti, dum vita manebat/quique pii vates et Phoebo digna locuti.

[69] Hebrews conflates vengeance with divine judgment, since it views willful sin as a pollution of Jesus' blood, a sacrilege that deserves vengeance (Heb. 10:30–31). *Aeneid* 12.948–9: Pallas te hoc volnere, Pallas immolat et poenam scelerato ex sanguine sumit ("Pallas who sacrifices you with this stroke, and takes retribution from your guilty blood!").

Judaism does not have, the author portrays Jesus as a purifying priest who then is granted admittance into heaven.

4. The Founding Son

Hebrews offers us the new idea that Abraham anticipated a city designed and built by God (Heb. 11:10). This stands in contradiction to the narrative bias in Genesis against cities. Yet in Hebrews, we encounter a midrash that faithful people were longing for a "homeland" (11:14) and a "country" (11:16). It is true that Jesus is not explicitly described as a city-founder. Still, Moses is among those who sought for a divinely sanctioned city (Heb. 11:13–16, 23–29), and Moses is said to have chosen the reproach of the Christ over the treasures of Egypt (11:26). Moses' object, then, is grouped together with the heavenly country and city that are described as the objects of Enoch through Sarah's faith (Heb. 11:5–12). The enduring, heavenly city reappears in a reprise of this theme in Hebrews 12:28; 13:14. Is the quest for an enduring homeland or city in Hebrews an idea that is rhetorically significant for author and first audience of Hebrews because of the basic plot of Virgil's master story of Augustan theology?

According to a careful reading of Augustan theology, Aeneas does not found Rome. He founds cities in Sicily according to Dionysus of Halicarnassus, before going on to Italy where he founds a city where the sow rests, Lavinium, even though he knows it will not be the final resting place of his people.[70] Still, in popular expressions of Augustan theology, Aeneas is closely linked with the founding of Rome, as this stanza of Horace's *Carmen Saeculare* illustrates:

> If unscathed from Ilian flames, Aeneas,
> Blameless chief survivor of perished homeland,
> Led the way, predestined to found a city
> Greater than ever.[71]

And in similarity to the wandering and homesick people of Hebrews 11, Augustan portraits of Aeneas and his band of Trojans carry the

[70] Dionysus of Halicarnassus, *Ant. Rom.* 1.52.4; 1.56.1–57.1.

[71] This stanza of Horace, *Carmen Saeculare* is quoted from Zanker, *Power of Images* 171.

sense that they wandered and endured hardship before finding a home.[72] Ovid routes them through Delos, Crete, Phaecia, Sicily, Carthage, a return to Sicily, the Aeolian islands and then to the Italian peninsula with perhaps a stronger sense of wandering than we find in Virgil's *Aeneid*.[73] In the *Aeneid*, some of the women followers of Aeneas long for a city.[74] Helenus, priestly son of king Priam, also provides a long oracle to Aeneas on his destiny to found a city in Italy that drives the expectations of Aeneas and his band (*Aen.* 3.374–462). It also must be said that in Augustan theology, Aeneas founds a people. Whether in the *Aeneid* or in Augustan sculpture, the figure of Aeneas stands for the Roman people.[75]

The divine sons in both the *Aeneid* and in Hebrews go through a time of training themselves and become able to supervise others' training as well, a training that occurs during the wandering. The heavy emphasis on education cannot be escaped when reading Hebrews 5:11–6:3.[76] This recurs with the cluster of paideia words in Heb. 12:7–11. Paideia is not simply classroom instruction; "[i]t includes theory and practice, preparation and testing."[77] Just as Aeneas experiences testing in the *Aeneid*, so does Jesus, according to Hebrews.

Jesus as hero of Hebrews is a learner.[78] Because of his trials he is perfected (Heb. 2:10) and thus uniquely qualified to help others (Hebrews 2:18; 5:8–9), just as Dido finds rest after trials (*Aeneid* 1.630) and Aeneas is to endure whatever fortune brings (5.710).[79] The trials of life qualify one to help and educate others. Jesus' trials have given him the experience that qualifies him to help others (Heb. 2:18; 4:15–5:2). The trials of Jesus also include his actual death, which Hebrews views not just as a trial that strengthens or educates, but as a sacrifice that carries atoning and sanctifying significance (Heb. 9:26; 13:12).

Where would the author of Hebrews get the idea that God's son had to learn through trials? Prophetic texts in the Old Testament that

---

[72] G. Karl Galinsky, *Augustan Culture: An Interpretive Introduction* (Princeton: Princeton University Press 1996) 246–47 emphasizes the toil and cost involved in founding Rome as a dominant theme of the *Aeneid*.

[73] Ovid, *Met.* 13.626–14.451.

[74] urbem orant in 5.617.

[75] Galinsky, *Augustan Culture* 248; Zanker, *Power of Images* 202.

[76] See Koester, *Hebrews* 301–3, 308–9.

[77] Koester, *Hebrews* 527.

[78] This is noted by all commentators. See also Aune, "Heracles and Christ" 14.

[79] Koester, *Hebrews* 290 makes the connection between *Aeneid* 1.630 and Hebrews 2:18; 5:8.

New Testament writers configure to fit their evolving ideas of a messiah are little help here. Joseph is described as a hero who learns through his trials, but there are no explicit signals that the author of Hebrew is relying on the Joseph cycle here. As David Aune has observed, Heracles may account for Hebrews's use of the hero as learner and sufferer of trials topoi.[80] In addition, Virgil's Aeneas and Hebrews' Jesus are both loyal to their fathers, behaving as sons who are paragons of piety. These sons then become teachers of others (*Aeneid* 8.515–17).

Heracles certainly is a hero who gains divine status and enters heaven because of his labors, as does Christ in Hebrews.[81] Indeed, Heracles's last three labors all deal with victory over death, a trait of the hero in Hebrews as well.[82] The Heracles stories are older than Virgil's *Aeneid*, and indeed the latter work owes much to the Heracles stories. Virgil portrays his hero as targeted for destruction by the same goddess who stalked Heracles. *Aeneid* 8 contains a lengthy scene in which Evander entertains Aeneas and his men at a meal of meat sacrificed to Heracles at the site of one of Heracles' labors and retells that labor as an act of sacred commemoration, and concludes with Evander's and Aeneas's men singing a hymn to Heracles.[83] Both Jesus and Heracles conquer death (Seneca, *Hercules Furens* 889–90 and Hebrews 2:14).[84] Even Virgil's title for his epic, Αἰνηίς, is made on the analogy of the Ἡρακληίς.[85]

Is the influence I am tracing from Augustan theology to Hebrews rather due to a primary connection between the Heracles stories and Hebrews? Since the heroic traits of Heracles have influenced Virgil's *Aeneid*, the relationship I'm proposing between this primary text of Augustan theology and Hebrews would then be reduced to a secondary one, based on no direct allusions but on these texts' common debt to Heracles. Still, because of Hebrews' emphasis on its hero as a pious, priestly son who helps to found a homeland for a wandering people, it seems more likely that the Heracles material that is certainly evident in Hebrews has entered through the mediation of Augustan theology.

---

80 Aune, "Heracles and Christ" 14–17.

81 Aune, "Heracles and Christ" 18–19. See the account of Heracles' death and ascension to heaven in Apollodorus 2.7.7 cited by Aune (19).

82 Heb. 2:14–15; H.J. Rose and C.M. Robertson, "Heracles," *Oxford Classical Dictionary* 2nd ed., 498, exegete the last three labors as "variants of one theme, the conquest of Death."

83 *Aeneid* 8.172–305.

84 I am indebted to David Aune, "Heracles and Christ" 7 for the Heracles reference.

85 C.G. Hardie, "Virgil," *OCD*, 2nd ed., 1125; Fitzgerald, *Aeneid*, "Postcript," 405.

The integration of Heracles into Augustan theology is already very evident in book 8 of Virgil's *Aeneid.*

Hebrews' debt to an Augustan theology that includes the Heracles material also seems likely when one considers this New Testament book's singular emphasis on endurance. The bold endurance that Hebrews ascribes to both Moses and Jesus and enjoins on its readers (Heb. 6:15; 10:32, 36; 11:27; 12:1–3, 7; 13:13) is a virtue named more often in the *Aeneid* and the Heracles legacy than in the scriptures explicitly quoted by Hebrews. Nor is endurance specifically described as a virtue in the canonical gospels, some of whose traditions may have been known to Hebrews' author. By contrast, Virgil places the programmatic statement on the lips of Nautës, who tells Aeneas, "All Fortune can be mastered by endurance." Virgil works this theme out by charting Aeneas's course from Ilium to Latium, and by making explicit mention of Heracles' endurance.[86] Hebrews' Jesus as a son of God who has to endure a set of trials and sufferings in order to enter his full reward or his full status as divine owes more to Augustan theology than to historical Jesus traditions or expectations from the Jewish scriptures.

After being faithful through his sufferings and trials, Jesus becomes the presiding leader in a training contest in which the rest of those who believe in him are involved (Heb. 12:2). The contest is well known in the Aeneas material, mentioned both by Virgil and Dionysus.[87] The conjunction of comparing those in a contest to a cloud and the encouragement to keep eyes on the end of the race is an echo of the description given of the race in book 5 of the *Aeneid*. Indeed, Craig Koester has found a significant number of parallels between the *Aeneid* and Hebrews in these scenes.[88]

So the wandering people that Aeneas and Jesus lead long for a homeland, endure sufferings in imitation of their leaders, and participate in a contest that encapsulates their existence on this earth as a quest for a divinely provided homeland. Yet the object of the Trojans' longing is not simply for a homeland; it is also for rest. In this Augustan epic,

[86] *Aen.* 5.710 (quoted from 5.922 in Fitzgerald); 6.261; 8.291–93 (Heracles).

[87] *Aen.* 5.104–603; Dionysus of Halicarnassus, *Ant. Rom.* 1.50.3.

[88] "At this/They toed the line; and when they heard the signal,/Suddenly given, broke from the starting post/And made off on the track like an outriding/Rack of storm cloud. As they marked the finish,..." (Fitzgerald 5.403–407). "Haec ubi dicta, locum capiunt signoque repente/corripiunt spatia audito limenque relinquunt,/effusi nimbo similes. simul ultima signant,..." (*Aen.* 5.315–317). Koester, *Hebrews* 523, 525, 530, 535–36.

entering one's rest after death is considered a positive transition for a human; if someone misses the rest appointed for them after death, the problem must be remedied.[89] Otfried Hofius's dissertation focuses on the well known theme of rest in Hebrews and makes no reference to the *Aeneid*.[90] We are therefore in good company if we imagine that the meditation on rest in Hebrews 3:7–4:11 comes simply from the author's artful exegesis of Psalm 95:7–11, but it is possible that the long meditation on entering rest is influenced by the *Aeneid*'s repeated emphasis on the rest that Aeneas and his followers sought.[91] This would at least account for the concluding statement that presupposes that Joshua failed to give the Israelites rest, a direct contradiction to Joshua 21:44. The author of Hebrews must make this move because he assumes first with Virgil that the military leader who brings his followers into a homeland is supposed to provide rest. Dionysus of Halicarnassus says that Aeneas built the cities of Aegesta and Elyma for the Trojans already living in Sicily and that he granted ἀνάπαυσις to those from his own group who wished to remain there.[92]

Hebrews' portraits of Jesus as founder or pioneer may arise from the expected description of divine son, whether Heracles or Aeneas, as a founder. Jesus is the ἀρχηγός of faith in 12:2. David Aune has noted that Dio Chrysostom once refers to Heracles as ὁ ἀρχηγὸς ὑμῶν Ἡρακλῆς when addressing an assembly from Tarsus.[93] The Vulgate's equivalent, auctor, is used repeatedly in the *Aeneid*. It can refer to the counsel of a god or goddess.[94] It can refer to the founder of a rite of worship.[95] It is used to describe how Aeneas "sought Italy at the call of fate."[96] It is used specifically to describe Dardanus, the founder of Troy.[97] And it is used as the founding ancestor.[98] The most significant semantic parallel for the ἀρχηγός of faith in Hebrews 12:2 in Virgil is

---

[89] *Aen.* 3.378; 6.221, 444; 7.822.

[90] Otfried Hofius, *Katapausis*, WUNT 1.11 (Tübingen: J.C.B. Mohr [Paul Siebeck], 1970).

[91] References to "rest" in the *Aeneid* include 1.205 ("sedes . . . quietas"); 3.495 ("vobis parta quies"); 7.598 ("mihi parta quies"). Cf. Fitzgerald 1.281; 3.657; 7.822.

[92] Dionysus of Halicarnassus, *Ant. Rom.* 1.52.4.

[93] Dio Chrysostom, *Or.* 33.47 as quoted by Aune, "Heracles and Christ," 16.

[94] 5.17; 8.336; 12.159; 12.405.

[95] It is used to describe Potitius, founder of a rite of worship for Heracles in 8.269.

[96] 10.67; trans. H. Rushton Fairclough; Italiam petiit fatis auctoribus.

[97] 6.650; 8.134 (Dardanus, Iliacae primus pater urbis et auctor).

[98] 3.503; 4.365; 7.49.

Anchises' prediction that Aeneas's descendants Procas, Capys, Numitor and Silvius Aeneas will found a city of "faithfulness."[99]

The divinely founded city is coterminous with a heavenly fatherland or country in a manner that has its most secure antecedent in Rome's identification as both a homeland and a city (Heb. 11:14–16). In a direct hit against the accepted doctrine of Rome as the eternal city, Hebrews 13:14 claims that here we have no lasting city.[100] The letter's author stands with its readers among those who like Abraham are looking for an eschatological city.

What sort of reader would resonate with the idea that heroes of faith of the Old Testament, and Jesus himself, are leading people to a divinely provided city? The only city worth pursuing in the Old Testament is terrestrial Jerusalem, but even so the divinely favored people follow Moses not in search of a city, but in search of the land God has promised them. It is true that the Deuteronomic literature highlights "the place" in its Jerusalem centered theology, but still the people are not described as searching for a city.[101] The center of the apostle Paul's symbolic universe—despite all his assertions of independence from it—was terrestrial Jerusalem (Gal. 1:18–19; 2:1–10; Rom. 11:26; 15:25–27). But the author of Hebrews has no concern with terrestrial Jerusalem. The city to which he looks is "Mount Zion . . . the city of the living God, the heavenly Jerusalem" (Heb. 12:22). This author looks forward to an enduring city (Heb. 13:14). It is possible that one could form the goal of an enduring city from such texts as Psalm 48:1–8. It is also possible that the author has a minor fixation on the "enduring city" because Jerusalem has just fallen. But the term "enduring city" is not found in the Old Testament, while it is found in Virgil's *Aeneid*, a story about a hero who leaves one city that cannot be defended for a city that the gods decree will endure forever. On Delos, Aeneas prays to Apollo for "an enduring city" (mansuram urbem; *Aen.* 3.86)

[99] 6.773—hi tibi Nomentum et Gabios urbemque Fidenam.

[100] mansuram ubem (3.86); "abiding city" (Fitzgerald 3.119). See Herbert Braun, *An die Hebräer* 469 for the Augustan parallels on "lasting city."

[101] I accept C.L. Seow's emphasis that the deuteronomistic writers did not invent the idea of Zion as a chosen city (*Myth, Drama, and the Politics of David's Dance*, HSM 44 [Atlanta: Scholars, 1989], 185). Still, this corpus certainly follows the idea wholeheartedly, as e.g. in Deut. 12:10–12; 14:23–26; 15:20; 16:2–16; 17:8–10; 18:6; 26:2; 31:11; 2 Sam. 5:5–14; 1 Kgs 11:13, 32, 36; 15:4; 2 Kgs 21:4, 7; 23:27. See also Bernard M. Levinson, *The Hermeneutics of Innovation: The Impact of Centralization upon the Structure, Sequence and Reformulation of Legal Material in Deuteronomy* (Ann Arbor: University Microfilms International, 1991).

and immediately receives a favorable oracle from Apollo. Celaeno the Harpie refers to the city Aeneas is to found as a "datam...urbem," an appointed city.[102] When they finally land near Rome, the pioneer Aeneas and his men go exploring for the city: "by separate ways they search out the city and boundaries and coasts of the nation."[103] With the "reproach of Christ" (11:26) and "founder" terminology (12:2) as christological signals, it appears that Hebrews portrays Jesus as a pioneer who helps his followers reach a divinely founded city (11:10, 16; 12:22; 13:14).

I make no claim to be able to articulate in detail the intentions of the author of Hebrews, much less to specify the author's political identity. But it is a reasonable claim that with the string of references to kingdoms or cities that are described as shaken/unshakeable (12:26–28), non-enduring/enduring (13:14—"we have here no enduring city, but we are searching for one that is to come") so near to the final greeting from "those from Italy" (Heb. 13:24), the author is making a statement that stands in dialectical tension with standard Roman ideology of the Principate explicitly formulated in the *Aeneid*. Rome was founded on an unshaken rock and would endure through time, according to Virgil. At the deaths of the Trojans Euryalus and Nisus, Virgil writes:

> Fortunate, both! If in the least my songs
> Avail, no future day will ever take you
> Out of the record of remembering Time,
> While children of Aeneas make their home
> Around the Capitol's unshaken rock,
> And still the Roman Father governs all.[104]

The kingdom to which Jesus leads his followers is also unshakeable (Heb. 12:28). Whether the author of Hebrews is consciously subverting material from the *Aeneid* or not, it appears evident that he accepts a basic presupposition of Augustan theology that is otherwise not emphasized in his Old Testament: the son of God leads a people to a divinely founded city. We may then gloss the point being made about Jesus as founder of a people and their homeland or city as follows: *Unlike Aeneas,*

---

[102] *Aeneid* 3.255: sed non ante datam cingetis moenibus urbem (Fitzgerald 3.347: "But you may never wall your destined city").

[103] Fairclough trans.—urbem et finis et litora gentis diversi explorant (7.149–50).

[104] Fitzgerald 9.633–638; *Aeneid* 9.446–449—Fortunati ambo! Si quid mea carmina possunt,/nulla dies umquam memori vos eximet aevo,/dum domus Aeneae Capitoli immobile saxum/accolet imperiumque pater Romanus habebit.

the divine son of Augustan theology who founded an empire for his people that is centered around an unshakeable city that will supposedly endure forever, Jesus God's son leads those who follow him to a truly unshakeable and enduring city.

Time would fail me if I pursued all the connections between the *Aeneid* and Hebrews such as the common use of ekphrasis,[105] the appeal to "today,"[106] the use of the symbol as portal to a deeper meaning,[107] the tendency to look for the true meaning of a name,[108] and the shared view of faith as something which yields nothing certain in this life.[109] I make no attempt at locating the echoes of Augustan theology in an intentional dependence that the author of Hebrews has on the *Aeneid*. But when one sees, in an analogous way, how pagan Greek philosophical arguments could be recycled with little alteration in Jewish and Christian writings, it makes the case for contact between Augustan theology and the book of Hebrews more probable.[110] I have limited the comparison to three main lines in which Aeneas serves to model Jesus' significance for the author of Hebrews. These three lines of comparison, the pious son, the priestly son and the founding son, lead us to consider what the letter is saying about its hero's people.

5. The Superiority of the Divine Son's People

All that remains in this foray into Hebrews' connection with Augustan theology is to observe that this Christian letter uses another people's master text, the Jewish scriptures, in order to portray the followers of Jesus the divine son as replacing the Jewish people. This tactic has already been employed by Virgil in the master text of Augustan theol-

[105] See Michael C.J. Putnam, *Virgil's Epic Designs: Ekphrasis in the Aeneid* (New Haven: Yale University Press, 1998) and Heb. 9:1–7; 13:18–29.

[106] See Heb. 3:13–15; 4:7 and Knauer, *Die Aeneis und Homer* 295–96, who also notes the use of "today" in Homer's *Iliad*.

[107] See Viktor Pöschl, *The Art of Vergil: Image and Symbol in the Aeneid*, trans. Gerda Seligson (Ann Arbor: University of Michigan Press, 1962) and Heb. 9:8–10, 23–25; 10:1, 19–22; 13:10.

[108] See Heb. 4:8a; 7:2 and J.J. O'Hara, *True Names: Vergil and the Alexandrian Tradition of Etymological Wordplay* (Ann Arbor: University of Michigan Press, 1996).

[109] Nusquam tuta fides (*Aeneid* 4.373; "Faith can never be secure" Fitzgerald 4.514). See Heb. 11:1, 13, 35–40.

[110] Jaap van Amersfoort, "Pagan Sources in the Pseudo-Clementine Novel," in *Religious Identity and the Problem of Historical Foundation: The Foundational Character of Authoritative Sources in the History of Christianity and Judaism*, eds. J. Frishman, W. Otten and G. Rouwhorst, Jewish and Christian Perspectives 8 (Leiden: Brill, 2004), 265–74.

ogy, for the *Aeneid* uses the framework of Homer's *Odyssey* to portray pious Aeneas the divine son and his people the Romans as superior to crafty Odysseus and the Greeks. According to Hebrews, the followers of Jesus, the author and perfecter of faith, supersede the Jewish people. Is there any sense in which Hebrews is also showing that the followers of Jesus supersede the Roman people? Hebrews 13:14 seems to be a direct criticism against the idea of an eternal Rome, but beyond that verse, there is scant evidence for a conscious subversion of the values of Augustan theology or direct criticism of its political regime. So in terms of the peoples being compared in this letter, the main comparison is that between the followers of Jesus and the Jewish people. I am not arguing that the author of Hebrews intentionally used the *Aeneid* because it was written to supersede the *Odyssey*. It is probably rather a case of tragic serendipity, in which an author attempting to write a sermon of epic dimensions was influenced not only by a competing theology's depiction of its hero, but also by the social implications of this depiction in which one divinely favored people replaced another.

The people who follow the divine son in Hebrews replace the members of Judaism as God's people (Heb. 4:8–11; 8:8a; 13:9–10). While the supersessionism of Hebrews is well-observed in the literature on Hebrews, its origin is seldom considered.[111] Commentators take different approaches to this supersessionism, including Gordon's attempt to situate it within prophetic critiques and alongside the supersessionism that Judaism also displays toward the animal sacrifices of the Jewish scriptures. Still, Gordon's approbation does not satisfy: "*Hebrews*, it could fairly be claimed, is exemplary as a supersessionist text for the way in which it argues its case without rancour or abuse."[112]

Hebrews is more supersessionist than Paul's letters. It is one generation removed from the apostles and Paul (Heb. 2:3). The blame is more firmly put on the Jews for a change in covenant arrangements (Heb. 8:8a). The Jews' covenant with God is not to be established (cf. Rom. 3:31) or considered the Jews' irrevocable possession (cf. Rom. 11:29). Instead the Jews' covenant with God is about to disappear

[111] Hays for example, acknowledges this characteristic but examines other books of the New Testament: "In short, Matthew (alongside the letter to the Hebrews) is the preeminent canonical voice of supersessionist Christian theology: the church *replaces* Israel" (Richard B. Hays, *The Moral Vision of the New Testament* [New York: Harper Collins, 1996], 424, his emphasis).

[112] Gordon, *Hebrews* 27–28; quotation from 28.

(Heb. 8:13). Exegetically, since Romans 9–11 is the one place where a New Testament author explicitly considers Judaism in light of the promises God made to the Jewish people, it deserves priority in our reading of the New Testament's ambivalent position toward Judaism. Ethically, since Romans 9–11 finds God's promises to the Jewish people as irrevocable (11:29), it appears that this section should be privileged to keep us from reverting to the anti-Semitism found in other parts of the New Testament.

As we read Hebrews, then, we should reject any statement the author makes about Jewish culpability for the ending of the Mosaic covenant (Heb 8:8a), a possibility never envisioned in the Mosaic covenant itself. Similarly, Hebrews' assertion of the Abrahamic or Mosaic covenant's terminal status (Heb. 8:13) must be regarded as unreliable, since these covenants are affirmed as irrevocable in the one place where a New Testament author self-consciously addresses the question of Christ-less Judaism (Rom. 11:29). Since the church now regards Israel as an end in itself, and not simply a foil or preparation for the church, we should consider Hebrews' message about the futility and end of Judaism as now proven false, a model for relating Israel and the church that cannot work and must be discarded.

We have seen in the section above entitled "The Priestly Son" how Hebrews distorts the Jewish scriptures in directions congruent with Augustan theology. At places where Hebrews exegetes the Old Testament in order to show Jesus as greater, we should therefore monitor its exegesis with extreme caution, and refuse to accept any assertion that runs against the plain sense of the Old Testament text. For example, when Hebrews says that the blood of bulls and goats never took away sin (10:4), we should reject this statement since it is not only patently against the symbolic world of the Jewish scriptures, but effectively undermines the whole temple cultus that forms the basis for the Christian doctrine of sacrifice.

These negative implications for our use of Hebrews arise logically from our understanding of this letter's debt to Augustan theology and the tendency toward corporate supersessionism that such theology evokes. So we must ask regarding the book of Hebrews the very question Aeneas asks regarding territory that cannot be held: "Where's the crux?... What strongpoint shall we hold?"[113] I suggest the following positive assertions that can still be retained from the book of Hebrews.

[113] Fitzgerald 2.432–33; quo res summa loco... quam prendimus arcem? (*Aen.* 2.322–3).

First, the model of learning towards piety is useful for Christian discipleship. It provides a portrait of Jesus that can result in ethical living among those who follow him. Second, the grammar of purification within the portrait of the priestly son is a useful language to use when discussing Jesus' death, an event various parts of the New Testament attempt to identify, whether as tragedy, choice or necessity. This grammar of purification includes the arena of the religious subject's conscience, which again is ethically useful for Christians and should be retained. Third, the portrait of Jesus as founding son is a helpful check against the magnetic pull of the nation state on the self-understanding of people today. Such caution seems consistent with some exegesis of Paul's letters, which finds them questioning the idolatry required by the Roman empire.

6. Conclusion

In this article I argue that the model for a divine son that the author and first audience of Hebrews employ seems to derive its categories of pious son, priestly son and founding son more from Augustan theology than from the scriptures used by the first century church. David Aune states in regard to his examination of Hebrews that "many of the important and vital functions attributed to Heracles as a Hellenistic savior figure were understood by some early Christians as applicable to Jesus to an even greater extent than they were to Heracles."[114] I am extending Aune's comparison by including Heracles within the conceptual framework of Augustan theology, since this theology had explicitly absorbed Heracles into its pantheon of heroes and value system (*Aen.* 8.102–350). It cannot be proven that the author of Hebrews is consciously depending on Virgil's *Aeneid*. Rather, in order to make its point about Jesus as divine son, Hebrews employs categories ascribed to the divine son and that son's people that were current in the Augustan theology of the first century.[115]

---

114 Aune, "Heracles and Christ" 19.

115 It is a privilege to be able to contribute this article as a way of honoring and thanking my teacher, Robert M. Grant. I wish also to thank the New Testament Trial Balloon Society of St. Paul, Minnesota, who discussed an earlier version of this paper. The designated respondent of that discussion, Steve Reece, especially deserves recognition. The errors and oversights in this paper remain my own responsibility.

THE TWO THIRTEENS: ROMANS AND REVELATION

Graydon F. Snyder

Historically some biblical texts have had a powerful influence well beyond the intent of the biblical author. Often that impact is, in the minds of some, very negative, or at least a serious misappropriation of the meaning intended by the author. Scholars have approached these texts in at least two different ways. Some show, usually correctly, that the text has been misunderstood or even deliberately misexegeted.[1] While this is true, proper exegesis will not solve the historical/social issue.[2] The damage has already occurred. In order to sanction a differing social/political perspective, such as racial equality or feminism, other writers show how the text has been inappropriately abused[3] Though this methodology also can be useful, the historical abuse of the text cannot be suppressed. We propose here a different approach to misappropriated texts. We will show that each abused passage has in the Bible a clear counterpoint (Two Thirteens, if you wish). As we shall see these counterpoint passages balance the misappropriated passages, even in post-biblical times. We will reflect on five examples:

---

[1] In *Noah's Curse: The Biblical Justification of American Slavery* (Oxford: Oxford University Press, 2002), Stephen R. Haynes speaks of what I call "misappropriated" as the "reading" and disagreement with the text as "counterreading" (pp. 177–200). My method here is to describe the tradition history of other texts that stand over against the misappropriated text. I speak of them as countertexts.

[2] Writing on homosexuality in the Hebrew Scriptures, Frederick Gaiser assumes re-exegeting the key texts used against homosexuality will have little value. So he seeks to clarify the function of parallel texts (such as Isaiah 56:1–8). He doesn't, or can't, trace a tradition history of that particular text, however. See his "A New Word on Homosexuality? Isaiah 56:1–8 as Case Study," in *Word and World* 14/3 (1994) 280–293. Condensed in *The Christian Century* 123 (May 2, 2006), 26–27.

[3] Using yet another method Willard Swartley discusses major social issues in terms of their place in the biblical material and later impact in Christian history. He does not deal with any specific misappropriated text, but his evaluation of the specific issues is quite valuable. Willard M. Swartley, *Slavery, Sabbath, War, and Women* (Scottdale, PA: Herald Press, 1983), 228–234.

1. Slavery and Racism (Gen. 9:25; 10:6)

A. *The Misappropriated Text*

וַיֹּ֖אמֶר אָר֣וּר כְּנָ֑עַן עֶ֥בֶד עֲבָדִ֖ים יִֽהְיֶ֥ה לְאֶחָֽיו׃

25 he said, "Cursed be Canaan; lowest of slaves shall he be to his brothers."

וּבְנֵ֖י חָ֑ם כּ֥וּשׁ וּמִצְרַ֖יִם וּפ֥וּט וּכְנָֽעַן׃

6 The descendants of Ham: Cush, Egypt, Put, and Canaan.

While it would be historically incorrect to maintain that the Curse of Ham caused slavery and racism, certainly the Genesis 9–11 texts were used, particularly in the southern United States, to sanction slavery in the seventeenth century and even today defend racial differentiation. While black people were distinct in the ancient world (hence the name Ethiopian) there is little evidence for racial discrimination.[4] Nevertheless, Ham was reviled by the early fathers as the symbol of man in isolation, hot with impatience (like the heretics)."[5] Despite the obvious intent of the Genesis tradition to place Ham in black Africa (Kush/Ethiopia with Egypt), color became an issue much later. Only after Europeans began to explore southern Africa, did the association of black with Ham begin to appear. In the middle of the15th century a Portuguese scholar offered Noah's curse as the basis for black slavery.[6] Later, during antebellum years, the Curse of Ham was used in the United States as the biblical authorization for slavery. More recently, postbellum. the text has been used to substantiate racial differentiation.[7] For example, in pre-Mandela years Genesis 9–11 was used by the Dutch Reformed Church of South Africa to defend apartheid.[8]

---

[4] So David Goldenberg, *The Curse of Ham: Race and Slavery in Early Judaism, Christianity and Islam* (Princeton: Princeton University Press, 2003), 9. Also Frank M. Snowden, *Before Color Prejudice: The Ancient View of Blacks* (Cambridge: Harvard University Press, 1983), 88–108.

[5] Augustine, *City of God*, XVI: 2.

[6] Gomes Eannes de Azurara, *The Chronicle of the Discovery and Conquest of Guinea*, trans. Charles Raymond Beazley and Edgar Prestage (New York: B. Franklin, 1963), I, 54; see also II, 319, ftnote 69 and 321, ftnote 81.

[7] Sylvester A. Johnson, *The Myth of Ham in Nineteenth-Century American Christianity* (New York: Palgrave Macmillan, 2004), 31–45.

[8] Willem Vorster, "The Bible and Apartheid 1," in John W. DeGruchy and Charles Villa-Vicencio, *Apartheid is a Heresy* (Grand Rapids: Eerdmans, 1983), 94–111.

B. *The Countertexts (Psalm 68:32; Acts 8:27–38)*

יֶאֱתָ֣יוּ חַ֭שְׁמַנִּים מִנִּ֣י מִצְרָ֑יִם כּ֥וּשׁ תָּרִ֥יץ יָ֝דָ֗יו לֵאלֹהִֽים׃

[31]Let bronze be brought from Egypt; let Ethiopia hasten to stretch out its hands to God.

[27]καὶ ἀναστὰς ἐπορεύθη. καὶ ἰδοὺ ἀνὴρ Αἰθίοψ εὐνοῦχος δυνάστης Κανδάκης βασιλίσσης Αἰθιόπων, ὃς ἦν ἐπὶ πάσης τῆς γάζης αὐτῆς, ὃς ἐληλύθει προσκυνήσων εἰς Ἰερουσαλήμ,[28] ἦν τε ὑποστρέφων καὶ καθήμενος ἐπὶ τοῦ ἅρματος αὐτοῦ καὶ ἀνεγίνωσκεν τὸν προφήτην Ἠσαΐαν.

So he got up and went. Now there was an Ethiopian eunuch, a court official of the Candace, queen of the Ethiopians, in charge of her entire treasury. He had come to Jerusalem to worship[28] and was returning home; seated in his chariot, he was reading the prophet Isaiah. (Acts 8:27–28)

[36]ὡς δὲ ἐπορεύοντο κατὰ τὴν ὁδόν, ἦλθον ἐπί τι ὕδωρ, καί φησιν ὁ εὐνοῦχος· ἰδοὺ ὕδωρ, τί κωλύει με βαπτισθῆναι;[38] καὶ ἐκέλευσεν στῆναι τὸ ἅρμα καὶ κατέβησαν ἀμφότεροι εἰς τὸ ὕδωρ, ὅ τε Φίλιππος καὶ ὁ εὐνοῦχος, καὶ ἐβάπτισεν αὐτόν. (Acts 8:36–38)

As they were going along the road, they came to some water; and the eunuch said, "Look, here is water! What is to prevent me from being baptized?"[38] He commanded the chariot to stop, and both of them, Philip and the eunuch, went down into the water, and Philip baptized him.

In contrast to some of the other misappropriated texts, the exegetical problems with the Curse of Ham are quite obvious. According to the text Ham did observe the nakedness of his father, Lot, and Lot did recognize what Ham had done. Lot did pronounce a curse, but on the son of Ham, Canaan, not Ham himself. It is Canaan who will be a slave. No explanation for this shift seems obvious. However, as we have noted, an exegetical critique of the said text will not change its history. The Curse of Ham text was used from the fifteenth century on as a biblical authorization of slavery of blacks and then segregation.[9]

The countertexts seem less than obvious but have proven highly important. The major independent churches of sub-Sahara Africa (the major locus for the earlier slave trade) consider their origin to be Ethiopian. They see in the Bible two major defining texts.[10] In the first, Psalm 68:32, they find the Hebrew Scriptures affirming a faith relationship between the

---

[9] Edwin M. Yamauchi, *Africa and the Bible* (Grand Rapids: Baker Academic, 2004), 27–29.

[10] Edward Ullendorff, *Ethiopia and the Bible* (London: Oxford University Press, 1968), 9–10.

people of כּוּשׁ and Elohim. The second text plays an even more important role. In contrast to those readers who might have supposed Cornelius was the first non-Jew to be converted (Acts 10:1–11:18), the author of Acts describes the Ethiopian Eunuch as the first non-Jewish convert. Cornelius represented the mission to Gentiles as it went northwest to the ends of the earth (Acts 1:8). The Ethiopian Eunuch represented the mission to the Gentiles as it went south to the other end of the earth, Africa, especially black Africa.

Present awareness that homo sapiens emerged from Africa thousands of years ago and all "modern" people have the same DNA basis makes any designation of race irrelevant. Differences are due to climate, forestation, agriculture and solar exposure. So the first Gentile Christian, the Ethiopian Eunuch, represents also that original source of humanity and makes the Curse of Ham totally insignificant.[11] Awareness that race and color are not genetic differences has rendered prejudice inappropriate.

2. Anti-Semitism/Anti-Judaism

A. *The Misappropriated Text (Matthew 27:25)*

> 25καὶ ἀποκριθεὶς πᾶς ὁ λαὸς εἶπεν· τὸ αἷμα αὐτοῦ ἐφ' ἡμᾶς καὶ ἐπὶ τὰ τέκνα ἡμῶν.
>
> Then the people as a whole answered, "His blood be on us and on our children!"

By any standard Matthew 27:25 has been the most destructive text in the New Testament.[12] Along with John 19:6 this text has sanctioned, even caused, Christian attacks on Jews and eventually the Holocaust itself. To be sure, pagan conflicts with Judaism did exist before the writing of the New Testament, so attacks on Jews cannot have started with this appearance of this text (ca. 90 C.E.). In fact during the early decades

[11] For an excellent survey see Wells's *The Journey of Man: A Genetic Odyssey* (Princeton: Princeton University Press, 2002). Accounts of the procedures and some results, planned by Spencer Wells can be found at www.nationalgeographic/genographic. See also Steve Olson, *Mapping Human History: Discovering the Past Through out Genes* (Boston: Houghton Mifflin, 2002), 38–39.

[12] Gerd Lüdemann, "*The Unholy in Holy Scripture: The Dark Side of the Bible*," (Westminster John Knox Press, 1997), 76 to 127.

it was relatively peaceful: sometimes permissive (e.g., in North Africa) and sometimes confrontive (because of conversionary efforts, e.g. Justin Martyr's Dialogue with Trypho). But by the end of the second century the Matthean deicide text was beginning to appear in Christian writings. Melito of Sardis (ca. 180) might have been the first:

> Bitter therefore for you is the feast of unleavened bread, as it is written for you:
> *You shall eat unleavened bread with bitter flavours.*
>
> Bitter for you are the nails you sharpened,
> bitter for you the tongue you incited,
> bitter for you the false witnesses you instructed,
> bitter for you the ropes you made ready.
>
> O unprecedented murder! Unprecedented crime!
> The Sovereign has been made unrecognizable by His naked body,
> and is not even allowed a garment to keep Him from view.
> That is why the luminaries turned away,
> and the day was darkened,
> so that He might hide the one stripped bare upon the tree,
> darkening not the body of the Lord
> but the eyes of men. (Peri Pascha lines 93–97)

The first verbal vicious attack on Jews came from Chrysostom in his eight homilies entitled *Adversus Judaeos.*[13] Speaking of the synagoue he writes (among other vituperative sentences):

> For, tell me, is not the dwelling place of demons a place of impiety even if no god's statue stands there? Here the slayers of Christ gather together, here the cross is driven out, here God is blasphemed, here the Father is ignored, here the Son is outraged, here the grace of the Spirit is rejected. Does not greater harm come from this place since the Jews themselves are demons? In the pagan temple the impiety is naked and obvious; it would not be easy to deceive a man of sound and prudent mind or entice him to go there. But in the synagogue there are men who say they worship God and abhor idols, men who say they have prophets and pay them honor. But by their words they make ready an abundance of bait to catch in their nets the simpler souls who are so foolish as to be caught of guard. (Dialogue I, VI, 3)

While Chrysostom was only verbal, his colleague Ambrose permitted the Christian burning of synagogues. The other contemporary, Augustine

---

[13] Robert L. Wilken, *John Chrysostom and the Jews: Rhetoric and Reality in the Late 4th Century* (Berkeley: University of California Press, 1983). James Carroll, *Constantine's Sword: The Church and Jews* (Boston: Houghton Mifflin Company, 2002), 191.

(North African) was more permissive than Ambrose with a bipolar attitude toward Jews (let them survive, but don't encourage growth) much like the *Sicut Judaeis* of Gregory (7th century).[14] Despite the continued support of *Sicut Judaeis* eventually the anti-Judaism (a religious conflict) of the early period of Christianity shifted to anti-Semitism (a racial conflict).[15] The racial conflict erupted with the expulsion of the Jews in 1492 from Spain, and then appeared in one of history's greatest catastrophes—the Holocaust in Germany. The theological basis for the Holocaust came largely from the pen of Alfred Rosenberg whose vituperative depiction of the New Testament Jews strikes the reader as nauseating and incredibly absurd.[16]

B. *Countertexts (John 4:22)*

> [22] ὑμεῖς προσκυνεῖτε ὃ οὐκ οἴδατε· ἡμεῖς προσκυνοῦμεν ὃ οἴδαμεν, ὅτι ἡ σωτηρία ἐκ τῶν Ἰουδαίων ἐστίν.
>
> You worship what you do not know; we worship what we know, for salvation is from the Jews.

The John 4:22 countertext has significant implications.[17] At the same time, unfortunately the text is found in that Gospel considered by many to be the most anti-Judaic. The "crucify him" passage in 19:6 parallels Matthew 27:25. And the accusation the Jews are children of the devil (8:44), though not as devastating as Mt. 27:25 does purport to come from the mouth of Jesus rather than the gospel editor. In any case National Socialists like Rosenberg spoke of the anti-Judaic Fourth Gospel as the Golden Gospel. While it has been my intent to deal with the historical affect of these texts, it is difficult not to note that the Gospel of John intends to divest the gospel of sociological involvements. In that sense it is far closer to Gnosticism than anti-Judaism.[18] John 4:22 does not play a significant role in early Jewish-Christian relationships. Other "countertexts" deal with reconciliation or equality of participation between

---

[14] Augustine, *City of God*, Bk. 18, chp 46. See Carroll, *Constantine's Sword*, 208–219.

[15] Dominic Crossan, *Who Killed Jesus?: Exposing the Roots of Anti-Semitism in the Gospel Story of the Death of Jesus* (San Francisco: HarperSanFrancisco, 1995), 32.

[16] Alfred Rosenberg, *Der Mythus des 20. Jahrhunderts: Eine Wertung der Seelischgeistigen gestaltenkämpfe Unserer Zeit* (München: Hoheneichen-Verlag, 1930).

[17] See Rudolf Pesch, *The Trial of Jesus Continues*, trans. Doris Glenn Wagner (Allison Park, PA: Pickwick Publications, 1996), 75–78.

[18] Graydon F. Snyder, "The Social Context of the Ironic Dialogues in the Gospel of John," in *Putting Body and Soul Together: Essays in Honor of Robin Scroggs* (Valley Forge: Trinity Press International, 1997), 3–23.

Jews and Gentiles. Galatians 3:27 and Ephesians 2:14–18 speak of a new people of God that includes all people.

However the John countertext goes deeper than simply reconciliation. Salvation itself derives from the revelation given to the Jews, and Christians may share in that. Following the Holocaust, attempts have been made to articulate the John 4:22 position. In 1948 the French Jewish scholar Jules Isaac wrote in *Jésus et Israël* that the Matthew text was tendentious, deicide was never intended and a rupture between Jews and Christians should never have occurred.[19] The position of Isaac had considerable influence on Christians. After it was presented to the Vatican in 1965 Pope Paul VI issued a declaration entitled *Nostra Aetate* in which he essentially concurred with Isaac. Salvation was of the Jews!

> Thus the Church of Christ acknowledges that, according to God's saving design, the beginnings of her faith and her election are found already among the Patriarchs, Moses and the prophets. She professes that all who believe in Christ—Abraham's sons according to faith—are included in the same Patriarch's call, and likewise that the salvation of the Church is mysteriously foreshadowed by the chosen people's exodus from the land of bondage. The Church, therefore, cannot forget that she received the revelation of the Old Testament through the people with whom God in His inexpressible mercy concluded the Ancient Covenant.

The document does not mention Matthew 27:25, but does note that the "crucify him" passage in John 19:6 references Jewish authorities, not the Jewish people. *Nostra Aetate* was followed soon thereafter by Protestant studies, referred to as The New Perspective, that also strove to erase any gap between Paul, Jesus and Judaism.[20] That is, Christianity is a historical extension of God's intent as seen in the Hebrew Scriptures. Salvation is of the Jews.

3. Papal supremacy (Matthew 16:18–19)

A. *The Misappropriated Text*

[18] κἀγὼ δέ σοι λέγω ὅτι σὺ εἶ Πέτρος, καὶ ἐπὶ ταύτῃ τῇ πέτρᾳ οἰκοδομήσω μου τὴν ἐκκλησίαν καὶ πύλαι ᾅδου οὐ κατισχύσουσιν αὐτῆς. [19] δώσω σοι

---

[19] Jules Isaac, *Jesus and Israel*, trans. Sally Gran (New York: Holt, Rinehart and Winston, 1971), on John 4:22 see p. 196.

[20] James Dunn, "Echoes of Intra-Jewish Polemic in Paul's Letter to the Galatians," *JBL* 112/3 (1993), 459–77. E.P. Sanders, *Paul, the Law, and Jewish People* (Philadelphia: Fortress Press, 1983), 171–179.

> τὰς κλεῖδας τῆς βασιλείας τῶν οὐρανῶν, καὶ ὃ ἐὰν δήσῃς ἐπὶ τῆς γῆς ἔσται δεδεμένον ἐν τοῖς οὐρανοῖς, καὶ ὃ ἐὰν λύσῃς ἐπὶ τῆς γῆς ἔσται λελυμένον ἐν τοῖς οὐρανοῖς.
>
> And I tell you, you are Peter, and on this rock I will build my church, and the gates of Hades will not prevail against it. I will give you the keys of the kingdom of heaven, and whatever you bind on earth will be bound in heaven, and whatever you loose on earth will be loosed in heaven.

In contrast to the Curse of Ham and the Blood Curse, it would be difficult to evaluate the misappropriation of Matthew 16:18–19. The issues are primarily centralization of power, inclusion and exclusion. To be sure some Roman Catholics have used their power to do damage and encourage violence. On the other hand, in many areas Roman Catholics have been persecuted, excluded and held in contempt. In other words, the misappropriation of the text has worked both ways. Essentially the Matthew text stands alone in the New Testament. The Markan and Lukan parallels deal with the identity of Jesus and the Messianic secret rather than the authority of Peter. Possibly 1 Peter, and more so 2 Peter, were written to express that authority in the Asia Minor area. And Jesus' adjuration of Peter in John 21:15–19 may reflect the authority of Peter even in the Ephesian bailiwick.

Otherwise the primacy of Peter may have first appeared in the writings of Clement of Alexandria (*Who Is the Rich Man That Is Saved?* 21:3–5 [200 C.E.]). About as early as Clement would be the reference to the keys in Tertullian (*Antidote Against the Scorpion* 10 [211 C.E.]). The power of the Matthew passage appears clearly at the Council of Ephesus as stated by the Roman Apostolic See:

> There is no doubt, and in fact it has been known in all ages, that the holy and most blessed Peter, prince and head of the apostles, pillar of the faith, and foundation of the Catholic Church, received the keys of the kingdom from our Lord Jesus Christ, the Savior and Redeemer of the human race, and that to him was given the power of loosing and binding sins: who down even to today and forever both lives and judges in his successors' (session 3 [431 C.E.]).

The evolution of Peter's Primacy followed the expansion of the Holy Roman Empire. Eventually the successor of Peter became the infallible (verse 17) head or co-head of that Empire.

B. *Countertexts*

Denials of Peter's infallibility occurred immediately in the Gospel of Matthew.

Jesus spoke of the suffering Messiah (addressing the identification in 16:16) and was rebuked by Peter for his redefinition of messiahship. Jesus retaliated with exceptionally strong words:

> But he turned and said to Peter, "Get behind me, Satan! You are a stumbling block to me; for you are setting your mind not on divine things but on human things." (16:23)

And regarding the Rock and the Keys, of all the Gospels, Matthew stresses most the power of the faith community to make corporate decisions:

> Truly I tell you, whatever you bind on earth will be bound in heaven, and whatever you loose on earth will be loosed in heaven.
>
> Again, truly I tell you, if two of you agree on earth about anything you ask, it will be done for you by my Father in heaven.
>
> For where two or three are gathered in my name, I am there among them." (18:18–20)

But far more important for the history of the church we find in the Gospel of John a person who rivals Peter as the Primate of the church. Again and again the author of the Gospel makes Peter subservient to the beloved disciple, the "apostle" of Ephesus:

The beloved disciple is called prior to Peter (1:35–42). The author of John picks up the Matthean implication that Peter is of the devil (6:68–71). At the last supper Peter sits at the table in such a position that he must ask the beloved disciple for the words of Jesus (13, especially vv. 23–24). Because of his sword Peter is chastised by Jesus (18:10–11). Though Peter denied Jesus the beloved disciple did not deny him and could enter the courtyard of the high priest (18:15–27).

The primary Johannine countertext comes in John 19:26–27:

> [26]'Ιησοῦς οὖν ἰδὼν τὴν μητέρα καὶ τὸν μαθητὴν παρεστῶτα ὃν ἠγάπα, λέγει τῇ μητρί· γύναι, ἴδε ὁ υἱός σου.[27] εἶτα λέγει τῷ μαθητῇ· ἴδε ἡ μήτηρ σου. καὶ ἀπ' ἐκείνης τῆς ὥρας ἔλαβεν ὁ μαθητὴς αὐτὴν εἰς τὰ ἴδια.

> When Jesus saw his mother and the disciple whom he loved standing beside her, he said to his mother, "Woman, here is your son." Then he said to the disciple, "Here is your mother." And from that hour the disciple took her into his own home.

In the Gospel of John Jesus doesn't name a primary disciple to lead the community of the faithful. Rather he names a person who replaces him, a new child of Mary. The Ephesian disciple is the new Jesus.[21] An astounding affirmation that surely trumps Matthew 16:18–19. And in fact though tradition has Peter the first to see the empty tomb, that "honor" goes to Mary Magdalene and the beloved disciple (20:1–10).

The Gospel of John offers another primate for the early Christian church. While the bishop of Ephesus was never the head of the ancient or medieval church, there was sufficient struggle regarding power and theology that the eventually the eastern church split from Rome in 1054.[22] About five hundred years later the British also split to form the Church of England (1534 C.E.). Both insisted on apostolic succession, but both denied the primacy of Peter. About the same time the Reformation started in German and Switzerland. Protestants, however, did not generally (note Swedish Lutherans) accept apostolic succession as source of authority.[23]

4. The Silence of Women in Church (1 Corinthians 14:33b–36)

A. *The Misappropriated Text*

[33b] Ὡς ἐν πάσαις ταῖς ἐκκλησίαις τῶν ἁγίων[34] αἱ γυναῖκες ἐν ταῖς ἐκκλησίαις σιγάτωσαν· οὐ γάρ ἐπιτρέπεται αὐταῖς λαλεῖν, ἀλλὰ ὑποτασσέσθωσαν, καθὼς καὶ ὁ νόμος λέγει.[35] εἰ δέ τι μαθεῖν θέλουσιν, ἐν οἴκῳ τοὺς ἰδίους ἄνδρας ἐπερωτάτωσαν· αἰσχρὸν γάρ ἐστιν γυναικὶ λαλεῖν ἐν ἐκκλησίᾳ.[36] ἢ ἀφ' ὑμῶν ὁ λόγος τοῦ θεοῦ ἐξῆλθεν, ἢ εἰς ὑμᾶς μόνους κατήντησεν;

(As in all the churches of the saints,[34] women should be silent in the churches. For they are not permitted to speak, but should be subordinate, as the law also says.[35] If there is anything they desire to know, let them ask their husbands at home. For it is shameful for a woman to speak in church.[36] Or did the word of God originate with you? Or are you the only ones it has reached?)

---

[21] Graydon F. Snyder, "John 13:16 and the Anti-Petrinism of the Johannine Tradition," *Biblical Research* XVI (1971): 1–11. Kevin Quast, *Peter and the Beloved Disciple: Figures for a Community in Crisis* (Sheffield: Sheffield Academic Press, 1989), 95–97.

[22] *The Primacy of Peter: Essays in Ecclesiology and the Early Church*, ed. John Meyendorff (Crestwood, NY: St. Vladimir's Seminary Press, 1992). For the Orthodox reading of the Matthean primacy text see Meyendorff's essay "St Peter in Byzantine Theology" (pp. 67–90).

[23] Charles Journet, *The Primacy of Peter from the Protestant and from the Catholic Point of View*, trans. John Chapin (Westminster, MD: Newman Press, 1954), ix–x; 73–102.

In certain historical sense this text has not been misappropriated. That is, it cannot be considered the ancient cause for the subordination of women.[24] Male dominance prevailed in most of the Mediterranean cultures adjacent to Israel (much of Africa was matriarchal)[25] as well as Judaism itself.[26] The Hellenistic world differed very little.[27] If anything, earliest Christianity differed from it social context, as we shall see, because it did encourage female participation in its corporate life. Nevertheless, I Corinthians 14:33a–36 has been the battleground text for the role of women in the church. The rule against verbal participation became formal rather quickly: 1 Timothy 2:11–12b; 5:5:9–16; Titus 2:3–5.[28] The data on the early church does not allow us to state exactly when women clearly were no longer allowed to speak in the congregational setting. Tertullian (ca. 180) used 1 Cor. 14 to enforce the silence of women:

> It is not permitted to a *woman* to speak in the church; but neither (is it permitted her) to teach, nor to baptize, nor to offer, nor to claim to herself a lot in any manly function, not to say (in any) sacerdotal office. (De virginibus velandis, 9)

Women were not permitted to speak formally in church until the 19th century. The first break occurred with the Quakers who, because of their Spirit theology, would not maintain that the Spirit spoke only in men. In 1660 Margaret Fell wrote a pamphlet rejecting the 1 Cor. text. It was entitled: *Women's Speaking Justified, Proved and Allowed of by the Scriptures, All Such as Speak by the Spirit and Power of the Lord Jesus And How Women Were the First That Preached the Tidings of the Resurrection of Jesus, and Were Sent by Christ's Own Command Before He Ascended to the Father (John 20:17)* [London, 1666]. Even so it was two centuries after Fell's writing before women began to be ordained and were encouraged to participate in public

---

[24] Edgar Krentz, "Order in the 'House' of God: The Haustafel in I Peter 2:11–3:12, in *Common life in the Early Church: Essays Honoring Graydon F. Snyder.* Edited by Julian V. Hills (Harrisburg: Trinity Press International, 1998), 279–285.

[25] Cheikh Anat Diop, *The Cultural Unity of Black Africa: The Domains of Patriarchy and of Matriarchy in Classical Antiquity* (London: Karnak House, 1989), 47–64.

[26] Letha Dawson Scanzoni and Nancy A. Hardesty, *All We're Meant to Be: Biblical Feminism for Today.* Grand Rapids: Eerdmans Publishing, 1992), 47–70.

[27] Luise Schottroff, *Lidias ungeduldige Schwestern: Feministische Sozialgeschichte des frühen Christentums* (Gütersloh: Chr. Kaisar Verlag, 1994). See especially her discussion of Cicero and the Roman sense of family (formal) in contrast to the Judeo/Christian (relational [pp. 40–53]).

[28] John Dominic Crossan and Jonathan Reed, *In Search of Paul: How Jesus's Apostle Opposed Rome's Empire with God's Kingdom* (New York: HarperSanFrancisco, 2004), 110–123.

worship.[29] That occurred primarily in Free Churches while several groups such as Roman Catholic, Latter Day Saints, Orthodox and for the most part Southern Baptists still hold to the 1 Cor. prohibition.

B. *The Countertexts: (1 Cor. 11:4–5)*

> [4]πᾶς ἀνὴρ προσευχόμενος ἢ προφητεύων κατὰ κεφαλῆς ἔχων καταισχύνει τὴν κεφαλὴν αὐτοῦ.[5] πᾶσα δὲ γυνὴ προσευχομένη ἢ προφητεύουσα ἀκατακαλύπτῳ τῇ κεφαλῇ καταισχύνει τὴν κεφαλὴν αὐτῆς· ἓν γάρ ἐστιν καὶ τὸ αὐτὸ τῇ ἐξυρημένῃ.

> [4]Any man who prays or prophesies with something on his head disgraces his head, [5]but any woman who prays or prophesies with her head unveiled disgraces her head—it is one and the same thing as having her head shaved.

Whatever we assume Paul meant in the "silence" passage, it must also be stated that Paul either encouraged or allowed women to speak in the church. Earlier in 1 Corinthians he describes how a woman praying or prophesying must be dressed. Since prophesying referred to the explanation of a text from the Hebrew Scriptures, there is hardly anyway to avoid the conclusion that women in the Corinthian house churches "preached". Furthermore women in other Pauline churches must have engaged in a speaking role. Phoebe was the minister (διάκονον) of the church at Cenchreae:

> Συνίστημι δὲ ὑμῖν Φοίβην τὴν ἀδελφὴν ἡμῶν, οὖσαν [καὶ] διάκονον τῆς ἐκκλησίας τῆς ἐν Κεγχρεαῖς, (1 Cor. 16:1)

And it would be difficult to believe that Junia, a relative of Paul, an apostle, and a woman converted to Christ before Paul, would have been prevented from speaking in the churches:[30]

> ἀσπάσασθε ᾿Ανδρόνικον καὶ ᾿Ιουνιᾶν τοὺς συγγενεῖς μου καὶ συναιχμαλώτους μου, οἵτινές εἰσιν ἐπίσημοι ἐν τοῖς ἀποστόλοις, οἳ καὶ πρὸ ἐμοῦ γέγοναν ἐν Χριστῷ. (Romans 16:7)

> Greet Andronicus and Junia, my relatives who were in prison with me; they are prominent among the apostles, and they were in Christ before I was.

---

[29] Richard L. Greaves, "Introduction,"*Triumph Over Silence: Women in Protestant History*, ed. Richard L. Greaves (Westport CN: Greenwood Press, 1985), 3–12, especially p. 7. See also Roland H. Bainton, *Women of the Reformation in Germany and Italy* (Boston: Beacon Press, 1977), 9–14.

[30] See Eldon Jay Epp, *Junia: The First Woman Apostle* (Minneapolis: Fortress Press, 2005). Epp discusses the translation biases as well as the textual variations.

The secondary Pauline texts about women appear to be part of an early Christian Haustafeln used by Paul and other writers to avoid unnecessary criticism from opponents in an unfriendly social context. However, 1 Cor. 14 does not read like a Haustafeln. Even though it may be a misplaced text, it addresses a particular problem. Had the freedom of women to speak already gone beyond what the early community intended? In any case nascent Christianity spawned groups in which women participated fully.[31]

Whatever we understand by the translocal remarks in the early "fathers", at least some local communities must have been inclusive of women. For example, in early Christian catacomb art the primary human figure was a woman, the Orante, who symbolized a person delivered from conflicts of the Mediterranean culture. In the Roman catacomb of Priscilla women are seated at the Agape meal found in the Capella Greca. The story of Susanna and the Elders (a threat to women) occurs several times in the Priscilla catacomb. Gradually the mainline church became more strict regarding the participation of women. That left only service as a deaconess or participation in the monastic life. Nevertheless the inclusion of women in sectarian church life, possibly the reason for the misuse of 1 Cor. 14, did continue. In 1200 the Waldensians allowed both men and women to speak. And starting in 1415–1419 the Hussites did the same.

5. Obey the Governing Authorities Romans 13

A. *The Misappropriated Text*

> [1] Πᾶσα ψυχὴ ἐξουσίαις ὑπερεχούσαις ὑποτασσέσθω. οὐ γὰρ ἔστιν ἐξουσία εἰ μὴ ὑπὸ θεοῦ, αἱ δὲ οὖσαι ὑπὸ θεοῦ τεταγμέναι εἰσίν.
>
> Let every person be subject to the governing authorities; for there is no authority except from God, and those authorities that exist have been instituted by God.

Because of its minority status in the Roman Empire, and the occasional persecutions, the first Christians did not apply Romans 13 to Rome.

---

[31] Elaine Pagels, *Beyond Belief: The Secret Gospel of Thomas* (New York, 2003), 50–73. See Gospel of Thomas, 114.

That occurred first, after Constantine, in the writings of Augustine.[32] While medieval emperors appropriated the biblical authority, it was Jacques-Benigne Bossuet (1627–1704) who first articulated the concept of a Divine Right of Kings:

> It appears from all this that the person of the king is sacred, and that to attack him in any way is sacrilege. God has the kings anointed by his prophets with the holy unction in like manner as he has bishops and altars anointed. But even without the external application in thus being anointed, they are by their very office the representatives of the divine majesty deputed by Providence for the execution of his purposes.[33]

Regardless of our exegesis of Romans 13, the Jews did consider the State a subsidiary of divine rule. Even before King David, the Lord created rulers for the people:

> Then the LORD raised up judges, who delivered them out of the power of those who plundered them. (Judges 2:16)

But more central to divine political leadership is the Lord's deeply influential and powerful promise to David:

> Your house and your kingdom shall be made sure forever before me; your throne shall be established forever. (2 Samuel 7:16)

Even more than the Davidic State, the writers of the Hebrew Scriptures generally recognize that political structures are a gift of God:

> By me kings reign, and rulers decree what is just;
> by me rulers rule, and nobles, all who govern rightly. (Proverbs 8:15–16)

While most of these texts apply to Israel as a State, even Nebuchadnezzar was mentioned by Jeremiah as one whose authority was given by God:

> It is I who by my great power and my outstretched arm have made the earth, with the people and animals that are on the earth, and I give it to whomever I please. [6] Now I have given all these lands into the hand of King Nebuchadnezzar of Babylon, my servant, and I have given him even the wild animals of the field to serve him. [7] All the nations shall serve him and his son and his grandson, until the time of his own land comes; then many nations and great kings shall make him their slave. (Jeremiah 27:5–7)

[32] Augustine, *City of God*, Book 5, 21. God "gave a kingdom to the Romans". But Augustine doesn't actually reference Romans 13.

[33] Translated in James Harvey Robinson, ed., *Readings in European History* (Boston: Ginn and Company, 1906), 2, 274.

Nevertheless, great kingdoms, like beasts, arose from the sea and did evil toward the people of God:

> [I] saw in my vision by night the four winds of heaven stirring up the great sea,[3] and four great beasts came up out of the sea, different from one another. (Daniel 7:2–3)

As we shall see in the countertext (Rev. 13) the beast(s) of the sea have been associated with tyrannical states, so when Paul wrote Romans 13 he indeed had a Jewish background for understanding the State as a human structure of good given by God. But he also had the background that inferred the Roman Empire was a beast rising from the sea. Why did Paul write positively about the State in Romans 13? He had rejected the authority of the State in an earlier letter:

> When any of you has a grievance against another, do you dare to take it to court before the unrighteous, instead of taking it before the saints?[2] Do you not know that the saints will judge the world? And if the world is to be judged by you, are you incompetent to try trivial cases?[3] Do you not know that we are to judge angels—to say nothing of ordinary matters?[4] If you have ordinary cases, then, do you appoint as judges those who have no standing in the church?[5] I say this to your shame. Can it be that there is no one among you wise enough to decide between one believer a and another,[6] but a believer goes to court against a believer—and before unbelievers at that? (1 Corinthians 6:1–6)

In the same Corinthian letter Paul assigned the Roman rulers to the realm of theological ignorance because they crucified the Lord of glory (1 Cor. 2:8). Given the lack of positive statements about the Roman authorities why was Romans 13:1–7 included?

Many explanations have been offered for the anomaly of Romans 13:1–7: John C. O'Neill considers this passage the most damaging in the New Testament and assumes Paul never wrote it.[34] Ernst Bammel considers this passage historically the most influential text of the New Testament and could not have been written by the Jewish Paul.[35] Carrying the Jewishness of Paul to an extreme, Mark Nanos does not believe the governing authorities were Roman, but, instead, rulers of the

[34] John C. O'Neill, *Paul's Letter to the Romans* (Harmondsworth: Penquin, 1975), 207–209.

[35] Ernst Bammel, "Romans 13," *Jews and the Politics of his Day*, eds. Ernst Bammel and C.F.D. Moule (Cambridge: Cambridge University Press, 1984), 365.

synagogue in Rome.[36] Others do not believe the intent of the passage is so much to grant authority to Rome as to quell the enthusiasm of aberrant and Gnostic Christians who allow their heavenly citizenship to override earthly existence.[37] Most modern writers assume a type of Haustafeln here in which Paul calls for socially acceptable behavior.[38] The passage can be seen as a continuation of the ethical admonitions of chapter 12.[39] More radically some scholars see the passage as a Ghandhi like non-violent opposition to the Roman state.[40]

Despite the overwhelming use of the text as a basis for governmental authority, most readers do warn that it doesn't apply to tyrannical states.[41] Under such circumstances they may reject Romans 13 or appeal to the famous counter text: Revelation 13:1–4.

B. *Countertext (Rev. 13:1–4)*

18 Καὶ ἐστάθη ἐπὶ τὴν ἄμμον τῆς θαλάσσης. 1 Καὶ εἶδον ἐκ τῆς θαλάσσης
θηρίον ἀναβαῖνον, ἔχον κέρατα δέκα καὶ κεφαλὰς ἑπτὰ καὶ ἐπὶ τῶν
κεράτων αὐτοῦ δέκα διαδήματα καὶ ἐπὶ τὰς κεφαλὰς αὐτοῦ ὀνόμα[τα]
βλασφημίας. 2 καὶ τὸ θηρίον ὃ εἶδον ἦν ὅμοιον παρδάλει καὶ οἱ πόδες αὐτοῦ
ὡς ἄρκου καὶ τὸ στόμα αὐτοῦ ὡς στόμα λέοντος. καὶ ἔδωκεν αὐτῷ ὁ δράκων
τὴν δύναμιν αὐτοῦ καὶ τὸν θρόνον αὐτοῦ καὶ ἐξουσίαν μεγάλην. 3 καὶ
μίαν ἐκ τῶν κεφαλῶν αὐτοῦ ὡς ἐσφαγμένην εἰς θάνατον, καὶ ἡ πληγὴ τοῦ
θανάτου αὐτοῦ ἐθεραπεύθη. Καὶ ἐθαυμάσθη ὅλη ἡ γῆ ὀπίσω τοῦ θηρίου 4
καὶ προσεκύνησαν τῷ δράκοντι, ὅτι ἔδωκεν τὴν ἐξουσίαν τῷ θηρίῳ, καὶ
προσεκύνησαν τῷ θηρίῳ λέγοντες· τίς ὅμοιος τῷ θηρίῳ καὶ τίς δύναται
πολεμῆσαι μετ' αὐτοῦ;

1 And I saw a beast rising out of the sea, having ten horns and seven heads; and on its horns were ten diadems, and on its heads were blasphemous

---

36 Mark Nanos, *The Mystery of Romans: The Jewish Content of Paul's Letter* (Minneapolis: Fortress, 1996), 289.

37 Ernst Käsemann, *Commentary on Romans*, trans. Geoffrey W. Bromily (Grand Rapids: Eerdmans, 1980), 351.

38 Luke Timothy Johnson, *Reading Romans: A Literary and Theological Commentary* (New York: Crossroad, 1997), 186. E.F. Scott, *Paul's Epistle to the Romans* (London: SCM 1947), 68–69. Paul J. Achtemeier, *Romans* (Atlanta: John Knox Press, 1985), 203–207.

39 Philip F. Esler, *Conflict and Identity in Romans: The Social Setting of Paul's Letter* (Minneapolis: Fortress, 2003), 231.

40 John Howard Yoder, *The Christian Witness to the State* (Newton, Kansas: Faith and Life Press, 1964), 73. Surprisingly Karl Barth insisted that resistance to the State only increases its power and violence. Karl Barth, *The Epistle to the Romans*, trans. Edwyn C. Hoskins (London: Oxford University Press, 1933), 481–492. Submission will undermine its power.

41 James D.G. Dunn, "Romans 13:1–7—A Charter for Political Quietism?" *Ex Auditu* 2 (1986), pp. 55–68 (68).

> names.[2] And the beast that I saw was like a leopard, its feet were like a bear's, and its mouth was like a lion's mouth. And the dragon gave it his power and his throne and great authority.[3] One of its heads seemed to have received a death-blow, but its mortal wound had been healed. In amazement the whole earth followed the beast.[4] They worshiped the dragon, for he had given his authority to the beast, and they worshiped the beast, saying, "Who is like the beast, and who can fight against it?" (Rev. 13:1–4)

In contrast to Romans 13, Rev. 13 describes the origin of the State in terms of the mythological dragon, Leviathan. While Leviathan, or the dragon, does not lie outside the divine creation, it represents that power of chaos (water) which God conquered in creation:

> [20] καὶ εἶπεν ὁ θεός ἐξαγαγέτω τὰ ὕδατα ἑρπετὰ ψυχῶν ζωσῶν καὶ πετεινὰ πετόμενα ἐπὶ τῆς γῆς κατὰ τὸ στερέωμα τοῦ οὐρανοῦ καὶ ἐγένετο οὕτως [21] καὶ ἐποίησεν ὁ θεὸς τὰ κήτη τὰ μεγάλα καὶ πᾶσαν ψυχὴν ζῴων ἑρπετῶν ἃ ἐξήγαγεν τὰ ὕδατα κατὰ γένη αὐτῶν καὶ πᾶν πετεινὸν πτερωτὸν κατὰ γένος

> [20] And God said, "Let the waters bring forth swarms of living creatures, and let birds fly above the earth across the dome of the sky."[21] So God created the great sea monsters and every living creature that moves, of every kind, with which the waters swarm, and every winged bird of every kind. (Genesis 1:20–21)

Using the Genesis 1:20–21 passage, the author of Daniel describes four successive beasts coming out of the sea. The four were the great tyrannies of the ancient world, the most terrifying of which was the fourth beast. That beast was noted for its ten horns. While few texts of the New Testament are more complex than Revelation 12–14, the intent of its author can hardly be misunderstood. Using the Daniel text, the author has made the ten horn beast be Rome of the first century C.E. Rome received its power from the mythological dragon, Leviathan, the chaos monster (i.e. Satan; 12:9). This one beast of Revelation has all the marks of the beasts in Daniel. In contrast to Daniel, of course, the beast of Revelation suppresses new Christian communities, not the Israelites of the second Temple period. In Revelation 13:1–4 the sea-beast refers to the State, but later in chapter 13 a second beast arises out of the earth. The beast is a vicious person, a tyrant whose number is 666 (13:18).[42] Few people would deny that Revelation 13 refers to the tyrannical

[42] David E. Aune, *Word Biblical Commentary: Revelation 6–16*, Volume 52b (Nashville: Thomas Nelson Publishers, 1998), 768–773.

Roman Empire (the first beast), but the identity of the second beast has been much debated. Most readers assume 666 refers to Nero and therefore the Neroninc persectution.[43] But data for a persecution by either Nero or Domitian is lacking.[44] It may well be then second beast refers to Roman culture in general.

So Revelation 13 clearly stands as a countertext to Romans 13:1–7 and it would be difficult avoid that conclusion. Of course, it has been controversial to ascertain what groups of early Christians were being threatened by the beasts.[45] In a sense the issue of primary addresses does not concern our countertext methodology. Shortly after the appearance of Revelation it was used as an anti-imperial document.[46] That observation needs further reflection. If Revelation was written to the seven churches, and if there was no actual persecution in Asia Minor, then the book has been written to support, encourage or warn a smaller group of Christians about the potential assimilative or oppressive power of the dominant culture. In like manner throughout history Revelation has encouraged and supported the minority position overagainst the majority, the sectarian versus the governing power. The original minority recipients have been reproduced again and again throughout history.

That is the fascination of Revelation 13 and its tragedy. If we had not already described Romans 13:1–7 as a seriously misappropriated text, we might as well have said Rev. 13:1–4 is one of the most misappropriated texts in the New Testament.[47] It is the source for constant pseudo-divine

---

[43] For example, Shirley Jackson Case, *The Revelation of John: A History of Interpretation* (Chicago: University of Chicago, 1919), 319; Charles C. Torrey, *The Apocalypse of John* (New Haven: Yale, 1958), 60; John A.T. Robinson, *Redating the New Testament* (Philadelphia: Westminster, 1976), 235.

[44] Paul B. Duff, *Who Rides the Beast? Prophetic Rivalry and the Rhetoric of Crisis in the Churches of the Apocalypse* (Oxford: Oxford University Press, 2001), 4–5. Adela Yarbro Collins, *Crisis and Catharsis: The Power of the Apocalypse* (Philadelphia: Westminster Press, 1984), 69–73. Charles H. Talbert, *The Apocalypse: A Reading of the Revelation of John* (Louisville: Westminster John Knox, 1994), 8–11.

[45] David Aune suggests the communities at risk are the seven churches in chapters 2–3. See Aune, *Word Biblical Commentary: Revelation*, I, lxix–lxx; 130–132. In his *Imperial Cults and the Apocalypse of John: Reading Revelation in the Ruins* (Oxford: Oxford University Press, 2001) Steven J. Friesen, assumes Revelation was written to the smaller community of churches (pp. 180–181).

[46] Friesen argues that in Revelation there is no legitimate place for an earthly empire. "John was not just anti-Roman; he was anti-empire." (*Imperial Cults*, p. 208)

[47] Robert Grant called Revelation "the most enigmatic book in the New Testament"; *A Historical Introduction to the New Testament* (London: Collins, 1963), 235. I first heard Robert Grant speak at a meeting of the Chicago Society of Biblical Research. He spoke

attacks on organizations and persons. To see that one needs only to check popular literature like the "Left Behind" series or topics like 666 or Revelation 13 on the internet. All governments, and church organizations like the National Council of Churches, the World Council of Churches or the Roman Catholic Church, have been positively identified as the beast from the sea. The beast from the land, 666, includes Hitler, Stalin, any pope, and all presidents of the United States, to name a few.[48] Furthermore, from the passage (13:5) dates have been deciphered in such a way to predict an immediate end of the world or, at least, our participation in such an earthly demise.[49]

Despite the incredible abuse of this countertext, it has been a lynchpin for the message of the New Testament in the Western and African worlds. While in the words of Jesus there is no call for violent attack against the State, neither is there a direct support for imperial rule.[50] Haustafeln like 1 Peter 2:13–7 and 1 Tim 2:1–2 also call for subordination to the State, but we cannot determine the impact of such a standard form. Despite the presence of Romans 13:1–7, the New Testament essentially does not recognize the lasting and ultimate power of the State. Eschatologically speaking the Reign of God "supercedes" the reign of Caesar (Rev. 20).

Through history then Rev. 13:1–4 has represented the New Testament relativization of the State or any final human authority. The original anti-state impact lasted for two centuries until the time of Constantine (Theophilus [Theophilus To Autolycus, XI], Melito of Sardis, *Antoninus Caesar*, Tertullian, *Ad Scapula*, I). Though through the Middle Ages various groups denied the validity of Romans 13, it was the Reformation that returned to Rev. 13. Martin Luther refused any political authority

guardedly about the canonicity of Revelation. The same caution can be seen in his *The Sword and the Cross* (New York: Macmillan, 1955), 56–57. At a somewhat later CSBR I read a paper on Ignatius of Antioch. Grant was there. He invited me do a translation and write a commentary on the Shepherd of Hermas. It was my entrée into the academic world. I am very grateful to for that opportunity and pleased for this opportunity to express my appreciation.

[48] Talbert, *The Apocalypse*, 1–2.

[49] Barbara R. Rossing, *The Rapture Exposed: The Message of Hope in the Book of Revelation* (Boulder: Westview Press, 2004), 33–46; 115–122.

[50] Depending on how one interprets the tax story (Mt. 17:24–27) or the coin response (Mt. 22:15–22). Edgar Krentz, "Order in the 'House' of God: The Haustafel in I Peter 2:11–3:12, in *Common life in the Early Church: Essays Honoring Graydon F. Snyder.* Edited by Julian V. Hills (Harrisburg: Trinity Press International, 1998), 278–285.

other than the Bible.[51] The Anabaptists called on Rev. 13 to support their break with the State and the state church.[52] More than State was involved, however. Rev. 13 was used by other groups to substantiate their break with dominant authorities. For example, the Quakers used the text in their struggle with the Church of England and Roman Catholicism.[53]

> From an apostate she [the Roman/Anglican church] becomes a persecutor. 'Tis not enough that she herself decline from ancient purity; others must do so too: she will give them no rest, that will not partake with her in that degeneracy, or receive her mark [Rev 14:11]. Are any wiser than she? Than Mother Church? No, no: Nor can any make war with the beast she rides [Rev 13:4/17:3], those worldly powers that protect her, and vow her maintenance against the cries of her dissenters.

Since the Reformation the Countertext has encouraged Free Churches, or as Friesen calls them, "the not necessarily confessing" faith communities, to maintain the separation of Church and State.[54] Sometimes the biblical basis for such separation is a modification of Romans 13. That is, the State no longer reflects the will of God.[55] At other times, Revelation 13 is placed directly against Romans 13.[56]

More recently the Rev. 13 has been used in various types of liberation theology to counter the negative impact of Romans 13. For example the authors of the 1985 South African Kairos document describe, at great length, the abuses of Romans 13 and then shift to Revelation 13:

> If we wish to search the Bible for guidance in a situation where the State that is supposed to be "the servant of God" (Romans 13:16) betrays that calling and begins to serve Satan instead, then we can study chapter 13 of the Book of Revelations. Here the Roman State becomes the servant

[51] Robert H. Stein, *Interpreting Puzzling Texts in the New Testament* (Grand Rapids: Baker Books, 1996), 289–294.

[52] John Howard Yoder, *Discipleship as Political Responsibility* (Scottdale, PA: Herald Press, 2003 <1964>), 23–32.

[53] *William Penn on religion and ethics; the emergence of liberal Quakerism*, ed. Hugh S. Barbour (Lewiston NY: Edwin Mellen Press, 1991 <1682>). (Studies in American religion, 53), 160.

[54] Friesen, *Imperial Cults*, 215.

[55] John Howard Yoder, *The Politics of Jesus: Vicit Agnus Noster* (Grand Rapids: Eerdmans, 1972). Revelation 13 and Romans 13 are often balanced with each other. Christians must measure the State. If the State is orderly then use Romans 13, if evil then reference Revelation 13 (p. 202). See also Oscar Cullmann, *The State in the New Testament* (New York: Charles Scribner's Sons, 1956), 3.

[56] Oscar Cullmann, *The State in the New Testament*, 5. The two texts are juxtaposed throughout the NT.

of the dragon (the devil) and takes on the appearance of a horrible beast. Its days are numbered because God will not permit his unfaithful servant to reign forever. (2:1)

6. Conclusion

The balancing system doesn't solve the original meaning and doesn't change the historical use of abused passages. It does allow the present day Christian to see biblical alternatives when they object to the use of the Bible to support racial prejudice, anti-Semitism, excessive ecclesiastical authority, subjugation of women, and a divine basis for governmental authority.

PART THREE

PATRISTIC STUDIES

NOTES ON DIVESTING AND VESTING IN *THE HYMN OF THE PEARL*

Robin Darling Young[1]

The *Hymn of the Pearl* is a ballad about a quest[2] for one magic jewel and a set of magical or religious garb. Seemingly composed in the second century, it survives in only two manuscripts, both preserved in the British Library.[3] This conventional title is not original; neither are two other titles by which the ballad is known: the "Hymn to the Redeemer" and the "Hymn of the Soul."

These later titles, however, indicate a continuing problem within the scholarly interpretation of the composition: although it sings a tale whose details are specific, if mystifying, the *Hymn of the Pearl* seems to attract metaphorical interpretations that are retrojected as its genuine meaning. In that way, it resembles in miniature certain canonical works; a theological imperative of some kind propels later readers to insist, as the *Pirkē Aboth* says of Torah, that "everything is in it." It is Gnostic; it

[1] Early last spring I asked Robert Grant whether *The Hymn of the Pearl* was a Gnostic composition. It was a propitious day and occasion to inquire—an annual St. Patrick's Day party to honor with libations a mysterious hero who, like the youth in the *Hymn*, charmed and exorcised snakes. This was a question I had neglected to ask as a student in his 1977 seminar on Gnosticism, but now the time was ripe to approach the oracle. All fellow disciples of Professor Grant will savor his gnomic reply: "Not necessarily." Unlike Grant, other scholars, less ambivalent, have been more certain about the gnostic origins of the *Hymn*. It is to Professor Grant, then, and to his learned caution that this article is gratefully dedicated, for instruction received since then *viva voce* and in numerous illuminating publications. From him I have learned an important lesson: far more questions in the study of early Christianity remain open than stamped with the deadening letters: case closed.

[2] For a recent discussion of the possible ancient purposes of the tale of the hero's quest, see Walter Burkert, *Creation of the Sacred: Tracks of Biology in Early Religions* (Cambridge, MA and London: Harvard University Press, 1996), pp. 56–78. To Burkert's list of examples could be added modern ones like *The Lord of the Rings* and other works of J.R.R. Tolkien, and (*pace* Burkert, who thinks the quest tale is being replaced by visual media), massively multiplayer online (video) games World of Warcraft or the single-player AdventureQuest, as well as the film *The Matrix* and its videogame spinoff.

[3] See P.-H. Poirier, "L'Hymne de la Perle des Actes de Thomas: Etude de la tradition manuscript," *Orientalia Christiana Periodica* 205 (Rome, 1978): 19–29, and ibid., *L'Hymne de la Perle des Actes de Thomas: introduction, texte-traduction, commentaire* (Louvain-la-Neuve: Centre d'histoire des religions, 1981), pp. 27–304.

is Persian; it is Buddhist; it is Manichaean; it is orthodox Christian; it is Jewish Christian. Its earliest interpreters among the Syriac-speakers of Edessa (where it probably originated) and Mesopotamia were the author of the Acts of Judas Thomas in the second century, and the third- and fourth-century teachers Mani and Ephrem the Syrian. The first included the ballad as a song of the apostle of *enkrateia*; the second read it as an oracle of himself and his mission; and the third, Ephrem, adopted it for his interpretation of apostolic Christianity in the *Hymns on the Pearl*.

Beautiful and fascinating, the *Hymn of the Pearl* has shown itself to be true to the skill of its hero, the anonymous "young man" and his heavenly, aquiline letter;—it has exercised a kind of magic over its readers. Almost every interpreter has pointed to a different aspect or reminiscence in the song and has suggested, and sometimes insisted, that the feature determines the song's origin and meaning.

The history of interpretation is, as Professor Grant knows, a useful exercise, and the *Hymn of the Pearl*'s recent interpreters have still not exhausted its possible context and meaning. After all, the song exists in roughly contemporary Syriac and Greek versions, and it is possibly Christian in origin; therefore, the cultural worlds of the eastern Mediterranean as well as Mesopotamia and Parthia or early Sassanid Persia can also be invoked as explanatory contexts.

But what have all these worlds been invoked to explain? The ballad is, as mentioned above, the story of a quest. In the tale, a young boys' parents strip him of his royal robe and toga, inscribe his heart with a covenant and send him from their home in the East down to Egypt, where he is to steal a pearl from a dragon.

Notwithstanding the inscribed covenant, he eats the local food and falls asleep. Not until a letter arrives from his parents' court does he awake, put a magic spell on the dragon, seize the pearl and, led by the shining letter along the same path, receive his clothing again. The animate clothing recognizes its wearer and embraces him; then he is ready to enter his parental court.

As an essay composed in gratitude for the work of Robert Grant, the present article has two sections. The first is a survey of recent interpretation of the boy's clothing in *The Hymn of the Pearl*. The second makes a new suggestion about the robe, one that reflects the likely Edessan and Syriac origin of the ballad. I wish to suggest that the author may have in mind the high-priestly robe that attracted so much attention in second Temple Judaism and whose reputation passed, even after the vestments were destroyed in the conflagration of 70 A.D., into both post-destruction Judaism and early Syriac-speaking Christianity, inasmuch as the two could be clearly separated in the second century in Mesopotamia and northern Syria.

Interpretation

Here is the question with which this essay approaches the *Hymn of the Pearl*: how are its readers or listeners to take the passages about the clothing of the hero? Those royal garments he stripped off at the beginning of his journey, and put back on at its end, have usually been taken as clues to the *Hymn*'s core meaning as a Gnostic allegory. The true meaning of the clothing, and of the *Hymn* as a whole, can then become a universal metaphor for humanity's catastrophic descent into the material world of alienation and reascent into the tranquil world of the spirit.

Suppose, however, that every word of the *Hymn of the Pearl* is neither an allegory nor a metaphor invoked to cloak some other experience. If the scholar should begin an investigation by stripping off convenient labels and supposing that a real experience lies not under, but within, the words of the *Hymn*, then its nearly universal scholarly interpretation as Gnostic can tabled for a time, and placed at the start of the *Hymn*'s Nachleben. Like Mani, scholars of the nineteenth and twentieth centuries have enjoyed a dualistic interpretation of the *Hymn*; unlike Mani, a genuine shaman, they have done so because they do not know how to apprehend a text which tells how a hero charmed a dragon in Egypt, slept, was awakened by a luminous eagle-letter, stole the dragon's treasured pearl, and returned to a royal court in Parthia.

Mani took himself to be the subject of the *Hymn* and gave it a dualistic interpretation to make it a befitting typological prophecy of himself. Mani was all: descending youth, priceless pearl, heavenly companion, reunited double at the court of the king of kings. Mani was not the vehicle of a divided mind, though—he actually saw an abyss running through the center of the cosmos, and took the *Hymn* to predict his own mission as savior and healer.[4]

---

[4] For an early study of the process, see W. Bousset, "Manichäisches in den Thomasakten, Zeitschrift für neutestamentliche Wissenschaft 18 (1917–1918): 1–39. See also Jason BeDuhn, *The Manichaean Body: In Discipline and Ritual* (Johns Hopkins University

What, then, is the remedy for the modern misprision of the *Hymn*, or for that matter of any ancient communication that speaks of experiences unknown and incomprehensible and unutterable in the present day? To understand why it has received the description given it since its first publication in 1871; to put that description in perspective by understanding the history of scholarship as an expression of the politics and preferences of the twentieth century schools where it was studied; to turn away from that and all later descriptions, to the text word-for-word, and the rich world of powers, human and invisible, that the text bespeaks.

It is a testimony to the ancient and continuing appeal of typological interpretation that the *Hymn of the Pearl* continues to be described as a Christian text despite the complete absence of the name of Jesus or the title Messiah, or the label Christian. Even its inclusion in *The Acts of Thomas* is no proof of its Christian content, as the example of Old Testament quotations in the New Testament readily show.

The work, which should be called rhythmic interpretation following its presumably original, Syriac title *madrosho*, instead recites in first person the story of an unnamed boy who, in the course of his adventures, becomes a young man. Many of the human beings and objects that feature in the *madrosho* are already known from previous stories in the scriptures of ancient Judaism, and many of these had been applied already to Jesus or his teaching, symbolically, in the first-century scriptures about him—the pearl, the dragon, the robe, the kingdom, the finding of the lost, for instance. Yet neither Jesus nor any follower of his appears in the *madrosho*, and the assumption that the work is Christian rests upon the typological interpretation that assumes the youth to be Adam, Adam-Christ, or a Christian. Again, its inclusion in the *Acts of Judas Thomas*, an adventurous Christian recounting of the missionary journey of the ascetic preacher Thomas, has led to the widespread assumption that although separately composed the work is rightly assigned to early Syriac Christianity.

Press, 2000), and idem, "The Leap of the Soul in Manichaeism," in *Il Manicheismo: Nuove Prospettive della Richerca*. A. Van Tongerloo & L. Cirillo, eds. (Turnhout: Brepols, 2005), pp. 9–26.

In addition, the work has long been assumed to be a Gnostic composition. In a brief and admiring entry on the work, Klauck[5] remarks that although certain "biblical motifs" that figure in the work "presents a possible link to a theology that is found elsewhere in non-Gnostic Syriac Christianity," he also insists that "this text lends itself with great facility to a gnostic reading."

If salvation through knowledge this is the criterion for early Christian (heretical) Gnosticism, then one of the themes of *The Hymn of the Pearl* is certainly germane. The forgetfulness and untimely sleep of the hero and his rescue from that state via a letter sent from above, setting into motion a chain of events that leads to his reunion with a garment and its "motions of knowledge" and affection in which he sees himself reflected.

The uncertainty that attends this text bespeaks the central problem of gnosticism as a heretical movement or interpretation within Christianity which is that the features of Gnosticism are also the features of much of Greek-speaking Christianity itself. Often forgotten is the assertion of two gods as a teaching by which early Christians identified heretical versus acceptable teaching.

Of key importance here is the opinion that a certain text "lends itself . . . to a gnostic reading." Long before the discovery of the Nag Hammadi texts, with their promise of greater first-hand knowledge of Gnosticism, scholars thought that the song fit that description.

This interpretive trend was aided by the lack, at the time, of acquaintance with Aramaic-speaking Christianity or its Jewish analogue the Babylonian Talmud, or studies of the connections between the Jewish communities and early Christianity, now being explored for both early Aramaic-speaking Christianity and in the period of the fourth century.[6] Considering that an examination of the Second Temple and rabbinic Jewish context for the *Hymn of the Pearl* is work that remains to be done, it is interesting to see that an entirely different tack has been taken with regard to the *Hymn of the Pearl*—an attempt to identify it with the culture of Parthia, to the east of Edessa where the madrosho was arguably composed.

---

[5] Hans-Josef Klauck, *The Religious Context of Early Christianity: A Guide to Graeco-Roman Religions*, trans. by Brian McNeil (Studies in the New Testament and Its World). (Edinburgh: T&T Clark, 2000).

[6] See, for example, Sebastian Brock, "Jewish Traditions in Syriac Sources," *Journal for the Study of Judaism* 30:2 (1979): 212–232.

James Russell, on the other hand, has recently argued that the hymn "is an epic... [that] might have been designed... to convey a Gnostic ideology, of Christian or Manichaean character or both, specifically to Armeno-Iranian listeners." Epic poetry was a characteristics of idiom Parthian nobility, and conveyed "martial valor, heroic values, and romantic dalliances," recited by a bard. (p. 33) This epic genre was "in the Iranian East... not an isolated genre among many, but the central social narrative of the Parthian period." Its subjects could be royal chronicles of war, a romance, or religious teaching, and although composed in Syriac and translated into Greek, in the polyglot marchlands between the Roman and Persian empires it could allude to earlier epics or romances, or religious teachings from varying religious communities.

Russell writes:

> The later documents of gnostic and mystical religion in the Iranian area show that the *Hymn of the Pearl* was indeed calibrated to address and impress an audience in that world—nowhere else does it fit so securely into a tradition of intimately-understood imagery (64)

Russell has located a Parthian analogue for nearly every item in the *Hymn of the Pearl*; of particular interest here is the robe which is stripped off before the journey and in which the boy is re-clothed at journey's near-end. In the robe, Russell finds the robe of honor adorned with the image of the king of kings to be reminiscent of the brocaded robes of Sasanian Iran. Russell remarks:

> No Aramaic speaker familiar with the story of Creation in Genesis would have failed to appreciate the way the poet takes the familiar portrait in brocade, sanctifies it with a Biblically marked term, and then makes of it a tableau vivant. The brilliant robe seems to be more than raiment—it is both a part of the Prince's restored spiritual body, and his astral self. (82)

Whatever might be meant by "astral self," it is time to turn to the garment itself as one of the central features of the madrosho.

The young boy received a burden (mawbla) from his royal parents (gazzan); this load itself is paradoxically large and light (*saggi'ā w-kallilā*, and includes, gold, silver, chalcedony, topaz, and diamond.

Providing this burden is the prelude to the divestiture of the robe of glory "which they had made for me in their love, and my purple toga that was woven to fit my stature." The stripping of the youth seems to allow for the inscription of the agreement in the heart to gain the pearl from the serpent in the midst of the sea of Egypt, because only after this agreement has been fulfilled will the youth be able to regain "the glorious robe and the toga that covers it."

In the course of the youth's descent to the serpent's lair, he disguises himself in the clothes of the Egyptians, which leads him to forget that he is the son of a king, and forget about the pearl. The letter that subsequently arrives from his parents and their court reminds him of his birth, the pearl, the robe and toga. This robe is a necessary precondition to his attainment of rule with his brother our grand vizier (pasgriban) and inheritance of the kingdom. The letter itself changes clothing: it has a voice, flies like an eagle, and itself represents a light, since it shone "like an imperial beacon" and is even capable of affection ("by its love it drew me ahead").

Thanks to the voice of the letter, the youth was able to avoid a dangerous place in Babylon and arrive at the border of his parents' kingdom. There he found "my splendid robe which I had shed, and the toga which covers it." Treasurers had carried it "from the heights of Hyrcania."

The history of the *Hymn*'s interpretation can be found in one of the most acute studies of the text, an expanded dissertation by Paul-Hubert Poirier. In Poirier's view, the hymn itself "must have originated in the Irano-parthian milieu at a date that cannot be fixed with certitude, but which only with difficulty could be after the beginning of the third century."[7] Poirier is mainly interested in the influence, and not the contents, of the *Hymn*; its manuscript history and the history of its interpretation both ancient and modern, and to provide a new critical edition of the Syriac text, with a translation. Therefore, apart from his plausible, but not original, conjecture that the text came from the part of the Syriac-speaking world in the Iranian domain, Poirier chiefly reports on the text as interpreted by others.

According to Poirier, that history can be divided into three stages: the first, from 1871–1904; the second, 1905–1933; and the third, 1933–1981. Each stage was dominated by a particular scholarly approach, in Poirier's view. The first period, opened by Wright's publication of

---

[7] Poirier has demonstrated that the *Hymn* is older than the *Acts of Thomas*, and was inserted in it at a later date: see Paul-Hubert Poirier, "*L'Hymne de la Perle* des *Actes de Thomas*: étude de la tradition manuscrite," *Orientalia Christiana Analecta* 205 (1978): 19–29, and *L'Hymne de la Perle des Actes de Thomas*: Introduction, texte-traduction, comentaire. Louvain-la-Neuve (Centre d'histoire des religions de Louvain-la-Neuve: 1981), pp. 169–304.

the Greek version of the *Hymn* within the Greek *Acts of Thomas*, was dominated by Preuschen's thorough analysis. Preuschen retreated from Nöldeke's attribution of the *Hymn* to Bardaisan, and interpreted it as an encoded Gnostic hymn to Christ and his descent into the flesh. In the second period, representing the approach of the religionsgeschichtliche Schule, Reitzenstein's work influenced other scholars to interpret the *Hymn* in the context of Iranian culture and religion. Finally, in the third period, Bornkamm's study of the *Acts of Thomas*, the *Hymn of the Pearl* becomes a pre-manichaean work—but gnostic—and thus adaptable to the self-presentation of Mani; Jonas agreed in considering the work "Irano-Manichaean." In this period, despite the widely-accepted character of Bornkamm's description, two scholars departed from the convention—Klijn and Quispel. Each approached the *Hymn* on the basis of wider studies of early Syriac-speaking Christianity, and each tended to see the *Hymn* as an outgrowth of the "encratite Christianity" of the region, or as a further interpretation of symbols found in the works of first-century Christianity. Menard combined the two approaches and saw the hymn as "pure gnostic doctrine" (159) in the context of Jewish Christianity.

Summing up his *Quellenforschung,* Poirier remarks that the "diversity of these hypotheses, which admit some variants according to which one makes of the hymn a work more or less gnostic, is indicative of the difficulty of interpreting the *Hymn of the Pearl* in one single perspective."[8] Poirier himself wants to interpret the *Hymn* from the perspective of the *Acts of Thomas*, and to concentrate, following Puech and Peterson, on "le thème thomasien de la gémellité." Seen from this angle, the *Hymn* represents "the salvation of the soul by the spirit, the restitution of man in his primitive and perfect syzygy, the conjunction of the psyche with the soma or the nous that has appeared to it."[9]

As Poirier demonstrates, scholars of the *Hymn of the Pearl* have largely, though not without exception, read the *Hymn of the Pearl* as if it were either Gnostic in origin or legitimate interpretation. In other words, it must be read as an esoteric work, because it is self-evidently one. Such an interpretation depends on the unexamined assumption that the work must be symbolic in the modern sense—that is, allegorical. The

[8] Poirier, p. 166.

[9] H.-Ch. Pueche, En quête de la gnose, II: Sur l'Evangile selon Thomas (Paris, 1978), p. 119.

descriptive words and actions in the *Hymn* must then become "metaphors" or "imagery," such that there is an esoteric meaning readily yielding itself to the interpreter with the proper literary key. Needless to say, this interpretation of a text by means of a key to unlock the true meaning beneath the veil of literality is itself an ancient practice, invented first to reinterpret Homer and then to make the Bible palatable, as Origen complained with respect to Heracleon's reading of the Gospel of John.

The company of scholars from Wright forward, despite its astonishing industry, has still stayed within very narrow confines. Modern scholarship on the *Hymn of the Pearl*, taken as an overall accumulation of interpretation, moves like iron filings toward the magnet of Gnosticism, or at least toward the magnet of the esoteric or referred sense. This approach also guides most Syriac scholars who have considered the *Hymn of the Pearl.* In his celebrated and influential study of early Syriac-speaking Christianity, Robert Murray addressed at length the fourth-century authors Aphrahat and Ephrem and their use of "clothing metaphors" for the incarnation.[10] Murray found that the declarative sentence *lbeš pagrā*, "he clothed himself with a body," the standard expression for the incarnation, appeared in the Acts of Judas Thomas, the originally Syriac Acts of John, and the *Doctrina Addai*, as well as the Syriac *Didascalia Apostolorum.*

Murray's concern, in part, was to show that Aphrahat and Ephrem employed the "regular, 'consecrated' use of a term which did not, after all, appear in the New Testament outside allusions to baptism in Rom. 13:14, Gal. 3:27 (or as "new man" Eph. 4:24, Gal. 3:10). But there was also more troubling appearance of this metaphor of Christ "putting on a body," which the "orthodox tradition... did not hastily abandon" even when "it could be exploited by heretics, whether docetists, using it to suggest an insubstantial body, or other Gnostics, using it of the psychikos Christos."[11]

An example of the latter, Murray thought, was in the *Hymn of the Pearl.* There, he wrote, "we find a variant of the 'clothing' image with features alien to the tradition reviewed so far." In the case of the young prince of the *Hymn*, "the application of the imagery is here dualistic

[10] Robert Murray, *Symbols of Church and Kingdom: A Study in Early Syriac Tradition.* Cambridge: Cambridge University Press, 1975.

[11] Murray, *Symbols*, p. 311.

and hostile to the body." Later, discussing the controversial tradition of the Holy Spirit as mother, which appears in another hymn preserved in the *Acts of Thomas*, Murray again refers to the meaning of the *Hymn*, which, in his opinion, differs from the ascetically-infused Acts in which it appears. This passage is worth quoting at length:

> The *Hymn of the Pearl* pictures the imprisoned soul as an exiled 'prince,' recalled by a letter from his Father the 'King of Kings', and his mother, the 'Queen of the East.' The latter is doubtless the Mother Spirit, the imagery of the whole poem serving to illustrate the Valentinian system or one like it. More explicitly related to our theme are the invocations of the Holy Spirit preceding baptism, which, like the *Hymn of the Pearl*, contain more Gnostic language than the narrative as a whole.[12]

The *Hymn of the Pearl* did not received sustained attention in Murray's book. In the short afterglow of the second Vatican Council, Murray, by training a scholar of the Old Testament, had turned to later Semitic authors to draw a comparison between their thought and that of western early Christianity on a topic that greatly occupied that Council—the nature of the church. Evidently Murray was influenced in his view of the *Hymn* by the views of A. Adam, whom he cites,[13] to view the *Hymn* as a Gnostic composition; but Murray does not argue the case. Apparently to Murray, as to most scholars, the *Hymn* is self-evidently Gnostic, and often viewed as an allegory of the escape of the spirit from the world of matter back, whence it came, to a heavenly kingdom.

One of the few scholars to depart from this assessment is the late Han Drijvers. Although he acknowledged that "a gnostic interpretation of the hymn is usual," he argued that, like the *Acts of Thomas* itself, the *Hymn* was a retelling of a common early Christian interpretation of Exodus. Still, Drijvers followed Klijn[14] in making the *Hymn* a symbolic interpretation of first-century Christian and Jewish belief. It is, Drijvers wrote, "a symbolic portrayal of the life of Adam, the man

---

[12] P. 317.

[13] A. Adam, *Die Psalmen des Thomas und das Perlenlied als Zeugnisse vorchristlicher Gnose, Beiheft zur Zeitschrift für die neutestamentliche Wissenschaft* 24 (Berlin, 1959).

[14] A.F.J. Klijn, *The Acts of Thomas*. (Supplements to *Novum Testamentum*. 5, 1972; 2ed. Supplements 108, 2003) Klijn's translation is based on William Wright's edition of the Syriac text in *Apocryphal Acts of the Apostles* (now repr. Piscataway, NJ: Gorgias Press, 2005).

who of his own free will left his Father's house, Paradise, with a part of his inheritance."[15]

Drijvers also indicates the importance of the divesting and re-clothing with a special garment. "The robe," he writes, "symbolizes the image of God, immortality, which man recovers when he is clothed with his heavenly second self, his twin brother Jesus." Here Drijvers interprets the *Hymn* by means of the *Acts of Thomas* with the latter's explicit reference to Jesus, the combat with Satan and corresponding ethical dualism, and the ultimate destination of a heavenly homeland.

He goes on to point out that the "symbolism" of departure and return that resembles the Exodus story of descent into Egypt and return to the land of promise has been bound, by the author of the *Hymn*, to the wedding garment of the heavenly bridal feast in Rev 3:5 and 19:7–9, where they are united to the heavenly bridegroom. Drijvers cites Sebastian Brock's analysis of "clothing metaphors" used in fourth-century Syriac writers, and in certain liturgical texts of the Syriac-speaking tradition. In a description of how the "robe of glory," understood both as the baptismal robe and the body of Christ, as well as the original nature of humanity by these sources, was also a high priestly robe, Brock points out that there is a connection between the first and second Adams in the temporal distribution of the robes: the first robe was the robe of glory given at creation, a characteristic of the angelic character of humanity; that robe was lost and replaced by "garments of skin"; the robe is regained thanks to the action of the Messiah, the second Adam, and conveyed in baptism, where humanity regains either its former state or its former state, improved, in view of the world to come.

Brock makes the intriguing suggestion, as far as I know unexplored in subsequent scholarship, that "the subsequent use of the robe imagery in Syriac literature could in fact be said to provide a remarkably illuminating commentary on the *Hymn of the Pearl*, the main difference lying in the much less negative evaluation of the world that is to be found in orthodox Syriac writers of later times."[16] Indeed, much of the imagery

---

[15] Han J.W. Drijvers, "The *Acts of Thomas*: Introduction," in *New Testament Apocrypha*, rev. ed., Edgar Hennecke and Wilhelm Schneemelcher, ET ed. by R. McL. Wilson, vol. 2: *Writings Related to the Apostles, Apocalypses and Related Subjects*. Louisville, KY: Westminster/John Knox Press, 1992, p. 332.

[16] Sebastian Brock, "Clothing Metaphors as a Means of Theological Expression in Syriac Tradition," in *Typus, Symbol, Allegorie bei den östlichen Vätern und ihren Parallelen im Mittelalter*, ed. M. Schmidt. Eichstätter Beiträge 4, 1982, pp. 11–38. Brock cites

in the *Hymn* finds a place in later religious literature of Mesopotamia, because it is already old by the time it is used in the *Hymn*.

Brock comments that "we have here, indeed, an excellent example of the Syriac genius for expressing profound theological truths in purely symbolic terms," and he points to an earlier work of Murray's as a confirmation.[17] For Brock, the *Hymn* is a "mysterious poem", but not so mysterious that it cannot be readily identified as an allegorical account, where Egypt is "the fallen world," and the robe is "his double."

At this point in the *Hymn* it becomes clear that there is a play upon doubling of identity, because the robe is a mirror to the youth, now older in age, as line 75 makes clear.

> Though I did not remember its rank (and dignity), having left it in my childhood
> At my Father's house,
> Yet suddenly when I faced the vestment, I felt as if seeing myself in a mirror,
> So closely it resembled me
> I saw the whole if it (reflected) in the whole of me, and again, all of me I faced in it.
> We were two by clear distinction, and yet one by identical form.

Not only is the robe a double of the youth; the treasurers who bring it are a double of each other; they are thus another image of the robe:

> The treasurers, too, who brought it to me, I saw in the same way,
> That, though being two, they were of the same form,
> For one and the same kingly character was stamped on them
> By the hand of my father who through them returned to me my deposit,
> My precious wealth.

The next sections of the madrāshā expand on the first lines having to do with the robe, by showing exactly how it is glorious or shining:

a prayer attributed to the martyr Cyriacus, whose acts are extant in Syriac: Hugo Gressmann, "Das Gebet des Kyriakos" in *Zeitschrift für die neutestamentliche Wissenschaft* 20 (1921): 23–35.

[17] In Brock's note 46, Murray's article, a summary of some of the themes of his book of the same year, is cited: "The theory of Symbolism in St. Ephrem's Theology," Parole de l'Orient 6/7 (1975/6): 1–20; as well as another work of Brock's, "The poet as theologian," Sobornost 7/4 (1978): 243–250.

> The glorious robe, decorated, bright and colorful
> With gold and beryls, chalcedonies and topazes,
> With sardonyxes of various hues, yet its coloring was constant
> With diamond stones all its seams were fastened
> And the full image of the King of Kings was depicted all over it in embroidery
> And variegated like the sapphire stone was again the coloring of this, too.

Immediately after this description it becomes apparent that the robe is animated and does, indeed, represent another self that merges with the narrator. For the moment, however, it is important to consider the features of the robe in relationship to the central jewel of the story. Only if he is clothed in the robe can the young man enter the court; but he will do so holding the pearl, as the last lines make clear. To the applause of the court and its servants, the king of kings will admit the boy "with the present of my pearl." (l. 105)

Here I would like to suggest two possible referents for the robe, ones that are closely connected by the time of the *Hymn*'s composition. The first one is the "robe of glory" known elsewhere in Syriac tradition, that signifies the original angelic appearance of the first man. The second one is the robe of the priest, allowing admission to the holy of holies and both reflecting and causing the transformation of the priest that allows him to keep company with divine beings.

Consider, for instance, the details of the robe. The hymn consistently calls the robe a "shining thing," zahithā, and refers to its zahiuthā, "brightness, or splendor." The same root appears in Dan. 2:31 and 4:33 to mean radiance, and ultimately goes back to *melammu* in Akkadian, to refer to the aura surrounding the gods and kings. (See also Syr. Ex. 34:29, on Moses' face).

More specifically, the stones mentioned as adorning the robe are both similar to some of the stones on the breastplate of the High Priest in Ex. 28:17–20, possessed by the King of Tyre in the Garden of Eden (Ezek. 28:13) and in the foundations of the New Jerusalem in Rev. 21:18–21. If the pearl itself is included, then the connection with those stones mentioned in connection with the New Jerusalem become even clearer: the twelve gates of the city are pearls, and the gates are "adorned with every jewel" (Rev. 21:19) The pearl in the *Hymn* was fashioned "on its height" (l. 84) referring to a temple, a high place, and perhaps heaven in the sense that it is occupied by the king, who has divine attributes in the poem. In addition, the stones have ancient associations with magical healing and with royalty.

In addition, the boy wears a scarlet toga: *tugā d'zhurithā*, in l. 10. That a scarlet toga is by this time a sign of imperial rule goes without saying; but in addition, the Syriac Old Testament uses the word for "red dye," zhurithā, for the threads of sacred cloth in the Temple: the paroqet at the entrance to the Holy of Holies, the screen for the entrance of the tablernacle, the screen for the gate of the court, the decorated band of the ephod, the breastplate, and the pomegranates along the edge of the high priest's robe. (Ex. 26:31, 26:36, 27:16, 28:8, 28:15, and 28:33).

As numerous recent studies have demonstrated, the first centuries B.C.E. and C.E. saw the production, among Jewish authors, of an extensive literature concerned with the Temple, its liturgy, and its priesthood, including the garments of the high priest.[18] Perhaps to the list of possible contexts of, and allusions in, the *Hymn of the Pearl* should be added the robe of the high priest, transferred to an Edessan context and adding meaning to a quest story related as well to the parable of the prodigal son and the pearl of great price.

[18] See C.T.R. Hayward, *The Jewish Temple: A Non-Biblical Sourcebook* (Routledge: London and New York, 1996) for translation and discussion of selected sources, not including sources from Qumran and canonical Jewish scripture, having to do with the Temple and its significance according to interpreters from Hecataeus of Abdera to Pseudo-Philo. See particularly his translation of, and comments on, Hebrew Ben Sira 45:6–22, pp. 63–72.

ORIGEN, CELSUS AND LUCIAN ON THE 'DÉNOUEMENT OF THE DRAMA' OF THE GOSPELS

Margaret M. Mitchell

Robert M. Grant is the master of the six-page seminal essay.[1] I am not. But in his honor I tried for once to emulate both his critical good sense and its formidable formal expression. I thought it might help that I was focusing on a single sentence in Origen's *contra Celsum*. I was mistaken.

> ἢ οἴεσθε τὰ μὲν τῶν ἄλλων μύθους εἶναί τε καὶ δοκεῖν, ὑμῖν δὲ τὴν καταστροφὴν τοῦ δράματος εὐσχημόνως ἢ πιθανῶς ἐφευρῆσθαι, τὴν ἐπὶ τοῦ σκόλοπος αὐτοῦ φωνήν, ὅτ' ἀπέπνει, καὶ τὸν σεισμὸν καὶ τὸν σκότον; (*c. Cels.* 2.55)[2]

The manner of the death of Jesus, as narrated in the gospels, especially Matthew, elicited from Celsus (in the name of his "Jew," and directed toward Jewish-Christians)[3] this head-wagging critique. The statement is part of a longer quotation from Celsus, but Origen thought the wording of this particular sentence important enough to quote again in 2.58. Right before our quotation the anti-Christian polemicist had trotted out the stories of other ancient heroes and gods (αἱ ἡρῳικαὶ ἱστορίαι [2.56]) who had died and then supposedly risen, as part of the larger argument seeking to falsify Christian claims on the grounds that Jesus had faked both his divine birth and his resurrection. Celsus then names the topic for scrutiny: Ἀλλ' ἐκεῖνο σκεπτέον, εἴ τις ὡς ἀληθῶς ἀποθανὼν ἀνέστη ποτὲ αὐτῷ σώματι ("But the point to be examined is whether anyone who *actually died* ever rose bodily"). Hence before critiquing the accounts of the resurrection (which he will famously do by attributing them to "hysterical women") Celsus has a preliminary

---

[1] For just two examples, see "Hellenistic Elements in 1 Corinthians," *Early Christian Origins. Studies in Honor of Harold R. Willoughby*, ed. A. Wikgren (Chicago: Quadrangle Books, 1961) 60–66; "'Holy Law' in Paul and Ignatius," *The Living Text: Essays in Honor of Ernest W. Saunders* (Lanham, MD: University Press of America, 1985) 65–71.

[2] Text of Marcel Borret, *Origène, contre Celse* (SC 132, 136, 147, 150, 227; Paris: Cerf, 1967–76; corrected ed. of vols. 1–2, 2005).

[3] All of bk. 2 of the *contra Celsum* is dedicated to "the Jew's" critique of Christians, bk. 1 to his face-off against Jesus himself (see 1.71; 2.1; 3.1).

charge: Jesus never really died, and hence never rose from the dead before being seen.[4] Whether Jesus *really* died depends entirely upon how one assesses the historical reliability of the gospel accounts of his death, especially when compared with other literary compositions, i.e., the Greek myths on the one hand, and the Jewish scriptural accounts on the other.[5] Celsus' rhetorical question insists that the Christian cannot have it both ways, i.e., deem the stories of those others μῦθοι while insisting their own narratives are something more, or something else.[6] Celsus and Origen, who as literary elites share the same παιδεία, use the same toolbox when it comes to testing narratives—μῦθοι and διηγήματα—for whether or not they are historically accurate.[7] Chiefly, as the passage itself sneeringly indicates, it comes down to whether an account can be demonstrated πιθανός, "persuasive."

Celsus' carefully worded riposte seems deliberately open to various interpretations. Some of the translation decisions involved are illustrated by a glance at the divergent renderings of Chadwick and Borret:

> Or do you think that the stories of these others[8] really are the legends which they appear to be, and yet that the ending of your tragedy is to be regarded as noble and convincing—his cry from the cross when he expired, and the earthquake and the darkness?[9]

---

[4] As Origen agrees: Ὁ γὰρ ἀληθῶς ἀποθανὼν εἰ ἀνέστη, ἀληθῶς ἀνέστη (*c. Cels.* 2.16).

[5] The method of σύγκρισις is common both to Celsus' charge and to Origen's defense (see *c. Cels.* 1.18; cf. 8.47–48).

[6] Origen makes the same argument in 1.31 about the historicity of the death of Jesus on behalf of others: Λεγέτωσαν οὖν οἱ βουλόμενοι ἀπιστεῖν τῷ Ἰησοῦν ὑπὲρ ἀνθρώπων ἀποτεθνηκέναι τρόπῳ σταυροῦ, πότερον οὐδὲ τὰς ἑλληνικὰς παραδέξονται καὶ βαρβαρικὰς πολλὰς ἱστορίας περὶ τοῦ τινας ὑπὲρ τοῦ κοινοῦ τεθνηκέναι καθαιρετικῶς τῶν προκαταλαβόντων τὰς πόλεις καὶ τὰ ἔθνη κακῶν· ἢ ἐκεῖνα μὲν γεγένηται οὐδὲν δὲ πιθανὸν ἔχει ὁ νομιζόμενος ἄνθρωπος πρὸς τὸ ἀποθανεῖν ἐπὶ καθαιρέσει μεγάλου δαίμονος καὶ δαιμόνων ἄρχοντος, ὑποτάξαντος ὅλας τὰς ἐπὶ γῆν ἐληλυθυίας ἀνθρώπων ψυχάς; On the charge of inconsistency, see 8.47: ἀποκληρωτικῶς τὰ μὲν σφέτερα παραδέχεσθαι τοῖς δ' ἀλλοτρίοις ἀπιστεῖν.

[7] See Robert M. Grant, *The Earliest Lives of Jesus* (New York: Harper & Brothers, 1961), 70, on how in *contra Celsum* Origen was facing down "an opponent whose way of looking at [the gospel stories] was much like his own."

[8] Zamolxis, Pythagoras, Rhampsinitus, Orpheus, Protesilaus and Heracles, all previously named as figures who falsified their deaths so as later to be regarded as risen (*c. Cels.* 2.55).

[9] Henry Chadwick, *Origen, contra Celsum* (Cambridge: Cambridge University Press, 1953), 109.

> Pensez-vous que les aventures des autres soient des mythes en réalité comme en apparence, mais que vous auriez inventé à votre tragédie un dénouement noble et vraisemblable avec son cri sur la croix quand il rendit l'âme, le tremblement de terre et les ténèbres?[10]

The most evident discrepancy here has to do with the translation of the Infinitive ἐφευρῆσθαι, for the term can mean either "find" or "invent."[11] Chadwick takes the former, and Borret the latter;[12] what is at stake in each case is whether the charge accents the *reception* of the gospels (taken as plausible) or their *rhetorical invention* (to be seen by others as plausible). In turn, the adverbs εὐσχημόνως and πιθανῶς would either be acting adjectivally in reference to τὴν καταστροφήν ("the ending of the tragedy is found to be honorable and credible"),[13] or adverbially to the infinitive ἐφευρῆσθαι ("the ending of the tragedy has been invented in a fashion that is honorable[14] and credible"). This is where what appears at first to be an uneven parallelism between εἶναί τε καὶ δοκεῖν[15] and ἐφευρῆσθαι is most suggestive. Perhaps Celsus (speaking as "the Jew") was deliberately using ἐφευρῆσθαι to imply both sides of εἶναί τε καὶ δοκεῖν—how true the gospels *really are* (based on their authors' inventions) and how true the gospels *seem to be* to their readers.[16] By the neat parallelism he in effect suggests that among Christians readerly credulity and authorial fabrication are but two sides of the same coin.[17] The following translation may better allow for both possibilities:

---

[10] Borret, *Origène, contre Celse*, 2.415.

[11] LSJ, *s.v.*: I.1. find, discover, find anywhere; 2. discover besides; 3. bring in besides; II.1. find out, invent, of arts; 2. find out, discover.

[12] So also John Granger Cook, *The Interpretation of the New Testament in Greco-Roman Paganism* (Studien und Texte zu Antike und Christentum 3; Tübingen: Mohr Siebeck, 2000; Peabody, MA: Hendrikson Publishers, 2002), 51: "but that you have invented a noble and persuasive denouement of your tragedy."

[13] Herbert Weir Smyth, *Greek Grammar* (Cambridge: Harvard University Press, 1920), para. 1097a; this is how Chadwick takes them.

[14] Here, too, we have a options: "with grace and dignity, like a gentleman," and "later also, noble, honourable" (LSJ, *s.v.* εὐσχημόνως; but note that the adjective can also have a negative meaning: "in a bad sense, with an outside show of goodness, specious in behaviour"). If we favor the latter, perhaps a translation "that confers purported honor" or "that appears to be noble" would be appropriate.

[15] Cf. Origen's Καὶ τοῦτο δὲ εἰ μὴ πλάσμα ἐστίν, ὥσπερ ἔοικεν εἶναι πλάσμα (*c. Cels.* 3.33), in reference to the tale of Cleomedes the Astypalean.

[16] The other use of the verb on the lips of Celsus is similarly ambiguous (*c. Cels.* 7.2).

[17] Surely Lucian would agree, as shown by the fact that his Peregrinus when play-acting a Christian both interpreted and composed literature (*Peregr.* 11: καὶ τῶν βίβλων τὰς μὲν ἐξηγεῖτο καὶ διεσάφει, πολλὰς δὲ αὐτὸς καὶ συνέγραφεν). We shall return to Lucian below.

> Or do you suppose that the exploits of these others both are and seem to be "myths," but in your case[18] the dénouement of the drama—that is, his utterance while on the stake when he was breathing his last, and "the earthquake" and the darkness—has found form as honorable or credible?

My translation also seeks to reflect an awareness of the critical vocabulary being used. It was standard fare in the *progymnasmata* to teach students how to confirm or refute[19] the historicity of μῦθοι or διηγήματα based upon the criterion of πιθανότης. Theon of Alexandria's advice for the composite elements of the τόπος of credibility is as follows:

> ἐὰν τοίνυν ἀνασκευάζωμεν τὴν διήγησιν ἐκ τοῦ ἀπιθάνου, οὕτως ἐπεξελευσόμεθα, δεικνύντες ὅτι καὶ τὸ πρόσωπον ἀπίθανόν ἐστι καὶ τὸ πραχθὲν καὶ ὁ τόπος ἐν ᾧ ἡ πρᾶξις, ὁμοίως δὲ καὶ ὁ χρόνος καὶ ὁ τρόπος καὶ ἡ αἰτία τῆς πράξεως (Theon, *prog.* 4.218 [Spengel 2.94]).[20]

Both fictional narratives and myths (the latter being for him by definition a false account)[21] can be differentiated from historical accounts by prov-

---

[18] Borret's translation effectively renders ὑμῖν twice, and the infinitive as though active voice which seems unacceptable. The word order with the μὲν/δέ accents the contrast between the "pagan" myths and those of the Christians. My translation tries to accent this by rendering the Dative ὑμῖν as a dative of relation or reference (Smyth, *Greek Grammar*, para. 1495, 1496). It is also possible, perhaps preferable, to take the ὑμῖν as a dative of agent with a perfect passive infinitive, with Smyth, *Greek Grammar*, para. 1488. Then one would translate: "has been invented by you in an honorable and credible way," or "has been regarded/found by you honorable and credible." But the former undermined by the semantic context, for Celsus's Jew does not accuse his addressees—"Jews who believe in Jesus"—of having invented the gospels, but the disciples of Jesus (see 2.13, 15, 16, 26; cf. 2.48), and Origen's response (2.56) shows he thinks the charge has to do with whether believers regard the gospels as myths (not whether they composed them). The syntactical and lexical ambiguity likely intended, should be reflected in the translation.

[19] The importance of the rhetorical techniques of κατασκευή and ἀνασκευή for Origen's exegesis was shown definitively by Grant, *Earliest Lives of Jesus*, 38–79.

[20] "Now if we refute a narrative on the basis of its being unpersuasive, we shall proceed in this way, demonstrating that both the person and the thing done and the place at which the deed was done are unpersuasive; likewise also the time and the manner and the cause of the deed."

[21] Simply put in Theon, *prog.* 3.172 [Spengel 2.72]: λόγος ψευδὴς εἰκονίζων ἀλήθειαν. The philosophical problem of how a false story can tell truth is of course more complicated, especially for one with Platonising tendencies. As scholars have long observed, Celsus is himself inconsistent in his attitude toward the traditional myths, our passage being the extreme point of scepticism (see Carl Andresen, *Logos und Nomos: die Polemik des Kelsos wider das Christentum* [Arbeiten zur Kirchengeschichte 30; Berlin: de Gruyter, 1955] 44–78, esp. 46–55 on the relationship between Celsus' philosophical and cultural commitments and his argumentative purposes). Perhaps some of the inconsistency is due to his invocation here of the dramatic metaphor, and the complex role of myth in drama (Andresen notes that Celsus connects μῦθος with comedy at 6.49). A key source here is of course Aristotle, who famously mediated the Platonic position in discussion

ing them unpersuasive on six grounds: the person involved, the action described, the place in which it occurred, the time, the manner and the cause of the deed. This may explain "the Jew's" phrasing, τὴν ἐπὶ τοῦ σκόλπος αὐτοῦ φωνήν, which accents the place from which Jesus' statement was uttered as a key to its unbelievability.[22] The darkness and the earthquake are presumably questionable under the category of inherent implausibility (not πραχθέντα that happen every day), or perhaps coincidence of time (χρόνος). While the term εὐσχημόνως is not found in the standard list of τόποι for discerning a true from false narrative, it fits nicely the criterion of πρέπον, "that which is seemly."[23] This accords with the fact that the adverb or adjective εὐσχήμων was commonly used among imperial period writers of a noble death (in at least one case, by influence of the wording of Euripides's tragic account of the death of Polyxena).[24] Hence the accusation suggests that the dishonor of the crucifixion (hardly meeting the tragic requirement of "dignity" or "seriousness"),[25] redounds to its implausibility—like any other μῦθος—on the grounds of manner (τρόπος) or even the cause

of μῦθος (his term for the "plot" of a tragedy) in its relationship to ἱστορία and truth (see the key passage in 1451a–b, and the valuable exegesis of it in James M. Redfield, *Nature and Culture in the Iliad* Durham: Duke University Press, 1994) expanded ed., original Chicago: University of Chicago Press, 1975] 52–68). We cannot here take up the important topic of tragedy and religious cult, but see, e.g., Eveline Krummen, "Ritual und Katastrophe: Rituelle Handlung und Bildersprache bei Sophokles und Euripides," *Ansichten griechischer Rituale: Geburtstags-Symposium für Walter Burkert*, ed. Fritz Graf (Stuttgart/Leipzig: Teubner, 1998), 296–325, with further bibliography.

[22] Elsewhere Origen does take up the content of the words, as at *c. Cels.* 2.36, where he counters the objection that what Jesus said from the cross can hardly compare with Alexander the Great's quotation of *Il.* 5.340 in reference to his blood as not being "ichor such as flows in the veins of the blessed gods" (see also 7.55).

[23] Theon focuses on the heading of πιθανόν; Aphthonius, for instance, includes also σαφές, δυνατόν, ἀκόλουθον, πρέπον, συμφέρον (*prog.* 6 [H. Rabe, *Aphthonius, Progymnasmata* (Rhetores Graeci 10; Leipzig: Teubner, 1926) 14]).

[24] Euripides, *Hecuba* 568–569: ἡ δὲ καὶ θνῄσκουσ' ὅμως, πολλὴν πρόνοιαν εἶχεν εὐσχήμως πεσεῖν ("but she, even in death, took chiefest thought decorously to fall" [trans. Arthur S. Way, LCL]). The passage is quoted by Ps-Lucian, *Demonsthenis Encomium* 47 (with some manuscripts reading εὐσχήμων for εὐσχήμως), who follows up with the question: "If a girl acted thus, will Demosthenes judge an ignoble death preferable to a noble death (Δημοσθένης δὲ εὐσχήμονος θανάτου βίον προκρινεῖ ἀσχήμονα...)?" See also Dionysius of Halicarnassus, *Isoc.* 5.17; Polemo, *Decl.* 2.55; Maximus of Tyre, *Dialexeis* 30.5.

[25] As emphasized by Malcolm Heath, *The Poetics of Greek Tragedy* (London: Duckworth, 1987), 33–35, who cites Aristotle's definition of tragedy as an imitation of a πρᾶξις σπουδαῖα, "serious action" (*Poet.* 1449b24), with the chief characters being σπουδαῖοι "serious men" (i.e., Homeric and other heroes). In *c. Cels.* 2.36, Origen responds to Celsus' sarcastic invocation of a Euripidean quotation with the insistence that, while Celsus jokes, the gospels are σπουδαῖα, "serious works."

(αἰτία) implied in this type of death.[26] Having been accused on such conventional grounds, Origen responds in kind.[27] He appeals to the τόπος of the action—while "impaled on a spike"—as a differentiating mark between the supposedly dead and raised heroes and Jesus. Since Jesus's death and burial took place in public,[28] cast before the very eyes of the Jewish populace, Origen argues, it could not have been a story merely fabricated (πλάσασθαι), like those told of the heroes in each of their separate locations.[29] Here we see another point of contact with the school tradition, in which one of four types of narrative (alongside μυθικόν, and in distinction from ἱστορικόν) is the δραματικὸν διήγημα ("dramatic narrative"), that is by definition a πλασματικὸν διήγημα, a "fabricated narrative," such as is found in tragedies.[30] This leads us to the main focus of this essay, "the Jew's" characterization of the gospel story of Jesus' dying moments as ἡ καταστροφὴ τοῦ δράματος.

---

[26] αἰτία/αἴτιον of course being the term also for judicial "charge" on which Jesus was executed (Mk 15:26; Mt 27:37; Jn 18:38; 19:4, 6; Lk 23:4, 14, 22).

[27] Grant wryly notes that Origen, though by this time in his life he had come to see the difficulty of proof of historicity (κατασκευή), still was caught in the rules of this game: "The only answer, after all, to historical criticism is more historical criticism" (*Earliest Lives of Jesus*, 71). Although Origen in general disputes the σύγκρισις Celsus has set up between the narratives of heroes and that of Jesus, he still argues the case on particulars, as well.

[28] Μή ποτ' οὖν *πρὸς ἄλλοις αἰτίοις* τοῦ σταυρωθῆναι τὸν Ἰησοῦν καὶ τοῦτο δύναται συμβάλλεσθαι τῷ αὐτὸν ἐπισήμως ἐπὶ τοῦ σταυροῦ ἀποτεθνηκέναι, ἵνα μηδεὶς ἔχῃ λέγειν ὅτι ἑκὼν ὑπεξέστη τῆς ὄψεως τῶν ἀνθρώπων καὶ ἔδοξεν ἀποτεθνηκέναι οὐκ ἀποτέθνηκε δὲ ἀλλ' ὅτ' ἐβουλήθη πάλιν ἐπιφανεὶς ἐτερατεύσατο τὴν ἐκ νεκρῶν ἀνάστασιν; (*c. Cels.* 2.56). Origen names this very purpose as a cause [αἴτιον] of Jesus' decision to die this kind of death, to publicly present his demise so no suspicion of its falsification would later be possible.

[29] Note the deliberate phrasing, in regard to the heroes: Ἕκαστος μὲν γὰρ τῶν λεγομένων *κατὰ τοὺς τόπους* ἡρώων βουληθεὶς ἂν ἐδυνήθη ἑαυτὸν ὑπεκκλέψαι τῆς ὄψεως τῶν ἀνθρώπων καὶ πάλιν κρίνας ἐπανελθεῖν πρὸς οὓς καταλέλοιπεν (*c. Cels.* 2.56). This fits the emphatic linking of each hero with a geographical place in 2.55: Ὅπερ οὖν καὶ Ζάμολξιν ἐν Σκύθαις φασί, τὸν Πυθαγόρου δοῦλον, καὶ αὐτὸν Πυθαγόραν ἐν Ἰταλίᾳ καὶ Ῥαμψίνιτον ἐν Αἰγύπτῳ... καὶ μὴν καὶ Ὀρφέα ἐν Ὀδρύσαις καὶ Πρωτεσίλαον ἐν Θεσσαλίᾳ καὶ Ἡρακλέα ἐπὶ Ταινάρῳ καὶ Θησέα.

[30] See Ps-Hermogenes, *prog.* 2.11–14 [ed. H. Rabe, *Hermogenes Opera* (Rhetores Graeci 6); Leipzig: Teubner, 1913]: Εἴδη δὲ διηγήματος βούλονται εἶναι τέτταρα· τὸ μὲν γὰρ εἶναι μυθικόν, τὸ δὲ πλασματικόν, ὃ καὶ δραματικὸν καλοῦσιν, οἷα τὰ τῶν τραγικῶν, τὸ δὲ ἱστορικόν, τὸ δὲ πολιτικὸν ἢ ἰδιωτικόν. That Origen knows such a schoolroom distinction is clear from his preamble to the argument defending the historicity of the gospels, in which he acknowledges how difficult it is—if not impossible—to prove any story true (*c. Cels.* 1.42: Πρὶν ἀρξώμεθα τῆς ἀπολογίας, λεκτέον ὅτι σχεδὸν πᾶσαν ἱστορίαν, κἂν ἀληθὴς ᾖ, βούλεσθαι κατασκευάζειν ὡς γεγενημένην καὶ καταληπτικὴν ποιῆσαι περὶ αὐτῆς φαντασίαν τῶν σφόδρα ἐστὶ χαλεπωτάτων καὶ ἐν ἐνίοις ἀδύνατον), because the two examples he gives are the stock ones of the Trojan war and the Oedipus cycle (as also, e.g., in Dio Chrysostom, *Or.* 11).

This expression, which forms the centerpiece of Celsus' sentence, is translated by Chadwick "the ending of your tragedy" and Borret "à votre tragédie un dénouement...." The nouns in apposition to it in the sentence unmistakably identify this καταστροφὴ τοῦ δράματος with three episodes in Matthew's Gospel: the darkness, the cry, and the earthquake (Mt 27:45–53).[31] The referent is easy, but what is the rhetorical weight of this characterization, put by Celsus on the lips of his fictional Jewish interlocutor? Do we have here a technical term, and if so, in what realm(s), and with what resonances? Is it a positive or a negative characterization? In particular, is it being used descriptively, as pointing to the gospel's actual suitability to dramatic categories, or rather should we see it as an ironic jab pointing to the opposite—that the gospel is so far from real drama that calling it such throws into relief the literary pretensions and misapprehensions of the gullible Christian readers? These questions are complicated by the ambiguity in the syntax of the sentence, noted above: in whose eyes does this gospel episode deserve the designation ἡ καταστροφὴ τοῦ δράματος—Celsus/the Jew, the Christian authors who so fashioned it, the Christian readers who accepted it as such, or educated non-Christians whom they presume will appreciate the work in this way?

Although the two nouns are quite common, surprisingly this exact phrase conjoining them occurs only six times in ancient Greek literature, all save one clustered in the last decades of the second and early decades of the third centuries.[32] To unpack the resonances of the double noun

[31] All three terms, σκότος, φωνή, and σεισμός, are in the narrative itself; perhaps disparagingly, Celsus uses the term σκόλοψ for the cross, rather than σταυρός (Mt 27:32), a predilection he shares with Lucian's depiction of Jesus' form of death (see Jacques Schwartz, "Du Testament de Lévi au Discours véritable de Celse," *Revue d'histoire et de philosophie religieuses* 40 [1960] 126–45, 128–29, 132; more on this below). In having to defend the Matthean account, Origen had to swallow some of his own discomfort with it (so Grant, *Earliest Lives of Jesus*, 98: "Origen is not much impressed by the story in Matthew, which refers to the 'fear' of the witnesses and makes their faith depend on miracles. He finds more meaningful the account in Mark, where the centurion understood the events in proportion to his ability to understand...he understood the real miracle, which was the quick death of Jesus, the one who had power to lay down his life").

[32] The three authors are Lucian (3: *merc. cond.* 10; *Alex.* 60; *Peregr.* 37), Celsus (1, cited twice by Origen, in *c. Cels.* 2.55, 58), and Clement of Alexandria (1: *Quis dives salvetur* 40.3, in reference to the end of a man's life); the single earlier use, in plural, not singular, is Polybius 3.48.8, cited below. In the total I have not included the four references in Byzantine literature which are allusions to either Polybius' or Clement's use (the former in John of Damascus, *sacra parallela* 95.1173; 96.141; the latter in Constantinus VII Porphyrogenitus, *de sententiis* 121.22–23; Nicephoros Gregoras, *historia*

phrase we must begin with the lexicographical possibilities for each term. In both instances we have a word with a range of senses: a simple sense (δρᾶμα as "action," καταστροφή "overturning"), a specialized use in the world of the theatre, and a metaphorical extension of the latter to real life events that are seen to partake of theatrical elements. LSJ gives 3 glosses for δρᾶμα in its theatrical sense: "action represented on the stage, *drama, play*; metaph. *stage-effect* of any kind"; also *tragical event*.[33] None of these limits the term δρᾶμα to "tragedy," per se (as Chadwick and Borret both render it),[34] though many ancient plays of course were tragedies, and could be referred to by the generic term for stage-works, δράματα. While the Christian reader might assume the death of Jesus was, as LSJ allows, a "tragic event," it is quite certain Celsus would not agree. In the context, Celsus more likely might have meant the second of these, "stage-effect," as he is arguing that Jesus faked his own death, so that when he "reappeared" he could claim he had risen from the dead, as he had foretold.

If the word δρᾶμα alone does not unambiguously refer to "tragedy," perhaps it is the conjunction with καταστροφή that has suggested this to translators. For καταστροφή, LSJ's second entry gives the following meanings: "*end, close, conclusion*" (noting the common phrase καταστροφὴ βίου, "i.e. death") and they cite a special theatrical sense, "in the drama, *dénouement, ending*."[35] Taking this into account, at the very least the word has a double sense when used of the death of Jesus—the "death-scene of the play" as well as "the ending of the play."

Yet as Celsus well knows, the Gospel of Matthew does not end with the death of Jesus, but the resurrection and commissioning scenes in chapter 28 that Matthew had added to Mark's cliff-hanger ending. Here Borret's French term "dénouement" has a special nuance Chadwick's "ending" does not. A loan word into English, as well, "dénouement" comes from the Old French "desnoer," from Latin *nodare/nodus*, meaning "to untie a knot." As such, it is a literal and deliberate equivalent of the Aristotelian conceptualization of the tragic plot as made up of δέσις and λύσις, literally "tying and unbinding": Ἔστι δέ πάσης τραγῳδίας

romana 3.72). There is also a cognate periphrasis, with the verb καταστρέφειν + the noun δρᾶμα in Heliodorus, *Aethiop.* 1.3.1, which I thank Mr. Jeffrey Jay for calling to my attention.

[33] Translations of LSJ, *s.v.* (p. 448).

[34] Borret appears to follow Chadwick here, substituting "dénouement" for "ending."

[35] LSJ, *s.v.* (p. 915).

τὸ μὲν δέσις τὸ δὲ λύσις.[36] The distinction (much studied, of course)[37] is meant to define an elusive but real shift in the plot movement of a tragedy, as Aristotle goes on to delineate it:

> λέγω δὲ δέσιν μὲν εἶναι τὴν ἀπ' ἀρχῆς μέχρι τούτου τοῦ μέρους ὅ ἔσχατόν ἐστιν ἐξ οὗ μεταβαίνει εἰς εὐτυχίαν ἢ εἰς ἀτυχίαν, λύσιν δὲ τὴν ἀπὸ τῆς ἀρχῆς τῆς μεταβάσεως μέχρι τέλους.[38]

If the moment of Jesus' death in Matthew's narrative is viewed as "the dénouement of the play," then it is the moment of μετάβασις, "tragic transformation," for the hero.[39] Whether from good to bad or bad to good of course depends on the eye of the viewer.[40] And that is perhaps precisely what the carefully-chosen adverb εὐσχημόνως (and the introductory ὑμῖν) is suggesting.[41]

Yet it is not unmistakably clear (as Chadwick and Borret assume) that Celsus's καταστροφή *is* simply equivalent to Aristotelian tragical λύσις, or his other key term, περιπέτεια ("dramatic reversal")—especially since Aristotle himself never uses the word καταστροφή for this aspect of a tragic plot.[42] Even if not a technical term used exclusively

---

36 Aristotle, *Poetica* 1455b. See Stephen Halliwell, *Aristotle's Poetics* (Chicago: University of Chicago Press, 1998) 211 n. 14 on Aristotle's use of the term, and various English translations.

37 See, for example, the fine treatment of Anne Pippin Burnett, *Catastrophe Survived* (Oxford: Oxford University Press, 1971) esp. 1–17 on various types of περιπέτεια (major, minor, positive, negative) in Aristotle and the tragedians.

38 *Poet.* 1455b: "I mean this, that the complication is the part from the beginning up to the point which immediately precedes the occurence of a change from bad to good fortune or from good fortune to bad; dénouement is from the beginning of the change down to the end" (trans. W. Hamilton Fyfe, LCL).

39 This has always been a sticking point for those who seek to understand the gospels as tragedy—i.e., how is Jesus like and unlike a tragic hero. Does he make a "tragic error (ἁμαρτία) imposed on him by "the limitations or contradictions of his culture," like Agamemnon, or suffer from those of others, like Achilles (on this understanding of Aristotle see Redfield, *Nature and Culture in the Iliad*, 88–107)? Is his moment of transformation from good to bad or bad to good, or neither? And how do scenes like Mk 8:27ff. function as an Aristotelian ἀναγνώρισις, when it is not the hero who has the recognition, but his disciples? For sample works, see Gilbert G. Bilezikian, *The Liberated Gospel: A Comparison of the Gospel of Mark and Greek Tragedy* (Grand Rapids: Baker Book House, 1977) and Stephen H. Smith, "A Divine Tragedy: Some Observations on the Dramatic Structure of Mark's Gospel," in David E. Orton, ed., *The Composition of Mark's Gospel* (Brill's Readers in Biblical Studies 3; Leiden: Brill, 1999), 230–52.

40 Aristotle thought the movement of the wicked from bad fortune to good the most "untragic" type of plot (ἀτραγῳδότατον [*Poet.* 1452b]), which is how the non-Christian viewer would presumably view the executed criminal Jesus' return from the dead.

41 That is, ὑμῖν, "in your eyes."

42 In 1452b Aristotle gives the μέρη τραγῳδίας as πρόλογος, ἐπεισόδιον, ἔξοδος, and χορικόν. Attempts to map the Aristotelian categories onto existing tragedies are

for a structural part of a tragedy, the word, in its sense of "ending," could be used in relation to tragedies. In book 3 of his *History* Polybius uses our exact same phrase (in the plural) in an analogy he brings against other historians who violated their craft by their treatment of Hannibal's crossing of the Alps:

> It is probably for these reasons that they fall into a situation like that of the tragedians (οἱ τραγῳδιογράφοι). For in all their cases the denouements of the dramas (αἱ καταστροφαὶ τῶν δραμάτων) have a need to add a *deus ex machina* (μηχανή), because they took as their initial plot lines[43] things that are false and beyond reason (διὰ τὸ τὰς πρώτας ὑποθέσεις ψευδεῖς καὶ παραλόγους λαμβάνειν). The historiographers (οἱ συγγραφεῖς) must of necessity be similarly affected, and make heroes and gods appear, since they have as their starting point (ἀρχαί) things that are incredible (ἀπίθανοι) and false (ψευδεῖς).[44]

Here Polybius uses our exact phrase to refer to tragic-styled endings in purportedly historiographical accounts, which are implausible and false.[45] The assumption behind Polybius' complaint is that tragedies and histories should be worlds apart; it is the former that are defined by their beginnings (ἀρχαί) and their dénouements (καταστροφαί),[46] which are of necessity inseparably linked, for an action which begins in falsehood must culminate in falsehood. What Polybius regards as the prototypical dramatic dénouement (καταστροφὴ τοῦ δράματος) is the μηχανή, the incredible arrival of gods and heroes lowered or otherwise contrived onto the stage to end the action.[47] When that happens, he infers, we all know we are in the realm of fiction, even if we read this from self-styled historians (συγγραφεῖς), for it is an index that, having

of course legion, and the problems well known. In Walter Jens, ed., *Die Bauformen der griechischen Tragödie* (Munich: Wilhelm Fink, 1971), the term καταστροφή plays no role in the analyses; nor is it found among the technical terms of Greek tragedy in, for instance, Heath, *Poetics of Greek Tragedy* (though he does use an English neologism "eucatastrophic" for happy endings in tragedy [17, 31]), or P.E. Easterling, ed., *The Cambridge Companion to Greek Tragedy* (Cambridge: Cambridge University Press, 1997).

[43] For this translation of ὑπόθεσις see Robert M. Grant, *Irenaeus of Lyons* (London: Routlege, 1997) 47–49.

[44] Polybius 3.48.8–9.

[45] F.W. Walbank, *A Historical Commentary on Polybius*, 2 vols. (Oxford: Clarendon, 1957) 1.382: "an end; but also the dénouement of a dramatic plot."

[46] Yet in introducing the dramatic conceit in 3.47.8 Polybius appears to treat καταστροφή as not identical with ἔξοδος.

[47] Decried also by Aristotle (*Poet.* 1454a–b, though he did allow it for an action outside the play itself), and parodied by Aristophanes, and others after him, including Lucian (Wieland Schmidt, "Der *Deus ex machina* bei Euripides," diss. Universität Tübingen, 1964, esp. 5–35).

not had facts from which to start, they must end in the wildly fictional and implausible (ἀπίθανος).

This passage has much in common with Celsus' charge against the gospels. Like Polybius, "the Jew" critiques the gospel accounts of Jesus from their ἀρχή forward, on the assumption that a man who lied about his birth would also lie about (and stage) his death.[48] By terming the narrative of the death of Jesus ἡ καταστροφὴ τοῦ δράματος he may be characterizing the evangelist Matthew as a tragedian who was stuck with the problem of how to end his narrative, and hence pulled improbable events out of the hat to do so. And yet both Celsus and Origen know well that that is precisely what the evangelist does not do—i.e., he does not bring Jesus down off the cross in a miraculous way,[49] employing a *deus ex machina* contrivance,[50] despite the fact that the earthquake and darkness[51] provide just the right theatrical setting for such an outcome. At any rate both Celsus and Polybius appear to use the phrase ἡ καταστροφὴ τοῦ δράματος to mock the literary pretensions of others, suggesting that what is meant as tragic, serious and true, because of its clumsy stage-engineering comes off as comic and disqualified by virtue of self-evident melodramatic unrealism.[52]

---

[48] *c. Cels.* 1.28–30.

[49] Origen also sought to rebut the charge that Jesus did no gennai=on e!rgon, "noble act," "geniuine act," on the cross (like laugh at his pain and mock his killers) by saying his noble act is the miracles wrought to this day in his name. Hence Origen agrees with Celsus that the plot raises literary expectations of an ensuing rescue (in the categories of Peter Burian, "Myth into *muthos*: the shaping of tragic plot," P.E. Easterling, ed., *The Cambridge Companion to Greek Tragedy* [Cambridge: Cambridge University Press, 1997] 178–208, 186–90), but he located that expected rescue in the time of the church.

[50] The statement which follows our passage points out the inconsistency that while alive, Jesus did not help himself, but after he died he rose and showed the signs of his woulds. See also Origen's statement at *c. Cels.* 2.69: Εἴπερ οὖν ἀπὸ τῶν εὐαγγελίων μεμαθηκότες ὅτι οὐ γέγονεν εὐθὺς ἀφανὴς ἀπὸ τοῦ σκόλοπος ἐγκαλεῖν οἴονται τῷ λόγῳ, *μὴ πλασαμένῳ*, ὡς ἐκεῖνοι ἠξίωσαν, τὸ εὐθὺς αὐτὸν ἀφανῆ γενέθαι ἀπὸ τοῦ σκόλοπος *ἀλλὰ τὸ ἀληθὲς ἱστορήσαντι*, πῶς οὐκ εὔλογον πιστεῦσαι αὐτοὺς καὶ τῇ ἀναστάσει αὐτοῦ...

[51] Earlier, in *c. Cels.* 2.33 Origen adduced the supporting testimony of Phlegon to verify the historicity of an enclipse during the reign of Tiberius (Grant notes that Origen had in fact doubted a world-wide eclipse in his Matthew commentary; see *Earliest Lives of Jesus*, 97).

[52] Grant, *Irenaeus*, 42–43, drew attention to Irenaeus' continual mocking of Gnostic myths for containing τραγῳδία πολλὴ...καὶ φαντασία (*Adv. haer.* 1.1.8). See also the same association of melodramatic death with tragedy in Heliodorus, *Aethiop.* 1.3.1–2, where Chariclea calls on her attackers to kill her and Theagenes by "bringing to an end the drama surrounding us" (δρᾶμα τὸ περὶ ἡμᾶς καταστρέψαντες). The narrator characterizes her speech as ἡ μὲν ταῦτα ἐπετραγῴδει (1.3.2). See also 7.8.1, where the end of brotherly enmity is described as εἰς κωμικὸν ἐκ τραγικοῦ τὸ τέλος κατέστρεφε, precisely the theme we shall be exploring below.

Both Celsus and Polybius were speaking metaphorically, of course, of textual composition being akin to stragecraft. An exact description of such a staged dramatic ending may be found in Hero, a mechanical writer of the second or late first century B.C.E. In his *Automatopoetica* he details the construction and employment of a "puppet-stage" for putting on mini-dramas for an audience:

> Now, the ancients employed a simple form of dramatic setting (διάθεσις).[53] For after the front panel of the puppet stage[54] was opened, a face appeared painted on it, and it closed and opened its eyes repeatedly. But when the front panel was closed and then opened again, the face was no longer to be seen, but painted figures which had been outfitted for some tale (μῦθος).

Hero then describes one theatrical production—of the μῦθος about Nauplius—that he thought was especially well done. It included episodes (separated by the opening and closing of the curtain panel) of ship-building so lifelike as to merit the designation καθάπερ ἐπὶ τῆς ἀληθείας, of ships sailing in a row on the open water, a simulated storm at sea, the shipwreck, a fire aboard, and then

> Ajax[55] appeared swimming... and a theatrical device (μηχανή) was raised up from above the stage, and when thunder rang out on the stage, a lightening-bolt struck Ajax, and the figurine of him disappeared. And thus, after the front panel was closed, the tale came to its dramatic end (καὶ οὕτως κλεισθέντος καταστροφὴν εἶχεν ὁ μῦθος).[56]

Here καταστροφή is associated both with the demise of a heroic figure and with hyper-dramatic or contrived endings, i.e., endings which draw on the *deus ex machina* or other sorts of mechanical props to bring the plot to a screeching close.

Contrivances by definition bring to life on the stage things καθάπερ ἐπὶ τῆς ἀληθείας, but at the same time draw ridicule from some for being so obviously *not true to life*. This can be seen in the way the satirist Lucian makes fun of just such a type of low-ball street tragi-comedy in his treatise, *de mercede conductis* 1, where he tells of men who regale their audiences at temples with stories of miraculous rescues from dire

[53] LSJ, *s.v.* διάθεσις: "representation in a play."

[54] See LSJ, 1405, *s.v.* πίναξ, 8 (with reference to this work specifically: "toy theatre for marionettes").

[55] "The Lesser," whose death at sea is told in *Od.* 4.499–511.

[56] *de automatis* 22.1–6.

danger at sea by a μηχανή of some sort that allows a safe arrival on shore, supposedly by the χάρις καὶ εὐμένεια τοῦ θεοῦ. This passage introduces Lucian's own admonitory account of those who dare to join themselves to wealthy households in the position of a hired tutor, a story that begins auspiciously but, alas, in his terms, has its own καταστροφὴ τοῦ δράματος (to the eye of the astute viewer, that is)[57] when the early rewards of the position devolve later into spurnings, accusations and abandonment.[58] The satirist in using this phrase is defining his workspace between tragic appearance and comedic reality. Is Celsus' Jew, also?

When one looks closely at LSJ's gloss of καταστροφή as "in the drama, *dénouement, ending*," what is striking is that, with the exception of Polybius, the references they list concern comedies, not tragedies. A fragment of Antiphanes, the 4th century B.C.E. comedic playwright, for instance, connects καταστροφή with comedy over and against tragedy, and in so doing points to what in his mind are key differences between the two, especially in regard to freedom of invention:

> The art of writing tragedy (ἡ τραγῳδία) is fortunate in every way. For, first of all, the stories (οἱ λόγοι) are well known to people in the audience even before a character speaks a word, so that the poet merely has to remind them. Let me but mention Oedipus, and they know all the rest: his father was Laius, his mother Iocasta; they know who his daughters were, his sons, what he will suffer, what he has done...And then, when the poets can say no more, and their dramatic resources have completely given out (κομιδῇ δ' ἀπειρήκωσιν ἐν τοῖς δράμασιν), they raise "the machine" as easily as lifting a finger (αἴρουσιν ὥσπερ δάκτυλον τὴν μηχανήν) and the spectators are satisfied. But we [comedy writers] have not these advantages; on the contrary, we must invent everything (ἀλλὰ πάντα δεῖ εὑρεῖν)—new names (ὀνόματα καινά), new plots (καινὰ πράγματα], new speeches (καινοὺς λόγους), and then the antecedent circumstances (τὰ διῳκημένα πρότερον), the present situation (τὰ νῦν παρόντα), the outcome (τὴν καταστροφήν), the prologue (τὴν εἰσβολήν).[59]

[57] ἐπὶ πᾶσι δὲ ἥτις αὐτοῖς ἡ καταστροφὴ τοῦ δράματος γίγνεται (*merc. cond.* 10).

[58] Lucian ends the treatise with the potent image that the masters in such circumstances are like decorative papyrus rolls which underneath the purple cloth πολλὴν τὴν τραγῳδίαν σκέποντες, such that if you unroll one, δρᾶμα οὐ μικρὸν εὑρήσεις Εὐριπίδου τινὸς ἢ Σοφοκλέους (*merc. cond.* 41).

[59] Antiphanes, fr. 191 (text T. Kock, *Comicorum Atticorum Fragmenta* [Leipzig: Teubner, 1880–1888] 2.90; as emended and translated by Charles Burton Gulick, LCL, Athenaeus, *The Deipnosophists* 6.222–223).

The comedic dramatist's satiric complaint is that he does not have the tight strictures of the tragedians, which release them from the obligations of creativity, but he for his part must invent (εὑρεῖν) characters, events, speeches, and the structure of his plot, from antecedent events to the present, to the καταστροφή—the comedic turn-about which completes the action. Most interesting for our purposes is the way Antiphanes contrasts the types of ending of tragedies and comedies—the former use the contrivance of the *deus ex machina*, whereas the comic playwright fashions his own καταστροφή for his play. One need not accept Antiphanes' claim on face value to appreciate the distinction he is purportedly trying to uphold for his art. This use of the term καταστροφή for the dénouement of a comedy in particular is found nearly 800 years later in Euanthius' *de fabula hoc est de comoedia*,[60] and in fragmentary remains of the grammarian Donatus (teacher of Jerome, among others), who wrote a commentary on the great comic poet Terence: *Comoedia autem diuiditur in quatuor partes: prologum* πρότασιν ἐπίτασιν καταστροφήν.[61] We can add here as well two scholia to Euripides, which characterize the endings of *Orestes* and *Alcestis* with the identical comment: τὸ δρᾶμα κωμικωτέραν ἔχει τὴν καταστροφήν ("the play has a more comic dénouement").[62]

This use of καταστροφή in writing about comedy suggests that Celsus may by his carefully crafted charge be suggesting that the way Matthew chose to present the death of Jesus—because of its overt theatricality and stage-effects like the earthquake (that still does not save our hero!)—while tragic in the eyes of the simple-minded, is more fittingly seen by the astute observer as a comedy. To capture the open ambiguity

[60] "Comedy is divided into four parts: prologos, protasis, epitasis, catastrophe… catastrophe is the overturning of things to pleasant ends, disclosed all at once by the recognition of deeds"—*comoedia per quatuor partes diuiditur, prologum protasin epitasin catastrophen… catastrophe conuersio rerum est ad iucundos exitus patefacta cunctis cognitione gestorum* (*Comicorum Graecorum Fragmenta*, ed. Georg Kaibel, vol. 1 [Berlin: Weidmann, 1899], p. 67).

[61] *Aeli Donati quod fertur Commentum Terenti*, ed. Paul Wessner (Leipzig: Teubner, 1902), "excerpta de comoedia," VII 1 (p. 27). In VII 4 he defines our term: "catastrophe is the explanation of a tale, by which its outcome is confirmed"—*καταστροφή explicatio fabulae, per quam euentus eius approbatur*.

[62] *Scholia in Euripidem*, arg Or. 1.28 and arg Alc.1.18. This judgment is echoed by modern critics; see, e.g., Burnett, *Catastrophe Survived*, 195, on *Orestes*: "The chorus cries out to Victory and the aerial chariot [holding Apollo and Helen, whom he has rescued] swings out of sight, as the most complicated finale of classical tragedy comes to its end… and then every one of these disasters fails. Apollo comes, the wedding march begins, and catastrophe becomes blessedness in the twinkling of an eye" (note that the loan word "catastrophe" in English overlaps, but not co-extensively, the Greek term).

of the phrase as used by Celsus, I have put it in inverted commas in my translation above, as "the dénouement of the drama."

Whereas Celsus drops the phrase laconically into one sentence in his anti-Christian polemic, Lucian of Samosata—the only other non-Christian author beside Polybius to employ the expression ἡ καταστροφὴ τοῦ δράματος—uses it fully three times,[63] in each case embedded in a narrative context that gives an overt and deliberate play on the ambiguity between comedy and tragedy. Not only the frequency but also the rhetorical employment Lucian makes of it, are strikingly akin to what we have seen in Celsus' taunt against the Christians. In Lucian's depiction of the demise of his anti-hero, the one-time Christian pretender, Peregrinus (Proteus), he is said to have delivered a dramatic cry to the parental gods (Δαίμονες μητρῷοι καὶ πατρῷοι, δέξασθέ με εὐμενεῖς), and then leapt on the deathly pyre. Subsequently, after reporting that Peregrinus vanished from the sight of all (οὐ μὴν ἑωρᾶτό γε),[64] Lucian the narrator turns to his addressee, Cronius, and says, Αὖθις ὁρῶ γελῶντά σε, ὦ καλὲ Κρόνιε, τὴν καταστροφὴν τοῦ δράματος: "Once again,[65] good Cronius, I see you laughing at the 'dénouement of the drama'!" (§37).[66] Earlier in the treatise Lucian had claimed to have been present at the time of the event, at which the spectators were divided into two discrete audiences by their reactions: some grieved (as at a tragedy) and others laughed (as at a comedy) (*Peregr.* 2). Lucian himself tells Cronius that he had retold the tale (διηγούμενος) in two different ways, depending on the demeanor of the hearer he later encountered—giving straight facts (τὰ πραχθέντα διηγούμην) to the educated, but embellishing the tale with tragic details (τραγῳδεῖν) for the stupid (*Peregr.* 39). These patently false tragic add-ons tellingly include two of the three things Celsus singles out as defining Matthew's καταστροφὴ τοῦ δράματος: an earthquake (σεισμὸς μέγας) and a human voice (φωνή) rising from the instrument of death (here, the bonfire), as a vulture sped heavenward, emitting a powerful exit line.[67] Lucian says with some delight that the simple-minded reacted credulously to these details by paying hommage,

---

[63] We have discussed the first instance, in *merc. cond.*, above.

[64] Note the same phrasing as in Hero, suggesting a stage-trick disappearance.

[65] As in the opening to the work, in §2.

[66] Note that the death-scene does not effectively end Lucian's treatise (the same as in Matthew). After further post-mortem adventures, Lucian uses the concluding phrase: τοῦτο τέλος τοῦ κακοδαίμονος Πρωτέως ἐγένετο (§42).

[67] C.P. Jones, *Culture and Society in Lucian* (Cambridge: Harvard University Press, 1986) 128 accepts Lucian's word that these were his own redactions to the tale, and notes in regard to the earthquake that Lucian added one also in *Philopseudes* 22.

προσεκύνουν (as did most of the disciples in Mt 28:17), and they so effectively spread the rumor[68] that he later met a old man who swore he had himself witnessed both Lucian's fabricated vulture *and* Peregrinus himself alive in white clothes after death (*Peregr.* 40).[69]

In his *Alexander the False Prophet*, Lucian uses the same language to the same effect:

> Such was the end of the tragedy of Alexander (Τοιοῦτο τέλος τῆς Ἀλεξάνδρου τραγῳδίας), and this was the "denouement of the entire drama" (αὕτη τοῦ παντὸς δράματος ἡ καταστροφὴ ἐγένετο), as if this sort of thing portrayed an act of providence, although it happened by chance (ὡς εἰκάζειν προνοίας τινὸς τὸ τοιοῦτον, εἰ καὶ κατὰ τύχην συνέβη) (*Alex.* 60).

Recent scholarship on Lucian has emphasized the frequency of his use of language and imagery from the theatre,[70] and understood that it constitutes the fulcrum on which his satiric art is balanced—what looks like tragedy he turns mercilessly into comedy.[71] This particular

---

[68] "Il joue au bon apôtre," as Pierre de Labriolle, *La réaction païenne: étude sur la polémique antichrétienne du Ier au VIe siècle* (Paris: L'Artisan du livre, 1934), 107, suggestively put it.

[69] The comparisons between Lucian's *Peregrinus* and early Christian sources have a very long history (for some episodes in that history see the insightful study by Manuel Baumbach, "Phönix aus lukianischer Asche: Peregrinos Proteus im Spiegel seiner Rezeption," in Peter Pilhofer, Manuel Baumbach, Jens Gerlach and Dirk Uwe Hansen, *Lukian: Der Tod des Peregrinos: Ein Scharlatan auf dem Scheiterhaufen* [SAPERE 9; Darmstadt: Wissenschaftliche Buchgesellschaft, 2005] 198–227). In my judgment it is a mistake to isolate the so-called "Christian chapter" (paragraphs 11–14.16) from the rest of the work, especially the death scene. The valuable notes by Peter Pilhofer, for instance, become very cautious about Christian parallels after ch. 16 (Pilhofer, Baumbach, et al., *Lukian: Der Tod des Peregrinos*, 57–93). Surely Lucian did not forget later what he exhibited knowledge of earlier! (i.e., Jesus' being worshiped after his resurrection, and his followers' mistaken belief that they would live on after death). Even parallels to the old man seeing Peregrinus after death in white clothes (ἐν λευκῇ ἐσθῆτι), such as we find in Mt 28:3; Lk 24:4; John 20:12 or Mk 9:2–3 Pilhofer considers "dem Neutestamentler allerdings nicht durchweg überzeugend" (p. 90). But the differences he points to between any individual New Testament pericope and Lucian's send-up seem to assume Lucian would be copying any individual text exactly, rather than playing with known motifs associated with Christian claims (on the general question of Lucian's knowledge of Christianity, and possible contact with the New Testament, see Hans Dieter Betz, *Lukian von Samosata und das Neue Testament* [TU76; Berlin: Akademie-Verlag, 1961] 5–13 with further literature).

[70] See especially Orestis Karavas, *Lucien et la tragédie* (Untersuchungen zur antiken Literatur und Geschichte 76; Berlin/New York: de Gruyter, 2005); also Ulrich Viktor, *Lukian von Samosata: Alexandros oder der Lügenprophet* (Religions in the Graeco-Roman World 132; Leiden: Brill, 1997) 55.

[71] Of course, Lucian is playing on the comic potentialities of tragedy itself, as shown in the same debate about whether the *deus ex machina* endings of Euripides' plays are

favored expression, ἡ καταστροφὴ τοῦ δράματος,[72] is one of a set of tools by which Lucian engages in parody of Christians (and of others) in his own secondary compositions which mimic dramatic form.[73] His Alexander, inversely, is deprived of the *deus ex machina* tragic καταστροφή that Ajax received (by lightening bolt), but is subject to a comedic reversal that focuses less on the unsavory gangrenous illness than the public revelation of his baldness.[74] The deaths of Peregrinus and of Alexander (significantly, these are precisely the two treatises in which Lucian mentions and satirizes Christians) are characterized as "dramas" which have as their dénouement a death scene for which the term καταστροφὴ τοῦ δράματου is a brilliantly ironic *quadruple entendre*, referring at once to:

- the death of the protagonist;
- the near-ending of the secondary dramatic setting in which that death is recreated;
- the interpretation of that death as the dramatic reversal bringing a comeuppance for a charlatan;

seriously tragic, comedic or ironic (see, e.g., Walter Nicolai, *Euripides' Dramen mit rettendum Deus ex machina* [Bibliothek der klassischen Altertumswissenschaften, Reihe 2, n.f. 83; Heidelberg: Winter, 1990], esp. 30–37).

72 Viktor, *Alexandros oder der Lügenprophet*, 55; Karavas, *Lucien et la tragédie*, 203–204, includes this phrase in his catalogue of Lucian's theatrical vocabulary, concluding: "Lucien emploie l'expression ironiquement pour décrire la fin de Peregrinos et d'Alexandre, le faux-prophète. Leurs histoires étaient déja présentées comme des τραγῳδίαι ou des δράματα; par conséquent leur fin ne pouvait que correspondre à une *exodos* tragique." Dirk Uwe Hansen sees its role as as an Aristotelian περιπέτεια (though he does not use the term): "Daher bezeichnet Lukian diesen Moment als die καταστροφή des Dramas, den Moment nämlich, in dem Peregrinos das in Parium angelegte Kostüm ablegt und wieder ist, was er war" ("Zwei Inszenierungen eines Selbstmordes," in Pilhofer, Baumbach, et al., *Lukian: Der Tod des Peregrinos*, 129–50, 147).

73 See Hansen, "Zwei Inszenierungen eines Selbstmordes," in Pilhofer, Baumbach, et al., *Lukian: Der Tod des Peregrinos*, 129–50, esp. 145–50: "Jedoch nutzt Lukian auch noch andere Gelegenheiten, seiner Beschreibung der Ereignisse einen theatralischen, allerdings nicht tragödien- sondern komödienhaften, bisweilen auch an das Satyrspiel gemahnenden Ton zu geben" (145).

74 See the careful analysis of this scene by R. Bracht Branham, *Unruly Eloquence: Lucian and the Comedy of Traditions* (Cambridge: Harvard University Press, 1989), 207–208: "Having lived his life as a theatrical pursuit, his comic reversal is that his death must conform to dramatic ideas of justice and propriety. He lives out the *telos* of his *tragōdia* of his own creation, but in an ironically reduced and literal form. Thus the climax (*katastrophē*: 60) of the son of Podaleirius' drama is to die unexpectedly from a disease of the *poda* ('foot')."

- the ambiguity of this self-styled δρᾶμα for the viewers/readers, who either credulously perceive in this re-enactment a tragedy, or (as it is, for those who know how to see correctly) a most delicious comedy.

All four of these elements appear also to be implied in Celsus' charge that the Christian gospel depiction of the death of Jesus is a καταστροφὴ τοῦ δράματος, though he uses the phrase in a more cryptic fashion than does Lucian, as a passing slap at the gospels' veracity within a larger argument about the relationship between history and myth in Christian claims.[75] This significant overlap in the rhetorical function to which both authors put this exact phrase, ἡ καταστροφὴ τοῦ δράματος, especially when we appreciate the surprising rarity of the expression in Greek literature generally, and the close proximity of these writers in the late second century, may make it an as yet unappreciated piece of evidence for the long-standing debate on the possible historical and/or literary dependence between these two second sophistic authors who villified the Christians.[76]

Already in the Byzantine scholia on Lucian it was assumed that the Celsus to whom Lucian sent his treatise on Alexander the false prophet (*Alex.* 1, 61) was the same Celsus who authored the ἀληθὴς λόγος.[77] This judgment was defended with extensive arguments especially by Theodore Keim in the late nineteenth century, on the historical grounds that both, despite being purported Epicureans, were eclectic Platonists, both engage in mockery of Christians as charlatans, and they are contemporaries in the co-regency of Marcus Aurelius and Commodus,[78] and in the twentieth it was buttressed by linguistic parallels amassed by Jacques Schwartz,[79] for whom the argument of literary dependency

---

75 Of course, the subject of history and myth (and credulity in either case) was of major concern to Lucian, as well. In *Quomodo historia conscribenda sit* he consistently contrasts ἱστορία and μῦθος (§9–10; the latter pleases only the unsophisticated); §42: Thucydides as the example of one who rejected τὸ μυθῶδες in favor of ἡ ἀλήθεια; and especially §60, on how Lucian says one can repeat a myth, but οὐ μὴν πιστωτέος πάντως, tellingly leaving it to the audience to determine veracity for themselves.

76 On the current stalemate, see Viktor (*Alexandros oder der Lügenprophet*, 132), who says the question "kann ohne neue Argumente nicht beantwortet werden."

77 *Scholia in Lucianum* 42.1: οὗτός ἐστι Κέλσος ὁ τὴν καθ' ἡμῶν μακρὰν γράψας φλυαρίαν ἐν ὅλοις ὀκτὼ βιβλίοις, ᾧ πρὸς ἰσάριθμον ἀντεξαγόμενος πρόθεσιν ὁ σπουδαιότατος ἀντεῖπεν Ὠριγένης....

78 Theodore Keim, *Celsus' Wahres Wort* (Zurich: von Orell, Füssli & Co., 1873) 275–93.

79 Jacques Schwartz, "Du Testament de Lévi au Discours véritable de Celse," *Revue d'histoire et de philosophie religieuses* 40 (1960) 126–45; idem, "La 'conversion' de Lucien

was linked to a controversial claim about date, for he sought to show that when he wrote his *Alexander* in the late 160s Lucian already had Celsus' ἀληθὴς λόγος in front of him. But because of the influential reservations of Chadwick and Borret, among others,[80] contemporary scholarship has been much more cautious, if not completely dismissive, of this identification.[81]

The chief counter-argument against the identification of the two men named Celsus has been that Origen's opponent does not fit the description of an Epicurean,[82] which is how Lucian identifies his friend. Chadwick and others have emphasized that Celsus' own passages more often than not display a Platonic outlook, and an allowance of magic and of providence that no Epicurean (and surely one who wrote a book κατὰ μάγων)[83] rightly could.[84] Indeed, it is impossible to dispute Origen's own judgment that Celsus speaks often like a Platonist (as he put it in 4.83: καὶ γὰρ ἐν πολλοῖς πλατωνίζειν θέλει). Yet none of the three documents in question is a systematic philosophical treatise which allows us to track strict or singular philosophical commitments, and all three are part of a late antique philosophical culture which is universally recognized as eclectic, so all judgments about where a figure's utterances in a (selectively reproduced) argumentative framework so stray over the line of what one could conceivably hold if identified with that school of thought are difficult to sustain.[85] This is further complicated

de Samosate," *L'Antiquité classique* 33 (1964) 384–400. Schwartz is the only one I have seen who has pointed to the common use of the phrase in Lucian and in Celsus ("Du Testament de Lévi," 132), but he did not appreciate the rarity of it in Greek literature generally, nor analyze its rhetorical function in both authors. Had he done so, it might have compromised his larger argument that the direction of influence was from Celsus to Lucian, rather than the other way around.

80 Chadwick, *Origen, contra Celsum*, xxiv–xxix; Borret, *Origène, Contre Celse*, 5.192–96.

81 See, e.g., Jones, *Culture and Society in Lucian*, 20, 133. Yet there are glimpses of openness to dissent from the consensus, as in Mark J. Edwards, "Satire and Verisimilitude: Christianity in Lucian's *Peregrinus*," *Historia* 38 (1989) 89–98; Cook, *Interpretation of the New Testament in Greco-Roman Paganism*, 79 speaks of Celsus' "possible friend Lucian."

82 As Origen himself states at the outset (*c. Cels.* 1.8), he knows Celsus is an Epicurean from his other writings, and speculates that Celsus had dropped his Epicurean viewpoint because it was less conducive to the present argument

83 As Lucian says in *Alexander*, 21.

84 Chadwick, *Origen, contra Celsum*, xxv–xxvi: "Celsus' philosophy is that of an eclectic Platonist... It is, accordingly, inconceivable that he can be identified with a well-known Epicurean." Good summary of arguments and references in Cook, *Interpretation of the New Testament in Greco-Roman Paganism*, 17–26.

85 The other issue of course is what comparanda one uses to construct what is typically Epicurean (or Platonic, for that matter).

by the crucial fact that all three works—Lucian's *Alexander*, Celsus' *True Word* and Origen's *Against Celsus* are self-consciously rhetorically playing with identity and personification, and using the same *topos* to tar their opponents with inconsistency[86] (hence also leaving their own flank open to the same charge!).[87]

Given these methodological difficulties, it falls more to the linguistic evidence to determine possible literary contact between Lucian's Celsus and the author of the ἀληθὴς λόγος. Borret admired the careful work done by Schwartz,[88] but was concerned that the parallels may be due more to common polemical phrases than direct influence.[89] He also noted correctly that evidence of literary contact in itself does not prove Schwartz's conclusion about the direction of the borrowing—from Celsus to Lucian: "comment décider que, s'il avait une influence d'un auteur sur l'autre, ce fut celle de Celse sur Lucien"?[90] The present study may be able to address both these reservations.[91] First, we have seen that ἡ καταστροφὴ τοῦ δράματος cannot be dismissed as a common expression, for four of the six extant uses in all of Greek literature occur just in these two authors, Celsus and Lucian. Second, both authors use the phrase with the same ironic contours, and in both cases the implausibility is linked in some way to the same telling redactional detail on a death scene—an added, thoroughly improbable earthquake. Given that ἡ καταστροφὴ τοῦ δράματος is a favorite phrase of Lucian (used three times, and one of them in a text addressed to a Celsus!), makes it inherently more likely that Lucian was the source for Celsus' riposte than the inverse. Above all, this is supported by the fact that in each case Lucian uses the phrase in a fully developed narrative context, and with a rhetorical purpose which is thoroughly consistent with the well-

[86] So Origen, *c. Cels.* 1.8: Ἐλεγκτέον δὴ ὡς τὰ ἐναντία ἑαυτῷ λέγοντα τὸν Κέλσον.

[87] A valuable resource for this question is Branham, *Unruly Eloquence*, 181–210, which demonstrates keenly how in *Alexander*—if viewed purely from the point of view of logic and doctrine—the Epicureanism of Lucian and his expected reader, Celsus, likewise meets with incompatibilities.

[88] "Ainsi, grâce à J. Schwartz, une connaissance plus étendue de certaines ressemblances entre les deux écrivains est désormais acquise" (Borret, *Origène, contre Celse*, 5.194).

[89] "la base de la comparaison ... étroite, limitée à des traits de polémique entre philosophes et lettrés" (Borret, *Origène, contre Celse*, 5.194).

[90] Ibid.

[91] In this one case; the linguistic argument of course is all the more strengthened by the plurality of convincing parallels, but discussion of the other parallels lies outside our scope here.

recognized use of tragic terms and plays on the tragedians (especially Euripides) throughout his oeuvre,[92] whereas the phrase is dropped in in short-hand fashion by Celsus, an author who does not display the same predilection for theatrical terminology Lucian has.[93] Consequently it seems quite clear that the direction arrow must go the other way than Schwartz proposed, and Celsus was dependent upon Lucian for the language and logic of this terse, mocking characterization of the passion scene in the gospels. This conclusion also satisfactorily eliminates the other major argument Borret raised against Schwartz's thesis of literary contact: that it requires a dating of the ἀληθὴς λόγος considerably earlier than most scholars place it, ca. 177.[94]

According to Origen, Celsus engaged in προσωποποιία, varying his own persona to introduce a battery of anti-Christian arguments representing different fundamental assumptions and presumably different sources. However, Origen chides, Celsus apparently did not learn to carry out this school exercise very well.[95] While it is well known that

---

[92] Another point of contact between Celsus and Lucian is that both favor Euripides (Lucian's preference for Euripides is well known; see Jones, *Culture and Society in Lucian*, 151; Karavas, *Lucien et la tragédie*, 175–82, 330; Celsus for his part quotes Euripides five times, but never Aeschylus nor Sophocles).

[93] Celsus (in the extant fragments) employs very few items in the catalogue of Lucian's theatrical terminology amassed by Karavas, *Lucien et la tragédie*, 191–216. He never uses such key terms as τραγῳδία or cognates, δρᾶμα (beyond this one passage), μηχανή, ὑποκριτής and cognates, or many others. He does use χορός twice (5.33, 42), and θέατρον in 6.78 (discussed in n. 99 below).

[94] The internal dating of Celsus' work is usually determined by the convergence of Christian persecution (per *c. Cels.* 8.69) in that date, as witnessed by the Letter of the Churches of Lyons and Vienne, and the co-regency (Marcus Aurelius and Commodus) that *c. Cels.* 8.71 seems to require. Neither point is incontestable (for discussion see Cook, *Interpretation of the New Testament in Greco-Roman Paganism*, 23–24). My proposal would require moving that date ahead just into the sole reign of Commodus (beginning in March, 180), as Lucian's *Alex.* 48 shows knowledge of the death and divinization of Marcus Aurelius (*merc. cond.* is in the same time period, *Peregr.* much earlier, sometime after 165). Placing the work under Commodus' reign is acceptable if one takes οἱ νῦν βασιλεύοντες in 8.71 as a generic statement rather than an indication of co-regency (see also 8.73; further discussion of the point in Chadwick, *Origen, contra Celsum*, xxvii; general table of the chronology of Lucian's works in Jones, *Culture and Society in Lucian*, 167–69).

[95] See Origen's school-masterly invocation of the rules of proper execution of προσωποποιία at *c. Cels.*7.36: ὅτι ἀρετὴ μὲν προσωποποιοῦντός ἐστι τηρῆσαι τὸ βούλημα καὶ τὸ ἦθος τοῦ προσωποποιουμένου, κακία δέ, ὅτε τὰ μὴ ἁρμόζοντά τις περιτίθησι ῥήματα τῷ προσώπῳ τοῦ λέγοντος. On this use of the "urbanity *topos*" in early Christian exegesis, see Margaret M. Mitchell, "Rhetorical Handbooks in Service of Biblical Exegesis: Eustathius of Antioch Takes Origen Back to School," *The New Testament and Early Christian Literature in Greco-Roman Context: Studies in Honor of David E. Aune* (NovTSup 122; Leiden: Brill, 2006), 349–67.

Origen frequently unmasks Celsus for espousing views inconsistent with his supposed Epicureanism,[96] it is equally telling that he likewise chides "the Jew" for displaying an unbecoming knowledge of the theatre[97] in quoting Euripides, *Bacchae* 498 (*c. Cels.* 2.34) in his complaint that the gospel plot did not, like a good tragedy, include an act of final retribution and recognition by the slain.[98] When the mask slips from the πρόσωπον of Celsus' "Jew"—who issues the theatrical slight on Matthew's passion narrative as a thoroughly dishonorable and implausible καταστροφὴ τοῦ δράματος—do we catch a glimpse of Lucian behind it?[99]

---

[96] E.g., 3.35; 3.80; 4.36; 4.54; 5.3; cf. 1.8.

[97] This did not prohibit Origen from displaying some knowledge of the theatre himself books later, when he rebuked Celsus for putting words in the mouths of Christians on the analogy that this is as laughable as Aristophanes' send-up of Euripides for using speech not in character (*c. Cels.* 7.36–37).

[98] "The Jew" derides the gospel account for not having Jesus follow appropriate tragedic precendent and, like Dionysus in Euripides' *Bacchae*, exact grotesque punishment on his accusers (as happened to Pentheus) for not recognizing him (*c. Cels.* 2.34.). Once again (cf. n. 49), Origen does not repudiate the comparison, but seeks to argue that the tragic pattern of the retribution scene (for the type, see Burian, "Myth into *muthos*," 187–88) is actually found in Matthew's Gospel, in the Matthean episode of Pilate's wife (Mt 27:19), which, he says, was selectively omitted from "the Jew's" literary analysis.

[99] In book 6 Origen quotes Celsus' invocation of an unnamed comic poet who tells of Zeus waking up and deciding to send Hermes to save the human race. He then derides Celsus for not acting like a philosopher, but invoking a comic poet who is sporting for a laugh. Ὅρα δὴ καὶ ἐν τούτοις τὸ ἄσεμνον τοῦ Κέλσου, ἀφιλοσόφως κωμῳδίας ποιητὴν γελωτοποιὸν παραλαβόντος (6.78; cf. also 6.49). Lucian would be proud!

ANTE-NICENE PREACHING IN RECENT LITERATURE

O.C. Edwards, Jr.

In its earliest days the Christian faith spread through the Greco-Roman world with remarkable rapidity. Around thirty years after Jesus' crucifixion in Palestine its adherents were disruptive enough in the city of Rome for Nero to regard them as the natural scapegoat on which he could blame the burning of the city. About 250 years after that, Christianity was legally tolerated throughout the empire and the religion favored by the emperor. Everyone recognizes that one of the major factors in the success of the movement was its preaching. It is therefore highly ironic that we have neither a great deal of knowledge of Christian preaching during that period nor much trace of it outside its remarkable results.

1. Books and Authors

Although the shortage of identified information makes it difficult to change that situation, there has recently been a number of books that have sought to summarize the available data. That in itself is a little surprising since the history of preaching has not been a field that many scholars have attempted to survey until recently. For almost a century the only major work in English was the study made by Edwin C. Dargan.[1] Along the way a short survey by the scholarly Swedish archbishop Yngve Brilioth appeared.[2] Also Werner Schütz published a helpful, but terse little volume in German.[3]

The most ambitious undertaking was a thirteen-volume work edited by Clyde E. Fant Jr. and William M. Pinson Jr.[4] While this set makes

---

[1] Edwin C. Dargan, *A History of Preaching*, 2 vols. (1905–12; reprint, New York: Burt Franklin, 1968).

[2] Yngve Brilioth, *A Brief History of Preaching*, trans. Karl E. Mattson, The Preacher's Paperback Library (Philadelphia: Fortress, 1965).

[3] Werner Schütz, *Geschichte der christlichen Predigt*, Sammlung Göschen, Band 7201 (Berlin: Walter de Gruyter, 1972).

[4] Clyde E. Fant Jr. and William M. Pinson Jr., eds. *20 Centuries of Great Preaching*, 13 vols. (Waco, Tex.: Word, 1971).

texts of many sermons available in English, the introductions to individual preachers are not all of the same quality, and the first eighteen centuries of the Christian era are dispatched in two and a half of the twelve volumes.[5] The only works discussed there from the period we are considering are *2 Clement* and the first of Origen's homilies on the Song of Songs. Thus until the very end of the twentieth century it could not be said that investigating the history of preaching in the Ante-Nicene church was a major sphere of scholarly production.

In the last decade, however, there has been a flurry of activity in this enterprise. Besides my own contribution,[6] there have been studies by Hughes Oliphant Old,[7] Ronald E. Osborn,[8] and David Dunn-Wilson.[9] In addition, Mary B. Cunningham and Pauline Allen have edited a collection of essays covering the period.[10] With the exception of the work of Dunn-Wilson, all of these are parts of multi-volume series. Each of the volumes under consideration, however, covers more than the Ante-Nicene period. All reach back into the biblical age to some extent and all but this first volume of Old's work extends into the Post-Nicene era.

These writers bring a variety of skills to their undertaking and have different aims in view. After writing a dissertation on Tatian under our honoree, I taught first New Testament and then preaching in seminaries. My curiosity about how and why preaching has changed over time is given rein in two long volumes, one devoted to a survey and the other to documents illustrating that development. Old was a scholarly parish pastor when he was invited to follow his interest in the relation of the reading of scripture to preaching in Christian worship at the Center of Theological Inquiry in Princeton. He is close to publishing the sixth of a projected seven volumes noting the various combinations in which those two elements have appeared through the ages. Osborn was a

---

[5] The thirteenth volume is an index.

[6] O.C. Edwards Jr., *A History of Preaching*, 2 vols. (Nashville: Abingdon, 2004). (Vol. 2 is on a CD-ROM.)

[7] Hughes Oliphant Old, *The Reading and Preaching of the Scriptures in the Worship of the Christian Church, vol. 1, The Biblical Period* (Grand Rapids: Eerdmans, 1998).

[8] Ronald E. Osborn, *Folly of God: the Rise of Christian Preaching* (vol. 1 of *A History of Christian Preaching*. St. Louis: Chalice, 1999).

[9] David Dunn-Wilson, *A Mirror for the Church: Preaching in the First Five Centuries* (Grand Rapids: Eerdmans, 2005).

[10] Mary B. Cunningham and Pauline Allen, eds., *Preacher and Audience: Studies in Early Christian and Byzantine Homiletics* (vol. 1 of *A New History of the Sermon*. Leiden: Brill, 1998).

church history professor and seminary administrator whose purpose was "to discern what was happening in and to preaching as an enterprise, as demonstrated through the work of notable practitioners, to recount major developments, and to analyze trends as exemplified by representative voices."[11] His untimely death prevented his publishing more than the first of his projected four volumes.[12]

Dunn-Wilson is a Methodist minister who has served for forty years in the United Kingdom, Central America, and East Africa, spending much of this time in academic work. At the time of his retirement he was dean of the faculty at Kenyan Methodist University. While he appears to know ancient languages well, his book suggests he suffered from the limited library of third world schools before retirement provided him with the more abundant resources of British universities. His intention is to show how preachers labored through the patristic period to "adapt their style and themes to the congregation's changing needs."[13] The volume edited by Cunningham and Allen is different from the others in several respects. It is not a survey of preaching during the patristic period but a collection of essays on various aspects of that area. It is not about all patristic preaching, but only that done in Greek. And the authors of the chapters are specialists in the field reporting their own research rather than generalists who have had to study up on each period they wrote about.

2. Defining the Subject

A major source of variety among these accounts is differences in the way they define the activity whose history they report. A result of this is a similar variation in the number of early Christian writings each author considers it appropriate to treat as examples of preaching. I, for instance, began my book by setting limits on what I would investigate by defining a sermon as

> a speech delivered in a Christian assembly for worship by an authorized person that applies some point of doctrine, usually drawn from a biblical

[11] Osborn, *Folly of God*, 1:xviii.

[12] His former student and research assistant, Prof. Joseph R. Jeter Jr., has been commissioned to complete the second volume, but arrangements for the final two had not been made by the publisher when I last heard of the matter.

[13] Dunn-Wilson, *Mirror for the Church*, xv.

> passage, to the lives of the members of the congregation with the purpose of moving them by the use of narrative analogy and other rhetorical devices to accept that application and to act on the basis of it.[14]

This definition focuses on the oral nature of preaching, identifying it as a transaction between a person (usually ordained) and a congregation. Some written record has to have survived or the sermon could not be discussed, but I limit my study to words spoken in so far as they can be ascertained. Furthermore, I was more interested in tracing movements in preaching than in listing everyone who had stood in pulpits during a particular period. Thus, to show what is known of what Ante-Nicene preaching was like, I thought it enough to concentrate on *2 Clement*, Melito's *Paschal Homily*, and the homilies of Origen, with slight reference to a few other documents that may or may not have been homilies.

By contrast, Dunn-Wilson seems to make patristic preaching co-extensive with early Christian literature. He accomplishes that by calling personal evangelism "informal" preaching, written works such as those of the Apostolic Fathers "epistolary" preaching, and referring to the Apologists as "the apologist-preachers."[15] This tendency to lump everything into one category is also seen in the way he treats the teachings of these Ante-Nicene writers synthetically. After brief introductions to their periods, his chapters on the Apostolic Fathers and the Apologists are summaries of the teaching of these writers as groups, as though they all said the same things. Oddly enough, less than a page is given to the preaching of Origen.[16] That occurs in the chapter on the Apologists, but it deals with his homilies rather than *Contra Celsum*, his apology.

Osborn also gave a definition of preaching at the beginning of his book, saying that it is

> public discourse concerning the gospel, inspired by it, and offering a biblical witness and Christian perspective on psychic or social or theological issues confronting the hearers.[17]

He went on to say that, while the earliest Christian proclamation was evangelical or missionary, he would include in his definition of preaching

[14] Edwards, *History of Preaching*, 3–4.
[15] Dunn-Wilson, *Mirror for the Church*, 9, 25, 35.
[16] Ibid., 36–37.
[17] Osborn, *Folly of God*, xvi. Subsequent page numbers from this work will be indicated parenthetically in the text.

"discourse addressed to the believing community, commonly though not necessarily spoken within the context of the liturgy" (xvi–xvii).

It worked out in practice that this last qualification covered not only the liturgical context but also whether the discourse was spoken or not. The elasticity of his definition appeared when he called the ministry of the Hebrew prophets the "emergence of preaching" (90), describing one of their oracles as "a public address applying to a contemporary situation the preacher's reflection on a divine word or on the sacred tradition" (93). Then he said that the pseudepigraphical literature may be considered preaching in a broad sense, "especially since in those days one rarely if ever sat alone perusing a scroll in silence, but rather heard it read aloud in a gathering of eager listeners" (4)—thus declaring all foods clean and all religious writing to be preaching.

While he had some good things to say about the development of cultic preaching and its liturgical context, the inclusiveness of his definition became clear in his discussion of the Apologists. He cleared the way for treating their works as preaching by saying that "the apology or defense was a recognized genre of public address and, in its published form, of literature" (337). In a paragraph entitled "Apology as Preaching," he developed that thought by saying:

> Through a dedication to the Roman Senate or the Emperor, some made a bid in pamphlet form for an audience the preacher had no other way of addressing. Others apparently represent speeches actually delivered in public to a general audience (338).

Thus he was able to conclude that "for the missionary preaching of the era these documents constitute our chief source" (ibid.).

Osborn did have a clear sense of differences of genre, however, listing the following as species of Christian preaching: apology, protreptikos, dialogue, testament, testimony, prophecy, homily, diatribe, encomium, catechetical lecture, and panegyric. He also enumerated the figures or devices used in these genres, including symbolic narrative, parable, contrast, mandate, exemplum, wisdom saying, paradox, prosopopoeia, and sermocinatio or discussion (413–14).

Old, on the other hand, is, as his title states, interested only in "the reading and preaching of scriptures in the worship of the Christian church." He does recognize five major genres of preaching: expository, evangelistic, catechetical, festal, and prophetic, but even there he gives expository preaching a preferred status and thinks that should be based on *lectio continua* rather than a lectionary cycle or passages chosen *ad hoc*.

Indeed, his tendency is so much in that direction that he recognizes as expository preaching activities that few others have identified as such. For instance, he says that "two passages in the Old Testament illuminate this genre with particular clarity": Moses' reading of the Law at Mount Sinai and Ezra's reading of the Law at the water gate.[18] He concludes his discussion of the Sinai event by saying:

> One thing should certainly be very clear from the Sinai traditions found in Exodus. The Word of God was read and preached to the worshiping assembly of Israel immediately upon its revelation.... The Law was written to be read as Scripture in worship.[19]

Old does not make clear whether he thinks this is an accurate historical account or that he believes that since it is written in scripture it is theologically normative. In his discussion of Deuteronomy, however, he shows that he is willing to entertain the position of Peter Craigie and Duane Christensen that the book contains the words Moses actually spoke at a covenant renewal service just before the entry into the land, but he also holds open von Rad's thesis that it is the work of Levitical preachers from the time of Micah and Jeremiah.[20] He shows a similar ambivalence over the historicity of the account of Ezra at the water gate when he says: "Whether the traditions of the synagogue shaped what is here [in Nehemiah 8] reported of Ezra's service or whether it was Ezra who shaped the synagogue tradition is not completely clear."[21] This retrojection of Calvinist ideals of worship into the Old Testament period is consistent with the way that he was equally willing to give many pre-Reformation Christian preachers the benefit of the doubt and treat them as what someone has called "precocious Presbyterians."

Cunningham and Allen also provide their own definition, although it is of "homily" rather than preaching in general. The definition "includes works prepared beforehand or delivered impromptu at ceremonies which had some kind of liturgical content, but which were not always held in a church building."[22] The editors go on to recognize the existence of "desk homilies," meant to be read rather than heard—an important distinction, since, as they acknowledge, it is not always possible to tell

---

[18] Old, *Reading and Preaching of the Scriptures*, 1:9.
[19] Ibid., 1:28.
[20] Ibid., 1:28–40.
[21] Ibid., 1:96.
[22] Cunningham and Allen, *Preacher and Audience*, 1.

from surviving manuscripts which documents having the form of a homily were actually delivered. The only preachers from our period whose work is considered in their pages are Hermas, Hippolytus, and Origen. This limitation, however, does not derive from exclusions by definition, but is a function of their book's being a collection of essays by a variety of scholars rather than a survey of the history of the period.

3. Treatments of Ante-Nicene Preacher

The Apostolic Fathers—Dunn-Wilson, Osborn, Old, and I identify *2 Clement* as the oldest Christian homily we have, with Dunn-Wilson saying little more about it than that.[23] A collection of essays like the volume edited by Cunningham and Allen cannot be expected to treat all significant homiletical documents. Osborn deals with *2 Clement* in less than a page, calling it "an informal but earnest discourse without rhetorical pretensions exhorting hearers to zealous devotion."[24] Old uses six and a half pages in his treatment of the work,[25] discussing its outline and noting its teaching on subjects that interest him, especially the relation of preaching to the reading of scripture in Christian worship. His basic interpretation is problematic. He says:

> This sermon is an expository sermon in the classic sense of the term. It is an exposition and application of a passage of scripture. It is the same sort of preaching that was done in the synagogue. One notices one significant variation. Instead of the primary text being taken from the Law, it is taken from the prophets, and instead of the secondary text being taken from the prophets, it is taken from the gospels.[26]

The difficulty with that analysis is that neither verse is mentioned again after its original appearance in chapter 2.

Better justice is done to *2 Clement's* use of scripture by Karl Paul Donfried's observation that in chapters 3–14, there is a pattern of (1) statement of theme, (2) scripture quotation, (3) exhortation, and (4) scripture quotation.[27] The theme of the homily as a whole is stated

---

[23] Dunn-Wilson, *Mirror for the Church*, 27.

[24] Osborn, *Folly of God*, 376.

[25] Old, *Reading and Preaching of the Scriptures*, 1:278–84.

[26] Ibid., 284.

[27] Karl Paul Donfried, *The Setting of Second Clement in Early Christianity*, NovTSup, no. 38 (Leiden: Brill, 1974), 96–97. Donfried is wrong, however, in saying that the genre of the work is that of deliberative speech rather than homily.

as a question in 1.3: "what repayment, then, can we make to [Jesus, who, like God is judge of the living and the dead], or what result commensurate with what he has given us?"[28] Thus the outline given by Grant and Graham is more accurate, beginning, as it does with "God's gracious creative action in Christ on our behalf (1.1–2.7)" followed by "The response of following him in deed (3.1–4.5)."[29] Attention needs also to be called to the wide assortment of biblical quotations and allusions in the work, including many from the Prophets and Psalms, most New Testament books except the Johannine literature, and even some apocryphal works.

While other writings of the Apostolic Fathers are mentioned in the studies being surveyed,[30] the only other one whose work is examined homiletically in detail is Hermas. Dunn-Wilson notes the *Shepherd's* oral quality by observing that it "promises blessings to those who listen to it 'with pure minds,'" says that it classifies sins into the three categories of sexual, those of excess, and those of speech.[31] Osborn says that Hermas' work "has the feel of a scrapbook kept by a prophet and teacher through a lifetime of ministry and minimally revised for publication."[32]

The most extensive discussion, however, appears in the chapter contributed to *Preacher and Audience* by Alistair Stewart-Sykes, a scholarly parish priest in England who has published a number of significant books on the Ante-Nicene church in recent years.[33] His understanding is that Hermas was the head of one of a number of household churches in Rome around the turn of the century, well before there was a monarchical episcopate in Rome. In addition to being the householder, he was also a prophet. "The question is whether his status as a prophet derived from his social status, or whether his prophesying represented a secondary but necessary qualification."[34] Stewart-Sykes decides on the latter option because others in the congregation were

---

[28] The translation is that of Robert M. Grant and Holt Graham, *First and Second Clement*, vol. 2 of *The Apostolic Fathers: A New Translation and Commentary* (New York: Thomas Nelson, 1965), 112.

[29] Ibid., 111.

[30] In an effective homiletical use of language, Osborn called the dying of the martyrs like Ignatius and Polycarp "the most convincing preaching of all (*Folly of God*, 335).

[31] Dunn-Wilson, *Mirror for the Church*, 26, 30–31.

[32] Osborn, *Folly of God*, 377.

[33] Alistair Stewart-Sykes, "Hermas the Prophet and Hippolytus the Preacher: The Roman Homily and its Social Context" in Cunningham and Allen, *Preacher and Audience*, 33–63.

[34] Ibid., 37.

also wealthy. Yet he was more of a traditional leader with charisma than a charismatic leader.

Since his purpose in addressing his congregation was ethical, he was a parainetic rather than a mantic prophet. In response to Aune's suggestion that Hermas' rhetoric and diction were inspired by homilies,[35] our author argues on the basis of function, content, form, and style that much of the *Shepherd* "is constructed from only slightly redacted homilies,"[36] a view similar to that of Osborn. He goes on to say that most of Hermas' homilies are not based on scripture because "biblical texts did not yet possess a clear canonical function within the church."[37] Hermas' homilies are addressed to the wealthy members of his congregation, urging them to give higher priority to their religion than their business, and to help the poor. Theye are, like him, affluent freedmen who are successful in business. The lack of education displayed by the work is consistent with this status. The poor to whom his hearers should show pity must not be members of Hermas' household church because they are never addressed directly in the *Shepherd*.[38]

4. A Homily of Hippolytus

Stewart-Sykes contrasts the preaching of Hermas with a Hippolytean homily from roughly a century later to show changes in the Roman churches over that time. Before that can be done, it is necessary to decide exactly who wrote that homily. A statue of Hippolytus survives and on the side of the chair of the seated figure is a list of books. Originally it was believed that they were all by the historical Hippolytus, but since then it has been thought that the works of at least two different writers are listed. Stewart-Sykes believes that the one certain homily that has been identified in that corpus[39] was written by the earlier author of those two, the one who wrote the *Elenchus* at the time of Zephyrinus and Callistus (198–222), rather than the later one from the time of Pontianus, the historical Hippolytus.[40]

---

[35] D.E. Aune, *Prophecy in Early Christianity and the Ancient Mediterranean World* (Grand Rapids: Eerdmans, 1983), 304.
[36] Stewart-Sykes, "Hermas the Prophet and Hippolytus the Preacher," 39, 42.
[37] Ibid., 41.
[38] Ibid., 46.
[39] Other potential candidates are listed on p. 47, n. 39.
[40] Ibid., 47 n. 40, 55.

This homily is extracted from the *catenae* on the Psalms.[41] The preacher argues that the Psalms have *dynamis*—power, authority, inspiration, "meaning." That authority extends even to the titles of the Psalms, even though a recent heretical group had claimed that the titles are not part of the canonical text of the Psalms. Their position has been identified by Rondeau as a belief that arose in reaction against the Montanism threatening the churches in Rome at the time, a belief that the Psalms were not Davidic and not inspired.[42] Stewart-Sykes says, "In defending the inspired status of the Psalms, Hippolytus was willing to stray slightly in the Montanist direction against those who wished to deny the possibility of prophecy entirely."[43] In fact, Stewart-Sykes believes that exegetical preaching was designated as prophecy in the Hippolytean community.[44] The interpretation of the Psalms in this homily is used to argue on the one hand for prophecy and on the other for order in the church's worship.[45]

From all this Stewart-Sykes goes on to propose an understanding of the Christian community in which the writer preached and the role of the preacher in it. The time of the sermon is later than but consistent with that mentioned by Eusebius when families of wealth and position became Christians in Rome.[46] The use of Greek suggests that this was a wealthy immigrant congregation. The writer's role as a teacher did not "necessarily imply high social status."[47] Indeed, he could have been dependent on a patron whom he would have been unwise to displease. Yet he was also a social conservative who thought people should know their place in both the liturgy and in society. He also had enough social homogeneity with the rest of the congregation to be well educated, homogeneity with his flock being a trait he shared with Hermas.

An aspect of Stewart-Sykes' reconstruction that is less than persuasive to me is his identification of the church in which the Hippolytean writer preached as a school because the homily is exegetical and "part

---

[41] P. Nautin, *Le dossier d'Hippolyte et de Méliton dans les florilèges dogmatiques et chez les historiens modernes* (Paris: Éditions du Cerf, 1953), 166–83.

[42] M.-J. Rondeau, "Les polémiques d'Hippolyte de Rome et de Filastre de Brescia concernant le Psautier," *Revue de l'histoire des religions* 171 (1967), 21.

[43] Stewart-Sykes, "Hermas the Prophet and Hippolytus the Preacher," 55. He refers to both writers as Hippolytus for convenience.

[44] Ibid., 61.

[45] Ibid., 48.

[46] Eusebius, *H.E.* 4.30.1.

[47] Stewart-Sykes, "Hermas the Prophet and Hippolytus the Preacher," 59.

of the scholastic enterprise was the study and exegesis of a text."[48] The sort of school to which he compares our preacher's community is that of a grammarian, but (a) an earlier school-holder such as Justin did not reflect that style or content, and (b) Origen, a contemporary of the preacher, only preached after his ordination and did so as a Christian *grammatikos*. Yet Stewart-Sykes' allusive way of referring to all this makes me suspect that he is aware of literature with which I am unfamiliar in which the identification of the Hippolytean community as a school is accepted.

The other writers surveyed in this essay have little to say about the preaching of the earlier writer whose works are listed on the statue of Hippolytus, and the only one who has much to say about the latter is Old. He looks to the *Apostolic Tradition* written by Hippolytus in the closing years of his rival papacy when his opponent was Pontianus (230–35) for information about the worship of the Roman church during that period.[49] Old does not have much sympathy for Hippolytus, saying that he is "just plain stodgy. He is not so much a rigorist as a stickler for details, often putting the emphasis on matters of tertiary interest."[50] The *Apostolic Tradition* thus "reflects the kind of churchmanship that is overly concerned with how cheese, olives, and oil are to be blessed at the Eucharist and how the evening lamps are to be lit at vespers."[51] He goes on grudgingly to say however: "While Hippolytus does not speak of how the Scriptures are to be read and preached at the dominical service, he does give us some indications of the preaching ministry which was maintained at daily morning prayer."[52]

5. Melito's Paschal Homily

All of our writers except the contributors to *Preacher and Audience* refer to the *Homily on the Passover* of Melito of Sardis, although Dunn-Wilson barely does, calling it a "veritable homiletic tour de force" and saying that, along with Tertullian and Cyprian, its author is "expert in rhetoric

---

[48] Ibid., 60.
[49] Old, *Reading and Preaching of the Scriptures*, 1:273–77. Old, however, does not refer to the existence of two or more authors of the Hippolytean corpus.
[50] Ibid., 273.
[51] Ibid., 274.
[52] Ibid., 275.

and an admirer of Stoicism."[53] He includes him with the Apologists and Eusebius does include a fragment from an apology by him, but that is all that survives.[54] Osborn credits Melito with the earliest known "full-scale appropriation of classical rhetoric" in a Christian sermon, identifying his style as that of the Second Sophistic.[55] He lists the figures of sound and thought employed and describes them as "devices of epideictic declamation."[56] While oratorical fireworks characterized the *genus dicendi* devoted to praise or blame, it is more exact to recognize these devices as the Gorgian figures of which Plato is so scornful.[57] Osborn also laments, as one must, the polemic against the Jews that occupies almost a third of Melito's text. One could mention the extenuating circumstances, the enormous size of the Jewish community in Sardis and the martyrdoms of Polycarp and eleven other Christians in nearby Smyra around that time in which Jewish agitation was considered to be a factor, but that does not excuse the tone of Melito's address.[58]

In the ten pages that Old devotes to Melito's homily, he covers most of the ground the rest of us did, but also had some pointed things to say about the typological interpretation that characterizes the work. While he can find it acceptable up to a point, he notes that in Melito's view, "with the establishing of the church and the proclamation of the gospel, the prefiguration has become vain and Israel has lost its reason to exist."[59] The problem with that, he says, is that "it can become an argument against Christian use not only of Old Testament typology in Christian preaching but of the Old Testament in general."[60] He connects this attitude with the decline of the reading of the Hebrew Bible in both the Byzantine and Roman liturgies and also with the encouragement of anti-Semitism among Christians. He also has a good bit to say in this section about the early development of Christian liturgy. I know too little of the scholarship in this area to be able to evaluate what he has to say on that subject beyond recognizing that he obviously knows more than I do.

---

[53] Dunn-Wilson, *Mirror for the Church*, 36–37.
[54] Eusebius, *Hist. Eccl.* 4.26.5–11.
[55] Osborn, *Folly of God*, 377.
[56] Ibid., 378.
[57] Edwards, *History of Preaching*, 19–20.
[58] Ibid., 17–18.
[59] Old, *Reading and Preaching of the Scriptures*, 1:287.
[60] Ibid., 288.

6. The Preaching of Origen

All our writers are convinced of the superlative importance of Origen, the first Christian preacher from whom we have any considerable body of sermons. Dunn-Wilson, for instance, calls him "the one gigantic figure who towers over all the others," and goes on to say that he was "one of that select company of outstanding preachers whose vision and technique are truly innovative."[61] Yet he devotes less than a page to his preaching, while Osborn discusses his preaching in four pages and his biblical interpretation, along with that of others in another four.[62] I, on the other hand, use twenty-two pages to cover the subject and Old occupies forty-seven.[63] We both draw heavily on the work of Pierre Nautin,[64] although Old finds his reconstruction of worship in Caesarea "open to a number of serious objections."[65] And I would have been happier if Old had noticed that Origen's form of preaching derived from the model of the *grammatikos* and that some of his lack of rhetorical polish is due to his having to quit school at the end of his secondary education before rhetorical studies had been undertaken. Yet his study of Origen is very valuable. Old shows that Origen's hermeneutical method is best understood in terms of his statement of it in *De principiis*, he analyses a number of sermons in detail to show how Origen went about his preaching task, he analyzes the difference between allegory and typology, suggesting that the later is biblical and the former Platonic, and, as indicated, he comments on the liturgical situation in which Origen preached.

By far the most authoritative treatment of the preaching of Origen in these volumes, however, is the chapter contributed by Adele Monaci Castagno to the volume edited by Cunningham and Allen.[66] What makes her work so authoritative is that she is the only one of us who is a specialist who has done original research in the field. Indeed, she tells us that her chapter is an updated summary of a book she has written

---

61 Dunn-Wilson, *Mirror for the Church*, 36.

62 Osborn, *Folly of God*, 393–97, 402–06.

63 Edwards, *History of Preaching*, 27–48; Old, *Reading and Preaching of the Scriptures*, 1:307–52.

64 Pierre Nautin, *Origène, sa vie et son oeuvre* (Paris: Beauchesne, 1977) and P. Husson and P. Nautin, eds., *Homélies sur Jérémie*, 2 vols. (Paris: Éditions du Cerf, 1976 and 1977).

65 Old, *Reading and Preaching of the Scriptures*, 1:349.

66 Adele Monaci Castagno, "Origen the Scholar and Pastor" in Cunningham and Allen, *Preacher and Audience*, 65–87.

on the subject.[67] A good bit of her analysis, however, is devoted to the main themes on which Origen preached, which need not concern us here. In keeping with the volume in which her essay appears, she does try to analyze the audience to whom Origen preached in Caesarea, noting that in the congregation there were more converts from paganism than from Judaism and that Christians were a minority in the city.[68] Though there is little indication of the social class of his hearers, there appears to be a prevalence of those who were economically active in the buying and selling of goods. While he preached to both the baptized and catechumens, he had an ambivalent attitude toward the *simpliciores* among them, feeling the need to address them, but finding them uninterested in the spirituality he wished to teach.[69]

7. Conclusion

Probably the main thing to be learned from this survey of recent literature is how much more research needs to be done. In their introduction, Cunningham and Allen say that the primary purpose of their volume is to stimulate further research in the field.[70] If that is true of their work by specialists, it applies *a fortiori* to that of us generalists who have to summarize what they have discovered. The editors call attention to how much needs to be done in editing the texts of homilies, dating them, and identifying their authors. There are also problems in checking the accuracy of indications in the texts of the conditions under which they were preached, the relation of preachers to their audience, and other such issues. Identifying the genre of a homily is necessary, but one can be over-precise in efforts in that direction. And finally, scholars must look not only at homilies but other ancient texts that can shed light on transactions between preachers and their audience. What my survey of recent literature communicates more than anything else is how badly such research is needed if we ever hope to gain a clear and detailed picture of preaching in the Ante-Nicene church, the preaching that went so far toward converting the Roman Empire.

---

[67] Adele Monaci Castagno, *Origene predicatore e il suo pubblico* (Milan: F. Angeli, 1987.

[68] Castagno, "Origen the Scholar and Pastor," 70, 71.

[69] Ibid., 73.

[70] Cunningham and Allen, *Preacher and Audience*, 19.

THE EMERGENCE OF THE SPIRITUAL READING OF THE APOCALYPSE IN THE THIRD CENTURY[1]

Bernard McGinn

The Apocalypse of John is a contentious book even today when biblical literacy is in decline. Millions of fundamentalists read it as a blueprint for the geopolitical events of recent decades and for what lies ahead in such time as remains before the end. Many other Christians seem embarrassed by the book, scarcely knowing what to make of it. Biblical scholars investigate its confusing structure and rich symbolism as a resource for the study of first-century Christianity. Church historians point out that few books of the Bible have been as influential as its last, both for good and for ill. A good number of the literary and artistic monuments of Western culture have been deeply influenced by the Apocalypse and its remarkable imagery.

A study of the reception of the Apocalypse shows that the book has always been the subject of debate.[2] Perhaps even the Christians of the seven churches in Asia Minor to whom the wandering prophet John sent the book needed some help in making sense of it. Written most probably in the last decade of the first century C.E., the Apocalypse was praised and used by some second-century Christian authors, such as Justin and Irenaeus, but it was rejected by Marcion, who could scarcely have been happy with what has been termed the most Jewish book of the New Testament, due to its proximity to the apocalyptic literature of Second Temple Judaism. The objections to the Apocalypse

[1] A longer and somewhat different version of parts of this essay will appear under the title "Turning Points in Early Christian Apocalypse Exegesis," in a volume to be published under the auspices of the Pappas Patristic Institute of Hellenic College. I am happy to offer this essay in honor of Robert M. Grant, my friend and colleague for more than thirty-five years. Ad multos annos!

[2] There is no overall full history of the reception of the Apocalypse, though a helpful introduction can be found in Judith Kovacs and Christopher Rowland, *Revelation* (Oxford: Blackwell, 2004). For the reception in the early church, Ned Bernard Stonehouse, *The Apocalypse in the Early Church. A Study of the History of the New Testament Canon* (Goes, Holland: Oosterbaan & Le Cointre, 1929); Gerhard Meier, *Die Johannisoffenbarung und die Kirche* (Tübingen: Mohr, 1981); and Georg Kretschmar, *Die Offenbarung des Johannis. Die Geschichte ihres Auslegung im 1. Jahrtausend* (Stuttgart: Calwer, 1985).

made by Marcion were seconded by other Christians in the late second century, the "Alogists" of Asia Minor and Rome, who rejected both the Apocalypse and the Gospel ascribed to John.[3] We are not sure of the reasons for the attacks of the Alogists, though some have thought that they were rooted in efforts to combat Montanism, given the fact that the New Prophecy featured a revival of early Christian prophecy to the detriment of episcopal authority (as in the Apocalypse) and also believed in a new descent of the Holy Spirit (as in Jesus's predictions in John 16).[4]

The debate over the Apocalypse has also been tied to the issue of chiliasm or millenialism, that is, belief in the thousand-year reign of Christ and the resurrected saints on earth after the defeat of the forces of evil but before the end, as found in chapter 20 of the book.[5] The connection between chiliasm and the debates over the Apocalypse is real, but it should not be exaggerated for several reasons.[6] The first is that we do not know how widespread chiliastic beliefs actually were among Christians of the first and second centuries. Some apocalyptic texts, both scriptural, such as the Pauline letters, and non-scriptural, such as the *Didache*, are free of chiliasm. Justin and Irenaeus were millennialists, but other important figures, like Clement of Rome, Ignatius of Antioch, and Hermas, were not. As Charles Hill puts it: "A solidly

[3] The views of the Alogists are reported in several ancient witnesses, such as Irenaeus, *Adversus Haereses* 3.11.9; and Epiphanius of Salamis, *Panarion* 51. For a summary, see S.G. Hall, "Aloger," in *Theologische Realenzyklopädie* (Berlin: Walter de Gruyter, 1978) 2:290–95.

[4] For the anti-Montanist view of the Alogists, see Robert M. Grant, *Augustus to Constantine. The Thrust of the Christian Movement into the Roman World* (New York: Harper & Row, 1970), 139–40; Grant, "Literary Criticism and the New Testament Canon," JSNT 16 (1982), 39–40; and Stonehouse, *The Apocalypse*, 49. The extent to which the Montanists were chiliasts living in expectation of the imminence of the end has recently been put in question; see, e.g., Christine Trevett, *Montanism, Gender, Authority and the New Prophecy* (Cambridge: Cambridge University Press, 2002), especially 95–105.

[5] I will use chiliasm and millennialism synonymously as referring specifically to the expected reign of Christ and the saints on earth, often, but not universally, conceived of as lasting a thousand years. Millenarianism will refer to the wider phenomenon of any hope for a better future earthly age.

[6] The literature on millennialism is large. A helpful overview can be found in Robert E. Lerner, "Millenialism," in Bernard McGinn, ed., *The Encyclopedia of Apocalypticism. Volume 2. Apocalypticism in Western History and Culture* (New York: Continuum, 1998), 326–60. For the period under review, see Charles E. Hill, *Regnum Caelorum. Patterns of Millennial Thought in Early Christianity* (Grand Rapids: Eerdman, 2nd ed., 2001); and Clementina Mazzucco, "Il millenarismo cristiano delle origini (II–III sec.)," in Renato Uglione, ed., *"Millennium": L'attesa della fine nei primi secoli cristiani. Atti delle III giornate patristiche torinesi* (Turin: CELID Editrice, 2002), 145–82.

entrenched, non-chiliastic eschatology was present in the Church to rival chiliasm from beginning to end."[7] A second reason is the recognition that there was a variety of forms of chiliasm—it is not just whether there will be an earthly kingdom or not, but what form the kingdom will take, especially how materialistic it will be. John's description of the thousand-year reign in Apocalypse 20:1–6 is rather non-informative about the actual nature of the millennium. Other accounts, such as that ascribed to Papias, an early second century bishop, feature not only descriptions of incredible earthly fecundity and extravagant feasting, but also of enhanced sexual activity and bearing of children for the whole millennium,[8] echoing the language of some Jewish apocalyptic texts. We can conclude that chiliastic beliefs were not an integral feature of all groups of early Christians, as has been sometimes imagined, and that there was a wide range of sources for early Christian chiliasm besides John's revelation.[9]

Another factor in the debate over the Apocalypse in the late second and throughout the third century was Christianity's relation to Judaism. During this time, nascent orthodox Christianity struggled to work out its own interpretation of the Bible against its perceived opponents, especially the "hard-hearted and ignorant members of the circumcision," as well as the "members of the heretical sects," as Origen termed the two main groups of exegetical enemies in *De principiis* 4.2.1. Given the Jewish character of John's Apocalypse, part of the struggle over the book was how a text filled with Jewish apocalyptic imagery could be given the kind of reading that would make it useful for a church whose identity was formed in part by its anti-Jewish stance.[10] Just as Christians had vindicated Old Testament prophecies about the Messiah and his kingdom by reinterpreting them in spiritual fashion as pointing to Christ and the church, so too exegetes were called upon to show how the Apocalypse could be read as a message about the present life of the church as much as (or even more than) a prophecy about controversial events of the end time, events that some believers at least had interpreted in a literal, or "judaizing," fashion.

[7] Hill, *Regnum Caelorum*, 253. Mazzucco, "Il millenarismo," 174–77, also stresses the coexistence of millennial and non-millennial views throughout the Early Church.

[8] On Papias, see Eusebius, *Historia ecclesiastica* (hereafter HE) 3.39.

[9] This point is stressed by Mazzucco, "Il millenarismo," 155–62.

[10] Mazzucco, "Il millenarismo," 170–73, notes the anti-Jewish polemic found in many early Christian opponents to millennialism, suggesting that ongoing conflict with Jewish communities seen as religious competitors was a factor in the debates.

In the course of the third century a group of theologians and exegetes worked out the first systematic interpretations of John's Apocalypse, readings that emphasized the book's relevance for the present life of the church and of individual believers. These spiritualizing readings did not put a halt to all debates over the book and its authority, but they did provide a foundation for later uses of the Apocalypse in antiquity, the Middle Ages, and beyond. Such spiritual interpretations insisted that while the Apocalypse might contain a message about the last times, it was fundamentally a book about the life of the church in the "mid-dest," that is, in the period between Christ's departure from earth and his eventual return in glory. While the details of their readings may strike us as strained, what these exegetes attempted is worth pondering in a period when the debate over how to read the Apocalypse is still quite heated.

The four central Apocalypse exegetes of the third century were Hippolytus, writing early in the first decades of the period, Origen active ca. 220–53, and Methodius and Victorinus who wrote in the second half of the century. Hippolytus was a key figure in the development of Christian eschatology.[11] Although influenced by Irenaeus's view of the last things as set forth in book five of the bishop's *Adversus Haereses*, he did not share the bishop's chiliasm. He also strove to curb expectations of the imminence of the end by calculating the first coming of Christ to the middle of the last millennium of the seven-thousand year view of history, rather than to its end. The focus of Hippolytus's interest is on the present life of the church under Roman rule, toward which he took a decidedly negative stance.

Earlier patristic studies, on the basis of some ancient testimonies and a statue discovered in the sixteenth century with an inscribed list of works, viewed Hippolytus as a Roman priest of the early decades of

[11] For treatments of Hippolytus's eschatology and view of the Apocalypse, see Stonehouse, *The Apocalypse*, 99–109; Hill, *Regnum Caelorum*, 160–70; Brian E. Daley, *The Hope of the Early Church. A Handbook of Patristic Eschatology* (Cambridge: Cambridge University Press, 1991), 38–41; David G. Dunbar, *The Eschatology of Hippolytus of Rome* (Drew University, Ph.D. Dissertation, 1979). Most recently, see Allen Brent, *Hippolytus and the Roman Church. Communities in Tension before the Emergence of the Monarch-Bishop* (Leiden: Brill, 1995); and Enrico Norelli, "L'attesa della fine. 'Ippolito' e la sua tradizione," in *"Millennium": L'Attesa della Fine nei Primi Secoli Cristiani*, 65–99. For a discussion of Hippolytus's contribution to the Antichrist legend, see Bernard McGinn, *Antichrist. Two Thousand Years of the Human Fascination with Evil* (New York: Columbia University Press, 2000, 2nd ed.), 60–63.

the third century.[12] In the past half century this consensus has dissolved. In 1947 Pierre Nautin questioned whether all the works traditionally ascribed to the Roman presbyter could be from the same pen, and recent research seems to favor distinguishing two "Hippolytuses"—the writer of exegetical works such as the *Commentum in Danielem* and the treatise *De Antichristo*, and a second author of the chronographical and anti-heretical works formerly ascribed to "Hippolytus."[13] Although the treatise on the Antichrist and the commentary on Daniel (both written shortly after 200 C.E.) display a keen interest in the final events, Hippolytus was not fundamentally apocalyptic, at least in the sense of expecting an imminent return of Christ.[14] The new form of Christian eschatology pioneered by Hippolytus demanded a new kind of reading of John's revelation.

Hippolytus's interpretation of the Apocalypse was in part defensive—a rebuttal of the Alogists. The only Alogist writer known by name is the Roman priest Gaius active in the late second century.[15] Eusebius tells us that Gaius was an anti-chiliast who disputed with a Montanist named Proclus. According to the Father of Church history, Gaius held that the heretic Cerinthus was the true author of the Apocalypse and its chiliasm—"Cerinthus, who through revelations attributed to the great apostle, lyingly introduces portents to us as though shown him by angels, and says that after the resurrection the kingdom of Christ will be on earth and that humanity living in Jerusalem will again be a slave of lusts and pleasure."[16] Gaius's writings do not survive, but something of his views can possibly be recovered from Hippolytus's *Capitula adversus Gaium*. The problem is that the *Capitula* themselves also do not come

---

[12] See Eusebius, HE 6.22, and Jerome, *De viris illustribus* 61. For an account of the statue and the debates it has engendered, Brent, *Hippolytus and the Roman Church*, chaps. I–V.

[13] For recent judgments, see Norelli, "L'"attesa della fine. 'Ippolito'," 67–68; and Brent, *Hippolytus and the Roman Church*, chaps. IV–V.

[14] Hippolytus's *Commentum in Danielem*, the earliest surviving free-standing Christian biblical commentary, was edited by Georg Nathanael Bonwetsch, *Hippolyt Werke. Erster Band. Erster Teil. Kommentar zu Daniel* (Leipzig: Hinrich, 1897. GCS 7). Here I will use the second improved edition of Marcel Richard (Berlin: Akademie Verlag, 2000). For the *De Antichristo*, see the edition and commentary of Enrico Norelli, *Ippolito, L'Anticristo. De Antichristo* (Florence: Nardini, 1987. Biblioteca Patristica).

[15] Gaius is mentioned by Eusebius, HE 2.25.6–7, 3.28.1–2 and 31.4; and 6.20.3; and also Jerome, *De viris illustribus* 59. For modern studies; Emanuela Prinzivalli, "Gaio e gli alogi," *Studi storico religiosi* 5 (1981): 53–68; Maier, *Die Johannisoffenbarung*, 69–85; and Stonehouse, *The Apocalypse*, 92–99.

[16] Eusebius, HE 3.28.2.

down to us. Scholars of the early church used to be fairly confident that some passages of the *Chapters* could be found in the twelfth-century Syriac apocalypse commentary by Dionysius bar Salibi, as well as in other fragments of materials on the Apocalypse attributed to Hipplytus in Greek, Syriac, Coptic, and Arabic sources.[17]

The recovery of Hippolytus's defense of the Apocalypse against Gaius is further complicated by the fact that Jerome and other sources attributed a commentary on the Apocalypse to Hippolytus.[18] How, then, are the surviving fragments ascribed to Hippolytus to be construed? Are the texts to be assigned to one of the other work, the *Chapters* and the *Commentary*, or, as it has seemed more likely to some recent scholars, were the two works really the same? Most scholars today doubt the existence of a separate commentary on the Apocalypse;[19] some have even questioned the existence of the *Capitula adversus Gaium*, arguing that the debate between "Gaius" and "Hippolytus" found in Dionysius bar Salibi is a more recent construct based on Hippolytan materials filtered through a long chain of tradents.[20] Without attempting to settle these issues, if we compare the references to the Apocalypse in authentic Hippolytan texts, such as the work on Antichrist and the commentary on Daniel, with the fragmentary and controversial texts that reflect,

---

[17] For an edition, commentary, and English translation of the fragments of Hippolytus's *Adversus Gaium* found in the Apocalypse commentary of Dionysius Bar-Salibi, see Dr. Gwynn, "Hippolytus and his 'Heads against Caius'," *Hermathena* 6 (1888): 397–418. There is also a German translation in the first volume of *Hippolytus Werke. Erster Band. Zweiter Teil. Hippolyt's kleinere exegetische und homilitische Schriften*, edited by Hans Achelis (Leipzig: Hinrich, 1897. GCS 7), 241–47. In the same volume (229–38) Achelis also provided a translation of XXII other fragments, I–XXI from a medieval Apocalypse commentary in Arabic, and XXII from Old Slavic. The texts in Bar Salibi were translated into French and commented upon by Pierre Prigent, "Hippolyte, commentateur de l'Apocalypse," *Theologische Zeitschrift* 28 (1972): 391–412. Achelis's Arabic fragments, as well as some citations ascribed to Hippolytus by the sixth-century commentator Andreas of Caesarea, were translated and studied by Pierre Prigent and Ralph Stehly, "Les fragments de Du Apocalypsi d'Hippolyte," *Theologische Zeitschrift* 30 (1973): 313–33. Recently Sebastian Brock has published more Syriac fragments from a sixth century manuscript at Mount Sinai. There is an Italian translation and discussion of these by Alberto Camplani and Emanuela Prinzivalli, "Sul significato dei nuovi frammenti siriaci dei *Capitula adversus Caium* attribuiti a Ippolito," *Augustinianum* 38 (1998): 49–82. Recent discussions of the fragments include Brent, *Hippolytus and the Roman Church*, 144–84; and Norelli, "L'Attesa del fine. 'Ippolito'," 69–75.

[18] Jerome, *De viris illustribus* 61.

[19] See, e.g., Prigent, "Hippolyte, commentateur," 411–12, and "Les fragments," 332–33; Brent, *Hippolytus and the Roman Church*, 144–84; and Nolli, "L'Attesa del fine. 'Ippolito'," 70.

[20] For this argument, see Brent, *Hippolytus and the Church of Rome*, 173–84.

however distantly, his debate with Gaius, we do get the sense of an original exegetical program, one that can be said to form an alternative to the Alexandrian current soon to reach its crest in Origen.[21]

The conflict between Gaius and Hippolytus, although it reaches us in a much edited form, preserves the echoes of a serious exegetical and theological dispute at the end of the second and in the early third centuries. From the perspective of the meaning of Christian beliefs about the end, especially the role that John's Apocalypse should play, the anti-chiliasm of Gaius appears to be linked to a view of the Apocalypse that saw the book as an example of "judaizing" literalism at odds with the true predictions of the end time found in Paul and the Synoptic Gospels. The debate between "Hippolytus" and "Gaius" found in Dionysius bar Salibi features a series of objections made by Gaius to passages from the Apocalypse showing the opposition between what these passages predict and apocalyptic prophecies from Paul and the Synoptics. Hippolytus rebuts these objections by demonstrating that the conflict is only apparent. John's view of the last events, he argues, fully agrees with the scriptural predictions of both the Old and the New Testaments.[22] For example, commenting on the eschatological sign of the blowing of the trumpets in Apocalypse 8 and 9, Gaius is said to have claimed such open predictions contradict Paul's statement that the last things "will come like a thief in the night" (1 Thess. 5:2). Hippolytus responds by noting the concordance between the seven plagues against Egypt and the seven plagues of the Apocalypse (thus suggesting the kind of parallelism to be explored by later Apocalypse commentators, such as Joachim of Fiore), and by arguing that Paul's thief in the night does not refer to the suddenness of the end, but rather to the fact that the wicked will be surprised by the coming of the Lord because they dwell in the darkness of sin. Concerning the prediction in Apocalypse 9:14–15 about the sixth trumpet, when the four angels bound at the Euphrates will be loosed to kill a third of the human race, Gaius says, "It is not written that the angels will make war, nor is it written that 'a third of the human race will be destroyed'," but rather 'nation will rise against nation'" (Mt. 24:7)—thus contrasting the Gospel view of the end with that found in John's revelation. Hippolytus answers by

[21] On the originality of Hippolytus's exegetical program, Camplani and Prinzivalli, "Sul significato," 76.

[22] For a study of the objections, see Camplani and Prinzivalli, "Sul significato," 66–72, who emphasize the attempt to harmonize John and Paul in the text.

identifying the angels with the nations which they oversee, a position found in Daniel and followed by a number of Christian writers.[23]

Given the role that chiliasm played in the debates over John's revelation, it is not surprising to see that the thousand-year kingdom was also part of the confrontation between Gaius and Hippolytus. Gaius contrasted the promise of the binding of Satan at the time of the millennial kingdom (Apoc. 20:2) with the words of Matthew 12:29: "How can anyone enter a strong's man house,... unless he first ties up the strong man?" In other words, since Christ has already bound Satan during his time on earth, there can be no future binding and therefore no millennial kingdom. Hippolytus's refutation of Gaius's position is evidence of an emerging non-literal view of the millennium. He argues that it is evident that Satan is still at work in the world and therefore he was not bound in the past. For Hippolytus the binding and the millennium are still to come, though they are not to be interpreted in a literal way. Hippolytus insists that "the number of the years [i.e., a thousand] is not the number of the days, but it represents the space of one day, glorious and perfect, in which, when the King comes in glory with his slain, the creation is to shine..." Accordingly," he says, "when with the eye of the Spirit John saw the glory of that day [i.e., the sabbath day], he likened it to the space of a thousand years; according to the saying, 'One day in the world of the righteous is as a thousand years' (Ps. 90:4). And by that number he shows that day to be perfect for those that are faithful."[24] This rather elliptical statement is scarcely a literal form of chiliasm. An even more spiritualized reading is found in Hippolytus's *Commentary on Daniel*, where he identifies the seventh age, or thousand-year period, with the kingdom of the saints (Dn. 7), the endless reward Christ bestows on the just after the general resurrection.[25]

Hippolytus's use the Apocalypse in his two major eschatological texts, the *Treatise on Christ and Antichrist* and the *Commentary on Daniel*, often provide parallels, at least in general, with the later Coptic, Arabic, and Syriac fragments ascribed to him, even those that do not directly men-

[23] Gwynn, "Heads against Caius," 402.

[24] Fragment VII from Dionysius bar Salibi (Achelis, 246–47).

[25] For the view of the sabbath as a purely eternal kingdom based on Apoc. 21–22, see *Com. in Dan. 2.37.4* (on the saints as already judging); 3.31–2–4; and 4.10–11, 23, 58. See also *De Antichristo* 65 which fuses the first and the second resurrections. There is a discussion of these texts in Hill, *Regnum Caelorum*, 162–69.

tion Gaius.[26] Without attempting a complete examination, a look at some key passages concerning Apocalypse 12 can provide a good perspective on the originality of his reading of John's enigmatic revelation.

Seven of the surviving twenty-two Arabic fragments of the Apocalypse commentary ascribed to Hippolytus deal with chapter 12.[27] The same chapter is also used extensively in chapters 60–62 of the *Treatise on Christ and Antichrist*.[28] A comparison of these interpretations suggests that Apocalypse 12 began to emerge in the third century as a key component of the new ecclesiological and tropological interpretation of John's book.[29] As Pierre Prigent has argued, Apocalypse 12 can be considered "the center and key to the whole book" in the new spiritual interpretations.[30]

Hippolytus reads Apocalypse 12 in an ecclesiological and Christological way.[31] The Arabic fragments contain an extensive interpretation of the first part of the chapter (Apoc. 12:1–6), the encounter of the heavenly woman and the dragon. It begins with a explanation of 12:1: "Hippolytus, the Roman bishop, is of the view in his exposition of this verse that the 'woman' means the church and the 'sun' with which she is clothed means our Lord Christ, because he is named the 'Sun of Justice' (Mal. 4:2). The 'moon' under her feet is John the Baptist, and the 'crown of twelve stars' on her head signifies the twelve apostles."[32] The exposition found in the fragments continues with the historical identification of the seven heads of the dragon (12:3–4) as seven kings, emissaries of the devil, who persecute the people of God, both in the

[26] For a discussion, see Prigent, "Hippolyte, commenteur de l'Apocalypse," especially 392–410.

[27] Fragments IV–X (Achelis, 232–33).

[28] *De Antichristo* 60–62 (ed. Norelli, 140–46, with notes at 254–61). There are only two brief references to Apocalypse 12 in the Daniel commentary.

[29] According to the first three volumes of the *Biblia Patristica*, there are only 14 references to Apoc. 12 among second and early third century authors, but no less than 73 in the third and early fourth centuries (23 by Hippolytus; 24 by Methodius, and 13 by Victorinus). Origen refers to chap. 12 some 29 times, but this count is misleading, as will be seen below.

[30] Pierre Prigent, *Apocalypse 12. Histoire de l'exégèse* (Tübingen: Mohr, 1959), 1. This useful volume gives an overview of the history of the interpretation of Apocalypse 12.

[31] Prigent, *Apocalypse 12*, 4–5, provides a helpful chart of the surviving traditions concerning Hippolytus's reading of the chapter.

[32] Fragment IV (Achelis, 232). This reading is also reflected in the newly-discovered Syriac fragments a/b (Camplani and Prinzivalli, "Sul significato," 55–57 for the text in translation and 73–75 for discussion). In *De Antichristo* 61 (ed. Norelli, 142–44) we find a similar reading, save that the moon is given a generic reading as "heavenly glory."

time of the Old Testament and the New.[33] In the treatise on the Antichrist, Hippolytus provides a reading of verse 5 that emphasizes the church's continual role in bearing Christ in the world—"the church, always bringing forth Christ, the perfect man child of God, who is declared God and man, becomes the instructor of all the nations. And the words, 'her child was caught up unto God and to his throne,' signify that he who is always born of her is a heavenly king and not an earthly."[34]

The second part of Hippolytus's exegesis of Apocalypse 12 (Apoc. 12:7–17) concerns the meaning of the cosmic struggle between the dragon and the forces of good in the ongoing life of the church.[35] This fits well with his concern for the interim time between Christ's first and second comings.[36] Chapter 61 of *De Antichristo* reads vv. 13–14 (the dragon's pursuit of the heavenly woman, and the two wings given her to fly off for a time, times, and half a time) as the church's coming flight during the 1260 days of Antichrist when her faith in Christ's outstretched arms on the cross will be a protection for believers.[37] The Arabic fragments also contain an exegesis of vv.16 and 17 in which, after the river spit out by the dragon is swallowed by the earth, the dragon "went off to make war on the rest of her children, those who keep the commandments of God and hold the testimony of Jesus." The swallowing up of the river, the Arabic commentator says, can either be interpreted in an external way as predicting that the followers of Satan who persecute the church will actually be swallowed up the way Dathan and his group were at the time of the Exodus (Num. 16:32 ff.), or in an interior fashion, as signifying that the wicked wander here and there and miss the goal of their journey, "as Hippolytus says." Finally, the Arab commentator insists that those who keep the commandments and adhere to Jesus's testimony (v. 17) must be prepared to follow Christ not only in mind, but also in practice, even to the acceptance

---

[33] Fragment VI. The seven kings are Nebuchadnezzer, Kores the Mede (Cyrus), Darius, Alexander, the four successors of Alexander, the Roman empire, and Antichrist. The ten horns are identified with the ten kings who precede Antichrist. These verses are not exegeted in *De Antichristo* 61.

[34] Hippolytus, *De Antichristo* 61 (ed. Norelli, 142–44).

[35] Arabic Fragment VII reads "the great voice from heaven" (v. 10) as coming from the angels, but there are no surviving aspects of the exegesis of vv. 7–9 and 11–12.

[36] Dunbar, "The Delay of the Parousia," 318, notes, "The advance made by Hippolytus on earlier Christian thinkers is that he focuses attention on the time between the first and the second advents."

[37] Arabic Fragment VIII (Achelis, 233) reads the two wings as hope and love.

of martyrdom.[38] From these details, both those in the authentic works and those in the debatable fragments, it is clear that Hippolytus had a coherent ecclesiological reading of chapter 12 of the Apocalypse, one which saw the text as a summary of salvation history—past, present, and to come. There is also some, if minor, appeal to the moral, or tropological, significance of the text as a guide to how Christians should act both in the present and at the time of the end.

When we come to the second great Apocalypse exegete of the third century, Hippolytus's younger contemporary Origen, we find a use of John's revelation that goes even further in its ecclesiological emphasis. Among early Christian exegetes, Origen is noted for the way in which he directed his interpretation of scripture toward the goal of deeper understanding of revealed truth in the service of an anagogic appropriation of the message of the Word hidden under the external letters of the sacred text.[39] Origen's deeply spiritual view of the Bible might seem to have led him to oppose John's lurid revelation. This was not the case. The Alexandrian considered the Apocalypse as canonical, and he cites it, implicitly or explicitly, quite often in his surviving writings.[40] Unfortunately, Origen never got to write the commentary on John's revelation he tells us he wanted to compose.[41] His use of the Apocalypse, as Adele Monaci has shown, concentrates on undermining literal futuristic apocalyptic interpretations in the service of a realized Christological eschatology that adheres to a dogmatic, and not historical, sense of the biblical prophecies.[42] Somewhat surprisingly, Origen

---

[38] Fragment X (Achelis, 233). See also Prigent, "Les fragments," 325–26. Here the Arab commentator disagrees with Hippolytus, though the context makes the source of conflict difficult to interpret.

[39] For a good account of the tropological and anagogical aspects of Origen's exegesis, see Karen Jo Torjesen, *Hermeneutical Procedure and Theological Method in Origen's Exegesis* (Berlin: Walter de Gruyter, 1986).

[40] According to the references compiled in the *Biblia Patristica. Vol. III. Origène* (Paris: CNRS, 1980), 466–69, Origen references the Apocalypse 416 times, but many of these citations are generic at best. Origen seems to have been aware of the disputes over whether John actually wrote the book. In his late treatise *De Pascha*, he refers to "the Apocalypse said to be John's" (O. Guéraud–P. Nautin, eds., *Origène sur la Paque* [Paris: Éditions du Cerf, 1979], 119). On Origen's use of the Apocalypse, see Stonehouse, *The Apocalypse*, 117–123, Manlio Simonetti, "Il millenarismo in Oriente da Origene a Metodio," *Corona Gratiarum. Miscellanea Patristica, Historica et Liturgica Eligio Dekkers O.S.B. XII Lustra complenti Oblata* (Bruges: Sint Pietersabdij, 1975) 1: 37–58; and Adele Monaci, "Apocalisse ed escatologia nell'opera di Origene," *Augustinianum* 18 (1978): 139–51.

[41] See *Matthaei Commentariorum Series* 49 (GCS 11: 105.8): . . . exponentur autem tempore sui in Revelatione Iohannis.

[42] Monaci, "Apocalisse ed escatologia," 142–43, 149–50.

does not indulge in much personal appropriation of the images of the book for moral and mystical development. This dimension was to be taken up in more detail by those who came after him.

Origen's comment on the "Little Apocalypse" in Matthew 24–25 provides an example of what he might have done in a full commentary on the Apocalypse, by showing how a spiritual reading of the images of resurrection and final judgment in Matthew could avoid the extremes of rejection of the truth of prophecy, on the one hand, and the literalism of some of his predecessors, on the other.[43] Origen's understanding of the resurrection of the body, suggested in Matthew 25:31–46 and endorsed in Apocalypse 20:11–15, has come in for study in recent years.[44] His treatment of the gospel predictions about the Second Coming and the Last Judgment also demonstrate a concern for reinterpreting the details of the scriptural picture of the last events in the service of the dogmatic meaning of the symbols. For example, he argued that the particulars of the judgment scene presented in Matthew should not be taken as literal prophecies of what is to come, but rather as revealing various aspects of how Christ will manifest himself spiritually to all humans at the end of time—in glory to those who have been perfected in virtue and in judgment to the wicked.[45] Therefore, it is clear that there could be no real millennium for the Alexandrian exegete. Origen attacked such a view as Jewish literalism in *De principiis* 2.11.2–3, as well as in many places in his writings, basing his argument on the exegetical principle set forth in book 4 that "in all the prophecies concerning Jerusalem... the scriptures are telling us about the heavenly city...." (4.3.8).[46] For Origen, the thousand-year kingdom predicted in Apocalypse 20 is the heavenly intermediate state in which the souls

[43] For a sketch of Origen's re-reading of scriptural apocalypticism, see Daley, *Hope of the Early Church*, 47–60, who speaks of Origen's program as a form of demythologizing (48). Also see Hill, *Regnum Caelorum*, 176–89, on his attitudes towards chiliasm and exegesis of Apocalypse 20.

[44] See Daley, *Hope of the Early Church*, 51–55; and Caroline Walker Bynum, *The Resurrection of the Body in Western Christianity, 200–1336* (New York: Columbia University Press, 1995), 63–71.

[45] The most extensive discussion is in *Matt. Comm. Ser.* 32–73 (GCS 11: 57–174). See also the *Commentum in Matthaeum* 12.30–32 (GCS 10: 133–43); and *Contra Celsum* 5.14–17 (GCS 2: 15–19).

[46] Origen, *De principiis* 2.11.2–3 and 4.3.8 (GCS 4: 184–86, 333–35); see also *Contra Celsum* 7.28–29 (GCS 2: 178–81). Origen's insistence the eschatological Jerusalem is a heavenly, not an earthly, city runs directly counter to Irenaeus's claims that the prediction of the descent of the heavenly city to earth must be read literally (AH 5.35). Origen attacks literal readings of the millennium in many places; e.g., *Selecta in Psalmos* Ps. 4:6

of the just await the Last Judgment and the final Sabbath rest of the kingdom of heaven.[47]

Given the Christological focus of Origen's interpretation of the Apocalypse, one in which the picture of the Rider on the White Horse of 19:11–16 takes a central role, it is strange that he made such little use of chapter 12, which Hippolytus had already developed in terms of the relation of Christ and the church. Although the Alexandrian references the chapter almost thirty times, his interest centers on the activities of the seven-headed dragon, that is, Satan (e.g., *De prin.* 2.8.3). The dragon's tail that drags down a third of heaven's stars (vv. 3–4) is mentioned in the fragments of the *Matthew Commentary* (Mt. 24:29–30), where Origen says he will not go into detail but affirms that the seven heads could either be seven evil princes (as in Hippolytus), or (in a tropological reading) "such great sins as lead to death." The stars that are dragged down are read as those who at one time did actually shine like stars in following Christ, but who later lost their way and were brought down by the devil.[48] (Whether Origen has heretics, or perhaps apostatizing Christians in mind is difficult to say.) Notices of verses 7, 9, and 10 also survive, but mostly as generic references to the role of "the devil and his angels" being cast down into this world (see, e.g., *De prin.* 1.6.3; *Contra Celsum* 7.17).

Origen's rereading of chiliasm and his sporadic use of the Apocalypse did not mean that the book had clear sailing in the Christian East from the second half of the third century on. Literal millenarianism was alive and well in the time of Origen's pupil, Dionysius of Alexandria, as we can see from the bishop's letters that survive in Eusebius's *Ecclesiastical History* 7.24–25. Dionysius's pamphlet *On Promises* (significantly the same title as *De prin.* 2.11) attacked the literal chiliasm of the deceased bishop Nepos whose followers had introduced "schisms and secessions of entire churches." By dint of long debate, Dionysius won back the schismatics. Eusebius quotes his argument proving that the Apostle John cannot have been the author of the book, thus distinguishing the Gospel from the Apocalypse, but as Dionysius insists, "I myself would never dare to reject the book of which so many good Christians have a very high opinion, but realizing that my mental powers are inadequate to

(PG 12: 1149); *Commentum in Cantica Canticorum*, prol. (GCS 8: 66); and *Commentum in Matthaeum* 17.35–36 (GCS 10: 698–99).

[47] See the discussion in Hill, *Regnum Caelorum*, especially 176, 181, and 189.

[48] Origen, *Matt. Comm. Ser.* 49 (GCS 11:105–06).

judge it properly, I take the view that the interpretation of the various sections is largely a mystery..."[49] This was a standard humility topos, however, because Eusebius notes that Dionysius went on to examine the whole Apocalypse, "proving the impossibility of understanding it in a literal sense." Despite the efforts of Origen and Dionysius, the Apocalypse continued to be suspect in the East for some centuries, even among some of Origen's followers. As Robert Grant has demonstrated, Eusebius himself seems to have had two views of it—an early more favorable position, and a later suspicious one, although he never directly rejected the book (see HE 6.25.10).[50]

Origen did not got to write his commentary on the Apocalypse. The exegesis of the book by Hippolytus and Dionysius comes down to us only in fragments. The earliest surviving attempts at extended interpretations of the Apocalypse date from the second half the third century—the sections devoted to the Apocalypse in the *Symposion* of Methodius of Olympus and the Apocalypse commentary of the Dalmatian bishop Victorinus of Poetovio. These works constitute a major turning point in the history of the reception of John's revelation. In different ways they show how the images of the prophecy could be related not only to the understanding of the life of the church, as emphasized by Hippolytus and Origen, but also to the lives of individual Christians in their struggle for virtue.

Methodius is something of a mystery-man. He was not known to Eusebius, and therefore we have to go on very fragmentary evidence outside his own writings. Thought to be a bishop of Asia Minor in the later third century, he is said to have died a martyr in 311.[51] In the late

[49] Eusebius, HE 7.25.2. Dionysius's demonstration of why the Apocalypse could not have been written by the Apostle John, as found in HE 7.25, constitutes in Robert Grant's words, "the high water mark of ante-Nicene grammatical analysis, at least in so far as it has been preserved for us" ("Literary Criticism and the New Testament Canon," 40).

[50] For positive views of the apostolic authority of the Apocalypse, see, e.g., HE 3.18.1, 3.20.9, and 3.23.6. Later he followed Gaius in ascribing the work to Cerinthus; e.g., HE 3.28.2, 3.24.18, and 3.25.2 and 4. For a discussion, see Robert M. Grant, *Eusebius as Church Historian* (Oxford: Clarendon Press, 1980), 130–36. The two different views parallel the divergent accounts of Papias found in the HE, as shown by Grant, "Papias in Eusebius' Church History," in *Mélanges d'histoire des religions offerts à Henri-Charles Puech* (Vendome: Presses universitaires de France, 1974), 209–13.

[51] Jerome, *De viris illustribus* 83. On Methodius, see L. G. Patterson, *Methodius of Olympus. Divine Sovereignty, Human Freedom, and Life in Christ* (Washington, D.C.: Catholic University Press, 1997); and Herbert Musirillo, "Introduction," *St. Methodius. The Symposium. A Treatise on Charity* (Westminster: Newman Press, 1958), 3–37, whose translation

seventh century the most widely-diffused of all post-biblical apocalypses, the *Revelationes Methodii*, was ascribed to him, though today we know it was originally composed in Syriac about 690.[52] Little of Methodius's extensive corpus remains. Among the authentic works, the *Symposion*, a philosophical dialogue in the style of Plato, occupies the central place. Methodius comes down to us as an opponent of Origen, due to his attack on the Alexandrian's conception of the pre-existence of the soul and of a purely spiritual resurrection, but his exegesis is deeply Origenistic. Of the eleven discourses praising virginity that constitute the *Symposion*, four treat three different sections from the Apocalypse. Two are fairly brief, the passages in discourses 1.5 and 6.5 that take John's vision of the 144,000 virgins of Apocalypse 14:1–5 and 7:9 as predictive of the "very small number" of virgins found in the church.[53] The more extensive passages are found in discourses 8 and 9. The text in discourse 9 concerns the true meaning of the millennium. This discourse, the speech of the virgin Tusiane concerning the account in Leviticus of the Feast of Tabernacles (Lev. 23:39 ff.), sees the feast as a type of the image of heavenly realities found in the earthly church, which are, in turn, types of what is to come, namely "the resurrection and building of our temple...in the seventh millennium [when] we shall celebrate the great feast of the true Tabernacle in that new creation where there will be no pain, when all the fruits of the earth will have been harvested, and men will no longer beget nor be begotten, and God will rest from the work of his creation."[54] In explaining this heavenly conception of the millennium, Methodius invokes texts from the Apocalypse's account of the "first resurrection" (Apoc. 20:6), as well as from its picture of life in the heavenly Jerusalem come to earth

---

will be used here. The standard edition is that of G. Nathanael Bonwetsch, *Methodius* (Leipzig: Hinrich, 1917. GCS). On Methodius's chiliasm, see Simonetti, "Il millenarismo in Oriente," 54–58; Clementina Mazzucco, "Il millenarismo di Metodio di Olimpio di fronte a Origene: polemica o continuità?," *Augustinianum* 26 (1986); 73–87; L.G. Patterson, "Methodius' Millenarianism," *Studia Patristica* 24 (1993): 306–15; and Emanuela Prinzivalli, "Il millenarismo in Oriente da Metodio ad Apollinare," *Annali di Storia dell'Esegesi* 15 (1998): 125–51. See also Hill, *Regnum Caelorum*, 39–41; and Daley, *Hope of the Early Church*, 61–64.

52 On the *Revelationes Sancti Methodii*, see the new critical edition of the original Syriac text by G. Reinink, *Die Syrische Apokalypse des Pseudo-Methodius*, 2 vols. (Louvain: Peeters, 1993).

53 See *Symposium* 1.5 (ed., 13–14; trans. 47–48), and 6.5 (ed., 69–70; trans., 95).

54 *Symposium* 9.1 (ed., 114; trans. 132). For a survey of the ninth discourse, see Patterson, *Methodius*, 105–13.

(Apoc. 22:1 and 13).[55] The discussion shows that in the case of Methodius we are not talking about a literal millennialism, but rather, in the words of Emanuela Prinzivalli, "an almost evaporated millennialism."[56]

If the ninth discourse emphasizes the church to come, the eighth provides us with Methodius's view of the present church, as seen through the prism of the Apocalypse. This discourse, ascribed to the legendary virgin Thecla, supposedly a convert of Paul, centers on an extended exegesis of Apocalypse 12.[57] The reason for choosing this chapter for commentary is that virgins, like the visionary John himself, are meant to soar aloft to heavenly visions (8.2), specifically the beholding of the ideal forms "of marvelously glorious and blessed beauty, and such as are difficult to describe" (8.3). While virgins often seem to already live in the "abundant light of the kingdom of heaven" (8.4), the afflictions and sorrows of the present life continue to trouble them; but, says Methodius, such clouds sent by the evil one "will be blown away by the Spirit, if only, like your mother the virgin who brought forth a man child in heaven, you will not be afraid of the serpent" (8.4). Methodius's use of Apocalypse 12 is paranetic rather than predictive, an exercise in applying the mythic paradigms of John's vision to the life of the Christian virgin. There is no emphasis on salvation history, especially the past, but rather a call to direct our attention to the a-temporal heavenly realities, a Christian version of Plato's vision of the forms.

Although Methodius admits the difficulty of John's revelation—he speaks of "the greatness of the mysteries of the text" (*to megethos tôn ainigmatôn tēs graphēs*)[58]—he constructs a powerful and seamless spiritual

[55] *Symposium* 9.3 (ed., 117; trans., 136).

[56] Prinzivalli, "Il millenarismo in Oriente," 127: "Si tratterebbe di un millenarismo quasi evaporato." Others agree. Hill summarizes (*Regnum Caelorum*, 41): "Methodius's 'millennium' is no longer chiliastic in the important dogmatic sense of it being an interim reign on this earth prior to the last judgment." Patterson, *Methodius*, 113, noting the dependence on Clement and Origen, concludes: "While neither Clement nor Origen have any room for a 'millennium' of even Methodius' highly modified sort, and while Methodius is the first we know of to offer a millenarian interpretation of the Feast of the Tabernacles, it is plainly along the lines suggested by Clement and Origen that his interpretation of the feast becomes a vehicle for discussing the true significance of the restoration of souls to bodies in anticipation of their full perfection."

[57] *Symposium* 8 (ed., 80–111; trans. 104–30). The eighth discourse forms the heart of the work and is discussed in detail by Patterson, *Methodius*, 95–105. On the link between the spiritualized readings of Apoc. 12 and 20 in the two chapters, see Mazzucco, "Il millenarismo di Metodio," 82–83.

[58] *Symposium* 8.9 (ed., 92.1; trans. 114).

reading of the symbols of chapter 12.[59] The woman who appears in heaven clothed with the sun and crowned with twelve stars is our mother the church, who represents "virgins prepared for marriage" (8.5). She stands on the watery moon "as a tropological explanation for the faith of those who have been purified from corruption by baptism" (8.6). In answer to the objection that such a reading must be wrong because the woman of the Apocalypse brings forth "a man child," Methodius responds by laying out a fundamental principle of his spiritual exegesis—"Remember that the mystery of the Incarnation of the Word was fulfilled long before the Apocalypse, whereas John's prophetic message has to do with the present and the future" (8.7). Therefore, chapter 12 is no longer to be read as about the past, but rather tropologically about the life of the church and her children, both now and in the time to come. The child who is taken up to the throne of God to be protected against the dragon is not Christ himself, according to Methodius, but rather "all those who are baptized in Christ [and] become, as it were, other Christs by a communication of the Spirit; and here it is the church that effects this transformation into the clear image of the Word" (8.8). Methodius concludes: "And thus it is that the church is said to be ever forming and bringing forth *a man child*, the Word, in those who are sanctified" (8.9). Though the theme of the birth of the Word in the soul was already known to Origen, this part of Methodius's treatise is one of its most forceful expressions in patristic literature.[60]

The second part of Methodius's exegesis concerns the figure of the seven-headed dragon and the details of his pursuit of the woman and her child. The dragon, of course, is the devil; the third part of the stars he drags down with his tail is "the seditious group of heretics" who have erred about the Trinity (8.10). The evisceration of all prophetic content in Methodius's immanentizing reading is most evident in the last part of his commentary. The wilderness into which the heavenly woman, i.e., the church, flees for 1260 days represents a paradoxical desert empty of what is evil and corruptible, but abounding in the fruit of virtues (8.11), while the 1260 days "signify the direct, clear, and per-

---

[59] For a summary of Methodius's spiritualizing reading of chap. 12, see Prigent, *Apocalypse 12*, 10–11.

[60] On the birth of the Word in the soul, see Hugo Rahner, "Die Gottesgeburt: Die Lehrer der Kirchenväter von der Geburt Christi aus den Herzen der Kirche und der Gläubigen," in *Symbole der Kirche: Die Ekkelesiologie der Väter* (Salzburg: Müller, 1964), 7–87, who discusses Methodious on 35–40.

fect knowledge of the Father, Son, and Spirit, in which, as he grows, our mother rejoices and exults during this time until the restoration of the new ages..." (8.11)—a reference to Methodius's spiritual reading of the millennial kingdom. After a brief survey of the number symbolism underlying this interpretation (8.11–12), Methodius returns to the paranetic center of his reading, briefly commenting on how the defeat of the dragon signifies that the Christian virgin overcomes his seven heads or vices by practicing the opposing virtues, while she conquers his ten horns by combating sins against the ten commandments (8.13). Thus, Methodius made the symbols of Apocalypse 12 directly applicable to the moral life of the ideal Christian, that is, the virgin.

A similar line of interpretation is found in the *Commentary on the Apocalypse* by bishop Victorinus of Poetovio in modern Slovenia. This text, written perhaps as early as 260, is the earliest full exposition of the book. Despite Jerome's aspersions on the intelligence of this martyr bishop, the commentary is a remarkable and original reading.[61] Perhaps Victorinus was able to provide a complete commentary because he discovered a key aspect of the structure of the Apocalypse that during the past century has once again been revived by exegetes—*recapitulatio*, the notion that the work is organized according to repeating patterns of sevens. As he puts it in commenting on the relation of the seven trumpets to the seven vials (Apoc. 8:6–9:21 and 16:1–21), "Do not regard the order of what is said, because the sevenfold Holy Spirit, when it has passed in review the events leading to the last times and the end, returns once again to the same events and completes what it had said more briefly. Do not seek the temporal order in the Apocalypse, but look for the inner meaning" (*Nec requirendus est ordo in Apocalypsi, sed intellectus requirendus*)."[62] Victorinus's view of the recapitulation that provides the clue for the confusing repetitions of the Apocalypse was part of a wider theological agenda, inherited at least in part from Irenaeus, that made

---

[61] Our knowledge of Victorinus is largely dependent on Jerome, *De viris illustribus* 74. The most recent study is Martine Dulaey, *Victorin de Poetovio. Premier exégète latin*, 2 vols. (Paris: Institut d'Études Augustiniennes, 1993). Dulaey presents Victorinus's chiliasm in Vol. 1: 255–70. Dulaey's view of Victorinus is summarized in her "Introduction," in *Victorin de Poetovio. Sur l'Apocalypse et autres écrits* (Paris: Les Éditions du Cerf, 1997. SC 423), 15–41. See also Carmelo Curti, "Il regno millenario in Vittorino di Petovio," *Augustinianum* 18 (1978): 419–33; Daley, *Hope of the Early Church*, 65–66; and Hill, *Regnum Caelorum*, 35–39. Victorinus is traditionally said to have died in the Great Persecution in 303. Dulaey (*Victorin de Poetovio* 1:12) argues for a more likely date of ca. 283–84.

[62] Victorinus, *In Apocalypsin* 8.2 (ed. Dulaey, 88).

recapitulation the key to salvation history. Just as Christ recapitulates all ages and the stages of human life in himself, so too the Apocalypse, the final book of the Bible, gathers together all that had gone before it, both in the Old and the New Testaments.

Victorinus is not only the first author to provide a synoptic reading of the Apocalypse, but he was also an innovator in how he used the book's symbols to reveal the unity of the revelation of the Word in both the Old and the New Testaments. Much of the symbolism that earlier and later interpreters regarded as prophetic of events to come Victorinus inteprets as a revelation of the agreement between the preaching of the Old Law and that of the New, or as signs of Christ's fulfillment of prophecy. This is evident in the structure of his commentary.[63] The comment on the first six chapters is fundamentally Christological, a study of Christ's presence in the church. Apocalypse 1–3, the vision of the Son of Man who sends letters to the seven churches, is read as the manifestation of Jesus the God-man sending his sevenfold Spirit to the universal church manifested in seven forms (*In Apoc.* 1.7). The throne vision of chapters 4–5 signifies the unity of the preaching of the two Testaments. Speaking of the wings of the four living creatures in Apocalypse 4:8, for example, Victorinus says, "The wings are the testimonies of the books of the Old Testament, and that is why there are twenty-four, the same number as the elders seated on the thrones. Just as an animal cannot fly without wings, so too the preaching of the New Testament is not trustworthy without the prior testimonies of the Old Testament by which it is lifted up from the earth and flies."[64] In chapter six the lamb opens the books sealed with seven seals, that is, Christ by his death and resurrection opens up the inner meaning of the Old Testament.

The account of the seven seals in Apocalypse 6–9 is read both synchronically and diachronically, as Victorinus's exegesis begins to adopt a more historical stance. Although the seals were opened all at once in Christ's revelation of the meaning of the Old Testament, they also show the progress of the church through time. The first seal is the universal preaching of the Gospel, the second through fourth announce the persecutions of the church, while the fifth seal indicates the desire of the

[63] See the discussion of the structure in Dulaey, *Victorin de Poetovio*, Vol. 1, chap. III, which is summarized in the "Introduction," *Victorin de Poetovio. Sur l'Apocalypse*, 30–35.

[64] *In Apocalypsin* 4.5 (ed. Dulaey, 70).

dead for the Parousia.[65] The sixth seal represents the final persecution of Antichrist and the seventh seal is the "beginning of eternal rest," not its conclusion, as the recapitulation of the patterns of sevens in the rest of the book shows (*In Apoc.* 6.6). The later accounts of the seven trumpets and the seven vials Victorinus reads as filling in the details about the final persecution of the sixth seal. In the interpretation of chapters 10 and 11 Victorinus reprises his reading of the Apocalypse as the key to the bible. The strong angel who descends to earth with the open book (Apoc. 10:1–4) is Christ holding the Apocalypse, the revelation of all the mysteries of the Old Testament.

Victorinus's application of recapitulation enables him to read chapters 11 through 22 of the Apocalypse as a repeating, but incrementally increasing, revelation about the last persecution and the coming millennium predicted in chapters 20 and 21. The exception to this is his reading of chapter 12, a passage the bishop interprets as a special vision of the whole of history, past, present, and to come. The vision begins with the past because the woman crowned with the sun of verse 1 is identified as the "ancient church of the patriarchs, prophets and holy apostles," which groaned for Christ's coming.[66] The dragon is Satan who is not able to devour the woman's child because the devil had no power to hold Christ in death. The rapture of the child into heaven (v. 5) is Christ's Ascension. In unique fashion, Victorinus then turns to the present and future, reading the woman of vv. 6–14 as referring to "the whole catholic church, in which the one hundred and forty-four thousand will come to believe in the last time under the preaching of Elijah."[67] This *populum binum*, consisting of Gentiles and the Jews who will be converted at the end, is both the contemporary church subject

[65] Hill, *Regnum Caelorum*, 37–38 and 245, notes Victorinus's exegetical ingenuity in maintaining the old chiliastic view that all souls, even those of the martyrs, have to wait in Hades until Christ's inauguration of the millennium. Victorinus achieves this by distinguishing between the golden altar of heaven and the bronze altar of the earth under which the souls of those who died for Christ are waiting (Apoc. 5:3–4). See *In Apocalypsin* 6.4 (ed. Dulaey, 80–82).

[66] *In Apocalypsin* 12.1 (ed. Dulaey, 98–100). Victorinus's reading is unusual, as are its details. The sun is the hope of resurrection and reward, the moon is the bodily death of the ancients, which nonetheless does not extinguish their hope in Christ, while the crown of twelve stars indicates the choir of patriarchs who are Christ's bodily ancestors. On Victorinus's reading of chap. 12, see Prigent, *Apocalypse 12*, 7–9.

[67] *In Apocalypsin* 12.4 (ed. Dulaey, 102): ***Mulierum autem uolasse in deserto auxilio alarum magnae aquilae***... ecclesiam omnem catholicam, in qua in nouissimo tempore creditura sunt centum quadraginta quattuor milia sub Helia propheta.

to persecution by the dragon's seven heads, that is, Roman emperors, and the future church of the time of the final assault of Antichrist, which will flee into the desert and be protected by God during the three and a half years of his reign (*In Apoc.* 12.4–7).

After the defeat of Antichrist, Victorinus believed that there would be a millennial reign of Christ and the saints as predicted in Apocalypse 20. Jerome, who re-edited Victorinus's commentary about 380, was scandalized by this and replaced the bishop's discussion with his own exegesis of the passage.[68] Victorinus's chiliastic views are both archaic and innovative. He is old-fashioned in claiming two resurrections (*In Apoc.* 20.2) and making use of many of the material descriptions and biblical passages found in earlier Christian chiliastic texts (e.g., *In Apoc.* 21.1–6). He also identifies the thousand-year reign promised in Apocalypse 20:1–6 with the descent of the heavenly Jerusalem described in chapter 21, as some earlier authors had.[69] But when it comes to the details of this final sabbath age, the bishop, in line with the Origenist view, provides allegorical and spiritual readings of the joys of the coming kingdom that often make it difficult to distinguish it from the eternal bliss of heaven.[70] Victorinus's moderate view of the millennium represents an attempt at fusion between the literal chiliasm of many early Christians and the spiritualization of the millennium that had grown strong in the third century.[71]

The emergence of a spiritualized, or allegorical, reading of the Apocalypse in the third century did not come without a cost. In the concluding chapter of his *The Letter and the Spirit*, Robert Grant noted that the allegorizers of the early church, "tended to empty history of meaning," because "history was at best an imperfect representation of eternal truth."[72] Grant also recognized that the allegorizers did so at

[68] On the relation of Jerome to Victorinus, see Martine Dulaey, "Jérome 'éditeur' du *Commentaire sur l'Apocalypse* de Victorin de Poetovio," *Revue des Études Augustiniennes* 37 (1991): 199–236.

[69] Conflating the thousand-year reign of Apoc. 20:1–6 with the account of the descent of the Heavenly Jerusalem of Apoc. 21 can be found in such authors as Justin (*Dialogus* 81.1), Tertullian (*Adversus Marcionem* 3.4), and Commodianus (*Institutiones* 1.41 and 44).

[70] For a study of these spiritualized readings, see Curti, "Il regno millennario in Vittorino," 431–32.

[71] Recent interpreters of Victorinus have stressed the moderate nature of his chiliasm. See Dulaey, *Victorin de Poetovio* 1:255–70, and "Introduction," 39–41; and Curti, "Il regno millennario in Vittorino."

[72] R.M. Grant, *The Letter and the Spirit* (New York: Macmillan, 1957), 107.

least in part because "they were convinced that revelation had meaning not only in the past but in the present."[73] The ongoing tension between the spiritualizers and the historically-minded, which Grant showed had continued on into the theological situation of a half-century ago, takes on a particular power when it comes to the proper interpretation of the only prophetic book of the New Testament. Despite the general triumph of spiritual readings in East and West in the fourth century, the continuing re-emergence of literal interpretations of the Apocalypse is one of the most salient features in the reception history of the book. Such attempts at literal historicizing readings over the centuries have all proven false—and many of them were also the source of conflict, persecution, and violence. Today literal readings of the Apocalypse as a blueprint for what is soon to come abound. There can be no denying that they serve their purpose in making the book real and present for many fundamentalist believers, but one can question if this form of presence is either legitimate or helpful. Historicizing literalism, however, is not the only option. Perhaps an appreciation of the efforts of the great exegetes of the third century who pioneered the spiritual reading of John's dangerous book can suggest other interpretive possibilities worth exploring in our own much changed historical context.

[73] Grant, *The Letter and the Spirit*, 105.

EUSEBIUS ON PORPHYRY'S "POLYTHEISTIC ERROR"

Robert Lee Williams

Robert M. Grant is known as a church historian. His research has illuminated as well the developments in patristic theology from the church's interaction with religion and philosophy indigenous to its Greco-Roman culture. Christian theology has added texture from this vantage point. The present study reflects this contribution in relation to Eusebius, a figure familiar to our mentor and friend.

"Except for Origen, Eusebius outdistances all Greek Church Fathers in research and scholarship."[1] The largest portion of our author's work is in response to Porphyry, Neoplatonic philosopher and opponent of Christianity. The publications reflect a combination of historical works and theological works.[2] While best known for his *Ecclesiastical History*, Eusebius was more prolific in his theological writings.[3] This paper focuses on his theological response to Porphyry in *Preparation for the Gospel*. In particular, we shall find our author emphasizing the inadequacy of Porphyry's polytheism in providing a god who is creator of all and is good to that creation. Porphyry in fact lacks integrity and is not to be trusted. His writing betrays a deviousness laced with forced logic and intended to impress the populace with a deluding interweaving of mythology and philosophy.[4]

Understanding Eusebius's response to Porphyry will be facilitated by knowing personal and ideological features of their relationship. Regarding personal matters, Eusebius was an admirer of Origen.[5] Porphyry's work of fifteen books *Against the Christians* was an attack on the esteemed Origen as well as an important part of the pagan struggle underlying

---

[1] Johannes Quasten, *Patrology* (4 vols.; Westminster: Newman, 1963), 3:311.

[2] The *Chronicle*, in particular, was a response to Porphyry. See my *Bishop Lists: Formation of Apostolic Succession in Ecclesiastical Crises* (GD 16; Piscataway: Gorgias, 2005), 196–203.

[3] Aryeh Kofsky, *Eusebius of Caesarea Against Paganism* (Boston: Brill, 2002), 1.

[4] Similarly Kofsky, ibid., 271, has observed that Eusebius's argument was that "the [mythological] tradition that Porphyry sought to interpret...could not sustain Porphyry's interpretation."

[5] Ibid., 12.

the persecution in Eusebius's own day.[6] Parallel to Origen's eight books addressing Celsus's *True Word* in the third century (*Hist. eccl.* 6.36.2),[7] our author answered Porphyry's work with twenty-five books *Against Porphyry* (Jerome, *Vir. ill.* 81),[8] though the philosopher had probably died by the time of the work against him.[9] Porphyry's *Against the Christians* was arguably also the motivating force[10] behind Eusebius's most prodigious work, "the most majestic and disdainful of all polemics,"[11] an apologetic of thirty-five books divided into two parts, the more polemical *Preparation for the Gospel* of fifteen books and the more apologetic *Demonstration of the Gospel* with twenty (*Praep. ev.* 1.1.12–13).[12]

---

[6] Ibid., 4, 18. Eusebius quotes Porphyry as having met Origen. The philosopher was "very young" at the time (Eusebius, *Hist. eccl.* 6.19.5; Kirsopp Lake et al., ed. and trans., *Eusebius: The Ecclesiastical History* [2 vols.; LCL; repr., Cambridge: Harvard University Press, 1994], 2:58–59). If Origen died about 253 (Joseph Wilson Trigg, *Origen: The Bible and Philosophy in the Third-century Church* [Atlanta: John Knox, 1983], 243), the encounter was evidently while Porphyry was in his teens. Eunapius places Porphyry's birth in Tyre in 233 (*Lives of the Philosophers and Sophists* 455; Wilmer Cave Wright, ed. and trans., *Philostratus and Eunapius: The Lives of the Sophists* [LCL; London: Heinemann, 1922], 352–53; R. Joseph Hoffmann, *Porphyry's Against the Christians: The Literary Remains* [Amherst: Prometheus, 1994], 155). Porphyry had suffered abuse by Christians. Robert Grant, "Porphyry among the Early Christians," in *Romanitas et Christianitas*, ed. W. den Boer et al. (Amsterdam: North-Holland, 1973), 181, surmises that a "beating" of Porphyry by Christians in Caesarea, reported by Socrates (*Hist. eccl.* 3.23.38–39; Günther Christian Hansen, ed., *Sokrates Kirchengeschichte* [GCS NF 1; Berlin: Akademie Verlag, 1995], 222–23. ET: A.C. Zenos, trans., *The Ecclesiastical History of Socrates Scholasticus* [NPNF ser. 2; repr., Grand Rapids: Eerdmans, 1976], 2:93), is perhaps best understood as a "verbal defeat" in debate with Christians.

[7] See Kofsky, *Eusebius*, 77, for comparison of the two works.

[8] Earnest Cushing Richardson, ed., *Hieronymus: Liber de viris inlustribus; Gennadius: Liber de viris inlustribus* (TU 14, 1a; Leipzig: Hinrichs, 1896), 43. ET: Thomas P. Halton, trans., *Saint Jerome: On Illustrious Men* (FC 100; Washington: Catholic University of America Press, 1999), 114. On behalf of Origen, Eusebius had already assisted his mentor Pamphilus in a *Defence of Origen* addressing Christian critics (*Hist. eccl.* 6.33.4; LCL 2:88–89), completing it after the death of Pamphilus about 310 (Quasten, *Patrology*, 2:145).

[9] Porphyry's death is dated around 305 (Andrew D. Barker, "Porphyry," OCD, 1226). Eusebius composed his work between 312 and 324 (Kofsky, *Eusebius*, 74–75).

[10] Ibid., 18. See Jean Sirinelli, *Les vues historiques d'Eusèbe de Césarée durant la période prénicéenne* (Faculté des lettres et sciences humaines. Publications de la section de langues et literatures 10; Dakar: Université de Dakar, 1961), 165.

[11] Timothy D. Barnes, *Constantine and Eusebius* (Cambridge, Mass.: Harvard University Press, 1981), 175.

[12] The entire work is also captioned by the author *Demonstration of the Gospel* (*Praep. ev.* 1.1.1). Jean Sirinelli and Edouard des Places, ed. and trans., *Eusèbe de Césarée: La préparation évangélique. Introduction générale. Livre I* (SC 206; Paris: Cerf, 1974), 96, 102–4. Hereafter SC 206. ET: Edwin Hamilton Gifford, trans., *Eusebius: Preparation for the Gospel* (2 vols.; repr., Grand Rapids: Baker, 1981), 1:1, 4–5.

If the work by Porphyry was a motivating factor, it was not the purpose of Eusebius's apologetic. His intention for the work as a whole was "to present Christianity, what it is, to those who do not know" (1.1.1).[13] The approach consisted of four parts, responses to three questions raised by Greeks and Jews, followed by a presentation of Christian doctrines as fulfillment of Jewish prophecy.[14] The *Preparation*, in particular, addressed two of the questions raised by Greeks and Jews about Christianity (1.1.11, 13).[15] The issues were treated sequentially: Books 1–6 concerned Christians "withdrawing from the ancestral gods"; Books 7–15, their adopting "foreign and spurious mythical narratives of the Jews" (1.2.2–3).[16] Eusebius critiqued Porphyry in Books 3–5, justifying Christian departure from the ancestral religion by demonstrating its shortcomings, especially regarding its concept of deity.

Porphyry was the most influential Greek philosopher and promoter of contemporary pagan religion in Eusebius's day.[17] As the enemy of Christians, Porphyry is cited for two purposes, for supporting testimony against pagan religion and for critique of his views by Eusebius.[18] Eusebius registers his opposition to Porphyry in interaction with five of his works. Their order of writing is illuminating for our study. Our author's critical "response" was primarily to Porphyry's early works, *On Images* and *Philosophy from the Oracles*, presumably from Porphyry's study under Longinus in Athens, before his Neoplatonism and published opposition to Christianity.[19] Eusebius employs Porphyry's subsequent *Epistle to Anebo* and *On Abstinence* from his times in Rome, when he was with Plotinus (262–268), and then in Sicily,[20] in criticizing the earlier works.

---

13 SC 206: 96. ET: 1.

14 Kofsky, *Eusebius*, 78–79. Sirinelli, SC 206: 46.

15 SC 206: 102–4. ET: 4–5. The third question is addressed in Books 1–2 of the *Demonstration* (Kofsky, *Eusebius*, 79).

16 SC 206: 104–6. ET: 6–7.

17 For Eusebius Porphyry was more the adversary than Plotinus, his prominent mentor (Odile Zink, in *Eusèbe de Césarée: La préparation évangélique. Livres IV–V, 1–17*, Edouard des Places, ed., and Odile Zink, trans., (SC 262; Paris: Cerf, 1979), 20. Hereafter SC 262.

18 Kofsky, *Eusebius*, 253. Ironically our author employs the pagan philosopher considerably more often for support than for critique.

19 Eusebius briefly addresses the later *Against the Christians*, probably from the period 270–275 (ibid., 72–74) in Book 5.

20 Grant, "Porphyry among the Early Christians," 182.

His treatment of Porphyry is, therefore, artificial to an extent.[21] The philosopher's later perspectives, as cited by Eusebius, departed from polytheism to embrace Plotinus's Neoplatonism with its "intellectualist mysticism," promising ecstatic union with the "One."[22] In addition to this, Porphyry is commonly thought to have developed skepticism toward popular religion, though his universalist syncretism is well recognized.[23] Eusebius certainly felt the threat that Porphyry's skepticism and syncretism posed to Christianity.

With this background on Eusebius and Porphyry we proceed to our author's responses to his popular opponent. The *Preparation* is primarily polemical in the first six books, regarding ancient myths and subsequent interpretation of them, and apologetic in most of the subsequent books,[24] concerning the antiquity and superiority of Hebrew thought. Eusebius's objections to Porphyry fall within the polemical part and commence with his considering the "refinements" of the recent philosophers who "attempt" to combine Platonic ideas of a "mind of creation" and "rational powers" with earlier "myths" (*Praep. ev.* 3.6.7).[25] This trend, exemplified by Porphyry, "has exalted with greater delusion the promise of the myths," "greater" than did the earlier physical theory used to interpret them symbolically. The delusion was greater evidently because of the appeal of the "correct reasonings" from Platonic philosophical developments and was exacerbated by the "boastfulness" Eusebius finds in the presentation (3.6.7).[26] Eusebius's response unfolds in critique of two works, first *On Images* and then at more length *Philosophy from the Oracles*.

---

[21] Kofsky, *Eusebius*, 270–71, notes, "Porphyry bore a certain resemblance to Eusebius in the spirit of his theological concepts and in his tendency to asceticism.... Eusebius displays a great tactical finesse" in making public that "Christianity's dangerous enemy had once been captivated by oracles and sacrifices."

[22] "Plotinus," ODCC, 1301. Erik Robertson Dodds and John Myles Dillon, "Plotinus," OCD, 1199. Porphyry's "openness" and "desire to reform pagan religion" were exploited as weaknesses by Eusebius (Kofsky, *Eusebius*, 271).

[23] Barker, "Porphyry," 1227. "Porphyry," ODCC, 1309. Jeffrey W. Hargis, *Against the Christians: The Rise of Early Anti-Christian Polemic* (New York: Lang, 1999), 79–81.

[24] Books 13 and 15 are exceptions, resuming polemic against Greek philosophy.

[25] Edouard des Places, ed. and trans., *Eusèbe de Césarée: La préparation évangélique. Livres II–III* (SC 228; Paris: Cerf, 1976), 178–180. Hereafter SC 228. ET: 106.

[26] SC 228: 180. ET: 106.

1. Against "On Images": God is creator of all

Eusebius begins response to Porphyry's polytheism by examining *On Images* (3.7.1–14.2).[27] We find four items: representation of the invisible with visible forms (3.7.1–8.2), treatment of an Orphic hymn (3.9.1–11.21), Greek and Egyptian gods as natural powers (3.11.22–13.4), and a second discussion of the invisible in visible forms (3.13.5–14.2).

Current "physiology," as promoted by Porphyry, claims that "men have revealed God and God's powers through images suitable to sense perception representing the invisible with visible forms" (3.7.1).[28] Including figures of human reproductive organs, Porphyry's presentation is "shameful" in social sensibility as well as "forced" in logic (3.7.4–5).[29] Plausible though it is, the discussion is in truth "artifices" (*sophismata*) of the recent philosophers, not perspectives of the ancients who initially made statues. In Kofsky's words, such ideas "had never occurred to the ancient thinkers in their wildest dreams."[30] The respected names of Plutarch and Plato serve for refutation of the current physical explanations of statues, superficial though their comments are for the issue at hand.[31] Plutarch indicates that wood and sometimes ivory, not stone, gold, or silver, were the materials of choice for the earliest statues (3.8.1).[32] Then Plato is quoted in objection to gold, silver, ivory, iron, and bronze as ignoble materials for associating with gods (3.8.2).[33]

Next, in a lengthy passage Eusebius differs with Porphyry in interpreting an Orphic hymn about Zeus (3.9.1–14.2).[34] Our author first implies that Porphyry has misinterpreted the oracle with his symbolic approach. Porphyry understands the oracle to represent Zeus as both the world and the mind from which it is created (3.9.3).[35] Porphyry's interpretation is anachronistic. There was no belief in a mind creating the world at the time of the Orphic poem (3.9.14).[36] Such interpretation

[27] SC 228: 180–248. ET: 106–35.
[28] SC 228: 180. ET: 106.
[29] SC 228: 182–84. ET: 107.
[30] *Eusebius*, 265.
[31] Ibid., 265.
[32] SC 228: 184–86. ET: 108.
[33] SC 228: 188. ET: 108–9.
[34] SC 228: 188–248. ET: 109–35.
[35] SC 228: 192. ET: 110.
[36] SC 228: 198. ET: 112.

is "craftily devised" (3.10.3), not based on fact.[37] Furthermore, it is impious not to distinguish God from the creation (3.10.3–4).[38]

Then Eusebius turns to Porphyry's second interpretation with a more lengthy critique. He has already protested Porphyry's claim that the Orphic verses intended to represent Zeus as the creating mind. He now contests the reasonableness, implied by Porphyry, of representing in human form (Zeus) the mind which creates. Since an image can not even be made of visible things (!), certainly none can be made of God as mind (3.10.14).[39] Eusebius disregards the evident parallel that like God a human being has a mind and creates with it. Focusing instead on the statuary image of a human body, he notes its difference from the mind of God in corporeality and multiplicity of parts (3.10.15).[40] "The rational and immortal soul and the impassible mind in the nature of a human" is what preserves "God's image and likeness" (3.10.16).[41] The "God of all" and the "mind creating all" is not the Zeus "in the bronze or the dead ivory." Nor can that mind be the Zeus who is "the father of Hercules" and others who have proved to be mere mortals (3.10.19).[42] Similarly Zeus can not be the mind responsible for all creation if he has a father, Kronos, and a grandfather, Uranus, even if the two names represent the phenomenon of time and the location of heaven (3.10.22–23).[43] For Eusebius "the disparity between mythological tradition and its philosophical interpretation according to Porphyry" was a legitimate basis for refuting Porphyry.[44]

Continuing critique of the Orphic hymn, our author asserts that the mind of Zeus can not be the creating mind because Zeus's mind is identified with ether and is thereby "body," that is, material, not immaterial, as is presupposed for the mind behind creation (3.11.2).[45] Related to ether, the philosopher cites the "theologians" as understand-

---

[37] Kofsky, *Eusebius*, 266, astutely observes that "Eusebius cannot reject Porphyry's idealistic interpretation" and contents himself instead with its being ill-founded on the hymn.

[38] SC 228: 200. ET: 113.

[39] SC 228: 204. ET: 115.

[40] SC 228: 204. ET: 115.

[41] SC 228: 204. ET: 116. Eusebius's view is close to his opponent's. Kofsky, *Eusebius*, 266–67, poses two options. Eusebius has either misunderstood Porphyry's quotation or deliberately distorted it.

[42] SC 228: 204. ET: 116.

[43] SC 228: 208. ET: 117–18.

[44] Kofsky, *Eusebius*, 267.

[45] SC 228: 210. ET: 118.

ing Hera to be "the ethereal and aerial power" (3.11.5).[46] Eusebius then considers a reference to Leto, "symbol of the sublunar air" and "mother of Apollo and Artemis, the sources of light for the night" (3.11.5).[47] To such physical cause and effect Eusebius objects. Air is affected by sun and moon, not vice versa. Air, therefore, can not be "the mother of the sources of illumination" (3.11.6).[48] Furthermore, the physical explanations for Rhea, Demeter, and Zeus are "degrading" and "confusing." Rhea, "the mother of the gods," is associated with "rocks and earth" and the god Zeus with seeds, and Rhea and Demeter are distinguished in a way apparently unclear to Eusebius (3.11.7–8).[49] Similarly the "power of the earth," the phenomena of the air, and "the foul and licentious passions in human beings" are deified by Porphyry (3.11.17–20).[50] The one entity worthy of worship for our author is "the God of the universe," the one behind the earth's powers "for sustenance of the bodies of the animals upon the earth." Furthermore, human beings have received from this "sovereign ruler of the world" a soul with a nature "heavenly, rational, and immortal, able to perceive by the cleansed eyes of thought" (3.11.18).[51] Humans are by nature akin to God, beings higher than the earthly powers being worshipped. Such worship is not "befitting" to human beings. Silenus, representing air and revolution of the heavens, actually merits worship more than Adonis and Dionysus, corn-crops and tree fruits (3.11.19).[52] Finally, Eusebius moves from "his rival's absurdity" to impugning his "personal morals."[53] Satyrs and Bacchantes, the base human passions, are certainly worthy of no such solemn regard as they are accorded (3.11.20).[54]

Following treatment of the Orphic hymn Eusebius excerpts a lengthy passage from *On Images* (*Praep. ev.* 3.11.22–13.2)[55] and then registers a summary objection. Christians have justifiably deserted the Greek

[46] SC 228: 210. ET: 118. Eusebius is referring here to the text from Porphyry in 3.11.1, which is evidently a continuation of the text in 3.9.3–5, the allegorical explanation of "the theologians" (SC 228: 192; ET: 110).
[47] SC 228: 210–12. ET: 118–19.
[48] SC 228: 212. ET: 119.
[49] SC 228: 212–14. ET: 119.
[50] SC 228: 216–18. ET: 121–22.
[51] SC 228: 218. ET: 121.
[52] SC 228: 218. ET: 121–22.
[53] Kofsky, *Eusebius*, 267.
[54] SC 228: 218. ET: 122.
[55] SC 228: 218–34. ET: 122–28.

and Egyptian theology. "Sound judgment and reasoning" reject it as "shameful and unseemly" (3.13.3–4).[56]

At *Praep. ev.* 3.13.5 comes his concluding critique of *On Images*. Eusebius shifts to concern, for the second time, about Porphyry's transforming "visible" phenomena to certain "invisible and incorporeal powers."[57] His objection here is to resultant deification of multiple creating powers rather than only one power, as stated by Paul, "the power of God and the wisdom of God" (1 Cor. 1:24). Porphyry moves toward polytheism or pantheism (*Praep. ev.* 3.13.5–7).[58] This is related to "the most wise one's" erroneous ascription to the Egyptians of a "theology" of "incorporeal powers" (3.13.8–9).[59] Eusebius later explains his concern. Asserting that "God being one fills all things with various powers," "they (Porphyry and others) make into gods" the invisible powers in the visible world. They in fact lack integrity. They should simply "reject the shameful and unseemly myths about gods" and "celebrate the one and only and invisible God openly and purely" (3.13.22).[60] "Their long and manifold philosophy" and "their solemn meteorology and physiology" did not prevent Porphyry and his like from being "swept away with the polytheistic error of the ancients," both in their "words," the "physical theories," and in their "deeds" of sacrifice and worship (3.14.1–2).[61]

2. Against "Philosophy from the Oracles": God is good to his creation

At this point Eusebius shifts his critique from *On Images* to *Philosophy from the Oracles* (3.14.2–5.10.12).[62] Our author responds to this latter work more extensively than he did the former. His approach consists generally of making Porphyry appear, in Kofsky's words, "ridiculous and self-contradictory."[63] It involves five stages that build to a climax: the contradictory character of the oracles (3.14.2–17.3), pagan wor-

[56] SC 228: 234–36. ET: 128.
[57] SC 228: 236. ET: 129.
[58] SC 228: 236. ET: 129.
[59] SC 228: 236–38. ET: 130.
[60] SC 228: 244. ET: 133. Eusebius here acknowledges the opponents' claim of henotheism. His objection, therefore, shifts from their theology to their expression of worship (Kofsky, *Eusebius*, 268).
[61] SC 228: 248. ET: 134–35.
[62] SC 228: 248–60; SC 262: 70–130. ET: 135–217.
[63] *Eusebius*, 268.

ship of "evil powers" (4.1.1–5.9), "the kind of power" behind oracles (4.6.1–14.10), Apollo actually an evil daemon (4.14.10), and, as climax, all gods and daemons actually evil (4.15.1–5.10.12).

In the same spirit as the words and deeds of the contemporary philosophers, exemplified by Porphyry in the former work, these writers "record that the gods themselves agree with the stories about them" (3.14.2).[64] Our author thus establishes continuity between his preceding discussion and the one to come. From the latter work Eusebius cites oracles of Apollo, Asclepius, Hermes, and Pan. It is "most ridiculous of all" to attribute Apollo's birth to "the sun and a mortal woman" and then deem him a god (3.14.12).[65] By implication Eusebius considers the just noted accounts of Hermes and Asclepius worthy of similar derision (3.14.10–11).[66] Furthermore, the philosophers with their physical explanations—subsequently rejected as "artifices" from "perverse ingenuities of sophistic men" (3.16.4)[67]—have not improved the situation. An oracular word from Apollo regarding his identity "agree[s] with both the poets' legends and the philosophers' conjectures," and they are simply irreconcilable (3.15).[68] These oracles are not credible. Pan is properly understood not as either human or as symbolic of the universe but as a "daemon" who in fact "also published the oracle" (3.14.9).[69] Indeed, it turns out to be the "evil daemons" who are behind all oracles, working with both the "legends of the poets" and the pride-inducing "sorcery of the philosophers" (3.17.1).[70]

To further exploration of daemons Eusebius turns in Book 4,[71] continuing to scrutinize *Philosophy from the Oracles*. Greek theology has four tiers, the "first God," "the race of gods," daemons and heroes (4.5.1).[72] Order of obeisance is prescribed in two parts: "to *worship* first of all the gods of heaven and of the ether," then "the good daemons" and "the

[64] SC 228: 248. ET: 135. Their "agreement," of course, constitutes rejection of Porphyry's "physical-symbolic interpretation, thereby heightening the absurd effect" (Kofsky, *Eusebius*, 269).
[65] SC 228: 252. ET: 136.
[66] SC 228: 252. ET: 136.
[67] SC 228: 258. ET: 139.
[68] SC 228: 254–56. ET: 137–38.
[69] SC 228: 252. ET: 136.
[70] SC 228: 258. ET: 139.
[71] Zink, SC 262: 7, notes that the design of Book 4 and the first part of Book 5 "en effet, est de prouver que les dieux du paganisme ne sont que les demons de la tradition judéo-chrétienne."
[72] SC 262: 112. ET: 154.

souls of the heroes," and then "fourthly to *appease* the mean and evil daemons" (4.5.2).[73] He then shifts to what usually takes place. Pagan worship is in fact accorded only the "evil powers." Then juxtaposing the Christian view, "our divine oracles" consider all daemons evil, the only god is "the one cause of all," and "the gentle and good powers," created by the uncreated God, are distinguishable from the daemons by a "well-applied and intermediate name 'angels of God'" (4.5.4).[74]

With this contrast of theologies in mind Eusebius proceeds to "examine the character of the oracles" to determine "the kind of power" giving rise to them (4.6.1).[75] His strong and direct challenge to current philosophical thinking is implemented by singling out "the most notable of all in reference to the subject before us," "that very friend of daemons" and "their advocate," as the most knowledgeable on the matter. Our author at the same time undermines Porphyry's credibility by labeling him their friend and advocate.[76] He it is "who in our generation is celebrated for his false accusations against us" (4.6.2).[77] Eusebius explains that the author's *Philosophy from the Oracles* was intended to highlight the "excellence of the discourses about the gods"[78] and to encourage what he terms "Theosophy" (4.6.3).[79] They are an appropriate collection from which "to judge the soothsayers" and to determine "what kinds of power" they have (4.6.4).[80] More particularly, Eusebius plans to refute Porphyry from both his own words and his way of living (4.8.3).[81] Our author proceeds here similar to his earlier examination of the citation of the Orphic hymn to Zeus and Porphyry's commentary (3.9.1–5).[82] From *Philosophy from the Oracles* our author records an oracular "response of Apollo concerning their

[73] SC 262: 114. ET: 155.
[74] SC 262: 114–16. ET: 155.
[75] SC 262: 116–18. ET: 156.
[76] Kofsky, *Eusebius*, 269.
[77] SC 262: 118. ET: 156.
[78] The phrase is *tēs tōn theologoumenōn aretēs*. The translation of *theologeō* follows LSJ. In reference to *Philosophy from the Oracles* "discourses about gods" is preferred to Gifford's "the supposed deities" (ET: 156) and Zink's "ceux que l'on considère comme des dieux" (SC 262: 119).
[79] SC 262: 118. ET: 156.
[80] SC 262: 118. ET: 156.
[81] SC 262: 124. ET: 158. By "way of living" Eusebius evidently alludes to Porphyry's change of view on sacrifice from *Philosophy from the Oracles* to *On Abstinence*, on which he subsequently comments (4.8.4–10.3; see Kofsky, *Eusebius*, 269).
[82] SC 228: 188–92. ET: 109–10.

(the gods') worship" (4.9.1–2) and Porphyry's explanation (4.9.3–7).[83] Eusebius excerpts this material, which concerns animal and grain sacrifices, in order to show that his opponent contradicts himself in the later writing, *On Abstinence*. He states this purpose before the excerpt and outlines his argument following the excerpt (4.8.4–5, 10.1–3).[84] Then comes lengthy "demonstration" of the changes of Porphyry's perspectives on sacrifices (4.10.7–14.10).[85] Eusebius concludes the excerpt of *On Abstinence* in agreement with Porphyry that "no living (animate) being can with good reason be sacrificed to the gods," only to daemons (4.14.10).[86]

On the daemons, however, Eusebius parts company with Porphyry. There are two points of disagreement, first regarding Apollo and then regarding the distinction between good and bad daemons. From the "right reasoning" of Porphyry's *On Abstinence* Eusebius judges that the same writer's earlier record of Apollo's oracle in *Philosophy from the Oracles* renders "this dispenser of oracles" not a god or even a daemon good and free of deceit. "Therefore, as a deceiver and a cheat and an evil daemon must one openly denounce" him (4.14.10).[87] Eusebius thus casts a cloud over Porphyry's judgment in his earlier work by citing the philosopher's later judgment and in so doing calls into question the divine status of Apollo, the esteemed son of Zeus, supreme god of the Greeks.

Now he begins his case for understanding all daemons as evil, the climax toward which his theological opposition to Porphyry has been moving. Porphyry had consistently held that there were two kinds of daemons, good ones and evil ones. The issue was broached in Book 4 (5.4–5; 10.4, 7) with notice that it would be considered at a subsequent point.[88] Eusebius's "demonstration" consists of three steps: Porphyry's test for good and bad daemons (4.15.2–23.8), departure of gods and daemons after the appearance of Jesus (5.1.1–3.10), and a "sequel" against the existence of any good daemons (5.4.1–36.5).[89] He

[83] SC 262: 126–32. ET: 158–61.
[84] SC 262: 134–36. ET: 161–62.
[85] SC 262: 138–54. ET: 162–67.
[86] SC 262: 154. ET: 167.
[87] SC 262: 154. ET: 167.
[88] SC 262: 114–16, 136–38. ET: 155, 162.
[89] For our purpose of examining Eusebius's critical responses to Porphyry, this study will extend only to 5.10.12, where his critical responses stop, though his argument continues to the end of Book 5.

commences by noting that Porphyry acknowledges in his later work that the test of bad and good daemons is whether they are "evildoers" or "will not give trouble to us" (4.15.2).[90] There are incontrovertible internal contradictions between the *Philosophy from the Oracles* and *On Abstinence*.[91] By the standard in *On Abstinence*, those considered gods are proved to be evil daemons. Indeed, this holds with all gods and daemons "taking pleasure" in animal or human sacrifice (4.15.3–4).[92] Here Eusebius is apparently both referring back and looking forward. Gods accepting animal sacrifice in Porphyry's earlier *Philosophy from the Oracles* (4.9)[93] our author finds culpable from the enlightened vantage point of Porphyry's later work. Gods honored with human sacrifice, making the issue more emotionally charged, are "bloodthirsty powers" according to the records that Eusebius proceeds to introduce from Porphyry and others (4.16).[94] Eusebius is not focused on contesting Porphyry at this point. He is simply utilizing the philosopher's historical record. His use, however, is certainly different from Porphyry's. The philosopher's primary concern was evidently to indicate that societies have moved toward more humane religious practice. For example, "But that the human sacrifices in almost all nations had been abolished, is stated by Pallas, who made an excellent collection concerning the mysteries of Mithras in the time of the Emperor Adrian" (4.16.7).[95] Eusebius interpreted the cruelty of human sacrifice as a negative reflection on the welfare of the worshippers and the goodness of the god. Human sacrifice was "not harmless to the offerers" and was "unworthy of the gods" in the extreme, attributable solely to "utterly abominable and destructive spirits" (4.15.5).[96]

In Book 5 Eusebius continues his argument that those considered gods are neither gods nor good daemons, but "the opposite," evil daemons (5.1.1).[97] Here he registers his sole response to Porphyry's *Against Christians*. The philosopher had complained that the presence of "Asclepius and the other gods" was no longer evident in "public assistance" since "Jesus began to be honored" (5.1.10). The concern is that fewer

---

[90] SC 262: 156. ET: 168.
[91] Kofsky, *Eusebius*, 269.
[92] SC 262: 156–58. ET: 168.
[93] SC 262: 126–32. ET: 158–61.
[94] SC 262: 162–88. ET: 170–79.
[95] SC 262: 166. ET: 171.
[96] SC 262: 158. ET: 168–69.
[97] SC 262: 238. ET: 195.

are giving the gods their due. Eusebius challenges the concern with theological suggestions couched in sarcasm.[98] If the activities of the aforementioned figures "do not prevail over the power of Jesus" and they have all "fled," perhaps they are not gods and he is (5.1.11–12).[99] In contrast to his comments on the inhumane character of sacrifices to the gods, Eusebius expresses no concern for the public health problem noted by Porphyry (5.1.10).[100] Our author's endeavor was more theological than ethical in orientation. His polemic here was to persuade the people of the true God, not to express sympathy for their plight.

Finally, Eusebius contests Porphyry's belief that any good daemons even exist. The discussion falls within the "sequel" of the argument regarding "daemonical operation" begun in Book 4 (5.4.9).[101] This "sequel" extends from 5.4 to 5.36, the end of Book 5.[102] He addresses the issue with Porphyry in three items, countering him in some cases and agreeing with him in others (5.5.5–10.12).[103]

First, Eusebius divulges from *Philosophy from the Oracles* what Porphyry had urged to maintain as "secrets of the gods." Nine people reportedly died in a field where they were working at the appearance of Pan, one of the "good daemons" (5.5.8–6.1).[104] Eusebius clearly implies that such a daemon should be considered bad, not good, "learning this by practical experience" (5.5.9).[105]

Second, Eusebius objects that good daemons "are in service to amorous pleasures," "delight in drums and flutes and women's clatter," and "take pleasure in wars and battles." He associates these with three goddesses, Artemis of hunting, Deo of fruits of the ground, and Isis, "still mourning for Osiris," and the god Apollo, "uttering oracles" (5.6.4).[106] He suggests that Porphyry acknowledges the realities with

98 Kofsky, *Eusebius*, 271, notes that ridicule and derision are present in critique of Porphyry as elsewhere in the work.

99 SC 262: 244–46. ET: 197.

100 SC 262: 244. ET: 197.

101 SC 262: 258. ET: 202.

102 SC 262: 258–336. ET: 202–52.

103 SC 262: 276–310. ET: 207–17.

104 SC 262: 278–80. ET: 108–9. Eusebius claims that Porphyry "says [Pan] is good" (5.6.2; SC 262: 280; ET: 209) without explicit documentation. Our author may have inferred Porphyry's judgment from Apollo's verse about Pan's "smooth shrill-breathing pipe, that charms the gentle wood-nymph's soul" (5.6.1; SC 262: 280; ET: 209). Here the internal contradiction is, by Eusebius's view, self-contained in Porphyry's early work (Kofsky, *Eusebius*, 269).

105 SC 262: 278. ET: 208.

106 SC 262: 282. ET: 208.

approval. Such so-called good daemons, including somehow the divinities noted, confer no benefits on humankind (ibid.).[107] He proceeds to his "proofs" in three parts. First he offers two pieces of evidence of daemonic preoccupation with "amorous pleasures." From *Philosophy from the Oracles* Eusebius cites an oracle of Hecate which Porphyry understands to refer to "amorous indulgence" (5.7.1–2).[108] Then Eusebius cites from the *Epistle to Anebo* a disapproving reference from Porphyry regarding daemons' "leading those whom they meet into lawless sexual pleasures" (5.7.3).[109] Far from objecting to Porphyry's disapproval, Eusebius notes the phenomenon in the spirit of answering the philosopher's query at that point: Why do daemons not honor requests from one "defiled by sexual pleasures," nevertheless "lead" people into such? Our author's answer is simple, obvious to him: The daemons are evil, not good. Agreeing with Porphyry's concern, Eusebius disapproves of the philosopher's mental obtuseness.

The second of our author's three proofs addresses goddesses' lack of concern for "modesty." Again from *Philosophy from the Oracles* Eusebius disapprovingly notes Porphyry's non-disapproving record of an oracle with roles of the three abovementioned goddesses in the noisiness of music, female talking, and war (5.7.5–6).[110] For our author the roles of the goddesses are part of the less than consistent "proofs" that reputedly good daemons are in actuality evil.

The third and final part of a "mean and utterly wretched nature" involves theurgy and is presented in two parts. First Eusebius demonstrates that a "spirit" and an "emanation from the heavenly power" "suffer compulsion" (5.8.12–13).[111] Eusebius references Pythagoras and oracles from Hecate and Apollo. From Pythagoras Porphyry understands that gods invoked over sacrifices are "dragged by a certain necessity of following." They "come," "if I may so speak, by compulsion under the guise of persuasion" (5.8.1, 3).[112] In her oracle Hecate divulges that

---

[107] SC 262: 282. ET: 208. The evidence from *Philosophy from the Oracles*, however, has no apparent relationship to either good daemons or the divinities just mentioned. A "soul" in an oracle of Hecate Porphyry associates, apparently because of the goddess of the underworld, with hot temper and sexual promiscuity (5.7.1–2; SC 262: 282–84; ET: 209–10).

[108] SC 262: 282–84. ET: 209–10. Hecate, however, is goddess of the underworld, not a daemon.

[109] SC 262: 284. ET: 210.

[110] SC 262: 286–88. ET: 210–11.

[111] SC 262: 294–96. ET: 212–13.

[112] SC 262: 288–90. ET: 211.

she comes to earth from "persuasive prayer," "learned from heavenly counsels," "spells" that "charm immortal spirits" (5.8.4–7).[113] Then Apollo's oracle specifies the means of compulsion, his name, and the nature of the oracular activity, a "stream of heavenly light" that issues from the human speaker's welcome "voice" (5.8.8–11).[114] The second part of discussing theurgy is to show, regarding the spirits, that it is "not in their own power to withdraw" from the speaker (5.8.13).[115] Porphyry cites oracular verses indicating that the gods are "eager to withdraw" but that the human recipient must "dismiss" them in certain ways (5.9.1–8).[116] The quotations on theurgy show that there are indeed "spirits" involved but that they are not of such a nature as to be considered gods (5.9.10).[117] This brings the discussion back to daemons. These spirits are not "good daemons." They come only under constraint to those needing help (5.9.13).[118] Then they are subject to human manipulation for immoral purposes from "forbidden pursuits of sorcerers" (5.9.16).[119]

Eusebius concludes his proofs against the existence of good daemons with a quotation to that effect from Porphyry's *Epistle to Anebo*. The quotation is a lengthy extension of one found earlier in his proofs regarding sexual promiscuity (5.7.3).[120] A number of lines later in Porphyry's letter comes the statement that is important to Eusebius. Since supposed gods and daemons have offered, in Porphyry's words, "nothing sure or trustworthy in regard to happiness (*eudaimonia*), then they were neither gods nor good daemons (*agathoi daimones*), but only that deceiver (*planos*)[121] as he is called" (5.10.11).[122] For Eusebius these words stand without need of comment.

From this point forward our author cites Porphyry, sometimes at length, as in what follows immediately (5.11–16).[123] Our author provides as an apt summary statement regarding daemons and Christian

---

[113] SC 262: 290–92. ET: 211–12.
[114] SC 262: 292–94. ET: 212.
[115] SC 262: 296. ET: 213.
[116] SC 262: 296–98. ET: 213–14.
[117] SC 262: 300. ET: 214.
[118] SC 262: 302. ET: 214.
[119] SC 262: 302. ET: 215.
[120] SC 262: 482. ET: 210.
[121] The "deceiver," *planos*, is the source of the polytheistic "error," *planē*. The phrase appears in 3.14.1; 4.1.1, 15.6; 5.1.7, 2.3.
[122] SC 262: 308. ET: 217.
[123] SC 262: 310–28. ET: 218–22.

departure from them: "[T]heir gods were found to be daemons haunting the earth and enslaved to passions; wherefore it seems to me that I have followed sound reason in turning away from them" (5.15.3).[124] Reference to the philosopher is henceforth always in agreement rather than with some disapproval.

We conclude our study of Eusebius's response to Porphyry's "polytheistic error." The philosopher has contradicted himself in interpreting images as symbols for immaterial realities. He has raised questions about his credibility in acknowledging in one work the legitimacy of sacrifice and in another work the use of such only for evil spirits. These difficulties are attributable to two related shortcomings, a theological one arising from a personal one. Porphyry refuses to require that a single divinity, his henotheism notwithstanding, be responsible for creation of all things and that divinity, properly understood, be benevolent to the creation. Such refusal, in Eusebius's view, arises from his determination to reinterpret traditional mythology from contemporary philosophy for the sake of popular appeal, albeit at the cost of intellectual honesty and observable reality. Recent students of Porphyry, it deserves to be noted, have come to more positive views of Porphyry's philosophical motivations, though not of his perspectives on Christianity.

[124] SC 262: 324. ET: 221. Kofsky, *Eusebius*, 270.

A SIXTH-CENTURY PLEA AGAINST RELIGIOUS VIOLENCE: ROMANOS ON ELIJAH

L. William Countryman

The genre of verse sermon called a *kontakion* flourished in the Greek church of the fifth and sixth centuries, and its greatest practitioner was St. Romanos the Melode. He left a profound mark on the poetry of the Greek Church, even after the *kontakion* form was displaced by the longer and less unified *kanon*. Most of Romanos' works focused on broad Biblical and liturgical topics such as the Nativity, the Presentation in the Temple, the finding of the Empty Tomb, and the Resurrection appearances. Few of them have references to Romanos' own time and place. Those that do suggest that he was active in Constantinople between about 528 and 555, i.e. in the reign of Justinian.[1] According to the meager traditions about his life, he had come to the capital in the reign of Anastasius I (491–518). He was probably born at Emesa in Syria of Jewish parents and was ordained deacon in Berytus.[2]

The present essay focuses on Romanos' kontakion on the prophet Elijah.[3] Its portrayal of Elijah is a surprising departure from what had already become standard in Greek piety, where the prophet was treated as a model of devotion to God and a defender of religious purity. He was also seen as an early practitioner of askesis and an example for later monks.[4] Romanos' poem, by contrast, presents an Elijah who, though indeed a champion of righteousness and a friend of God, is also a great problem for God because zeal for righteousness is the only

[1] Paul Maas and C. A. Trypanis, eds., *Sancti Romani Melodi Cantica: Cantica Genuina* (Oxford: Clarendon Press, 1963), xv–xxiii.

[2] José Grosdidier de Matons, *Romanos le Mélode et les origines de la poésie religieuse à Byzance* (Paris: Beauchesne, 1977), 159–98.

[3] For the Greek text, see Maas and Trypanis, 367–80, and José Grosdidier de Matons, ed., *Romanos le Mélode, Hymnes*, vol. 1, *Ancien Testament*, SC, no. 99 (Paris: Cerf, 1964), 308–341. For the translations (all my own), I have followed the edition of Maas and Trypanis.

[4] Gustave Bardy, *"Le souvenir d'Élie chez les Pères Grecs,"* in [Gustave Bardy et al.], *Élie le prophète*, vol. 1, *Selon les écritures et les traditions chrétiennes* (Les études Carmelitaines; [Paris]: Desclée de Brouwer, 1956), 131–58.

value he acknowledges—even to the point of violence. He is entirely without human feeling.

Romanos both praises and criticizes Elijah. In the prelude to the work, the poet addresses Elijah directly, in terms of high honor:

> Foreteller and foreseer of the great deeds of our God,
> Elijah of great name—you
> that halted by your mere word the
> water-streaming clouds—
> intercede for us with *the only Lover of humankind*. (Proem)

The final phrase—"the only Lover of humankind"—which forms the refrain to be repeated at the end of each strophe, suggests the tension of the drama that is about to unfold. Elijah holds power over the natural world, but the God to whom Romanos turns Elijah's attention is here characterized not in terms of power but of love.

The poem retells the narrative of 1 Kings 17: Elijah curses the land with drought, then flees to the Brook Cherith and on to Sarephtha/Zarephath, where he is fed by the widow. The story culminates in the death of the widow's son and then leaps over the prophet's encounter with Ahab and his contest with the priests of Baal (1 Kings 18:1–40) to celebrate the return of the rains. The dramatic tension, however, is not between Elijah and Ahab or Israel, but between Elijah and God.

Three questions about the kontakion will occupy our attention in this essay. First, where does this treatment of Elijah come from? What sources or parallels may help situate it in the imaginative world of Romanos? Second, in what does the aesthetic coherence of the work lie? How has Romanos shaped his sources and to what ends? Third, can we identify in the circumstances of Romanos' time and place factors that would help us understand his choice of theme and treatment? Bringing these questions together promises to offer us a rounder understanding of the piece than any one of them by itself.

1. Sources and Parallels

Romanos drew on the Old Greek Version of the Bible for his basic narrative. But we also have two earlier documents in Greek that call for comparison. One is a fragment of an early kontakion, in which the widow of Sarephtha accuses Elijah of having caused the death of her son; he replies that this is unthinkable, since he has in fact benefited the family by keeping them alive through the famine. The widow is not persuaded, and Elijah is deeply distressed by her insistence on his guilt.[5] Romanos' kontakion similarly involves an extended exchange between widow and prophet, and the two works share at least one vivid image: the child's death as the pruning of a shoot.[6] But, over all, Romanos' treatment of their interchange is strikingly different. His is not a reasoned debate, but a passionate confrontation. And the widow dominates it to the degree that Elijah is barely allowed to speak.

The style of this kontakion fragment suggests that it dates from shortly before the time of Romanos' own early works. The speakers alternate strophe by strophe, in a way reminiscent of the Syriac *sugitha*; and the refrain is rather long and not well integrated into the verses. While we do not know the author of this fragment, one possible candidate is Elias I, Patriarch of Jerusalem early in Romanos' lifetime.[7]

The other Greek source is a sermon on Elijah by Basil of Seleucia, which Romanos follows closely at times, reproducing much of Basil's outline.[8] There are also echoes of thought and vocabulary (e.g., the prominence of the theme of God's *philanthropia*, "love of humanity"). The sermon has three parts. In the first, Elijah, concerned that God is too much given to *philanthropia*, decides to force God into punishing the wicked by swearing an oath that will give Elijah power over the rains; God, in response tries to teach Elijah a lesson in generosity by sending ravens to feed him during the ensuing famine. Basil explains that ravens are unclean, which suggests that the food they bring may have been tainted, and that they are violating their own harsh nature in feeding him, since they do not feed even their own young. But this makes no impression on the prophet.

In the second part, God sends Elijah to stay with the widow of Sarephtha, to whom God gives prophetic knowledge so that she recognizes the prophet when he arrives. The encounter with her does stir some human feeling in Elijah, for "he pities the mother starving with her children." Still, Elijah does not halt the drought; and in the third part, God makes one more effort to bring Elijah around by killing the widow's son. She attacks Elijah as responsible. Elijah turns to God but knows that if he asks God to raise the child, God will ask Elijah, in

[5] C.A. Trypanis, *Fourteen Early Byzantine Cantica* (Wiener Byzantinistische Studien 5; Vienna: Hermann Böhlaus, 1968), 102–104.

[6] Strophe 3.5 of the earlier poem; Romanos 21.2.

[7] Grosdidier de Matons, *Romanos le Mélode et les origines*, 17–18, 32, 53.

[8] PG 85, 148–57; quotations here are my own translation. Romanos also used Basil's sermons as sources for other kontakia; Grosdidier de Matons, 250.

return, to terminate the famine. Elijah yields. Death gives up the child with a speech full of fear and foreboding about the future erosion of its domain. At last, God, seeing that Elijah is again restive because sinners are not being punished, translates him to the heavens, where he will be a "fleshly fellow-citizen with the angels." God will then undertake a different and more generous response to human sinfulness.

What did Basil of Seleucia draw on for this astonishing treatment of Elijah? There are at least hints that point in the direction of Syriac-speaking Christianity and Rabbinic Judaism. Both traditions could speak of Elijah not only as a friend of God and a model of rigorous righteousness and orthodoxy, but also as an angry and violent figure. In both these communities, Elijah was certainly held in high reverence. But this did not mean, it seems, that he was beyond criticism. After all, the suffering he brought about fell on wicked and on innocent alike, and he did as much harm to Israel as many a foreign invader.[9] To be sure, there is plenty of evidence for such a characterization in scripture itself;[10] but it is routinely ignored in pious treatments of the prophet.

How these ideas reached Basil of Seleucia, we do not know, but his province of Isauria was related to the patriarchate of Antioch and doubtless open to Syrian influences. Elias of Jerusalem, too, if he was indeed the author of the kontakion fragment, might easily have known such traditions. If Romanos was from Syria and perhaps of Jewish birth, he may have adopted Basil's sermon as model partly because he recognized familiar themes. All three authors could have been immersed in the stream of Syrian and even Jewish tradition about Elijah.[11]

This kind of treatment of Elijah appears one other place in Greek, in a sermon ascribed to Chrysostom.[12] It seems to be a somewhat clumsy reworking of both Basil and Romanos. There are elements (for example, in the discussion of the ravens) that can only come from the former, but also verbal echoes that clearly point to the latter. The redactor's

---

[9] Michel Hayek, „*Élie dans la tradition syriaque,*" in [Bardy et al.], *Élie le prophète*, vol. 1, 159–78. Louis Ginzberg, *The Legends of the Jews* (Philadelphia: The Jewish Publication Society of America, 1968) vols. 4, 195–202; and 6, 316–25.

[10] Moshe Reiss, "Elijah the Zealot: A Foil to Moses," *JBQ* 32 (2004), 174–180; John W. Olley, "YHWH and His Zealous Prophet: The Presentation of Elijah in 1 and 2 Kings," *JSOT* 80 (1998), 25–51.

[11] Grosdidier de Matons argues that Romanos is unlikely to have known Syriac himself, 181.

[12] PG 56, 583–86. Efforts to date this work before both Basil and Romanos are unpersuasive; Grosdidier de Matons, 251, n. 54.

main contribution is an anti-Jewish preface that sits awkwardly alongside God's concern for Israel in the main body of the work. Apart from this one example, the treatment of Elijah by Basil and Romanos seems to have had little further influence in the Greek tradition, despite the ongoing popularity of Romanos' kontakia.

2. The Aesthetics of Romanos' Kontakion on Elijah

The fact that Romanos was drawing on an earlier source does not in itself tell us much about his kontakion. We must ask what he was trying to convey in his treatment of it. Preaching is a rhetorical exercise that fulfills certain liturgical requirements. Sermons may be motivated simply by the occasion, such as a feast day or a funeral, or by desire to exegete a text. But, in this case, Elijah does not come off well enough for the work to have adorned his feast day or to fulfill the usual expectations of piety. Why, then, resurrect a peculiar sermon from a previous generation?

One window on what Romanos was aiming at is to note ways in which he altered his source. However close their outlines, the two works are shaped by different interests and lead to different ends. Basil likes to explain things, sometimes at excessive length. Thus, he lays out exactly how Elijah's oath binds God as well as Elijah. He tells us perhaps more about ravens than we wish to know. He asserts, for exegetical purposes, that the widow knew who Elijah was when he arrived with his request for a piece of bread and explains that God had given her this prophetic ability in a dream. And he treats the raising of her boy as a foreshadowing of the salvation wrought by Jesus and the ultimate triumph over death and hell.[13]

Basil makes lively use of characterization and uses dialogue between Elijah and God and between Elijah and the widow to develop his interpretation. He steps inside the mind of Elijah to show the prophet's thinking about the obstacle that God's *philanthropia* poses for his efforts to punish the wicked—and inside the mind of God to explain God's plans to arouse human feeling in Elijah. He can spell out the unspoken motive behind God's speech: "'I am commanding,' God says, 'a widow

[13] In general, he proves a close reader of his texts. His exegetical rigor slips, however, at the end of the sermon when he refers to Isaiah as having prophesied before Elijah.

woman to feed you'—not saying 'Unless you're shamed by the food, you won't stop the suffering'" (152C).

A good deal of this material is repeated in Romanos, though typically with different proportions and emphases. Here, too, we meet an Elijah trying to get round God's generosity in order to punish the wicked, but Romanos emphasizes Elijah's effrontery more strongly:

> Then when the prophet saw the whole earth in its transgressions
> and the Most High not altogether angry, but patient,
> he was moved to madness and he called the Merciful One to witness:
> "I will take charge myself and punish the impiety of those who are making you angry!" (2, 1–4)

Accordingly, Elijah takes the oath that gives him power over the rain: "As the Lord lives, no dew or rain will come down, except by my word." The oath binds God as well, since God can violate it only at the cost of disowning a friend and champion of righteousness—an unthinkable breach of God's own constancy.[14]

God, then, must become very inventive in the effort not to force, but to awaken in Elijah enough human feeling that he can understand the suffering he is inflicting. First, God tries to work through the hunger that Elijah is experiencing along with everyone else. Romanos vividly describes "the stomach's inexorable demand" (7,5).[15] But the effort proves futile:

> ... [Elijah] remained unfeeling as a stone,
> possessed of zeal instead of any food—and content with that.
> When the Judge saw it, he tempered the distress to his starving friend
> not thinking it right for the just man to starve with the unjust and lawless—
> *the only Lover of humankind.* (8:3–7)

Elijah's asceticism allows him to subdue the body's demands, but will not keep him from dying.

Only then does God send the ravens to feed Elijah. Rather than explain the rationale of this decision to us directly as Basil does, Romanos has God lecture the still-resistant Elijah about the heartless habits of the birds and how amazing it is that these creatures are feeding him. He should imitate them. "Let not your great love of the divine give you

---

[14] Basil gives a more detailed explanation of the social dynamics involved (149 B–C); Romanos is more interested in the emotional interplay between Elijah and God.

[15] Something like this appears in Basil, but only as hints in 149C and 152C.

a misanthropic disposition," God pleads (10, 1–2), deeply distressed at hearing the tears of infants and the bellowing of starving beasts (11, 5–6). Elijah "went wild" at this and tells God to have the ravens stop bringing food. He would "rather be destroyed by famine," since he "will still punish the impious" (12).

God's next device is to send Elijah off to Sarephtha to be cared for by the widow. As in Basil, there is a hint here of Elijah being humiliated by the choice of a Gentile host, but it is not the main point.[16] Romanos develops the relationship between these two people dramatically. He begins by having Elijah come up to her "in a completely rude way" and say, "Woman, I'm ordered to collect what you owe to the only Lover of humankind" (14).

She snaps back, "I don't have so much as a biscuit—just a handful of flour. I'm going indoors/to bake it and eat it with my children./Beyond my handful of flour lies only death." (15) As in Basil, Elijah is, for once, touched. He will die alone; she has the additional responsibility of children. He does not want to be responsible for her death or to "be reckoned a child-murderer in this hospitable house" (15–16). Accordingly, he bestows the blessing of unfailing flour and oil and settles in for the duration.

This is the most Elijah is prepared to yield. God has only one means left to reach him and that is through the child. Unlike Basil (153C), Romanos will not say that God killed the child, only that "God presented the widow's son as dead" (18, 5). The consequences are the same; but this time there is no debate between widow and prophet, only the mother's grieving fury over the child's death. She

> rose up against the prophet,
> saying, "I wish I had died of famine before I laid eyes on you!
> It would be better for me to have been long dead of starvation
> and not see my son laid out in your presence.
> Are these the wages of the beautiful reception I gave you? I was replete with children
> before you came, fellow. But you came and left me childless with all your talk of
> *the only Lover of humankind.*" (19)[17]

---

[16] The Jewish traditions think of her as Israelite and sometimes declare the son that was restored to life to have been the prophet Jonah; Ginzberg, vol. 4, 197. But Romanos is following Luke 4:25, where Jesus identifies her as a Gentile.

[17] Romanos is echoing material from Basil 153C.

Here, unlike the kontakion fragment, Elijah never has a chance to defend himself in words. The widow seizes him and drags him to court. Romanos shows us the event in its full violence. He evokes a woman who has lost everything of value to her and cares nothing about claims to authority—male, prophetic, or divine.

> The man who held power over clouds and rain found himself in a widow's grip;
> the man who constrained all people with a word was held back by one woman.
> And an utterly wretched woman, without a shred of power,
> grasps this man who thought he grasped the heavens by word and power—grasps him like a criminal.
> With a crazy wrestling hold, she dragged him like a murderer into court, shouting out,
> "Give me the child you killed! I don't need your flour! Don't feed me and play host,
> *you 'only Lover of humankind.'*" (20)

Elijah is appalled by the child's death and shamed by being dragged through the streets. He suffers her withering irony when she addresses him by the title reserved elsewhere for God: "only lover of humankind." He is for once *feeling* human distress and suffering. This is not about theology, but about human feeling. Elijah has to discover it in himself. He is being made to suffer for something that he did not directly do, but at last he understands suffering. He shares a little of the insight that makes God "the only lover of humankind."

Elijah knows at once that the child's death is a divine act, not something in the natural order of events. And he knows that God has won their contest of wits:

> This is the device of your wisdom, Sinless One;
> you've engineered against me a merciful necessity so that when I ask you,
> 'Raise up the widow's dead son,' you can answer me straightway,
> 'Pity my son Israel, now in torment—and all my people,' for you are
> *the only Lover of humankind.* (23)

Elijah submits. And God, saying "I cannot bear to be reconciled without you," reaffirms their friendship and sends him off to Ahab to announce the coming of the rains.

The widow and her son have momentarily disappeared from view. After all, the central thing Romanos is after is Elijah's conversion from righteous violence to compassion. But they reappear in the midst of general rejoicing, a passage in which all sorts of new life spill together in a rush of relief and delight:

Reverencing the command, then, the prophet ran to Ahab
  and declared good news to him as the Compassionate One had said.
And at once the clouds, at their Maker's behest,
  big with water, swam through the air, gushing rain.
And the land rejoiced and glorified the Lord. The woman
  received her boy, risen from death. The earth and all beings delighted
    in and blessed
the only Lover of humankind. (29)

This is the climax of the kontakion; and it could perhaps be criticized as too brief to bear the weight required of it. But it is not the end. As in Basil, there is a kind of epilogue, though it is shaped differently. Instead of a typology between the boy's resuscitation and the resurrection of Jesus followed by a generalized assertion of the mercy of God, Romanos emphasizes the concluding struggle between God and the prophet. Elijah again grows restive, and God, seeing that he cannot live with people who "offend," invites him to "come over here and inhabit the sinless realms of my friends." God will go down instead, not to punish but to rescue. In the final strophe, Elijah's ascension becomes the type of Jesus' and the dropping of his cloak to Elisha a foreshadowing of the sending of the Spirit.[18]

The poem as a whole is vivid and passionate. It is less theological than Basil's homily, but works to evoke the hearers' fear, pity, gratitude, and generosity. It shocks with its abrupt, rude, uncompromising presentation of the prophet. Elijah is violent toward human beings and angry and harsh with God. God tolerates even this because Elijah is God's friend. But, ultimately, Elijah must learn that there is more to God than righteousness. *Philanthropia* is the divine power that creates new possibilities.

Maas and Trypanis, in the introduction to their edition of the kontakia, write, with specific reference to the kontakion on Elijah, that "A number of [the poems]—especially those that display an 'epic' rather than a 'dramatic' impulse—tend to be excessively long and tedious."[19] I was surprised to discover this judgment of a work had struck me as characterized rather by vivid detail, emotional intensity, and, in the scene with the angry mother and the ensuing restoration of rain, breakneck pacing. But the tension of the poem lies not on the surface of it, but rather in the way it recasts both the Biblical narrative and the usual

[18] Two comparisons not found in Basil.
[19] xxii.

Greek portrait of Elijah, pressing the hearer or reader to reevaluate a good many presuppositions about God, righteousness, punishment, and love.

3. The Situation

What kind of situation might have occasioned the writing of this unusual work? Two things suggest that the kontakion may have come from fairly early in Romanos' career.[20] First, he is more heavily reliant on a single source than is usual in his later works. He used Basil's sermon with considerable freedom and reshaped it toward rather different ends. Still, the sermon provided the basic outline of the kontakion.

Second, the poetic technique is occasionally awkward. Several strophes (21, 25, 27) force Romanos to make significant alterations in the refrain—more than just changing cases. By way of contrast, the kontakion on the Presentation of Christ in the Temple (probably written in 542), uses the same refrain and avoids such problems.[21] We do not know exactly how these refrains were performed—whether sung by the soloist or by a choir or even by the congregation as a whole. But their constant recurrence served to keep bringing the sermon back to its central theme. This would lose some of its effect if the words were not always the same.

An early date in Romanos' career would also place the kontakion relatively close in time to its Greek predecessors. Basil's see, moreover, was in Isauria, oriented ecclesiastically toward Antioch, and Elias and Romanos were both at home in this same region. If we ask what these associations in time and place suggest as to the reason for their use of the Elijah story, it is difficult to ignore the fact that Monophysite Christianity was shifting from a theological party to a separate ecclesiastical organization. While many of the critical struggles and decisions in this process occurred in the imperial court at Constantinople, Syria was the terrain in which early organizing efforts under figures such as Severus of Antioch and Jacob Baradaeus transformed the actual face of Christianity.[22]

---

[20] Perhaps even while he was still in Berytus; Grosdidier de Matons, 244.

[21] On its dating, cf. Maas and Trypanis, xix–xx.

[22] W.H.C. Frend, *The Rise of the Monophysite Movement: Chapters in the History of the Church in the Fifth and Sixth Centuries* (Cambridge: University Press, 1972) 201–20, 284–87.

Basil of Seleucia was directly involved in the conflicts before and after the Council of Chalcedon. He has been described as a kind of "Vicar of Bray" because of his tendency to try to please all sides.[23] It is possible that he was indeed looking out primarily for his own interests. It is also possible that, like many later theologians, he saw no value in the increasingly finer slicing of theological distinctions. Such a bishop might well have thought it reasonable to preach a sermon suggesting that too much zeal even for the right could be a bad thing.

Elias of Jerusalem suffered directly from the movement toward church division. As Patriarch of Jerusalem, he was a proponent of Chalcedon and, accordingly, a target for the Emperor Anastasius and for Severus after he became Patriarch of Antioch. Severus managed to drive him from his see.[24] Unfortunately, the fragment we have of the earlier kontakion on Elijah is not extensive enough to let us see what the direction of the full work may have been. We can only say that the dialogue between Elijah and the widow is consistent with a work intended to show the prophet's conversion to a less intransigent kind of religious practice.

Whether Romanos was in Berytus or Constantinople when he wrote his kontakion on Elijah, he was near one of the epicenters of church division. Severus was a law student at Berytus before he was converted to asceticism and the anti-Chalcedonian perspective.[25] Constantinople, in turn, harbored both Chalcedonians and Monophysites under the respective protection of Justinian and Theodora. Romanos expressed his Christology in Chalcedonian language, but he never attacked the Monophysite party as such.[26] This suggests that his position was not unlike that of Basil—Chalcedonian but reluctant to press matters in an absolutist way.

In either context, Romanos' "target" would have been those who insisted on absolute conformity and resisted efforts to bring the two sides together. If we think of him in his years at Berytus, the likeliest candidates would be monastic stalwarts like Peter of Iberia, the ascetic whom Severus regarded as his mentor, or even Severus himself, who may even have had something to do with Romanos' departure from

[23] Frend, 33, n. 1.
[24] Frend, 54, 228.
[25] Frend, 202.
[26] Maas and Trypanis, xxiii; Grosdidier de Matons, 267–68.

Berytus.[27] Given the long-standing tendency to understand Elijah as an ascetic (Romanos emphasizes how little he was affected by his own starvation), this would be an easy connection. But there were comparably intransigent figures later on as well.

On the other hand, there were examples on the Chalcedonian side as well of officials who used force to make anti-Chalcedonians conform. Indeed, Justinian eventually took this path.[28] Is it possible that Romanos was bold enough to challenge even the Emperor, albeit in oblique fashion? The poet died in the good graces of court and church, as demonstrated by his prompt canonization,[29] which suggests that Justinian at least did not detect criticism of himself. In principle, however, the problematic Romanos set up embraced both sides.

In any case, Romanos was not simply attacking Elijah. He is careful to treat the prophet with honor as well as to criticize. He emphasizes God's friendship for him and reaffirms that Elijah was right to prize righteousness. God does not dismiss Elijah's single-mindedness but attempts to soften and transform it with human feeling. Romanos can be read as treating the leaders of either or both parties with a certain respect while also trying to convey that God is less rigorous, intransigent, and violent than they. He is polemicizing not for one or the other party but against the increasingly routine resort to force on both sides.

This helps explain the sermon's aesthetic approach, which seeks to shape an emotional response, indeed a conversion. Romanos, having created a portrait of the harsh, intransigent Elijah, brings him round to human feeling step by step from his first meeting with the widow of Sarephtha through the death of her son to his own humiliating public exposure by being dragged through the streets. Even in the work's conclusion, where God speaks of the forthcoming incarnation, the emotional tone remains intense.

> If you cannot live with people who offend, prophet,
> come over here and inhabit the sinless realms of my friends.
> And I—strong enough to carry the strayed sheep
> on my shoulders—I'll go down and call to those who stumble,
> 'All you sinners running at full speed, come to me and rest. For I have come

[27] Frend, 202; Grosdidier de Matons, 185.
[28] Frend, 272–83.
[29] Grosdidier de Matons, 266–67.

not to punish those whom I have made, but to snatch them back from
their irreverence,
the only Lover of humankind.' (32)

This is not a work of ideas, but of spiritual experience, aiming at conversion. It stands out for its willingness to contradict the growing tendency of Christians to resort to violence in defense of what they conceived as righteousness.

SUBJECT INDEX